ORACLES OF EMPIRE

ORACLES

OF

EMPIRE

*Poetry, Politics, and Commerce
in British America,*

1690–1750

David S. Shields

THE UNIVERSITY OF CHICAGO PRESS

Chicago and London

DAVID S. SHIELDS is associate professor of English at the
Citadel in Charleston, South Carolina.

The University of Chicago Press, Chicago 60637
The University of Chicago Press, Ltd., London
© 1990 by The University of Chicago
All rights reserved. Published 1990
Printed in the United States of America

99 98 97 96 95 94 93 92 91 90   54321

Library of Congress Cataloging in Publication Data

Shields, David S.
    Oracles of empire : poetry, politics, and commerce in British
America, 1690–1750 / David S. Shields.
        p.   cm.
    Includes bibliographical references.
    ISBN 0–226–75298–4
    1. American poetry—Colonial period, ca. 1600–1775—History and
criticism.   2. Political poetry, American—History and criticism.
3. United States—Intellectual life—18th century.   4. Imperialism
in literature.   5. Commerce in literature.   6. Colonies in
literature.   I. Title.
PS312.S5   1990
811'.109358—dc20   90–10836
                                                        CIP

For

J . A . LEO LEMAY

Contents

Acknowledgments

As a Samuel Foster Haven Fellow of the American Antiquarian Society I investigated the interworkings of print and manuscript literary culture in New England. Conversations with the late Stephen Botein aided me in forming the picture of literary practice found in part 2 of this study. Chapters 6 and 7 benefited from the criticisms of David D. Hall, director of the American Antiquarian Society's Program on the History of the Book in American Culture. My analysis of manuscript culture should be viewed as an extension of the concerns of the "History of the Book" movement into the manuscript realm of taverns, clubs, and salons.

A National Endowment for the Humanities summer research grant in 1987 enabled me to search archives in the mid-Atlantic region for poetry upon the affairs of state.

The Citadel Development Foundation supplied research support to purchase microfilms of early American newspapers, to underwrite the microfilming of literary manuscripts, and to pay for travel to Scotland and New York. The foundation's generosity did much to allay the difficulty of writing this book while teaching 4 course loads each semester. I must also thank Prof. E. F. J. Tucker for his efforts to secure release time for the final preparation of this manuscript.

The American Philosophical Society underwrote travel to London to examine archival collections for the literary remains of Archibald Home and his circle. An incidental product of this search was the information about West Indian poetry incorporated into chapter 4.

Portions of chapter 2, in a somewhat altered form, appeared as "James Kirkpatrick; Laureate of British American Mercantilism," in *The Meaning of South Carolina History; Essays in Honor of George C. Rogers, Jr.* (Columbia, S. C.: University of South Carolina Press, 1990). I thank the University of South Carolina for permission to reprint this material.

The poetry of William Becket contained in manuscript Am .0165, "Notices and Letters Concerning Incidents at Lewes Town, 1727–1744," is printed courtesy of the Historical Society of Pennsylvania. I owe particular thanks to Linda Stanley, curator of manuscripts, for her patient answers to inquiries on a number of issues.

The poetry of Gov. Lewis Morris of New Jersey contained in the Robert Morris Papers, Special Collections and Archives, appears courtesy of Rutgers University Libraries.

Lewis Morris, Jr.'s verse epistle, "Mr Gales Letter To his constituents in answer To one They wrote To him that he would Inform them what the assembly were doing," Lewis Morris Literary Writings, is published courtesy of the The New-York Historical Society.

Joseph Green's satires of Governor Belcher contained in the Smith-Carter manuscripts and the F. L. Gay manuscripts are printed by permission of the Massachusetts Historical Society, as are the pasquinades drawn from the Benjamin Walker Diary.

Passages from Captain Thomas Walduck's 1710 letter from Barbados to James Petiver, Sloane MS 2302, appear by permission of the Trustees of the British Library. Permission has also been granted for printing passages of Thomas Dale's letter to Rev. Thomas Birch.

Excerpts of the anti-Cosby satirical ballads composed by David Humphreys and James Alexander, Miscellaneous Papers, (Cosby Songs 21, 24), appear courtesy of the Rare Books and Manuscripts Division, The New York Public Library, Astor, Lenox and Tilden Foundations.

I owe a debt of gratitude to librarians, archivists, and staff researchers in a host of institutions. These include Sherman Pyatt of the Daniel Library, the Citadel; Thomas Johnson of the South Caroliniana Library, the University of South Carolina; Harlan Greene and Cam Alexander of the South Carolina Historical Society; the staff of the Charleston Library Society; David Moltke-Hansen, director of the Southern Historical Society Collection, Wilson Library, University of North Carolina at Chapel Hill; William R. Erwin, Jr., senior cataloguer, Manuscript Division, Perkins Library, Duke University; Howson Cole of the Virginia Historical Society; the staff of the manuscript department, Alderman Library, the University of Virginia; the staff of the Rare Book Department, Earl Gregg Swem Library, the College of William and Mary; L. Eileen Parris and John O. Sands of The Colonial Williamsburg Foundation; the staffs of the rare book department and manuscript department of the Library of Congress; Donna Ellis, manuscripts librarian, Maryland Historical Society; Linda Stanley, archivist of manuscripts, Historical Society of Pennsylvania; the staff of the manuscript collection, the American Philosophical Society; the manuscript department of the University of Delaware; Ronald L. Becker, curator of manuscripts, Alexander Library, Rutgers University; Earle E. Coleman, university archivist, Seeley G. Mudd Manuscript Library, Princeton University; Robert

Burnett of the New Jersey Historical Society; the manuscript department of The New-York Historical Society; the staff of the research libraries, the New York Public Library; Robert Goler of the Fraunces Tavern Museum in New York City; James Campbell, Whitney Library, New Haven Colony Historical Society; the staff of the Connecticut Historical Society; Barbara Trippel Simmons, curator of manuscripts, American Antiquarian Society; the staff of the manuscript collection, Massachusetts Historical Society; Barbara Ward, the Essex Institute; Roger Stoddard, Houghton Library, Harvard University; the librarian, the Boston Atheneum; the Portsmouth Atheneum; Nathan Kaganoff, librarian, American Jewish Historical Society; the staff of the Queens Library, Aberdeen University; Ian Hill of the Scottish Record Office; C. R. Davey of the East Sussex County Record Office; C. J. Pickford, county archivist of the Bedfordshire Record Office; the staff of the Manuscripts Department, British Library; the staff of the Rare Book Department, the Huntington Library.

Conversations with several scholars influenced the argument of this study. My undergraduate training at the College of William and Mary, which took place during the emergence of the "Chesopean School" of historians in the early 1970s, predisposed me to see certain figurations of trade, agricultural production, and labor in British American writings. I was fortunate, too, to have been introduced to neoclassical belles lettres by Robert Maccubbin and Carl Dolmetsch, two enthusiastic readers of eighteenth-century texts. My friendship with Bernard L. Herman, the historian of American material culture, since our days as students in Williamsburg has involved me in investigations of the relationship of writing to material constructs. While this issue is the explicit concern of other studies I have undertaken, it operates here implicitly.

As an ITT International Fellow at Trinity College, Dublin, I had the opportunity to study the operations of literary culture in a provincial center other than in British America.

I was fortunate to have arrived as a graduate student at the University of Chicago in 1975 at a time when critical debate had taken up the question of the value of literary history. The rehabilitation of literary history by Hans Robert Jauss, Wolfgang Iser, and other theoreticians of the School of *Konstanz*, the interest in the workings of time and narrative projected by the hermeneutic philosophy of Gadamer and Ricouer, and intimations of the New Historicism in the work of Jerome McGann offered new hope to students interested in treating the literary past. The ferment of ideas on campus could produce brilliant debate. There was no more cogent and brilliant debater than John A. Friedman, the psychoanalytic theorist, who was my roommate from 1975 to 1978. His zeal as a thinker remains for me a standard by which to measure intellectual activity.

Robert Streeter and Robert Ferguson exerted profound influences upon the conduct of my scholarship. Robert Streeter's Saintsburian breadth of reading suggested that the richest history encompassed the broadest horizon of information. Robert Ferguson became a sort of externalized historical conscience for me, prompting greater rigor in argument, greater concision in expression, and greater circumspection in making claims. He was kind enough to subject a draft of this study to a detailed critique, improving its matter and manner substantially.

Over the six years since I began writing *Oracles of Empire*, the observations of a number of friends and colleagues have affected my project. Correspondence with Pattie Cowell and Carla Mulford contributed greatly to refining the picture of literary practice in British America. John C. Shields proved a useful source of insight into British American classicism. My conversations with Daniel Williams, Dennis Barone, R. C. DeProspo, and Frank Shuffelton have been invariably informative. I regret that the length of time expended on this work precluded my refashioning it as a study for a general readership, as William Spengemann counseled.

J. A. Leo Lemay, the scholar to whom I have dedicated the book, serves as its ideal reader. A chance encounter with his *Calendar of American Poetry* in a secondhand bookstore in Chicago in 1980 gave rise to many of the questions that *Oracles of Empire* undertook to answer. Often during the course of research, I have called upon his expertise. An extensive, at times weekly, correspondence with him resolved many thorny problems of attribution, communicated new manuscript discoveries, and speculated on matters of ideology, institutional history, and biography. Only a modest portion of the information developed in the correspondence receives airing here. His generosity in supplying information, his diligence as a scholar, and his faithfulness as a correspondent all require acknowledgment in the most direct way available to me—by dedicating this book to him.

Whatever felicity of style this study possesses may be attributed to the criticism of my wife, Lucinda Emley Shields. Blessed with a musician's ear for graceful English, she is the best of editors: ruthless with leaden prose, encouraging when the language flows. The many hours she spent re-forming this study express a care so profound that no thanks can do it justice.

Thanks are due my father, John E. Shields, for applying his professional skills as an editor to the page proofs when the birth of a child and final exams were occupying much of my attention.

Introduction

The Issue of Empire in the Literary Self-Understanding of British Americans

In 1675 Benjamin Tompson, New England's civic poet, depicted in verse the declensions of his country, particularly the transgressions that had provoked "New Englands Crisis." King Philip, the Indian sachem who had instigated the "crisis," would have been startled to discover that his people had risen to express providential displeasure at New England's growing commitment to the global consumer culture. Because "Old *Pompion*" (pumpkin) was no longer "Saint" and Indian maize "was eat" no longer "with *Clamp-shells* out of wooden Trayes / Under thatcht *Hutts* without the cry of *Rent*," the vials of God's wrath were being poured upon the chosen.[1] The times of holy simplicity, it would seem, had receded into the past, into a golden age *in illo tempore* which existed

> ere the neighbouring *Virgin-land* had broke
> The Hogsheads of her worse than hellish smoak.
> Twas ere the Islands sent their Presents in,
> Which but to use was counted next to sin.
> Twas ere a *Barge* had made so rich a fraight
> As *Chocholatte*, dust-gold and bitts of eight.
> Ere wines from *France* and *Moscovadoe* too
> Without the which the drink will scarsly doe,
> From western Isles, ere fruits and dilicacies,
> Did rot maids teeth and spoil their hansome faces.
>
> (41–50)

Tompson's complaints were in vain. No jeremiad had the force to quell the New World's "carnal idolotry" for tobacco, chocolate, tea, coffee, wines, rum, "fruits and dilicacies." Nor could pulpit admonitions counter the spell of "cast fashions from all *Europe* brought." Fashionable goods exercised the most potent witchcraft worked in New England during the final decades of the century. While Tompson and Samuel Sewall fumed, New En-

I

gland became the habitation of the wig, the snuff box, the whalebone
petticoat, and the teapot.[2] These worldly pollutions quite literally brought
the world to New England, for the economic network that the Dutch
traders had instituted and the British had coopted brought commodities
from the farthest reaches of the globe to Portsmouth, Salem, Newport, and
Boston. While native poets hymned the saintly purity of Indian pudding,
they secretly sauced it with blackstrap shipped from the sugar refineries of
the West Indies. Soon, the traditional plaints that sanctity declined as
Boston grew were supplanted by poetic fretting over the decline in trade.[3]
By 1697 Tompson himself could address an ode "To Lord Bellamont when
entering Governour of the Massachusetts" identifying the "Sinking State"
of the province with the fact that "Hast-Pudding's Servd in stead of roast"
and "Wine's not to be had."[4]

Trade became the theme of New England's lamentations when poverty
ceased to be holy simplicity and the rising glory of the country appeared the
token of God's favor.[5] George Herbert's dictum in "The Church Militant"
that "gold and grace did never yet agree" and his conviction that America's
rising glory in empire and arts would necessarily subvert it to sin transmuted in a few brief decades into Henricus Selijns' faith in the "human
progress of our exile-race."[6] It is appropriate that a Dutch Reformed minister fashioned the attestation to the doctrine of human progress prefacing
Mather's *Magnalia Christi Americana* (1702), for Dutch protestants over the
course of the previous 140 years had made commerce the medium of human
progress. With the installation of a Dutch prince as co-regent on the British
throne in 1689 and with his sponsorship of Dutch commercial procedures
and institutions—banks, credit schemes, the Board of Trade, joint stock
companies—the imperial context was established for the development of a
British American sensibility.

New England did not originate the British American self; indeed, its
regional mythologies militated against the formation of an identity that understood itself in commercial enterprise and the creation of wealth. Yet just
as surely as the region of the saints began spawning Yankee traders, New
England revised its sense of self to absorb the Dutch mystique of commerce.
In a sense Captain John Smith, who named the region, was as much the
material father of provincial New England as he was of Virginia. In *Advertisements for the Unexperienced Planters of New England, or Any Where* (1631) we
see that his enterprising mind had grasped the lessons of the Dutch and the
practical problems of colonial governance. Yet his speculations upon how
British America should be developed would not (with the exception of the
head-right system of granting land) become elements of colonial policy until a half-century after his death, and then only in portions of Britain's new
world empire.

The British empire that eventually came into being was more unwieldy than the one Smith imagined. Mercantilism, the commercial policy which directed the empire, arose out of an uneasy synthesis of three elements: a conception of trade borrowed from the Dutch, a scheme of colonial authority (autarky) taken from the Spanish, and English laws and liberties. These elements were mutually contradictory. While the Dutch notion of enterprise stressed free trade, the Spanish scheme of autarky envisioned a vast protected market in which the central metropolis was enriched at the expense of the provinces and colonies. English principles of liberty and equity accorded poorly with this disproportionate contract. Yet the contract was tolerated because the security of the imperial market was a matter of real concern. Mercantilism operated in a world where imperial adversaries periodically disrupted trade and seized colonial outposts. So long as the perceived threat of the Spanish and French outweighed the disadvantage of the trading contract, Britain's mercantilist empire stood firm. When the greed and hubris of the metropolis eclipsed the threat in the 1760s, the empire began to fall apart.

England's commercial empire exerted a substantial informing influence upon Augustan poetry. Margaret Doody has argued with striking cogency how the appetitiveness, sumptuous imagery, and expansive form of Augustan verse owed much to the "imperial-commercial" ambience of the Restoration and early eighteenth-century Britain.[7] The same could be said about the texture of poetry written in the imperial provinces. Yet more noteworthy was the elaboration of an imperial thematics. Nearly all of America's poetry upon the affairs of state concerned one of three imperial issues: the promise of material wealth and cultural refinement extended by the imperial contract; the contest of provincial laws and liberties with metropolitan prerogatives; and the threat to provincial security posed by Spain, France, and France's Indian allies. This study will explore the literature generated by these issues, treating each matter in turn.

British American poetry on the affairs of state featured from 1690 to 1750 a discourse of empire amalgamating the myths of Britain as the New Rome and the British empire as the *imperium pelagi*, or "empire of the seas."[8] Poets argued that the British empire's warrant for dominion lay in its institution of British liberties in colonies around the world. The rule of British law in turn stood guarantee on British contracts. Trade would give rise to the "arts of peace" and the "fruits of civility." Imperial rhetoric concerning English liberty was attacked by radical Whigs in Britain and a variety of commercial and nativist bodies in America who argued that free trade rather than the metropolitan privilege of mercantilism constituted the proper basis of an imperial contract. British American literature never manifested an imperial consensus, rather an imperial debate. And over the course of the provincial era the vision of empire changed, influenced by the altering economic and political circumstances of the colonies. During the

1750s and 1760s the mercantile topos of exchange was supplanted by the topoi of agricultural production and territorial expansion.

The question of whether the literature of empire and British America can be deemed a species of American literature must be answered equivocally. On one hand, the notion of metropolitan privilege in power, wealth, and liberty is specifically what the republican literature of the United States defined itself against. On the other hand, certain imperial themes and images—the myth of the New Rome, the mystique of laws and contracts, the notion of trade as the ground of "the arts of peace"—would be appropriated to the use of the nation. Yet my principal concern is not to argue the connection or disconnection of the literature of empire to the literature of the United States; rather it is to understand the imperial literature upon the terms projected by its own texts and the texts it provoked in opposition.

That the first British empire failed and its literature was consigned to the limbo of neglect are circumstances that speak powerfully enough. To disinter the imperial corpus simply to damn the bones in the name of American civil religion, or a post-Marxist "ethic of liberation," would be an act of perversity. Consequently I do not undertake this project with a hermeneutics of suspicion in mind. I wish to write an experimental rather than a polemical history.

One impetus for my undertaking was a remark in Samuel Johnson's "Life of Savage." Dr. Johnson observed that among the exalted subjects of poetry was imperial enterprise: "The settlement of colonies in uninhabited countries . . . the appropriation of the waste and luxuriant bounties of nature . . . cannot be considered without giving rise to a great number of pleasing ideas, and bewildering the imagination in delightful prospects; and, therefore, whatever speculations they may produce in those who have confined themselves to political studies, naturally fixed the attention and excited the applause of a poet."[9] The passage struck me for the promise it extended to American poets: the history of their colonies would form the matter of the highest species of poetry. Yet where were the great British American poems on imperial enterprise? And how could politics be divorced from the expansion of imperial dominion, particularly when commerce rather than agriculture was the great prop of empire? Then, too, what were the political consequences when the land being colonized was inhabited? The present book came into being to answer these questions.

Before explicating the imperial mythology of British American poetry, I should give some picture of the provincial literary culture behind its expression. This picture, in fact, may be an unfamiliar one since so much of the study of early American culture is now dominated by Puritan hermeneutics. In the 1930s, as Kenneth Murdock, Samuel Eliot Morison, and Perry Miller were reproclaiming the genius of Puritanism, Lawrence Wroth and Ralph Rusk were attempting to organize the study of American neoclassicism. The task of establishing bibliographical control of British America's eighteenth-century polite letters, particularly poetry, proved so great that neither Wroth nor Rusk ventured often from the description of texts to their interpretation. Wroth's essays upon James Sterling, Ebenezer Cooke, and John Maylem remain solitary monuments to the larger project that both scholars envisioned. [10] In these essays an insight emerged that would determine subsequent inquiry into American neoclassicism: that when we read the English-language literature produced in provincial America from 1690 through 1763 we must be mindful of the British empire as context.

Wroth's insight was not without negative consequences. His identification of empire with provincial literature brought a critical ban in many circles; the "progressive" academy of the 1930s had made "imperialism" a historical taboo in its search for a usable American past. This political malediction, combined with the prevailing critical distaste for literary neoclassicism (a distaste objecting to neoclassicism's "derivativeness") condoned the neglect of British American letters. Consequently the principal historiographic contest of the 1930s and 1940s took place between those who credited the patriot writers with the first expressions of "American genius" in letters and those who sought, under the influence of the Puritan hermeneutic, an earlier origin for the American mind and self. Even the astute Leon Howard did not ask why literary neoclassicism proved so congenial a mode of expression for such patriot litterateurs as the Connecticut Wits. In general, there was no wish to see that the neoclassical mode adopted the atavistic myth of the New Rome with its "course of empire." It could be argued that only in the work of the literary historians of the southern colonies—Richard Beale Davis, Louis B. Wright, and their intellectual offspring—did the issue of empire receive prolonged and serious consideration.

Since 1968, however, the situation has changed: several literary scholars have made the empire central to their reflections. Within the Puritan hermeneutic attempts have been made to discuss the *translatio imperii* from "The Church Militant" to "The Redeemer Nation."[11] Ideological criticisms, too, have emerged concerning the Puritan errand's effects upon the native inhabitants of the wilderness and upon the wilderness itself. Greater novelty attaches to the recovery of secularized visions of empire found in early American literature. The New Historicists have made a fashion of inquiry into the imperial fantasies of late Renaissance England. Peter White and Raymond Dolle have turned attention to the ideology of Spanish conquest in the American south and southwest. Michael Murrin has been investigating the imperial epics of Spanish America. Norman Grabo writes a history of American literature that conceives "America" in continental terms, encompassing Spanish, French, Dutch, and Amerindian writings. Philip Barbour's long-awaited edition of the works of Capt. John Smith has issued from the press. These endeavors recover the humanist vision of empire—a vision refracted in British American neoclassicism.

William Spengemann is the most vocal advocate for writing the history of British American literature. His polemical essay, "Discovering the Literature of British America" (1983), rebukes critical indifference to the writings of the empire.[12] He insists that the vast library of volumes generated about colonial enterprise be incorporated in our understanding of early American writing. His sense of the imperial literature is broad, for he believes (quite rightly) that the empire gave rise to a transatlantic cosmopolitanism, which found expression in London as well as in the provincial centers. Spengemann's several admonitions are just, yet the practical recommendations he offers seem less valuable. The compilation of a meta-bibliography of British American publications will not serve as the means to generate the literary history of British America. Spengemann's call for such a work simply repeats the oldest and most insistent motif of the "other tradition" of early American historiography. The succession of magisterial bibliographies—Sabin, Wegelin, Evans, Shipton, Stoddard, Lemay—the labors of the American Antiquarian Society and the projects of Wroth and Rusk all testify to the intensity of the urge for bibliographical description among successive generations of scholars. But this great effort will not reveal British American literature, for it maintains an exclusive absorption with books and and other products of the press. It is precisely the fixation with the *printed* page that has prevented the "other tradition" from encountering the more artful of early American writings. Significantly, belles lettres was in large part a manuscript literature in British America.

The discovery of the literature of British America depends upon an understanding of the *mixed print and manuscript culture* that operated in the provinces. This understanding was provided by J. A. Leo Lemay, the last-named of the major bibliographers above. Twenty years ago in his landmark essay on the poet Richard Lewis, Lemay supplied the clarification permitting the discovery of the literature of British America.[13] His researches revealed the club to have been the crucial institution of American belletrism. Communicative transactions within the clubroom or in the coffeehouse tended to be either oral or dependent upon manuscript texts. His survey of such writings in *Men of Letters in Colonial Maryland* demonstrated both the quality and extent of manuscript production.[14]

Lemay has never systematically taken up the question of how British American belles lettres was relegated to the limbo of neglect. Nor has he speculated why it has languished there for so long. Even so, the following causes are clearly important. First, manuscripts proved inefficient vehicles and clubs transitory institutions for preserving the memory of literary works compared to printed texts (particularly books) and libraries. Second, the patriot writers of the 1770s and 1780s repudiated all British American precursors when they proclaimed themselves the first agents of American genius. Their political definition of American identity prevailed. Third, the first historians of American literature—Rev. Samuel Miller, John Neal, Isaiah Thomas, Samuel Knapp, and Samuel Kettle—emerged during the early years of the republic when the conduct of literary affairs was effectively dominated by the periodical and book markets. Their understanding of literary culture was colored by the judgments of the markets in two particulars: value was equated with the published text, and transatlantic publication of a text was an index of aesthetic worth. Fourth, the club culture of the late eighteenth and early nineteenth century (the club culture that the earliest literary historians knew firsthand) had mutated greatly from that in operation during the imperial heyday. When authorship became a profession, the club ceased to be a major arena of literary exchange, becoming instead a rehearsal hall for refining public performances. The consequences of this complex of circumstances have been the devaluation of the manuscript as a literary medium, the misperception of the role of the club as an institution of provincial literary culture, and the loss of a substantial body of British American belles lettres.

A provisional sketch of poetic practice in British America can be ventured at this juncture. The colonies participated in the international literary movement that historians have called neoclassicism. New World poets embraced three developments in neoclassicism with great ardor: the religious sublime, belletrism, and Augustan neopaganism. Other developments—physicotheology and Spenserianism for instance—held relatively modest attraction for Americans.

The religious sublime, the mode of devotional poetry popularized by Abraham Cowley, Elizabeth Singer Rowe, and Richard Blackmore, jettisoned the elaborate wit of the metaphysicals in favor of a hyperemotive language serving Longinus's imperative that effective verse must inspire exalted emotion in the reader. Benjamin Colman introduced the religious sublime to New England, where it became the doctrine of the reformed Christian writers who emerged during the 1720s—Mather Byles, John Adams, Jane Turell, and Matthew Adams. It remained the dominant mode of religious poetry in America until the 1790s.

Belletrism came into the English-speaking world from France, reputedly introduced by Edmund Waller. The cultivation of pleasure was its highest literary ideal, celebrating humankind for human delectation, the exercise of wit and compliment promoting "sociability." The tasks of judgment and moral instruction were generally eliminated from belles lettres, because as Shaftesbury observed, shared laughter was a truer and firmer ground for the *sensus communis*. It is difficult to identify the first practitioners of belles lettres in British America, since so much of the manuscript culture in which belles lettres flourished remains unknown. A few names, however, come immediately to mind. Henry Brooke in Pennsylvania, William Byrd in Virginia, Paul Dudley in Massachusetts, Ebenezer Cooke in Maryland, and Anthony Aston in South Carolina were among the first, operating in the first decade of the eighteenth century.

A more public mode of discourse was Augustan neopaganism, whose elements were perfected by Dryden during the Restoration, but whose fullness was not known until the reign of Queen Anne. It passed judgment upon men and affairs of state. The mode encompassed the poetry of civic humanism and Juvenalian political satire. Since the nature and fate of empire falls into the purview of this literary mode, the poetry of Augustan neopaganism will be the special concern of this book.

In British America the political turmoils attending the Glorious Revolution also ushered in a consciously political literary culture. Circles that operated like the mug clubs in England formed in many of the provincial urban centers to propagandize on behalf of political interests. Governor Bellomont of New York complained "of the constant Cabals and clubbs" of opponents "held dayly at Colonel Fletcher's lodgings (from when I have as great reason to believe) false reports and rumors are spread about the City and province, whereby mens minds are disturbed, and odium cast upon the Government."[15] Loosely following the model of the Whig scriptoria that operated during the reign of James II, the British American political clubs disseminated their most corrosive criticisms of their opponents in manuscript to avoid press censorship. When any political interest advanced a positive program of government it resorted to the press.

One notable historical development over the course of the eighteenth century was the increased willingness of opponents of established authority to print anonymous tracts. Printers risked incarceration with greater willingness after the middle 1750s, if only because the proliferation of presses made the identification of issue more difficult. The many pamphlets generated by the excise controversy during that decade mark the beginning of the decline of the manuscript culture that had flourished since 1690. Isaiah Thomas, the first historian of early American printing, portrayed a turning point in the institutional history of American literature, which he witnessed firsthand as an apprentice, in his narrative of the failed proceedings against the printer of the lurid anti-assembly tract, *Monster of Monsters* (1754).[16] Never thereafter would prudence repress zeal in the American press. On several occasions before 1755 bold printers ventured incendiary texts into circulation. John Peter Zenger's *New-York Weekly Journal* and James Franklin's *New England Courant* are, of course, the most famous of these. Other instances of audacious confrontation occurred. The pamphlets and broadsides that resulted require particular attention.

The methodological consequences of these pictures of British American literary culture and practice can be readily grasped. Both published and manuscript materials must be examined to achieve an adequate account of literary reflection upon affairs of state. Some determination of the authorship of a text should be made, if not *in propria persona*, at least in terms of the spectrum of politics or tradition of literature. Individual texts must be judged in terms of the manner of dissemination, their specific party or club contexts, and their intended audiences, as well as their rhetoric, employment of persona, and ideology. This methodological program may recall the practical recommendations for textual study offered by New Historicists such as Jerome J. McGann.[17] I do not deny the affinities, yet it seems to me that there is much of the old historicism in the work I have done. The polemical cast of many of the New Historicist texts runs counter to the spirit of "humility before the text" (to borrow Hans-Georg Gadamer's phrase) which animates these interpretations. My hope is to understand the "problem of empire" for those early Americans who cared enough about the issue to reflect upon it artfully. I seek this understanding fully cognizant that imperialism remains an unresolved problem in modern history, albeit constituted in different ideological, social, and aesthetic horizons in 1990 than in 1690.

Because of the large number of unfamiliar texts I am introducing, I have composed my book as a historical narrative rather than a critical excursus. The principal rhetorical virtues of narrative are that it permits a reader to assimilate much information and it projects an aura of coherence. A point of my argument is that the debate over empire in British America was coherent from the Glorious Revolution until the adoption of William Pitt's policy in the Seven Years' War. Yet narration inhibits long forays into reflection. Regrettably a number of important questions concerning the aesthetics, language, and literary reception of British American poetry are raised only incidentally here. I have resolved to confront these questions directly in a subsequent study. Postponing their consideration can be justified primarily because the poetry of empire, even in its oral and manuscript forms, invariably addressed a public and frequently did so to accomplish practical ends. Consequently, a "reception history" could be assayed, examining political actions as effects of reading (or listening to) texts.[18] The scholarship of the various editors of the *Poems on the Affairs of State* series and the critical work of Margaret Doody enabled an investigation of the political situation and the rhetoric of the poetry of empire.

Beyond my circumscribed field of inquiry, troublesome questions remain about the poetry of British America, particularly provincial belles lettres: how did poets justify their retention of the manuscript as a medium of communication when the print culture of literary celebrity was forming around Alexander Pope in London? Since colonial society differed in structure from that of the metropolis and lacked an aristocracy, did a patronage system emerge in British America to reward able writers? Since position may have been precluded by lack of a patronage system and fame forestalled by distance from the arena of celebrity in London, what gratification did poets seek in British America? If poets conceived themselves to be creators of civility, did they envision the scope of their action to be society at large, or the private society of clubs and salons? Did a culture of gentility emerge which distinguished itself from a vulgar or popular culture, or was literary culture more democratic in its symbolizations? Did new constituencies for poetry emerge in British America during the eighteenth century? Answers to these and other questions must be offered before any general understanding of British American poetry can be claimed.

Even within my limited field of inquiry, questions remain unresolved despite substantial effort to find answers. Why did no British American women write poems on the affairs of state until the Seven Years' War, while female wits such as Elizabeth Boyd, Susanna Centlivre, and Mary Pix repeatedly ventured their opinions in print in London? Why do so few literary manuscripts from the West Indies survive? Did the relative lack of urban development in the south hinder the employment of certain forms of manuscript satire, such as the posting of pasquinades? Were public ballad singers present in the towns of the West Indies? Did the Canadian maritime provinces produce any native poets during the first decades of the eighteenth century? In the ideal book of my imagining these questions would have been answered. In the real one, they are not, and consequently I must surrender them to the reader.

PART ONE

The British Empire and the Poetry of Commerce

Commerce Navigation and Trade ought to
be encouraged and accounted the most honourable of
all professions, for that it brings the greatest Morall Blessings
to Mankinde, for what one Country wants is supply'd from
another that abounds and anciently men were Esteem'd honourd
& dig nify'd according to the benefits and commodities
their Country had recvd from them—War is destructive to
humane nature, physick is of necessity, law is for the depravation
of manners. Philosophy is but an idle Speculation, the
Mathematicks & Machinicks wou'd be useless w{i}thout Trade
& commerce, to dispose of ye several comodities that
imploy the Industrious and ingenious of all ages{.} Solomon
shew'd more wisdom and acquir'd more Glory by sending
his Ships to Ophir than his father David did by all his conquests
and the Citys and inhabitants of Tyre & Sydon are by
the prophet call'd the crowning Cities whose
merchants are princes & whose traffickers
are the honourable of the earth, only in
respect of their trade.

—THOMAS WALDUCK, Barbados, 1710

1

The Literary Topology
of Mercantilism

During the first decades of the seventeenth century, Spanish imperialists conceived and established national economic self-sufficiency—autarky— by organizing a global network of subordinate principalities, colonies, territories, and zones of domination. The desire for self-sufficiency arose from political ambitions of ancient vintage, a legacy of the great classical empires. The global economic modus was Spain's creation. Or perhaps it was an English innovation, for the first theoretician of autarky in Spain was the English mariner, Antony Sherly, whose *Peso Político de Todo el Mundo* (1622), addressed to the duke of Olivares, laid out on the widest possible canvas the method by which the resources of the world might be exploited to the benefit of Philip III's imperial dominion.[1] Sherly's vision, composed out of practical considerations for the imposition of economic coherence upon the welter of territories that had fallen under Spanish sway, became, during the middle decades of the seventeenth century, the imperial program of his native country. There in a mutated form it became the doctrine of imperial administration called mercantilism.

Mercantilism was the economic policy that governed the commerce of the First British Empire, which unraveled with the American Revolution. This policy assumed an extensive protected market wherein the imperial center ("the metropolis") produced manufactured goods and exchanged them for raw resources to an ever-expanding network of trading outposts and colonies. Imperial projectors envisioned a global trading network producing limitless supplies of gold and silver. The Board of Trade in London administered the trade, restricting exchanges between colonies and foreign states, and between colony and colony. To compensate for the lack of free trade and the privilege granted the central metropolis, the mercantile scheme ensured a secure market for all goods produced in the provinces.[2] To keep the system firmly in place, the British government inhibited the development of a manufacturing economy in the hinterlands.[3]

A view of Charles Town the Capital of South Carolina in North America, 1738. Engraving by C. Canot after a painting by T. Mellish. Published in the year that James Kirkpatrick, the laureate of British American mercantilism, left Charleston, Canot's engraving depicts the metropolis of South Carolina as a center of trade. Viewed from the perspective of the imperial center, Charleston appears over an expanse of water as the destination of merchantmen bearing the union jack. Each of British America's port cities was conventionally depicted from a mercantilist viewpoint until the 1770s. Reproduced courtesy of the South Carolina Historical Society.

Mercantilism came into being during the early seventeenth century less as a coherent economic ideology than as a concretion of ideas and practices.[4] When discussed, it lent itself more readily to symbolic representation than to elucidation as a scheme of economic principles. Indeed it was only with Adam Smith's critique of mercantilism in *The Wealth of Nations* that a comprehensive, systematic account of mercantilism was assayed in economic terms.[5] During the seventeenth century, poetry became an effective vehicle for popularizing the iconology of imperial trade. Animated by British patriotism, poets first employed mercantile images and themes during the Anglo-Dutch wars of the seventeenth century. Dryden perfected the mode in his poetry on the affairs of state.[6] British American poets grasped its utility during the decade following the Glorious Revolution. By the 1720s its imagery dominated American verse about empire.

An iconology—a scheme of symbolism employed in literature and graphic arts—evolved to illustrate the mercantile program.[7] A brief survey of mercantile topoi will introduce more detailed investigations of the imagery of British American empire.

We begin with the most potent and comprehensive image—the "empire of the seas." The doctrine of a maritime empire maintained by global control of the trading lanes derived from English musings on the rise of the Dutch to trading preeminence.[8] Raleigh and John Smith both distilled lessons from the Dutch experience, which they then applied to their colonial ventures. Furthermore, Bacon explored the role of maritime dominion in the expansion of empire in his *Advancement of Learning*.[9] Bacon argued that trade rather than territory constituted the more peaceful and economical way to national prosperity. Consequently, colonization efforts should be undertaken not to conquer territory from native populations (Bacon explicitly rejected the imperial projects of Spain in the New World and of Britain in northern Ireland), but to establish secure bases from which to dominate commerce with a people.

The notion that maritime dominion should be global came about largely as a result of the religious interpretation of the economy of providence. After the discovery of the New World, theologians speculated about God's intention in distributing commodities about the earth in such a way that no single country possessed a sufficiency of what it needed or desired. They concluded that commerce taught man his need for his fellow being. Anne Bradstreet stated the belief in the last of her meditations: "God hath by his prouidence so ordered, that no one Covntry hath all Commoditys within it self, but what it wants, another shall supply, that so there may be a mutuall Commerce through the world."[10]

England asserted mastery over this commerce (thereby usurping God's intention) in the name of an atavistic ambition—a revival of the ancient urge to seize glory by world domination.[11] Nursed by generations of classically educated enterprisers, the atavistic myth proclaimed London the New Rome and Britain's expanding territories the new Roman empire. Just as the old Roman imperium justified world dominion by promoting the benefits of the Pax Romana, the New Rome rationalized its empire of the seas by declaring the benefits of "the Arts of Peace" resulting from British superintendence of world trade.

Britain devised an elaborate apologetic for its mercantile empire. It promoted the benefit of British laws, much as the Romans did the imperium. It prophesied the rising glory of London (Augusta) and its provincial capitals in terms of both material wealth and aesthetic refinement; the prophetic myth is generally termed the *translatio studii*.[12] It featured a comparison to demonstrate the ethical animus of Britain's empire: the morality of British trade was held up against the depravity of Spanish conquest, a depravity the conquistadors confessed in the Black Legend; or it was contrasted to the "Gallic perfidy" of France.

The mystique of British law suffused the rhetoric of mercantilism. This mystique manifested itself in the *translatio libertatis*, the myth of the westward spread of Britain's legal liberties. The legend found its quintessential expression in James Thomson's poem *Liberty* (1736), of which the American poet and imperial administrator, Dr. Thomas Dale, said, "I have seen some parts of Thompson's Liberty, I take him to be the Homer of our Island."[13]

The legal mystique also found expression in the cult of the contract. The morality of British trade derived primarily from its grounding in contract. Over the course of the eighteenth century, imperial morality mutated as the understanding of the nature of the contract evolved. At first, North America's Indian tribes were envisioned as the superintendents of New World resources. The benefits of European civilization would be bestowed upon the Indians in return for the medicines, metals, and foodstuffs they controlled.[14] As decades passed the contract altered, becoming an exchange of native land for cloth goods, metalwares, and alcohol. This mutation marked the shift away from a purely mercantile vision of empire to a mixed model in which expanding colonial bases consolidated ever-greater expanses of territory, obtained by purchase rather than by conquest. The colonies became Britain's primary partners in the trading contract, while the native populations became ancillary concerns. While many writers commented on this shift, Rev. William Smith in *Indian Songs of Peace* offered the most comprehensive literary exposition of the revised imperial program.[15] Written instruments stood warrant over exchanges between the metropolis and both colonists and Indians, testifying to the autonomy of the trading partners; these were the provincial charters on one hand, and the Indian treaties on the other.

Entrepreneurs and poets imagined the global economy in terms of profusion. Common belief held that each land harbored a surplus of some commodity that could be exchanged. In promotional literature colonial territories invariably appeared as cornucopias of commodity or potential commodity. Indeed, this article of faith proved so potent that Rev. James Sterling of Maryland in his *Epistle to Arthur Dobbs*, the projector of the Northwest Passage, imagined the arctic wastes harboring marketable goods ripe for exploitation.

> Say; Necessaries grow in steril Lands,
> To answer simple Nature's prime Demands.
> Ev'n there some Superfluities are made;
> That Arts and Elegance may spring from Trade. [16]

The poets of commerce conceived of a world blessed with a superfluity of products. Furthermore, as the implications of trade impressed themselves into poetic thought, they provided a new discursive dress for the ancient project of conceiving metamorphoses. The poets envisioned a world wherein the characteristic things and appearances of places had changed or been exchanged. Colonies, for example, were transformed from places of intrinsic value whose wealth was constituted in native resources (the presentation in exploratory literature) to regions capable of producing whichever of the world's consumer items suited the demand of the empire—silk, wine, coffee, tea, chocolate. The image of colonies as transmutable regions of exchange value (the locus of consumer wishes, if you will) prevailed during the heyday of mercantilism, the 1720s and 1730s, the era of "George's Peace." Invariably, however, the amorphous potentiality that the rhetoric of trade lent to the American colonies condensed into the reality of economic monocultures. In the southern colonies particularly the fantasies of cornucopia gave way to a literature reflecting the staple system—a discourse pervaded with the theme of production and the mystique of land. The economic necessity that forced the literature of commerce to change over the course of the colonial era was the shortage of labor.

From a global perspective one did not deem resources scarce or valuable. Labor and manufacture imbued commodities with value. In exchanges, therefore, manufactured goods were weighted more favorably than raw materials. Yet the scarcity of labor affected the New World side of trade more than it did the Old World. This scarcity led to the institution of chattel slavery and indentured servitude to stabilize a work force. [17] Forced labor by unskilled workers demanded that tasks be simplified and rationalized. The constitution of the work force as much as the demand of the markets encouraged the adoption of the staple system of agriculture in the New World even before Cromwell legislated the mercantile system into being. The Acts upon Trade and Navigation were a ratification of a practice designed to secure the efficiency of trade in perpetuity. Yet the creation of effective staple economies did not occur until late in the imperial era—in the 1750s in the Carolinas and the 1760s in Georgia.

With Virgil's *Georgics* providing models and Dryden's translations supplying a language, British and British American poets in the 1750s began celebrating the creation of an agricultural civilization in the New World founded on the staple system: Charles Woodmason's "Indico" (1758), James Grainger's *The Sugar-Cane* (1764), and George Ogilvie's paean to rice culture, *Carolina; or, The Planter* (1776), documented the rise of the staple system. At the same time they spoke to the moral dilemma of mercantilism: that its empire of trade had resorted to trafficking in souls to increase Augusta's wealth and render her colonies profitable.

Besides the specter of slavery, the imperial contract was haunted by the phantom of luxury. As the wealth of Augusta increased, theory held that the brokers of empire fell increasingly under the sway of decadence. Wealth corrupted. Leisure nurtured debility. The fulfillment of material ambitions only gave rise to further ambitions, until all sense of proportion was subverted by an avaricious hunger for gain. In the colonies, too, the dangers of luxury obtruded. As the benefits of trade made the provincial capitals great, the cities became morally imperiled. George Herbert in his apocalyptic prophecy,"The Church Militant," supplied the dialectics of the *translatio imperii* a half-century before luxury began to touch British America in any significant way. [18] When slavery and luxury combined, the danger of moral corruption became peculiarly intense. Thus Charleston, the West Indies, and the Chesapeake region assumed dire significance in the geography of imperial morality. [19]

As a counterweight to the peril of luxury, mercantilism embraced the cult of virtue. The roots of this cult took hold in the fertile ground of Reformed Christian piety—the famous "protestant ethic." Yet a thoroughly secularized version of the cult of virtue, bolstered by the "pagan moralists," had been elaborated by the 1720s. A factor's reputation for trustworthiness was counted to his credit. Industry, frugality, timeliness, enterprise, and all the other qualities Franklin recommended in his "Advice to a Young Tradesman" became the fruit of moral probity.

As an adjunct to the cult of virtue there developed a rhetoric of worthy authority. Generated during the Glorious Revolution around William and Mary and developed into the Augustan myth applied to the House of Hanover, it insisted that monarchial adherence to the protestant faith stood proof of a monarch's justice. Because colonial charters were issued by the authority of the crown, and because the empire's sole constitutional consistency lay in crown authority, the image of worthy authority assumed peculiar prominence in British America. It would lead to odd expressions of loyalty in unexpected places, such as the pious Roger Wolcott's panegyric to dissolute Charles II for issuing the charter of Connecticut to John Winthrop II. [20]

A subsidiary development in the rhetoric of worthy authority was the creation of cults of personality around William Penn and James Oglethorpe, the two persons most concerned in the expansion of British America subsequent to the Glorious Revolution. The eighteenth-century vision of "the ethical empire" owed much to the propaganda surrounding the creation of Pennsylvania and Georgia. A shared distinctive feature of both schemes had been the philanthropic invitation to European refugees of religious oppression, English debtors, and sturdy beggars to find economic redemption in the New World. The correlation of authority and philanthropy remained a feature of the mercantile thinking until it was eclipsed by the military hero-worship of the Seven Years' War.

The culminating topos of the mercantilist program was the notion of America's moral compensation for its undeveloped state. The wealth and economic privilege of England's manufacturing centers would not be the New World's, but in its place would be the greater simplicity, happiness, and virtue of American life. The life of agricultural production ensured the superior morality of Americans, because it put them in immediate contact with the supreme "source and monitor" of morality, Nature.

Mercantilism enjoyed a lifespan of approximately a century, from 1650 to 1750, before its internal contradictions and the force of circumstance caused it to succumb. The most troublesome of the contradictions for British Americans was that posed by the privilege of the imperial center in trade, for this ran counter to the promise of equitability extended by all contracts. In practice, the London factors proved fickle purchasers of staple goods; the prices for commodities were surprisingly volatile.[21] American producers and merchants advocated free trade and the abolition of metropolitan privilege with increasing vehemence over the eighteenth century. London resisted any alteration of the imperial arrangement, so the Americans increasingly ignored the legal requirements. They became smugglers.

In Britain, too, dissatisfaction with the "looseness" of mercantile political organization grew. As the British American provinces expanded in size, older notions of territorial empire under direct state jurisdiction became fashionable in Whitehall. Britain's imperial adversaries, France and Spain, contributed to this change of attitude. France's imperial designs in North America always proceeded from territorial ambitions. Once France had consolidated control over the center of the continent, the British developed anxieties about the limits being imposed upon their exploitation of resources and about the possible diversion of the Indian trade. France had to be checked on her own terms in a territorial war. The Seven Years' War marked the final repudiation of Walpole's policies of purchasing peace and extending trade. The empire of the seas gave way to Pitt's world empire of colonies and client states.

In North America tensions grew between inland freeholders and the coastal merchants and affiliated large planters who dominated political affairs. The hard-money credit system favored by the mercantile interest and professional classes was attacked by inland proponents of the easy credit policies of various land bank schemes.[22] In the south, where control over public affairs was maintained by the coastal oligarchies, a frontier resistance to this dominion developed. The Regulator Revolts, the Chiswell affair in Virginia, and the Paxton rebellion in Pennsylvania all pointed to the developing formation of a "land" interest, which opposed merchants and the mercantile domination of public policy.[23]

The decay of mercantilism in the 1750s did not signal the exhaustion of its symbolic language, merely the scheme of arrangement that held the images in a distinctive economic constellation. The "empire of the seas," the "ethical empire," the "cult of the written contract," the "virtuous trader," the "worthy authority," the "New Rome," the Virgilian "civilization of staples," the vision of an undeveloped yet morally enriched New World would all survive the Revolution to serve the citizens of the United States in their expressions of self-understanding. The myths of the *translatio studii*, *translatio imperii*, and *translatio libertatis* were conveniently shorn of their British imperial frame and applied to a republican myth of the rising glory of America.

2

The Tide of Empire

Most British Americans hailed the accession of George Frederick, the elector of Hanover, to the throne of Britain on August 1, 1714. The causes for celebration were several. The defeat of attempts by Bolingbroke and the Tories to crown the Pretender prevented the Catholic Stuarts from regaining the throne, a prospect greatly feared by the predominantly protestant colonists. The Hanoverian accession also meant the supremacy of the Whig interest in Britain, for the Whigs during the final years of Queen Anne's reign had championed the elector of Hanover's right to the throne. The Tory party, whose wealth was concentrated in land, was supplanted by a party whose wealth derived primarily from trade. Since the prosperity of the American colonies depended on the encouragement of trade, the Whig supremacy promised wealth. Though this wealth would be purchased at the price of greater conspicuousness (and thus more careful scrutiny) in an increasingly organized scheme of empire, British Americans appreciated the benefits to be accrued. Men of letters in the colonies adopted the Augustan mythology surrounding the House of Hanover and celebrated the mercantilist views propounded by the Whig imperialists.[1] Mather Byles, the principal poet of the generation of belletrists trained at Harvard during the 1720s, supplied a typical New World retrospective of George I's coming to power.[2]

> Record, O heavenly Muse, the illustrious day
> When joyful *Britain* own'd the sov'reign sway;
> Conceal'd for ever, lye the Acts which stain
> The last black Months of ANNA's reign;
> When secret treason work'd, when justice fled,
> And loud destruction threatned o'er our head:
> 'Twas then, by heav'n ordain'd, his happy hand,
> From ruin rescu'd the devoted land.[3]

Providence, having selected George I as its agent, secured "Britain" from the reign of lawlessness (i.e., Tory greed and Catholic tyranny). Byles foretold how, under George's guiding hand, "Albion" would prosper. "Albion's" revitalization would be figured in the improvement of "Augusta", George's capital city of London.

> Let thy tall towers, and shining turrets rise;
> Where riches glitter; mirth for ever sings;
> And smiling plenty spreads her golden wings;
> For thee, *Peru* her beamy face displays;
> For thee the orient shores of *Ganges* blaze;
> A thousand pleasures crown thy flowry plains,
> While GEORGE divinely o're thy kingdom reigns.
>
> (48–54)

Byles saw the metropolis as the premier beneficiary of the Whigs' global scheme of trade. What "Augusta" owed to Peru, or the Ganges, or the American provinces in compensation remained undiscussed. Yet trade assumed exchange and the contractual dispensation of value. As London grew, so too would Boston grow, as long as legal institutions remained to guarantee equal treatment under law.

To understand British American literature on the affairs of state, one must grasp the eighteenth-century imperial contract. Those who cannot see beyond the surface obsequy in the tributary odes by Americans to British authorities forfeit an understanding of the literature of British America during the imperial heyday. When Byles praised London and celebrated trade, he knew that the consequence of trade would be Boston's transfiguration into a city of Augustan splendor. When Byles lauded the king and hymned his rule, he honored that person whose authority bound Massachusetts Bay in the imperial scheme of commerce. The province's charter derived from royal decree. Byles praised the figure whose person constituted the one coherent nexus of imperial rule, rule that ensured that the fruits of trade would enrich the commonwealth. We must recall the disparate character of Britain's colonies during the reigns of the first two Georges—trading companies on the Indian subcontinent and East Indies, garrisons at Gilbraltar and in Canada, economic spheres of influence such as the logwood region in central America, the semi-self-governing colonies of North America, and a host of island settlements.[4] Only the king's authority comprehended all these entities. Under his protection the British merchant plied the seas around the globe spreading prosperity.

Imperium Pelagi

Edward Young's ode on British trade, "The Merchant," was the poetic testament of mercantilist imperialism. Occasioned by George II's return from signing the Treaty of the Triple Alliance in 1729, it previewed the benefits that the treaty would entitle, principal of which were industry and trade. Robert Walpole had engineered the alliance to purchase a hiatus in the imperial wars—a hiatus that would be exploited by English vessels plying trade unmolested throughout the globe. The British Merchant rather than the British Grenadier would be the avant-garde of Walpole's empire.

Young's apostrophe to "The Merchant" spoke of wealth proceeding from the circulation of products, rather than their production. Of commodities he exalted naval oak, the commodity that transported all others.

> On oaks nursed, rear'd by thee, wealth, empire grows:
> O golden fruit! oak well might prove
>   The sacred tree, the tree of Jove;
> All Jove can give, the naval oak bestows.[5]

Trade, according to Young, "cherished by her sister Peace" distributes gain on every place. "She draws a golden zone / Round earth and main,— bright zone of wealth and fame!" Britain would enjoy the harvests of all lands "blending" on its shores.

A global commerce enriched England above all other states because it encouraged industry and trade more assiduously than other nations—and because it controlled the seas. From the conclusion of the War of Spanish Succession in 1713 the Britannic oak dominated the trading lanes. "George's Peace," the peace promoted by Walpole and the Whig oligarchy, secured an opportunity to expand trade with relatively little interference. Young saw the spread of commerce as the precondition to an expansion of civilized "Arts".

> COMMERCE gives Arts, as well as gain
> By Commerce wafted o'er the main,
> They barbarous climes enlighten as they run.
> Arts, the rich traffic of the soul,
> May travel thus from pole to pole,
> And gild the world with Learning's brighter sun.
>   (II, 1)

The poet presumed that European culture eclipsed those of "barbarous climes," whether Asian, African, or American. The willingness of barba-

rous peoples to trade for goods of British manufacture testified to the superi-
ority of the arts that fashioned them.

Young, too, believed Britain to be the primary legatee of Christianity's
civil program to enlighten the world. The poet retraced the pattern of western history: just as Christianity had burgeoned when adoption by the Roman empire empowered it with civic authority, so protestant religion
would progress when the ethical commerce of Britain's righteous empire
expanded. A Christian neoclassicist, Young explored the analogy of British
and ancient empire thoroughly. Since both Greek and Roman empires had
failed, wisdom could be rendered from their histories of imperial conduct;
in particular, warnings could be derived concerning the corruption of industry and trade. The poet considered the rise and fall of Tyre as his moral
exemplum.

Tyre grew wealthy by controlling the Mediterranean trading routes.
"She call'd the nations, and she call'd the seas / By both obey'd." By dint of
industry she became "The Golden City," as paradisiacal in splendor "as
Eden Fair." Yet this glory dimmed. Venality tainted the government; greed
prompted "Her pamper'd sons" to revolt in hopes of seizing greater riches.
The resulting chaos wrecked the city. Distrust inspired by the self-
indulgence of Tyre's businessmen caused trade to fail. Young concluded that
Britain must impose a self-discipline to constrain luxury, corruption, and
pride. "Virtues should rise, as fortunes swell" (III, 2).

Young employed Locke at this juncture in the argument to justify the
rewards garnered by the enterprising. The argument: self-discipline permits freedom of enterprise, for regulation need not be imposed externally if
enacted internally. Consequently, the rewards of enterprise may be regarded
as an index of moral worth. "What is large property? The sign of good/ Of
worth superior." Young did not grapple with the problem that this axiom
posed—that Britain, an island of limited extent and modest resources, did
not offer a broad canvas upon which virtuous men could make their marks.
Rather, Young indicated that Britons, being natives of an island nation,
naturally sought to exercise their enterprise upon the sea.

> Britain, fair daughter of the seas,
> Is born for trade, to plough her field, the wave,
> And reap the growth of every coast:
> A speck of land; but let her boast,
> "Gods gave the world, when they the waters gave."
>
> (III, 6)

The idea that empire entailed a mercantile dominion of the seas distinguished the Whig imperialism of Britain from the territorial imperialism of
premodern Europe.[6] The explicit economic motive was distinctive. Hugo

Grotius, the great legal scholar, had written that there could be none "qui mari imperaret" (that no nation could lay claim to the seas), but in Britain, the legal vacancy of the sea seemed an invitation to occupy and employ it.[7] A practical hegemony over the ocean could be imposed, though political dominion should be impermissible. Edward Young dared to envision a boundless Britannia, which "sallies till she strikes the star" (V, 1). The task of British literature, according to Young, was to recognize trade as the predominant heroic action in the modern era. Classical denigration of commerce as a prosaic activity had to be shown to be critically inappropriate to the circumstance of modern Britain. He wished to see "the British mast with nobler laurels bound," and trade granted the same prestige that Virgil granted agricultural production in imperial Rome.

Young's project had its detractors. Champions of the ancients and apologists for the Tory interest repeatedly ridiculed verse attempting to render British trade heroic. Samuel Johnson had a particular aversion to the commercial muse, seen vividly in his criticisms of the work of John Dyer.[8] Despite critical opposition, a mercantilist poetry developed celebrating Britain's *imperium pelagi*, "empire of the seas." John Hughes created *The Court of Neptune* (1699); Joseph Browne composed *Albion's Naval Glory* (1704); William Diaper wrote *Neireides: or, Sea-Eclogues* (1712); Thomas Cook fashioned the masque "Albion; or, The Court of Neptune" (1724); James Thomson supplied the great maritime anthem, "Rule Britannia" (1740); Richard Glover composed "Admiral Hosier's Ghost" (1740); and Charles Dibdin made Jack Tar the most popular hero of the stage.

In British America, poets embraced the opportunity to view themselves as agents of a heroic enterprise linked to a global scheme of commerce. A provincial poet, such as Thomas Makin of Philadelphia, could commend his city because "to this long known and well frequented port/ From sundry places many shipps resort."[9] A cosmopolitan imperialist, such as Rev. James Sterling of Maryland, could appreciate the civilizing effects of British trade in abstract. Around the world uncivilized peoples confronted by Britain's "laden fleet" would

> Their Treasures of barbaric Pride unfold,
> The glossy Fur, Spice, Jewel, Balm, or Gold;
> In rev'rence of superior Natures bend,
> And high the sacred Calumet [peace pipe] extend.[10]

Of the company of British American commentators upon the "empire of the seas," Dr. James Kirkpatrick of Charleston, South Carolina, demands most study, for his *The Sea-Piece; A narrative, philosophical and descriptive Poem. In Five cantos* (composed 1717–38, revised and published 1750) was the most thorough-going and ambitious meditation on Britain's maritime destiny composed by any eighteenth-century poet. It was the British American testament to the empire of the seas.

"THE SEA-PIECE"

Elevation of commerce to the heroic sphere of poetry and the promotion of the merchant as national exemplar might seem bathetic if they were not acts of acute historical insight. The British empire was built with the efforts of its merchants, the industrial revolution indirectly financed by the profits garnered from Britain's global trade. Capitalism was engendered by the Promethean (to borrow Marx's metaphor) energies of the metropolis and its agents. [11]

James Kirkpatrick conceived himself as an agent of Britain's mercantile empire. Unlike the Puritan immigrant of the 1630s or 1660s fleeing from "Babylon" to a refuge in the New World, Kirkpatrick did not experience a mental parturition as he crossed the Atlantic. The passage entailed no baptism into a new civic identity, because the sea was not for Kirkpatrick the arena of God's providential interventions; rather it seemed the arena of British imperial destiny. While on the Atlantic, Kirkpatrick deemed himself still in Britain. Indeed, Kirkpatrick viewed his poetic calling to be the recorder of British imperial expansion upon the sea. Just as Drayton in the previous century had rendered the English landscape poetic, so Kirkpatrick claimed the ocean for British poetry: a "Boundless Realm . . . to Verse unknown/ And each Imperiall Billow's all my own." [12] (Here Kirkpatrick may have been responding to Drayton's invitation to George Sandys to give Virginia poetry: "Intice the Muses thither to repaire,/ Intreat them gently, trayne them to that ayre.")

Given Kirkpatrick's ambition to be laureate of empire, it is curious that history has bestowed fame upon his labors as a physician rather than as an author. Born near Carrickfergus, Ireland, as James Killpatrick, he matriculated at the University of Edinburgh in 1708, though he did not take a degree. Upon returning to Ireland Killpatrick met with little success, so in 1717 he emigrated to South Carolina where he had relatives. In Charleston he practiced medicine and sold drugs. [13] With the outbreak of smallpox in 1738, he stepped onto the public stage, championing inoculation as a method of controlling the epidemic. His treatment, eschewing the administration of a cantharide upon the first appearance of fever, brought him into controversy with the literate and capable Dr. Thomas Dale. [14] At the same time, his medical skill attracted the attention of George Townshend, commander of the fleet in British America, who urged Killpatrick to take his talents to London. This the inoculator did, changing his name to Kirkpatrick and gaining formal credentials as a medical practitioner. His *Analy-*

sis of Inoculation (London, 1754) justly won international fame. Kirkpatrick died in 1770, a celebrity in European medical circles.[15]

As a protestant native of northern Ireland, Kirkpatrick was peculiarly predisposed to an imperial identity. His verse portraits of the northern Irish cities before his embarkation to America illustrate the benefits of trade. First he supplied a vignette of Carrickfergus, a fortress town emblematic of England's old territorial imperialism; then, a panorama of the recently colonized Belfast, premier trading center in the north. Belfast's material advantage forestalls Carrickfergus's

> Riches, and attracts her Trade.
> From the thin Harbour thro' the vocal Town,
> The chearful Sailor's *Hail* is rarely known;
> Tho' echoing Ruins greedily repeat
> Each Clangor straggling thro' the grassy Street;
> Whilst on the Way, where Merchants drove before,
> *Plato* might muse, and Antiquaries pore:
> Yet still her Sons some Privileges claim,
> And still the Ruins hold a City's Name.
>
> (I, 65–73)

Kirkpatrick's choice of Carrickfergus as the symbol of provincial stagnation resonates strongly. The lover of literature thinks of Swift's first living as prebend of that parish and recalls his fervent pleas for economic reform in *The Use of Irish Manufactures* or *The State of Ireland*. The historian recalls that Arthur Dobbs, sometime mayor of Carrickfergus, composed an *Essay on the Trade and Improvement of Ireland*, a tract so searching in its examination of imperial economy that he was appointed governor of a more prosperous sector of the empire, North Carolina.[16]

A mercantile axiom holds that wealth increases where trade abounds. The lesson of Belfast was plain: fortune was to be made where markets flourish. The greatest opportunity to participate in trade existed in the newest markets—those of the colonies. Kirkpatrick removed to South Carolina in search of fortune.

Like Edward Young, Kirkpatrick realized that the wealth generated by trade entailed moral dangers. In a passage celebrating "Eblana" (Dublin), whose "Turrets deck the nether Sky, / And with *Augusta*'s only fail to vie" (I, 127–28), Kirkpatrick meditates on the decadence born of luxury. Dublin's public squares are theatres of "grimace"—the fashionable display of surface.[17] At the Thosel, or principal commercial exchange, "conscience may be sold, or Bargains made."

Kirkpatrick performed the moralist's duty, censuring luxury and vice, yet he preferred the role of moral philosopher to that of censor. In Canto III of his "narrative, philosophical and descriptive Poem," he imagined a utopian society embodying all social and economic virtues. This fanciful "Empire of Philosophers" located beneath the sea obeys the wisdom of Halfanax, archsage and monarch. (The echo of Lord Halifax's name is intentional.) Halfanax condescends to instruct the visionary traveler in the mores of his submarine society: moderation and competence. Moderation is an ingredient of virtually every eighteenth-century utopia worth noting; competence, the economic counterpart of moderation, is more distinctive.

> Various the Plenty which these Realms produce,
> Yet here is nought esteem'd for Show, but Use;
> Here none for Heaps of glitt'ring Metal pine,
> Nor idolize a Pebble, if it shine:
> And while abounding Nature fully grants
> Our simple Wishes, and unstudy'd Wants,
> None heaps, or hucksters, what Another needs,
> Nor One is famish'd, while his Fellow feeds.
>   (III, 164–76)

We can appreciate the reasonableness of refusing to treasure items of marginal utility. Considering that many a colonial scheme conceived of economic well-being arising from the cultivation of fashionable staples, such as tea, tobacco, and wine grapes, or silk, Halfanax's wisdom is well taken. All proved to be troublesome ways to wealth. The philosopher-king's other point—that a superabundance of those resources necessary for life would eliminate the distinctions between rich and poor—would become an article of republican faith by the end of the eighteenth century. So long as the citizen pursued his self-interest industriously, Timothy Dwight held, he would be assured of his competence, for nature provided abundantly; only sloth could cause poverty in the pre-industrial utopia of *Greenfield Hill*. [18] No doubt Kirkpatrick had read similar sentiments in James Harrington's utopian tract, *Oceana*. Yet one need not look to the political philosophers for the ancestry of Kirkpatrick's economic ideal. It is expounded in the work of neoclassicism's greatest poet, Alexander Pope: "Reason's whole pleasure, all the joys of sense,/ Lie in three words—Health, Peace, and Competence" (*An Essay on Man* IV, 79–80). Much of the final section of *An Essay on Man* treats the vanity of desiring more than that competence which nature allows to each virtuous man.

The economics of competence had social ramifications: whatever differences inhered in the conditions of men should arise from distinctions in virtue. Kirkpatrick's utopia rejected the notion of hereditary privilege:

> "None dreams of Lineage here, as all the Kind
> "Stream from one boundless comprehensive Mind;

"Whence, born alike, Distinctions only flow,
"As our Endowments shine, our Virtues grow.
(III, 215–18)

Meritocracy was the fondest wish of that class of gentleman to which
Kirkpatrick belonged—the college-educated professional man of modest
birth. The eighteenth century saw the expansion of this class which sought
influence and emolument on the grounds of ability rather than on blood or
inherited wealth. Since the nobility and gentry held greatest sway in the
metropolis, educated provincials and able middle-class enterprisers sought
their fortune where hereditary influence mattered least—in the new lands.

Kirkpatrick took meritocracy to its logical extreme, recognizing the talents of all stations of people. The virtues of the professional class received no
extraordinary emphasis in his account. Indeed, the common "vet'ran sailor"
earns more fulsome praise.

Your ceaseless Toils adorn, and grant Repose
To Britain's silken Belles, and Belle-like Beaus.
Ye leave no Wealth, no Tenements, nor Stocks,
But braving Mountain Waves and latent Rocks,
Froze near the Pole, ye fry beneath the Sun,
T'enrich and chear a Land, where ye have none.
(IV, 167–72)

Undercompensated, worn by toils, yet cheerful, capable, and free, the
common sailor commanded respect instead of eliciting sympathy. Kirkpatrick reserved his readers' sympathy for the figure who would become
the single most popular symbolic character in early American literature,
the prototype of heroic sailors, the American Aeneas, Christopher Columbus.

THE TRIBULATIONS OF COLUMBUS

Students of early American letters generally conceive of Columbus as a fig-
uration of the "genius of America." Columbus's tribulations at the hands of
decadent courtiers invited analogy with Americans injured by corrupt ministers. Samuel Nevill of New Jersey had promoted this "Whig sentimentalist" reading of the explorer's troubled career in his "History of the Continent
of America," published in the New American Magazine (1758–59). [19] Patriot
poets, particularly the contingent educated at Princeton, endorsed the vision. Philip Freneau's and Henry Brackenridge's commencement composition, "A Poem, on the Rising Glory of America" (1771) presented the

explorer's career in pathetic terms: "thro' various toils,/ Famine and death,
the hero made his way,/ Thro oceans bellowing with eternal storms."[20] Columbus's travails haunted Freneau's imagination through the 1770s. He
composed a lyric, "Columbus to Ferdinand," in Brackenridge's *United
States Magazine* (1779) and later expanded the piece to an eighteen-part dramatic poem, "The Pictures of Columbus" (1788). Freneau presented the
character in terms of a dichotomy between the visionary intuition of reason
associated with the New World and the decadent learning of the Old. Columbus is accused of delusion by Spain's first minister: "being us'd to sketch
imagin'd islands / On that blank space that represents the seas, / His head
at last grows giddy with this folly, / And fancied isles are turned to real
lands."[21] For Freneau, Columbus's brilliance lay in his willingness to exceed
the restrictions of decadent learning by heeding his imagination's call. His
regard for "Nature's bold design" and his reason's intuition of nature's proportion kept the imagination from degenerating into madness. Lesser men
cannot possess Columbus's insight into nature and are consequently alien-
ated from him. Genius entails a cost. Though Columbus's vision proves
real, he will suffer the ingratitude of the court, be imprisoned, and become
lost to public notice. At the conclusion of Freneau's poem, we see Columbus
exiled in Valladolid, consoled only by imagining that

> Some comfort will attend my pensive shade,
> When memory paints, and golden fancy shows
> My toils rewarded, and my woes repaid;
> When empires rise where lonely forests grew,
> Where Freedom shall her generous plans pursue.
> (XVIII, 3)

Freneau's poem supplied Columbus with the comfort of reputation.

For Freneau (and Barlow for that matter), the story of Columbus encouraged sympathy for those who would undertake visionary enterprise. The
explorer's history illustrated the inevitable opposition of established powers
to progressive designs. The progressive design the Revolutionary generation associated with Columbus's exploration was the creation of a new nation. The established powers hindering its accomplishment were the imperial authorities in London.

Kirkpatrick's Columbus, too, was a heroic visionary, a man allied to poets in his capable imagination.

> Bold was the Man, who dar'd at first to shew
> From the old World the Passage to a new;
> Who greatly went in Quest of Lands unknown,
> And for uncertain Regions left his own;

> Who o'er extensive Seas a Journey taught,
> Seas as extensive as a Poet's thought.
> (V, 29–34)

Kirkpatrick, like Freneau, believed the injury done Columbus was posterity's improper neglect of his reputation. No nation bore the explorer's name. The continent he discovered honored a fraudulent usurper of the Genoan's fame, Amerigo Vespucci. Kirkpatrick proposed belated compensation: the renaming of the continent as *Columbona*.

Given the unanimity of Kirkpatrick's and Freneau's visions of Columbus in so many elements, in what way did the imperial rendering of the myth differ from the nationalist? Only in Kirkpatrick's apter recollection that Columbus's enterprise had as its basis a commercial motive. The explorer sought a shorter route to Asia and the wealth the orient contained. Instead, he discovered a world that rivaled Asia in its profusion of commodities.

> Alike your Balsams sweat from od'rous Stems;
> Alike your Mountains teem with Gold and Gems;
> Choice Drugs, unknown before, thy Woods bestow;
> Unrival'd Rivers from thy Mountains flow,
> Which have endur'd with Time, and long shall stream,
> To water Empires yet without a Name.
> (V, 91–96)

For Kirkpatrick, Columbus was not so much the "genius of America" as the hero of commercial enterprise—the man who revealed the global extent of resources through his willingness to trust his profoundest intuitions.

Kirkpatrick was a typical Whig mercantilist to the extent that he could not divorce the consideration of commerce from the consideration of religion. The protestant animus of Whiggery prompted its adherents (Thomson, Young, Dyer) to view the expansion of British trade and British empire as concomitant to the spread of Reformed Christianity. Columbus, because of his difficulties with Catholic authorities in Spain, lent himself to protestant uses despite his Italian origin. Freneau in the tenth of his "Pictures of Columbus" depicted a Spanish friar damning Columbus in the name of dogma and received opinion.

> Did not our holy book most clearly say
> This earth is built upon a pillar'd base;
> And did not REASON add convincing proofs
> That this huge world is one continued plain
> Extending onward to immensity.
> (X, 1–5)

Kirkpatrick, too, saw Columbus as the opponent of superstition (Whig cant for Catholicism) and evangelist of renovated Christianity. The poet, playing on the explorer's name, has his muse deliver an oracle concerning Columbus's role in the global scheme of providence.

> "As the Dove of old
> "The first, the peaceful Testimony gave,
> "Of the dry Land's emerging from the Wave;
> "So as progressive Times that Age disclose,
> "When Superstition sinks, and Science grows,
> "To a new World a nobler Dove shall soar,
> "And bear MESSIAH to the vastest Shore."
>   (V, 76–82)

The prophetic mode was an important element of the Whig aesthetic. When commerce was at issue, the poet would present the anticipations of profit entertained by the enterpriser, and the improvements in arts and industry to be rendered to a society by trade. When the poet treated of religion, he foretold the global conquest of Christianity and the consequent rise of empire, the *translatio imperii*. When speaking of the spread of civilization he spoke of the westward spread of arts and learning, the *translatio studii*. Just as Whig history traced the progress of society politically, Whig poetry represented the progress of empire and arts. The "progress piece," with its review of past accomplishment, its celebration of present enterprise, and its prospect of future glory, expressed the essential optimism of Whiggery. Forward-looking men might suffer indignities and tribulations, but in the course of time merit would be recognized. The infant United States, for instance, remedied the neglect of the explorer's reputation by naming its capital the District of Columbia. The sea, throughout the eighteenth century, retained a powerful hold on the Whig imagination. Its amorphous potentiality came to symbolize the sense of possibility attached to the empire. Kirkpatrick's *Sea-Piece* is the most ample illustration of that possibility composed by a British American. Its preoccupation with that imaginative suspension between the anticipations of the Old World and the fulfillments of the New; its attempt to encompass the progress of history in its narrative of the past, description of the present, and philosophical consideration of the future; and its synthesis of commerce and evangelism—all make it a quintessential expression of Whig aesthetics. Kirkpatrick elaborated the one immutable doctrine of mercantilist imperialism: that the fortunes of Britain have been, are being, and will be made on the seas.

BLOOD AND BRINE

According to humanist legend (the tale may date back to Vincentius Placcius's 1659 epic upon Columbus), the discoverer of the New World wept when permitted in prophetic vision to see the future that his discoveries inaugurated. He saw an Eden despoiled and an innocent people enslaved. The Black Legend held Spain responsible for the disruption of New World peace. Spanish galleons freighted the gold wrested from Peru's mines by enslaved natives; Spanish armadas conveyed the conquistadors to virgin territories. These scenes became the gothic furniture of Whig fantasy. During the 1730s English resentments burgeoned. The bursting of the South Seas Bubble had exploded promises of increasing wealth and rising glory from trade. Walpole's rhetoric of prosperity through peaceful employment of the trading lanes began to sound increasingly suspect. Territorial conflicts between Georgia and Florida, the freebooting of the Spanish *guarda costa* in the Caribbean agitated Walpole's rivals arrayed around William Pitt. When Captain Robert Jenkins displayed his mummified ear, severed by the cutlass of a Spanish garda, to Parliament in 1738, indignation swept away "George's Peace." Pitt's circle of militarist Whigs redefined "the empire of the seas" to emphasize the dominion of British naval might. American oracles of empire thus took on a new martial sound. Typical was adventurer Edward Kimber's address to the metropolis.

> See, pale *Iberians* strike the obedient flag,
> Where e'er thy dreaded fleets triumphant ride;
> See, humbled *Gaul* with lowly aspect bends,
> And asks thy union, with dejected cry!
> See ev'ry region of the earth conspire,
> To waft their wealth to thy protecting ports.[22]

In subsequent decades as the War of Jenkins' Ear gave way to King George's War, and King George's War to the Seven Years' War, the "empire of the seas" became increasingly militaristic. Poets of the 1740s and 1750s did not neglect to represent the arts of peace arising from trade, yet invariably reminded readers that the ships of the line stood ready to deal with any adversary who dared disturb that trade. In 1761, the high-water mark of the First British Empire after the triumph of Pitt's war policy in the Seven Years' War, a young graduate of Princeton, Alexander Martin, using the pseudonym "Martius Scriblerus" published a bumptious ode in the pages of the *New American Magazine*. It can be viewed as a treasury of imperial clichés.

V.

Where Ocean laves
His silver waves,
On West, or East, great Princes call;
In wealth array'd,
They court thy trade,
Thy blessings flow around the ball.

VI.

Where yon bright Sun
Pours flaming noon,
Nations, beneath the burning line,
In *Asia*'s lands,
And *Afric*'s sands,
There *Britain*'s glory, grandeur thine.

IX.

The golden light
Ne'er takes his flight,
From all *Britannia*'s vast domain;
Spain haughty boasts
Thus of her coasts,
A rule, unlike the sounding MAIN.

XI.

Yon abject *shore*,
With daring pow'r,
Confronts the *Mistress* of the ball.
Whose Tyrant-Lord
Unsheaths his sword,
Presumptuous tempts the *Goddess'* fall.

XIII.

Ambition raves!
The world he craves,
The nations frights with wild alarm:
But now, vile *Gaul*,
Thy pride shall fall,
Crush'd by *Britannia*'s potent arm.[23]

Martin amplified the neoclassical ethos of his ode by wedding the pin-
daric form to a faux-Roman imagery. France was "vile Gaul" whom Britannia, the avatar of Rome, would crush with a "potent arm." Britannia's
global influence, however, did not derive from muscle, rather the "blessings" that "flow" around the globe where wealth might be had. The vir-

tuous Britannia reserved mayhem for "haughty" Spain and ambitious "Gaul" for daring to obtrude on Britannia's influence.

The passing of a very few years would find the author turned into an avid patriot, serving as the second governor of independent North Carolina, and composing paeans to American liberty.[24]

3

The Material Redeemers

The Stuart program of colonization disavowed two traditional aims of imperial expansion: the redeployment at a distance of discontented elements in the body politic, and the absorption of surplus population.[1] From 1660 through 1688 the thrust of colonization was toward the southern mainland and the West Indies. Settlement designs called for the enrichment of a planter aristocracy by African slave labor cultivating staple crops. The period marked the consolidation of plantation culture on the Chesapeake, the reformation of the island economies to sugar cultivation, and the foundation of Carolina. The Acts upon Trade and Navigation testified to the southern preoccupations of the Stuarts by emphasizing southern and island products among the "ennumerated commodities" subject to regulation. New England was a troublesome distraction, New York a mismanaged and marginally profitable fiefdom, New Jersey and Pennsylvania speculative fantasies.

The decline and fall of the Stuarts during the 1680s put their colonial program into limbo. William and Mary wished to preserve crown prerogatives, but the contests for power in Europe absorbed royal attention at the expense of provincial affairs. Amidst distractions an ideological reversal occurred. William Penn, the proprietor of Pennsylvania, reanimated the promise of empire that those who did not or could not prosper in the metropolis might find fortune in the new land. Penn's invitation to exchange penury for property, constraint for liberty, created a mystique about Pennsylvania and its proprietor. By proffering *The Excellent Priviledge of Liberty and Property*, Penn infused the promise of imperial wealth with a spirit of philanthropy.[2] Once the promise had been renovated, no mainland colony could afford to ignore the persuasive power of philanthropy. The settlement of Georgia in 1732 marked the ascendancy of philanthropic topoi in imperial discourse. James Oglethorpe's many writings about the colony he founded held out the redemptive promise of the New World to those classes that hitherto had been exluded from consideration: debtors, the poor, petty criminals.

Penn and Oglethorpe understood the need to manage perceptions of their colonial schemes. Both employed pen and press to manufacture an aura of virtue about their projects. Both synthesized religious and economic imagery to create compelling visions of philanthropy. The crucial strategy of their rhetoric was the socialization of the mercantile motif of exchange; that is, they advanced the idea that the colonies meant the exchange, to an individual's profit, of old lives for new. Thus, the material redemption of the commonality became (again) the central justification of colonial enterprise.

THE ARCHETYPE OF LIBERTY AND LAW

Only one of the founder-proprietors of Britain's colonies in America garnered the rewards that Kirkpatrick envisioned for Columbus. Only William Penn had his paternity of the colony memorialized by name; only Penn was honored by subsequent generations as the "presiding genius" of his country. Pennsylvania's enduring regard for the character and deeds of its founder merits study, for it entails something more than a just valuation of the real virtues of the proprietor. Furthermore, it is somewhat surprising, given the complexity of Penn's character. He possessed neither the monolithic, Roman composure of a Washington, nor the Grecian philosophy of a Jefferson—simple identifications that aided the transfiguration of these founding fathers into popular symbols.

Penn's transfiguration into symbol occurred despite the complexity of his personality. He was well born, yet avowed a Quaker faith that drew many of its adherents from the ranks of the lower and lower middle classes. He stood high in the councils of the Whig party in Britain, yet did not support the Glorious Revolution. He entertained apocalyptic visions about Pennsylvania, believing the colony to be the instantiation of the fifth monarchy predicted in the Book of Daniel, yet when expressing his visions, he mixed them with the most mundane, practical sorts of recommendations concerning methods of settlement.[3] A remarkable element of Penn's colonial design was his refusal to grant his coreligionists a favored status in the government. He possessed a serious concern for the welfare of his subjects, so much so that his Charter of Privileges of 1701 granted more than was sensible for the exercise of authority. Whatever political advantage might have accrued from his liberality was offset somewhat by a lamentable inability to select capable governors. Thus the period from the granting of the charter until Penn's death in 1718 was troubled politically.

During Penn's lifetime the colony's men of letters, with the exception of

Francis Daniel Pastorius and George Keith, possessed less literary skill and imaginative scope than the founder. When poets Richard Frame and Judge John Holme related the merits of the country and its founder, they spoke bluntly. Frame in his *Short Description of Pennsylvania* (1692) sacrificed eloquence for directness when communicating his message: "No doubt but you will like this Country well, / We that did leave our Country thought it strange / That ever we should make so good exchange."[4] Judge Holme provided something more than Frame's testimonial to the worth of Penn's promise. Holme measured the practical effect of Penn's rule upon the welter of nationalities that inhabited the area. Indians, Swedes, Finns, Dutch, Germans, Scots, Irish, and French were harmonized to good order by Penn's equitable government. Penn's installation as proprietor enhanced the attractiveness of the land for would-be colonists.

> [S]ome of all sorts,
> Fast unto this good land resorts;
> But the greatest number came here when
> The King granted Governor Penn
> To be Chief Lord and Ruler here:
> Then multitudes hither did steer,
> And the most part of them indeed
> Are English people, or Welsh breed.[5]

Penn's success in establishing an effective government won him the reputation that inspired American bards to memorialize his name in verse. After Penn's death this practical capacity to govern remained a principal motif in the literature that recalled the founder. A decade after his passing survivors of Penn's generation delivered summary judgments upon the success of his colonial project. Thomas Makin, the elderly ex-Latin master of the Quaker school in Philadelphia, declared how Penn's "prudent Conduct Crown'd with good success,/ Rais'd this great Province from a Wilderness."[6]

The generation of young poets that emerged during the 1720s and 1730s presumed this success, concerning themselves with discovering those qualities of mind and character capable of projecting the "great" Pennsylvania that came to be. In 1731 an anonymous poet envisioned Penn in much the same way that Kirkpatrick saw Columbus, as a prophet of empire whose vision had been annealed in the courts of Europe:

> Whose vast presaging Mind, and Sense profound,
> Was in the Courts of Kings and Princes own'd:
> He laid the Basis, and the Scheme he drew,
> Whence PEACE and PLENTY in his Country grew.[7]

Penn proved himself to be a true prophet by foreseeing the ends towards which his enterprise should lead—peace and plenty—and by intuiting the means of fulfilling these ends—a charter of liberties.

That Penn's identification with the Charter of Privileges is so strongly asserted in the poetry of the late 1720s and 1730s was a function of political circumstance. Seventeen twenty-seven marked the reemergence of proprietary power in the colony after a period of litigation among the Penn heirs over the founder's estate and power grabbing by Governor Keith and his henchman in the assembly, David Lloyd, that had reduced proprietary influence to a minimum. The death of Hannah Penn, William's second wife, and Springsett Penn, grandson of his first marriage, removed the principal contestants over the estate. Hannah's three sons, John, Thomas, and Richard, emerged with clear title and a unanimity of purpose. The recall of Governor Keith in 1726 diminished the power of their most capable opponent.[8] The appointment of Patrick Gordon, a Scot of great political ability, in Keith's place cemented the power of the proprietary. In London the Whig lords declined to act upon long-formulated designs to reform the colony into a royal province. Assured of his authority, Thomas Penn visited Pennsylvania in 1727. The visit elicited new appreciation of proprietary power. At the same time it provoked anxiety about the extent of the power, prompting people to appraise his ancestor's grant of civil liberties.

Several of the rising generation of poets offered their hopes in the public gazettes. The better of these writers devised an eloquent argument projecting from the Charter of Privileges the "reign of Peace." This "reign of Peace" conflated the founder's Quaker pacifism, "George's Peace," the economic prosperity consequent to Robert Walpole's trade policy, and the post-1727 political equilibrium under Governor Gordon and the Penn heirs. George Webb, the most "officious" of the younger poets, lauded the peace in all its ramifications.

> But what, O Pennsilvania, does declare
> Thy Bliss, speaks thee profusely Happy: Here
> Sweet Liberty her gentle Influence sheds,
> And Peace her Downy Wings about us spreads,
> While War and Desolation widely reigns,
> And Captive Nations groan beneath their Chains.
>
> While half the World implicitly obey,
> Some Lawless Tyrants most imperious Sway,
> No threatning Trumpet warns us from afar
> Of hastning Miseries or approaching War;
> Fearless the Hind pursues his wonted Toil,
> And eats the product of his grateful Soil.[9]

Pennsylvania's exceptionality is conceived in extravagant terms. "Peace," the guardian angel of the province, established a sanctuary from the global dominion of war. War and desolation reigned when "Lawless Tyrants" indulged their "imperious Sway." The association of lawless rule with "imperious Sway" was a rhetorical legacy of the anti-Stuart propaganda of the 1680s and 1690s. Arbitrary command—i.e., the prerogative unchecked by law or the will of the people—reduced society to the Hobbesian state of nature where the imperious struggle against one another in the service of appetite. Those unfortunate enough to be subject to these tyrants became slaves to an uncontrolled will. Webb's passage contrasted the unbounded aspirations of warring tyrants with the "gentle" pursuits of the "Hind" whose customs and duties constrain his will and satisfy his appetite by rendering to him the reward of the "product of his grateful Soil."

Webb argued that to the extent a ruler regulated his ambition, refusing to serve his own desire by redirecting his energies toward the welfare of his dependents, then that will assumed the beneficial character of law. Penn's surrender of much of his prerogative right by granting the 1701 Charter of Liberties marked the full redemption of his promise of the privilege of liberty and property. [10]

> No Unjust Sentence we have cause to fear,
> No Arbitrary Monarch rules us here;
> Our Lives, our Properties, and all that's Ours,
> Our happy Constitution here secures.
> What Praise and Thanks, *O Penn*, are due to thee!
> For this first perfect Scheme of Liberty.
>
> (49–54)

Webb's debt to the founder's thought appears in the conviction that the Old World brought misery upon itself, embracing war and misrule. In a protracted diagnosis of civic ills in *The Benefit of Plantations, or Colonies*, Penn observed that England had fallen victim to luxury, that the citizens had neglected their ancient discipline and addicted themselves to "Pleasure and Effeminacy". [11] He argued that the emigration of people would not injure England; rather, people emigrated because England was already injured, and the only possible means of restoring virtue in its citizenry was by enduring the trial of colonial enterprise. Webb tied Penn's critique to the doctrine of the *translatio studii* that the rise of the new empire is driven by the growing decadence of the old. In an untitled ode to Philadelphia published in the *American Weekly Mercury*, Webb declared that

> Here Themis loves to have her Altars blaze,
> And willing grants, whate'er her Votary prays,

> Not so, where the loud Trumpet, ever Sounds
> Where War and Desolation, Stalk around,
> The Goddess fires th' unhospitable Ground.
> Hence 'twas that 'erst She sought Arcadia's Plains,
> And taught the sacred Arts to rural Swains. [12]

The arts of peace, over which Themis presides, required peace as a precondition for their vitality. As Arcadia served in legendary times as a sanctum of amity and arts, so Pennsylvania would be the modern asylum of those civil refinements requiring leisure and contemplation. In the coda of the poem, Webb delivered his oracle:

> E'er Time has Measured out an hundred Years
> Westward from Britain, shall an Athens rise,
> Which soon shall bear away the learned Prize;
> Hence Europe's Sons assistance shall implore,
> And learn from her, as she from them before.
>
> (39–43)

Or, in the more pungent formulation of Webb's poem on William Penn, "Europe shall mourn her ancient Fame declin'd,/ And Philadelphia be the Athens of Mankind" (29–30).

Webb's conviction that the colonies would supplant their parent in greatness possessed more than prophetic audacity as warrant. History and literature provided several models of colonial supersession. Indeed, the most famous of imperial poems, Virgil's *Aeneid*, told that *Troy nova* (Rome) would be the greater Troy. The principle of metropolitan eclipse by a colony became a popular renaissance precept, employed by Bacon in "An Essay on Plantations" and by Machiavelli in *Discourses upon Titus Livius*. Nonetheless, it is novel that the cohort of poets residing in the raw capital being built on the Schuylkill should arrive at a general conviction that their country's ascendancy over Augusta was at hand. During the 1730s every element in Webb's prophecy received substantiation by other provincial poets. Jacob Taylor, the Quaker philomath and surveyor, [13] specified the political circumstance that made Pennsylvania the refuge of the world's lovers of peace:

> Oppressed Nations here for safety throng,
> From lawless Rage, and from vindictive Wrong:
> Here Britains fate do n'er with dread surprize,
> Sink under Taxes or foresee Excise.
> The painful *Belgian* can securely sleep,
> Nor dreads the dangers of th' uncertain deep:
> Distressed *Germans* here secure of Right,
> Fear not the force of titulary might:

No *Gallick Armies* can their Peace molest,
Destroy their Harvest or disturb their Rest:
The Hungry, Needy, and oppress'd with Ill,
Here seek thy Aid, and wait upon thy Will. [14]

"Ruris Amator" (Rev. Griffith Hughes?), [15] who published his compositions in the Philadelphia gazettes of the mid-1730s, suggested that the virtue of the country lay in its manifestation of the morality of nature. A
"noble savage"—a Chester County Indian named "Willigan"—instructed
the recent immigrant in the moderation of passion and indifference toward
the wars that passion impels.

He neither is concern'd to know
What Storms in Warlike *Russia* glow,
Nor what's the Fate of *Polish* Jars,
Of *Stanislaus*, or *Persian* Wars;
Or how, or when *Eugene* will curb
The short liv'd Joys of *Phillipsburg*:
More than a Monarch thus controuls
The various Passions of the Soul. [16]

Willigan's self-possession—his willing inclination to abide by the rule
of natural law—may be seen as analogous to William Penn's self-restriction
in law. Both exemplified self-government; both were presented as models
for emulation. Webb's use of Penn as a moral paragon was unembarrassedly
didactic. In the verse in Leeds's *American Almanack for 1730*, Webb noted
that Pennsylvania's "hopeful Youth in Emulation rise"—that the daughters
of the province evince wit "check't with Modesty" and Penn's own "sober
Sense." In subsequent decades this image of Penn as the archetype of virtue
and ability would remain vital. When Provost William Smith in 1753
hailed the promising youths of the Philadelphia Academy, he had William
Penn himself bestow a benediction on the rising generation.

I see my Spirit spread, ennobling, down
Thro' all your Country, and its GENIUS grown;
While by your softer Arts, and genuine Worth,
You rise the Wonder of the circling Earth.
But, with far higher Transports I behold,
Your glorious Plan the tender Thought t'unfold;
Where Emulation keens the virtuous Flame,
And Merit is the only Road to Fame. [17]

Thus Penn became the prototype of all virtuous Pennsylvanians; in a curious way the pattern of Penn's life became the general pattern of Pennsyl-

vania biography. Penn's virtue, and his self-government, were tested by the vicissitudes of experience. Webb reminded his reader that Penn's great deeds prevailed only after the experience of "Toils" and "Perils."

> How scorning Ease, didst tempt the raging Floods?
> How hew thy Passage thro' untrodden Woods?
> Thine was the Danger, Thine was all the Toil,
> While we, ungrateful We divide the Spoil.
>   (63–66)

Webb's tale of success through tribulation followed a form that we have already seen in Kirkpatrick's presentation of Columbus. It also fixed the pattern that most significant early Pennsylvania biography assumed. Franklin's account of his own rise from early hardships is, of course, well known. But others have survived. Joseph Breintnall's poetic account of the career of Aquila Rose is noteworthy. Rose fled England to escape a failed love affair, worked as a common seaman, shipped to Philadelphia, sickened in solitude, recovered from the brink of death by the ministrations of new friends, attracted the notice of great men by his talents, found new love, gained office and emolument, and died after winning renown.[18] Or we might think of Franklin's account in the *Autobiography* of poet George Webb himself. Webb gave up an Oxford scholarship to become a player, starved in London, signed indentures to the New World, and began his rise to reputation and appointment as official printer to South Carolina.[19] A life was considered noteworthy to the extent it followed the pattern of a rise from hardship. We know little about the careers of the Pennsylvanian writers who enjoyed life-long success—David French, William Becket, Henry Brooke, Jacob Taylor, Nicholas Scull—because contemporaries did not consider them worthy of comment. But the lives that did somehow embody the crisis of life in the Old World, the aspirations for asylum in a place of peace, the cultivation of the arts of peace in the New World—those lives were meaningful enough to be preserved in story.

One might suspect that the persons who sought refuge in Pennsylvania might have borne their old home ill will. But this was not always the case. William Penn, for one, stressed the need for a connection between New World and Old. Colonies provided for the relief of England, absorbing the country's excess population. Furthermore the life of virtuous labor in a rural setting produced citizens habitually disinclined to the luxuries of city living; these citizens would reinfuse republican simplicity into the body politic. So the colonies played a redemptive role in their relation to Britain, a role that would be forfeited if Pennsylvanians did not embrace the imperial connection.

Many of the early men of letters maintained an imaginative link with

Britain. Aquila Rose and his circle in the 1720s explored the experience of colonial expatriation by imitating Ovid's elegies of Scythian exile. "Ruris Amator" compared the natural education of the provinces with scholastic education, in an epistle to a friend at Oxford. And Webb in the third of his major poems on the *translatio studii*, an untitled paean to "George's Peace," detailed the manner of Pennsylvania's participation in the empire.[20]

The poem was a prophecy in which "the muse" witnesses a council of the gods called to weigh kingdoms in the scales of fate. Jove declares that "contending Powers/ Hesperian Realms disturb" and decrees that the "clarion shall be made to cease/ Since GEORGE and CAROLINA, call for Peace."[21] The British royal couple shall determine the peace, for "they more than we o'er Europe's Weal preside."

Jove's oracle would sound offensively deferential if it were not for the political circumstances that stood behind the declaration. George II and Caroline by 1731 had inaugurated a great era of European peace, having played an instrumental role in the establishment of the Quadruple Alliance. In Parliament Queen Caroline's favorite, Walpole, administered the peace policy. He promised that prosperity would arise from refusing to respond with armed might to Spanish depredations upon British shipping, for inaction would slow the drain on the exchequer. The peace policy enjoyed favor in the colonies more for what it promised than what it accomplished, for the Spanish troubled the West Indies trade upon which many a provincial fortune depended. Webb, writing at the moment when the promise of peace seemed brightest, invoked the prospect of tranquility with a fervor matched only by James Thomson's invocation in *Britannia*:

> Oh, *Peace!* thou Source, and Soul of social Life;
> Beneath whose calm, inspiring Influence,
> Science his Views enlarges, Art refines,
> And swelling Commerce opens all her Ports;
> Blest be the man divine, who gives us Thee!
>   (*Britannia* 122–26)

Webb, who died in 1731, did not live long enough to witness the failure of Walpole's policy with the War of Jenkins' Ear, nor did he feel Thomson's suspicion concerning the prime minister.[22]

Human greatness consisted for Webb in the ability of a person to exert a determinative civic influence beyond his or her mortal term. Penn survived in his Charter of Liberties, and Webb foresaw George II and Caroline undergoing a similar immortalization: "King and Queen shall quit their low abodes / And mount and mingle with their kindred Gods." Their heavenly influence would nurture their "Offspring" below. Philadelphia of all the "Offspring" would be accorded favored status, because its government had embraced the preservation of peace as its prime directive. In effect, the poem equated the rule of law as embodied in Penn's charter with the policies of George II and Caroline. Nicholas Scull, after hearing Webb recite the poem in a meeting of the Junto, recorded in verse what he thought notable in the performance. He said nothing about Philadelphia's promised greatness. Rather,

> Britania happy in the best of Kings
> How her great Monarch by judicious care
> Has gaind a peace without the cost of war
> that with a nod from his Imperial throne
> Contending nations lay their arms down.[23]

What was the imperial faith of the poetic beneficiaries of Penn's philanthropy? When a "judicious" king presides, then the empire inspires loyalty and gratitude. When his proprietary vicegerent abides by a charter of liberties that ensures the regulated conduct of affairs, then promises of future wealth and greatness are credited widely. Until the promise is fulfilled, it is the task of poets, as priests of the civil religion, to reiterate it. By its repetition the country and the Penn proprietors are reminded of their obligations in the social contract. Witness Rev. William Becket of Lewes writing to Thomas Penn in 1738:

> In future Times a City shall arise
> Whose lofty Top shal[l] stretch toward the Skies
> Far, Far remov'd from fam'd Brittannia's Shore,
> But guided Still by her auspicious Lore.
> An English Chiefs Descendents claim the Ground
> (A Chief for Wisdom & for Arms renown'd.)
> I see a mighty River wash her side
> And wealth still flowing in, with e'ery Tide.
> There stately Oaks, shall lofty Piles adorn;
> And yet perplex'd with various Weeds and Thorn
> Here Industry & Peace shall fix their Seat,
> & Plenty make her Pleasant, Happy, Great.
> There Liberty shall reign, & Bless her State,
> (The Subjects, Blessing, but the Tyrants Hate)
> Europa's sons observing with surprize
> So great a Town, in so few Years arise.
> Their golden Instruments the Muses string
>   And eccho'd back what great Apollo sing.[24]

THE BENEFACTOR

Georgia, the last of Britain's mainland settlements in the New World, attempted to elevate charity to a status commensurate with the other motives of colonization—procurement of religious liberty, the creation of wealth, and the sequestration of territory.[25] Attempts had been made before James Oglethorpe's expedition of 1732 to establish an English settlement south of Carolina. Robert Mountgomery in 1717 had promised bountiful wealth to all who would settle in his "Margravate of Azilia" south of the Savannah River.[26] But promises of wealth no longer sufficed in the second decade of the century, for the bursting of the South Seas Bubble and the collapse of the Mississippi venture had tarnished the promises of colonial adventure. Mountgomery's enterprise collapsed. Only when the profit motive was subordinated and a scheme of colonization devised to solve an enduring British social problem, poverty, were monies forthcoming to back settlement. Then the resources of "the philanthrophic movement" were thrown behind the project and a subsidy secured from Parliament. The Trustees of Thomas Bray and the other bodies contributing to the formation of Georgia believed their contributions to be a sort of "seed money" that would permit unfortunates in England to work themselves to prosperity in the New World.[27] Only when the opportunity to gain material sufficiency was extended to the class that could least afford to refuse opportunity—the impoverished of Great Britain—did a colony come into being. James Edward Oglethorpe, a friend of Bray and an active member of the philanthropic movement, presided over the birth.

Like Penn (who was a political ally of Oglethorpe's father Theophilus from 1689 to 1694), the founder of Georgia envisioned his colony as a refuge for those who did not enjoy the full fruits of liberty. Oglethorpe knew about the benefit of liberty firsthand, for he had won political reputation in the great parliamentary investigation of Britain's prisons. The four reports he composed condemning the arbitrary power of the corrupt wardens became landmarks in the development of British humanitarianism. When Oglethorpe turned to a consideration of what to do with the debtors whom prison reform had released into the streets of London, he reaffirmed the solution proposed by Penn: transportation to new lands. To Penn's notion of a refuge, Oglethorpe added a vision of territorial empire.

Military service, familiarity with the designs of the European powers gained from his Jacobite boyhood, and a distrust of Walpole's efforts to disarm Britain contributed to Oglethorpe's conviction that Georgia could perform a strategic service defending the southern frontier. Incessant Spanish harassment of Britain's West Indies trade convinced reluctant parliamentary backers of Walpole's peace program of the efficacy of the colony. So, binding charity to militant imperialism, Oglethorpe promoted the "British Peace" with a Roman notion of how to enforce the *pax civica*.

In the campaign to reform Britain's prisons, Oglethorpe had learned the value of conducting a publicity campaign to mold public opinion. When the trustees of Georgia organized, they assigned Oglethorpe the task of conducting the publicity for the new enterprise. The years 1731 and 1732 saw a flood of newspaper reportage about the proposed colony. Oglethorpe himself penned *A New and Accurate Account of the Provinces of South-Carolina and Georgia*, and he oversaw distribution of the two other major prospectuses sponsored by the trustees: Benjamin Martyn's *Some Account of the Designs of the Trustees* (1732) and *Reasons for Establishing the Colony of Georgia* (1733). [28] These efforts had two results: they secured a grant from the home government in support of the colony (a unique development in American colonization to that date) and stimulated a literary cult of personality around Oglethorpe. This cult erupted into ecstatic praise when Oglethorpe determined in 1731 to accompany the colonists as resident trustee.

In Charleston, "a muse from *India*'s savage plain" (perhaps James Kirkpatrick) celebrated the moral courage that prompted Oglethorpe to brave the crossing:

> Oceans in vain their bounds immense oppose,
> And speechless horrors to the eye disclose . . .
> Nor less in vain to stay his great efforts,
> The arts of cities and the pomp of courts:
> Senates, which lately charm'd, with ease he flies;
> While from neglect augmented glories rise. [29]

As a resident in the New World, the poet was not blind to the practical dimensions of the Georgia enterprise. He did not fall into the error of imagining Oglethorpe as some champion of utopian harmony founding a land "whose plains no armies vex,/ Nor purple gore with thy clear rivers mix" (Moses Browne[?], "To the honourable James Oglethorpe). [30] The American has Oglethorpe announce,

> "Iberia's motley race a bound shall know,
> "And slave contented in the mine below:
> "Nor Gallia's sons of new encroachments dream
> "Glad while they taste the Mississippi stream:
> "In peace 'till we preside, in war prevail,
> "And the new world allow the British scale."
> (49–55)

The thoughts expressed here more closely approximate Oglethorpe's thinking through the 1730s than do the imaginings of the London panegyrists. The Spanish at St. Augustine presented the primary threat, since Oglethorpe's settlements and fortifications encroached on territory claimed by Iberia. The French under Bienville at Mobile presented a more distant danger, but one that worried Carolinians greatly because of France's oft-repeated strategy of extending its hegemony through Indian proxies.

Oglethorpe would check the French threat by cultivating friendship with the Creek Indians. He arranged that Parliament provide a regular grant of "presents" to the Creek leaders. He befriended the chief of Yamacraw natives settled at Musgrave's trading post on the Savannah River where the English built their capital.[31] Chief Tomochichi in the legend surrounding Oglethorpe assumed much the same role that the Leni Lenape chief, Tammany, held in the mythology surrounding Penn. Both greeted the English founder with words of welcome and tokens of trust. Both were paragons of natural virtue who recognized a similar morality in their English counterpart. When Tomochichi accompanied Oglethorpe to London, the genuine signs of regard between the men seemed in the eyes of the trustees and the general public a proof of the humanitarian program. Poets attached to the philanthropic movement could not restrain themselves from proclaiming the foundation of the peaceable kingdom. Thomas Fitzgerald in an ode upon the Yamacraw chief used the Indian as a lash to whip the vices of Britons,

> dissolv'd in soft luxurious Ease,
>   Our ancient Virtue vanish'd soon away.
> Rare to be found is the old gen'rous Strain
>   So fam'd amongst us once for Patriot Zeal,
> Of try'd Good Faith, and Manners stanch and plain,
>   And bold and active for their Country's Weal;
> Clear from all Stain, superior to all Fear;
>   Alas! few such as These, few OGLETHORPES are here.[32]

Oglethorpe, the avatar of British virtue, and Tomochichi, nature's nobleman, carried more than the usual burden of moral paragons. They served more than the usual task of providing a standard by which to measure the declensions of contemporary character. They are the means by which the moral regeneration of fallen Britons will be accomplished.

> Oft hast thou seen with what assiduous Care
>   His [Oglethorpe's] own young Infant Colony he rears;
> Like a fond Parent anxious to prepare
>   His tender Offspring for maturer Years.
> To Love of Labour he subdues their Minds,
>   And forms their Morals with instructive Laws,
> By Principle their solid Union binds,
>   And Zeal that only heeds the Public Cause;
> Still with Example strenth'ning Reason's Call,
> Still by superior Toil distinguish'd from them all.
>   (71–80)

Patriarchs do not simply provide examples; they actively intervene in the reformation of the offspring. As Milton Ready has explained, the particular reformation sought by the projectors of Georgia was the weaning of the poor from the habits of indolence "to Love of Labour."[33] Oglethorpe "by superior Toil distinguish'd from them all" will "subdue" indolence by his "assiduous Care."

Armed with zeal and care Oglethorpe militated against the "relaxation of discipline and corruption of manners" that Locke and Defoe had identified as the cause of "the growth of the poor."[34] The reclamation of the poor would, in turn, assist in the improvement of public morals. The founding of Georgia must be viewed as a political counterpart to the great jeremiad the Augustan satirists directed against the decay of manners in Britain. "Scarce *Egypt*'s Land more dire Disasters knew," observed the author of one trenchant catalogue of England's woes published in the *Virginia Gazette*:

> Landlords who seize for Rent, when we've no Coin,
> Sour Ale, Small Beer, False Reck'nings, and Brew'd Wine;
> Guttling Church-Wardens, Overseers Rapacious,
> And Trading Justices of Law Tenacious;
> Canters, Quack-Doctors, Pettifoggers, Punners,
> Pimps, Parasites, and Usurers, and Dunners;
> Tip-Staffs, Tom-Turdmen, Messengers of State,
> The Pack'd-up Jury, and the Prison Grate.[35]

Oglethorpe harrowed the hell of prison; from the horrors of Britain's dungeons the "squalid wretches feel the day restor'd." The liberty of the street, Oglethorpe knew, was not liberty enough, for the freed debtor still suffered the bondage of his want. It was to the poor that we see Oglethorpe directing his secular beatitudes. "The muse from India's savage plain" codified in poetic language the benefactor's invitation:

>   "here let the wretch have peace,
> "Nor fear to pine, while wasting nature fails,
> "By tedious intervals of scanty meals,
> "The gaping young loud craving new supplies,
> "The weeping parent's wretched lot denies;
> "Nor as when shaking near the frosty pole,
> "They trembled more to heap the stinted coal.
> "Whilst here luxuriant forests gladly spare
> "The sweetest fuel for the choicest fare."
>   (37–46)

This is the Oglethorpe that the philanthropic literature preserved, the material redeemer of the poor and homeless—"Indulgent Providence has thee design'd,/ Its Blessings to diffuse to human Kind."[36] James Thomson concurred. In *Liberty*, the poet's most ambitious exposition of Whig ideals, he showed that Georgia's blessings were not restricted to distressed Britons; Oglethorpe provided

> a calm retreat
> Of undeserved distress, the better home
> Of those whom bigots chase from foreign lands;
> Not built on rapine, servitude, and woe,
> And in their turn some petty tyrant's prey,
> But, bound by social freedom, firm they rise.[37]

Thomson's claims were not fanciful; the infant colony did provide refuge for many of the distressed peoples of Europe. The Lutheran Salzburgers, Count Zinzandorf's Moravians, and a community of Jews found haven in Georgia. All were invited to settle except for Roman Catholics, presumably because they were the "bigots" who tyrannized the afflicted of Europe. Poets did not doubt that a "wand'ring Emigrant" who found refuge in Georgia would prove to be a useful citizen of the British empire. Gratitude for liberty and "the Men that did this Port provide" would inspire loyalty ("To James Oglethorpe Esq; on His late Arrival from Georgia"). The poets did not foresee how Oglethorpe's imperial designs on Florida would force the Moravians to move to Pennsylvania rather than bear arms for the colony; nor did they foresee that peculiarities of property ownership contained in the colony's charter (male entail, the prohibition on ownership of slaves, the absence of fee-simple land ownership) would eventually lead to unrest among the Scots Calvinists.

Benjamin Martyn explained the rationale for Georgia's peculiar treatment of property rights in *Reasons for Establishing the Colony of Georgia*. Large tracts would not be granted to settlers because "experience has shown the Inconvenience of private Persons possessing too large Quantities of Land in our Colonies, by which means, the greatest Part of it must lye uncultivated."[38] Fee-simple transfer of title would not be allowed because it would permit speculation in land. The trustees identified in the experience of Virginia and Carolina the immoderate appetite for gain that had turned Britain into a modern Egypt. If colonists were not allowed "to alienate their Lands without Leave of the Trustees, none certainly will go over, but with a Design to be industrious", since the fruit of the land and not the land itself would be the basis of wealth.

Reading Martyn's tract we can understand why in the philanthropic mythology Tomochichi must stand with Oglethorpe as archetype of the reformed Georgian. If labor alone could reclaim the poor, then the local workhouse might suffice. Yet once the workhouse had overthrown the indolence of the impoverished, the newly industrious would bend their energies to the immoderate accumulation of those things the society about them deemed valuable—real property, finery, consumer luxuries.[39] The poor must be taught not only to love labor, but to resist temptation. Tomochichi, the virtuous leader of a people who did not count real property as wealth, can be understood as a characterological model alternative to the prosperous citizen. His life, supported by the fruits of the land garnered by his own industry, illustrated to rich and poor the simple virtues of life lived in contact with nature.

The irony of the philanthropic myth was that the commodities the colonists would be producing in Georgia were in many cases the luxuries that fueled temptation in the Old World. Silk, wine, and tropical fruit were prominent among the items that Oglethorpe and Martyn believed to be the sources of profit. The American poets saw with more clarity than their English brethren the commercial possibilities of the infant colony. James Kirkpatrick [?] (the "muse from India's savage plain") in neighboring Charleston credited the visions of prosperity. When the "gloomy wood" had been converted into pasture and field and when cities arose where once the tiger ranged,

> Then may the great reward, assign'd by fate,
> Prove thy own wish,—to see the work compleat;
> Till *Georgia's* silks on *Albion's* beauties shine,
> Or gain new lustre from the royal line:
> Till from the sunny hills the Vines display
> Their various berries to the gilded day:
> Whence the glad vintage to the vale may flow,
> Refreshing labour, and dispelling woe.
> While the fat plains with pleasant olives shine,
> And *Zaura's* date improves the barren pine.
> Fair in the garden shall the lemmon grow,
> And every grove *Hesperian* apples show.
> The almond, the delicious fruit behold,
> Whose juice the feign'd immortals quaff'd of old.
> Nor haply on the well-examin'd plain
> Shall *China's* fragrant leaf be sought in vain;
> While the consenting climate gladly proves;
> The costly balms that weep in Indian Groves.
>
> (77–94)

Here revealed is the global consciousness that mercantilism had engendered. Indeed, Georgia has been transmuted into the world in the poet's imagining. The sole native product, the solitary image of intrinsic worth, is the gum drawn from "Indian Groves"—sap collected for pharmacological purposes, or for use in perfumes. Once the sap has been drawn and the groves cleared, the orchards will, like some horticultural garden, mix the cultivars of the several continents. No doubt the longitudinal analogies between Georgia and the holy land drawn in works such as Joshua Gee's *Trade and Navigation of Great Britain Considered* (1729) fired the fanciful visions of dates, olives, and citrus fruit.[40] But this exercise in wishful projection had other purposes. By conceiving the land relatively barren of native produce, Oglethorpe amplified the importance of labor. The settlers cannot thrive on the natural bounty of the land. Georgia is no lubberland where colonists may grow fat plucking fruit from "low-embowered limbs." The colonists would have to work to thrive; by such work they would be morally transformed.

Oglethorpe's fascination with silk production arose out of his considerations of the labor it entailed, a labor affording work to all members of a family. "It must be a weak Hand indeed that cannot earn Bread where Silkworms and White Mulberry-trees are so plenty. Most of the Poor in Great Britain, who are maint'd by Charity, are capable of this, tho' not of harder Labour."[41] Rev. Samuel Wesley conceived of the distribution of labor differently. Rather than the weakened poor managing the cocoons, the worms would be tended by women: "Here tend the Silk Worm in the verdant Shade,/ The frugal Matron and the blooming Maid."[42] In the hopes of making these visions a reality, one hundred thousand white mulberry trees were planted during the provincial era in the public garden at Savannah. The silk industry failed on the eve of the Revolution.

Of the many literary writings tempting Britons to transplant to Oglethorpe's utopia, Rev. Samuel Wesley's *Georgia* was the most influential writing contributed independently of the trustees' publicity campaign. Its repute stemmed more from reasons of circumstance than from literary merit. Wesley had early found Oglethorpe a subject worthy of literary treatment. The prison investigation prompted Wesley's *The Prisons Open'd*. The author's cousins, John and Charles Wesley, had voyaged to the colony to minister to the inhabitants. And he himself had become a friend of Oglethorpe. *Georgia* was prompted by Oglethorpe's second trip to the colony, after he had quieted the trustees' trepidations and mustered parliamentary support for the enterprise. Wesley explained the founder's absence to the people of the colony in an ancillary poem, "A Copy of Verses on Mr. Ogelthorpe's Second Voyage to Georgia":

> He comes, whose Life, while absent from your View,
> Was one continued Ministry for you;
> For you were laid out all his Pains and Art,
> Won ev'ry Will and soften'd ev'ry Heart.
> With what paternal Joy shall he relate,
> How views its Mother Isle your little State.
> (29–34)

In *Georgia* Wesley depicted Oglethorpe absorbed in imagining the colony's "prospects fair" while in transit across the Atlantic. He envisioned "Another BRITAIN in the Desart" and pictured the profusion of commodities that will be.

> Here the wild Vine to Culture learns to yield,
> And purple Clusters ripen through the Field.
> Now bid thy Merchants bring thy Wine no more
> Or from the *Iberian* or the *Tuscan* Shore . . .
> Delicious Nectar, powerful to improve
> Our hospitable Mirth and social Love.
>
> (249–52, 257–58)

Wesley's pleasant scenes of "this paradise of the world" so epitomized the philanthropic view of the enterprise that the colony's malcontents used it as the text for their critical reinterpretation of the province, *A True and Historical Narrative of the Colony of Georgia in America.* The malcontents, called the "Scotch Club," were Freemasons, whose discontents broke out during Oglethorpe's absence from the colony. One member of the circle was imprudent enough to be detected posting satiric poems at the pump and tavern and was brought to justice for libel.[43] When they next moved to literary endeavors, they sought the more congenial climate of Charleston where they printed their deconstruction of the Georgia of philanthrophic fantasy at Peter Timothy's press. With Patrick Tailfer and David Douglas, Hugh Anderson, a gentleman who had heeded the promise of Georgia, and found the labor too great and the recompense too small for his liking, ridiculed the Georgia of poetry point by point. "From the whole, we doubt not, the reader will look upon us as sufficiently punished for our credulity: And indeed, who would not have been catched with such promises, such prospects? What might not the poor man flatter himself with, from such an alteration in situation? And how much more might a gentleman expect from a plentiful stock of his own, and numbers of servants to set up with? Could a person, with the least faith, have questioned the committing of his interests to such guardians, and such a tender father as Mr. Oglethorpe was believed to be?"[44] These ironic questions cast doubt upon the crucial promise of philanthropic colonization, the material redemption of life.

Anderson and Tailfer attacked other aspects of the scheme as well. "As for those poetical licences touching the wine and silk; we do not transcribe them as a reflection upon the author; but as a satyr upon the mismanagement of those manufactures; since no measures were taken that seemed really intended for their advancement." Anderson's intentional misreading of Wesley's poem challenged the commercial fantasy attaching to the province, yet more on the grounds of the leadership of enterprises than the possibility of silk and wine production. "We no wise question the possibility of advancing such improvements in Georgia, with far less sums of money, properly flourishing of wine and silk can make a colony of British subjects happy, if they are deprived of the liberties and properties of their birth-right." Here the malcontents make their most telling points. The phi-lanthropic paternalism of "tender father" Oglethorpe did not permit the residents of Georgia a legislature, nor the range of property rights available to British subjects in other regions of the empire. While many might sym-pathize with Oglethorpe's disinclination to permit the ownership of chattel slaves, the limiting of inheritance to male offspring and the restrictions on land ownership cannot be considered anything except a relative curtailment of liberties.

The earl of Egmont, president of the Georgia trustees, observed in the margins of his copy of *A True and Historical Narrative of the Colony of Georgia*, "One would expect the Hyperboles of Poetry Should not have influenced so wise an Author as Mr. Anderson to quit his native Country. The meanest School boy makes due allowance for such flights."[45] Yet the images of mate-rial and moral regeneration were more potent than reason would allow. And the promises that had attached to Georgia made the languishing condition of the colony during the 1740s that much more distressing to those who believed in "the ethical empire."

Curiously, General Oglethorpe contributed to the poetic metamorphosis of Georgia from utopia to a New World purgatory. After his return to En-gland and his rustication from the army after the events of 1745, the bene-factor became involved with the literary circle superintended by Samuel Johnson. Oglethorpe's tales of the hardships of pioneer life in Georgia prompted Goldsmith to imagine the dire fate that awaited the dispossessed inhabitants of *The Deserted Village* on the banks of the Altamahata.

> Far different there from all that charm'd before,
> The various terrors of that horrid shore;
> Those blazing suns that dart a downward ray,
> And fiercely shed intolerable day;
> Those matted woods where birds forget to sing,
> But silent bats in drowsy clusters cling;
> Those pois'nous fields with rank luxuriance crown'd,
> Where the dark scorpion gathers death around.[46]

The imaginative legacies of Oglethorpe's experiment were not wholly tainted by the trials of the 1740s. In the evangelical community, Georgia became a vision of the attempt to make the Kingdom of God workable. The chrism of Georgia annointed the Wesleys and Whitefield. The latter's cam-paign to fund the Orphan House located in the colony became the warrant for his itineration. Oglethorpe, himself, retained something of the aura of benevolence for the remainder of his long life. Indeed, much later, when John Adams presented his credentials as first representative of the United States, he submitted them to the one person the English government chose to symbolize the nobility it attached to the lost American empire, the ancient General Oglethorpe.

4

Staples

Maryland, the only proprietary colony to be restored after the Hanoverian accession, treated the Calverts with greater circumspection than Pennsylvania did the Penns and Georgia, Oglethorpe. When the male Calverts converted to the Church of England after the death of the second Lord Baltimore in 1715, then rebuked the governmental excesses of their Catholic agent, Charles Carroll, the Anglican establishment in Maryland recognized the proprietors' good faith.[1] George I's restoration of proprietary privilege seemed in provincial eyes a demonstration of the family's entree to the Hanoverians. Access to the centers of power meant the possible redress of the one problem that obsessed natives—a tobacco trade that enriched English merchants at the expense of Maryland planters and factors. To a noteworthy degree, the provincial perception of the Calverts attached to the issue of tobacco. Tobacco dominated the economic life of Maryland. We see an instance where proprietary mystique was supplanted by a pragmatic concern with profit. Praise came to the Calverts when they enhanced the prospect for profit; blame when they failed. If anything possessed mystique in Maryland, it was the material upon which the colony's fortune was built: tobacco.

Tobacco's mystique arose in good part from negative factors. Of all the staples it was the most problematic. It was difficult to cultivate, falling victim to worms and disease. It inflicted injury on cultivators, the juice of green tobacco stinging like wasp venom when entering sores or cuts. It exhausted soil rapidly. It possessed no nutritional or medicinal value. Yet by 1714 a vast literature had been generated concerning "the bewitching vegetable." In hundreds of plays, tracts, and poetic squibs (the bulk of which were collected and described in *Tobacco—Its History Illustrated by the Books, Manuscripts, and Engravings in the Library of George Arents, Jr.*), the psychotropic effects, the fashionability, the frivolity, and the immorality of tobacco use received comment. The offense to common sense of placing a

burning vegetable in one's mouth in order to secure physical satisfaction
was so great that this staple alone of those produced in British America defied heroic treatment. Americans composed georgics upon the cultivation
of sugar-cane, indigo, rice, and, in the republican era, cotton. No one attempted to be a modern Virgil on behalf of "sot-weed." Its history was a
matter to be treated lightly—as in William Byrd's tale of its introduction
to the English court, recounted in the public version of the *Histories of the
Dividing Line betwixt Virginia and North Carolina*:

> These first Adventurers made a very profitable Voyage, raising at least a
> Thousand per cent. upon their cargo. Amongst other Indian Commodities, they
> brought over Some of the bewitching Vegetable, Tobacco. And this being the
> first that ever came to England, Sir Walter thought he could do no less than
> make a present of Some of the brightest of it to His Roial Mistress, for her own
> Smoaking.
>
> The Queen graciously accepted of it, but finding her Stomach sicken after
> two or three Whiffs, it was presently whispered by the earl of Leicester's Faction,
> that Sir Walter had certainly Poison'd Her. But Her Majesty soon recovering her
> Disorder, obliged the Countess of Nottingham and all her Maids to Smoak a
> whole Pipe out amongst them.[2]

Tobacco merchants, because of their avidity for instant wealth and their
ignorance of provincial ways, served as butts for two of early America's more
outrageous satires: Henry Brooke's "The New Metamorphosis" and Ebenezer Cooke's *The Sot-Weed Factor*.[3] The consumer of tobacco also inspired ridicule. One of the finer travesty poems of the Augustan era was Isaac Browne's
"A Pipe of Tobacco," which rhapsodized hyperbolically over the effects of a
smoke in the styles of the major poets of the day. Among the undergraduates at Harvard "A Satyr on Tobacco" circulated in manuscript, cherished as
an exquisite piece of wit.

> Tobacco, mortal Pest! of Weeds the worst
> When careful cut or when reduc'd to Dust.
> Drawn thro' a Tube, oft have I seen thy Fume
> In Clouds wide-spreading sail around the Room;
> Ascending slowly, with a lingring Grace,
> Curl from the Lips & play before th' Face;
> Still rowling on winds, taint the dying Light
> And o'er the Eye-Balls call the Shades of Night.
> So frowning Pluto, in his dark abodes
> Tremendous, grins behind a Gloom of Clouds;
>
> . . . .
>
> Inspir'd by thee Fops write heroick Strains
> And with thy Dung manure their barren Brains;
> By thee each clumsy Clown a Gallant grows
> And Awkward, guides thee to his nasty Nose;

Stung by thy Strength, into a dire Grimace
He wrings the horrid Features of his Face;
Redoubling Sneezes from his Lungs resound,
And all the laughing Croud bespatter round.[4]

Indeed, the single aspect of tobacco that did not lend itself to humor was
the economic effect of tobacco trade on the colonies. Because the economic
welfare of populations hung on this issue, the tobacco trade inspired serious
literary reflection.

TRADING WEED

In *A Description of the Golden Islands* (1720), one finds an aphorism about
wealth pertinent to the era of colonial venture. Robert Mountgomery observed, "There are but two safe Bottoms (in Designs of this Nature) on
which Men may build Expectations of Profit. One of these is *land*; the other
Trade".[5] The experience of the colonial with both land and trade differed
from that of an inhabitant of the British Isles. Colonials outside of Georgia
enjoyed the fee-simple transfer of land title, something Britons would not
have on a mass scale until the success of the enclosure movement at the end
of the eighteenth century. In trade, the colonist had to sell or exchange
goods according to strict parliamentary restrictions, enacted in 1696.
While certain commodities—wheat, fish, and maize most notably—were
exchanged on an international "free market", the "enumerated commodities"—tobacco, sugar, rice, mast timber, furs, indigo, whale oil, iron, and
pine tar—fell under the restraint of the Acts upon Trade and Navigation.[6]
James Oglethorpe was a pioneer in the resistance to the restrictive pattern of trade imposed upon the empire. In a series of parliamentary speeches
and in his promotional writings for Georgia, Oglethorpe laid out the argument on behalf of free trade. It rested on several propositions. Always an
imperialist, Oglethorpe held that might on the seas ensured British prosperity, and that trade was the greatest support of British sea might. He
noted that the merchant trade supplied an expanding pool of experienced
sailors available for use in the defense of British interests. He noted that the
effort required to prosper in trade accustomed people to look for recompense
from labor. "Spain . . . has great Countries and more Subjects in America
than we have, and yet does not navigate in that Trade a Tenth Part of the
Shipping that we do. By a lucky kind of Poverty our Dominions there have
no Mines of Gold, or Silver: We must be, and ought to be contented to deal
in Rum, Sugar, Rice, Tobacco, Horses, Beef, Corn, Fish, Lumber, and
other Commodities that require great Stowage".[7] The final strand of the
argument attacked the hierarchical presupposition that grounded the old

mercantilism. Oglethorpe argued that Britain's own success in trade resulted from her willingness to compete throughout Europe in the woolen market. Should colonies be relegated perpetually to economic disadvantage by suffering trade restrictions that the fatherland had cast off on its own way to wealth? No; the colonies should possess the same liberty to trade that the parent country enjoyed.[8]

Of the enumerated commodities, tobacco accrued the greatest wealth to Britain during the decades before the Revolution. Britain controlled the European market for tobacco.[9] The French purchased their supplies from British merchants at triple markup and distributed them within France through a monopoly. Strict control of trade coupled with heavy duties on importation drove the price up; consequently demand was dampened. In the tobacco colonies, Maryland and Virginia, the static demand created periodic crises in the economy, because the number of cultivators kept increasing. The consequence was a glut in supply. In the late 1720s Maryland suffered an economic depression because of a tobacco glut. The situation prompted the two foremost poets in the colony, Ebenezer Cooke and Richard Lewis, to confront the problems of production and trade.

Cooke, known to American literature as the author of "The Sot-Weed Factor" (1707), a burlesque on a greenhorn's experiences in Maryland as a tobacco trader, returned in 1730 to a consideration of his countrymen's staple crop. *Sotweed Redivivus* responded to the Maryland Assembly's attempt to spur demand by ordering the destruction of inferior leaf. The attempt was futile. Two circumstances prevented legislative efforts to find another source of revenue: the crop was the medium of exchange in the colony (its money in effect), and the planters were too timid to attempt cultivation of other revenue-producing crops.

Cooke offered two remedies: ratification of a currency bill, and the diversification of production. (These would be remedies that generations of colonial legislators would attempt to enact, with marginal success, in the ensuing decades.) The Maryland Assembly had considered a currency bill, but debate between proponents of hard money and inflatable paper currency frustrated passage. Cooke was impatient with such quibbling: "It's Money, be it what it will,/ In Tan-Pit coin'd, or Paper-Mill,/ That must the hungry Belly fill."[10] When considering the problem of sot-weed's oversupply, Cooke has Coucherouse, an experienced planter, advance a plan. Cultivation would be limited to six hundredweight per landowning citizen. The supply would thereby be restricted by a monopoly imposed at the source. The planter would receive the majority of his revenue from "Grain, Hemp, Flax, Rice" and "Cotton." Sheep and cattle would supply wool and hides.

Cooke does not consider the alternative remedy: the establishment of a free market for the commodity with Europe. This would break the artificially high price structure, stimulate consumption, and allow locals to prosper by continuing to cultivate the product they know best. Couche-rouse's method of driving up price by limiting supply sacrifices the one de-sideratum of all economies; an ever-expanding market. A second liability to Coucherouse's plan is that he suggests the colony produce those very things—sheep and cloth goods—that Britain views as its economic foun-dation. The parent country was not about to look favorably upon price com-petition from its own colonies. Despite these liabilities Coucherouse's advice has one thing to recommend it: it details a course of action that the settlers could take. This faith in the planters' ability to overcome self-interest and concert their wills reveals a public-spiritedness difficult to asso-ciate with the author of *The Sot-Weed Factor*. When Richard Lewis mused upon the remedies available to Maryland he placed his hopes in hands other than those of the natives.[11]

The difficulty of the tobacco trade was that the artificially high price lev-els the monopoly engendered were instituted to provide the king revenue—the benefits were disproportionately weighted toward London and the pal-ace. British botanists had discovered that tobacco could be grown in the British Isles, but a royal edict prohibited its cultivation to protect the king's revenue.[12] Because other monarchs could accrue similar benefits through-out Europe by instituting their own state monopolies supplied through the sole source (this was an artificially "rationalized" economic system), they did not attempt to break the British stranglehold on the commodity.

Lewis, unlike Cooke, held little hope for a restriction of production, per-haps because neighboring Virginia would seize the opportunity to dump its second-rate leaf on the market to fill the gap between demand and supply. Rather, he looked to the imperial hierarchy for remedy. The Calvert pro-prietors of Maryland heard repeated requests for intervention with the king on behalf of the colony. Lewis's pleas were designed to alert the Calverts of their own stake in the prosperity of the colony's planters. In an ode "To His Excellency Benedict Leonard Calvert, Governour, and Commander in Chief, in and over the Province of Maryland" (1728), Lewis calls upon the colony's leader

> To animate the PEOPLE, now dismayed,
> And add new Life to our declining TRADE;
> We hope to see soft Joys o'erspread the *Land*,
> And *happier Times*, deriv'd from *Your Command*.
> For should Your EXCELLENCY'S Plan take Place,
> Soon will returning *Plenty* shew its Face:
> The *Markets* for our STAPLE, would advance,
> Nor shall we live, as *now* we do, by CHANCE.
> No more, the lab'ring PLANTER shall complain
> How *vast* his *Trouble!* but how *small* his *Gain!*[13]

Calvert hoped to ease the restrictions of the monopoly. Lewis seized upon the hope Lord Baltimore extended for the advancement of the tobacco market. In *Carmen Seculare* (1732), a civic ode modeled on Matthew Prior's panegyric to King William, and occasioned by the hundredth anniversary of the founding of Maryland, Lewis hailed the arrival of Charles Calvert, Lord Baltimore, and his bride in the colony.[14] To acquaint the absentee proprietor with the concerns of the planters while commending the Calvert influence, Lewis inserted a special commendation of brother Benedict, "who unweary'd strove/ Our long declining Staple to improve."[15] To impress Lord Baltimore with the gravity of the problem the poet interrupted his ode with a complaint:

> TO long, alas! *Tobacco* has engross'd
> Our Cares, and now we mourn our Markets lost:
> The plenteous Crops that over-spread our Plains,
> Reward with Poverty the toiling Swains:
> Their sinking *Staple* chills the Planters Hearts,
> Nor dare they venture on unpractis'd Arts;
> Despondent, they impending Ruin view,
> Yet starving, must their old Employ persue.[16]

Having dramatized the colony's woe, Lewis declared its hope: "In this Distress to YOU they turn their Eyes,/ From YOU, My LORD, their Hopes of Comfort rise." Why Lord Baltimore? "Your happy Station in the British Court,/ Enables You your Province to support."

The hopes attached to Lord Baltimore's influence were not restricted to Maryland. John Markland, from tobacco-growing Virginia, in "To the Right Honourable CHARLES, Lord Baron of Baltimore," hailed him "whose Station is advanc'd so near/ BRITANNIA's other Hope, and Royal HEIR."[17] Markland played upon Baltimore's love of reputation with the flattering suggestion that Calvert's Maryland with its tradition of religious liberty served as model for Oglethorpe's Georgia.

> Already see! the brave Example fires,
> And *Oglethorpe* new Settlements enquires:
> A kind Regard to succour the distrest,
> To seek a Refuge for the poor opprest,
> Engages all his Charitable Breast.
> (43–47)

The support that Lewis and his contemporaries asked Lord Baltimore to supply was twofold: intervention with the king and king's counselors to break or diminish the stranglehold on trade, and encouragement of new industries. Calvert did little in either regard. Sir John Randolph of Virginia did more good for Maryland planters by complaining of the short-weighting of tobacco hogsheads by British factors; in his testimony before Parliament Randolph made his point by reminding the legislators that the short-weighting deprived the crown of its proper level of duties.[18] Thus the dreaded duty was marshaled as justification for the remedy of the planters' trouble. A graver disappointment attached to Calvert's apathy in encouraging the diversification of Maryland's economy. Lewis had hoped that Maryland could supply flax, silk, wine, fish, and ore. The colonies would prosper if they produced items (semitropical fruits for instance) that were incapable of being produced in Europe, or if they supplied at lower cost materials offered by England's European competitors (Maryland's in place of France's "nectareous Juice"; American linen, "finer . . . than *Germany* can yield"). Yet Lewis was not content with making Maryland an agricultural supply station. He realized that civilizations prospered only when they improved upon nature's bounty by cultivating arts and industry. The historical structure of *Carmen Seculare* emphasized the argument. The Calvert family had overseen the improvement of the colony from its natural state. Cecil, the founder, settled the country and applied his fortune to the furtherance of its success. He forestalled civil strife by granting the colony a religious liberty unavailable in the parent country. Cecil's son, Charles, tamed the "outrageous Natives" whose "daily Wars" hindered the exploitation of Maryland's natural bounty. Under Charles's care, the Indians "liv'd, persuing gainful Trade;/ And to their Parent-Land large Tribute paid." Lewis indicated that now the occasion had arrived for Charles's son, the addressee, to preside over the next stage of the country's development—the overcoming of the tobacco problem and the nurture of native arts and industry. Lewis hoped for the development of two industries particularly: linen manufacture and shipbuilding. Weaving would never enrich Maryland's coffers. But Lewis proved farsighted regarding shipbuilding. In the course of time both Annapolis and Baltimore would construct many a globe-circling vessel.

From the earliest era of settlement, the vast forests of the New World set English projectors dreaming of breaking the nation's dependency on Baltic timber. During the 1660s John Winthrop, Jr., alerted members of the newly formed Royal Society to the promise that the colonies held for shipbuilding.[19] Thenceforth, the dream of establishing colonial yards to build the empire's ships inspired enterprising minds. More important than the abundant supply was the size of American trees, fully equal to those in the great Scandinavian forests. Baltic trees had served as masts for Europe's vessels for centuries. The crown's use of New World timber for its navy is a commonplace of colonial history. Less well known is the story of Americans' attempts to make themselves the builders of the empire's ships.[20] Lewis conveyed the aspirations of America's shipbuilders in "To

Mr. Samuel Hastings, (Ship-wright of Philadelphia) on his launching the Maryland-Merchant, a large ship built by him at Annapolis."

Lewis's ode displayed history as a progress, illustrating "the slow Degrees . . ./ By which the Ship-wright to thy Skill arose."[21] Commencing with the primitive craft (which he likens to an Indian canoe) plying the *Euphrates*, Lewis traces the development of the industry through biblical and classical eras. His argument insisted upon the importance of the ship as vehicle of civil growth:

> by a Ship the *Greeks* their Freedom gain:
> To Ships, we owe our Knowledge, and our Trade,
> By them defend our own, and other Realms invade.
> Without their Aid, *America* had been
> To all, except its Natives, now unseen.
>
>   (77–81)

The poem posited a fateful association between the ship and the welfare of the colony. Maryland's prosperity depended on the trade that ships plied—"What Nature has to *Maryland* deny'd, / She might by Ships from all the World provide." Moreover, the ability of shipwrights like Hastings would turn the attention of the world to American shipbuilding—"So shall the greateful World proclaim his Name; / So shall my Bay exceed all Floods in Fame." This attractive prospect was juxtaposed to a warning to Marylanders who lived by tobacco cultivation. "The Factors whom they now employ / In *Britain*'s Isle their Interest betray."

Lewis had little liking for metropolitan privilege. He saw that his colony's principal hope of prosperity resided in industrial development, rather than the cultivation of a solitary staple; yet this hope directly contravened the policy of the Board of Trade that the provinces should remain undeveloped. For those of his countrymen whose livelihood depended upon tobacco, he offered a curt diagnosis of the protected market. The lack of competition enjoyed by the British traders in tobacco permitted them to gouge American planters. Only the institution of written contracts and strict accounts could forestall such gouging. "Let strictest Bonds some Merchant's Faith secure"; "an honest, plain Account of Sales to give." Only if contracts were violated would Lewis resort to the restrictive practices—boycotts and cutbacks—that Cooke counseled.

> Let such who have the Fortune to be Free,
> Refuse to send their Crops across the Sea;
> Let them in other Works employ their Hands,
> Nor with Tobacco vex their fertil Lands;
> 'Till they've enjoy'd a Rest of one short Year,

Then Trade shall in a richer Dress appear,
And with a higher Price reward the Planter's Care.

(213–17)

Boycott efforts in the early 1730s failed. The problem of securing contracts with factors persisted. The constrictions of mercantilism had given rise to the first generation of articulate complaint against the cost for Americans of the empire's inequitable apportioning of wealth. The economic seeds of the dissolution of the British empire in America were being sown. The economic allures of free trade were challenging the political directives of autarky.

DYER'S "FLEECE"

British Americans who opposed the staple system for its economic inflexibility faced a difficult task convincing the English Lords of Trade of the perils of specialization. English trade had long prospered on the husbandry of sheep and the manufacture and exchange of woolen goods. From 1700 to 1760 woolens accounted for roughly half of the value of Britain's exports: in 1700 bringing in £2,989,163 of a total £6,477,402; in 1760 bringing in £5,453,172 of £14,694,970.[22] In token of the commodity's importance, the ranking minister in Parliament sat on a woolsack.

John Dyer, the author of *Grongar's Hill*, became the laureate of wool, publishing in 1757 the four-book georgic, *The Fleece*.[23] It is an excellent poem of its sort, illustrating the imposition of economic significance on the traditional pastoral circumstance of poetry. The books present in turn (1) the husbandry of sheep, (2) the quality and advantage of English wool as a clothing material, (3) the dyeing and weaving of cloth, and (4) the conduct and scope of the wool trade. Heeding the English taste for variety in long poems, Dyer relieved his argument by interspersing digressions and narrative episodes throughout the four books: an apostrophe to trade, a recollection of Jason's expedition in search of the golden fleece, a pastoral dialogue between shepherds, and geographical vignettes of exotic locales touched by the wool trade. The poem's success lay in providing a serious discussion of the role of wool in Britain's economic welfare, while lending poetic charm to mundane matters of economic fact. Attempts had been made by earlier poets to illuminate the role of certain commodities in English life—John Philip's *Cider* being the most notable—but Dyer's georgic was the first to manage successfully the synthesis of information and poetry.[24] The accomplishment inspired imitation by three New World poets, who appropriated staples for poetry. Charles Woodmason, an English-born resident of South Carolina, composed "Indico"; James Grainger, a physician and friend of Dr. Johnson who moved to St. Christopher Island (present-day St. Kit's) in the West Indies, composed *The Sugar-Cane*; and George Ogilvie, a Scot who set up as a rice planter on the banks of the Santee River, wrote *Carolina; or, The Planter*.

Dyer supplied his New World imitators with several themes: the morality of labor, the necessity of scientific husbandry, the benefit of manufactures within a country, and the global benefits of trade. This last doctrine, which we have seen already as an essential element of Whig mercantilism, is rendered in *The Fleece* as a providential decree. Dyer supplies nothing less than a theology of trade.

Beliefs that God designed the world in such a manner that its constituent parts complemented each other in a material harmony, and that the residents of every locale had to engage in commerce with inhabitants of other areas to obtain those things requisite to life were long commonplace in Christendom. In the early modern era they enjoyed particular favor among physicians, who, adhering to the Galenic doctrine of signatures, believed that providence supplied a cure for every disease. Discovering the cure entailed reading the divine emblem in a natural object (eye diseases, for instance, were treated by aconite whose bloom resembles an eye). With the discovery of the New World a profusion of new natural objects came under the consideration of the medical community and with them the hope that cures would be found for long-untreatable ailments. This hope communicated itself to the public at large. Thus when Dyer introduced his theology of trade, he did not elaborate the immediate justification for English commerce—lack of native dyes forced Britain to seek foreign sources of supply—but exploited the popular hope for new, potent medicines.

> TRADE to the good physician gives his balms;
> Gives chearing cordials to th' afflicted heart;
> Gives to the wealthy, delicacies high;
> Gives to the curious, works of nature rare;
> And when the priest displays, in just discourse,
> HIM, the all-wise CREATOR, and declares
> His presence, pow'r, and goodness, unconfin'd,
> 'Tis Trade, attentive voyager, who fills
> His lips with argument.[25]

Dyer contradicted the aristocratic prejudice against business and men of business by animating the trader with a divinely inspired intuition. Worth did not course in one's veins, but in one's enterprising passions.

> To censure Trade
> Or hold her busy people in contempt,
> Let none presume. The dignity and grace,

And weal, of human life, their fountains owe
To seeming imperfections, to vain wants,
Or real exigencies; passions swift
Forerunning reason; strong contrarious bents,
The steps of men dispersing wide abroad
O'er realms and seas. There, in the solemn scene,
Infinite wonders glare before their eyes,
Humiliating the mind enlarg'd; for they
The clearest Sense of Deity receive,
Who view the widest prospect of his works,
Ranging the globe with trade thro' various climes.
                                                    (II, p. 118)

The trader, in his apprehension of the scope of God's creation, resembled the other great hero of the eighteenth century, the natural philosopher. Philosophic study of nature led to a humble appreciation of creation, in countless British and British American poems. The trader experienced a like humility, yet his appreciation of creation depended on a faculty "forerunning reason." Providence inscribed in the trader's passions (where disorder is commonly deemed to arise), an intuition that contravened human imperfections. Commerce became, by implication, sacramental—an occasion when divine design touched upon and superseded human motives, whether vain wants or "real exigencies."

Given the sacral character of commerce, the trader had to beware of two vices: laxity in the service of the divine intuition to enterprise (that is, indolence); and too great delight taken in the ends of trade rather than the act of trade (that is, indulgence in luxury). Dyer treats the "ill consequences of idleness" in Book III of *The Fleece*, proposing a system of county workhouses as a remedy. The poet warns against luxury by bringing before the reader the sad history of Tyre (by now a fixture in the admonitory literature of Whig mercantilism). We see in these passages the undiluted vitality of the protestant ethic subserving capitalism, for the individual trader is viewed as the sufficient actor, capable of willing himself out of idleness or away from luxury. The notion that impersonal economic forces might drive shepherds into idleness—the visions of ruined cottages that troubled Goldsmith and Wordsworth—had not impinged on the literary imagination of the Whigs.

Prospects of domestic stagnation did not disturb Dyer because he wrote during an era when trade brought unprecedented prosperity to much of Britain; furthermore, a more visible threat to prosperity absorbed him: competition. The competitors he most feared were the French. The project that posed the greatest peril to Britain's welfare was the attempt to introduce herding into western Louisiana, in present-day Arkansas and Kansas.

Ev'n in the new Colombian world appears
The woolly covering: Apacheria's glades

And Canses', echo to the pipes and flocks
Of foreign swains. While time [ ] down his sands,
And works continual change, be none secure:
Quicken your labors, brace your slack'ning nerves,
Ye Britons' nor sleep careless on the lap
Of bounteous nature; she is elsewhere kind.
See Missisippi lengthen—on her lawns,
Propitious to the shepherds.

(II, pp. 108–9)

Dyer incited countrymen to industry, then assured them that the quality of British wool gave it a great natural advantage over rival varieties. Yet the threat of a New World wool manufactory in the hands of the French must have haunted the thoughts of many an Englishmen. Under the imperial scheme wool production was not encouraged in British America. The colonies were supposed to be a secure market for British woolens. Having a source of supply in immediate proximity, even when manufactured by an imperial adversary, would tempt British American traders to forego English goods to avoid the transatlantic shipping cost. Or, if the French effort were successful, it might lure colonists to violate the ban and develop a wool trade on such a scale that the British would lose their readiest customers.

Dyer, when representing British America, employed much of the rhetoric the philanthropists applied to Georgia. The colonies offered opportunity to the excess population of Europe. They create the demand that employs Britain's weavers.

No land gives more employment to the loom,
Or kindlier feeds the indigent; no land
With more variety of wealth rewards
The hand of labor: thither, from the wrongs
Of lawless rule, the free-born spirit flies;
Thither affliction, thither poverty,
The arts and sciences: thrice happy clime,
Which Britain makes th' asylum of mankind.

(IV, p. 179)

Since trade presupposed exchange and since Britain's staple, its primary commodity to be exchanged, was wool, the prosperity of British America depended upon the maintenance of the imperial order. If Americans wished to extend the wool trade, the opportunity existed on their shores; they could trade with the Indian. Yet the wealth of America depended on its own specialized productions: "the silkworm's thread" in which Georgia's fortunes are bound; Carolina's "thirsty rice"; Virginia's "wealthy cultivations"; New England's "white fish." The value of these commodities would be converted into "num'rous towns, / On hill and valley" (IV, p. 179).

A solitary cloud shadowed the bright prospects of New World prosperity for Dyer, and that was slavery. The cultivation of the New World's agricultural staples demanded a great investment of labor. Since the availability of land was so great, any free man would choose to labor for himself on his own freehold rather than work for another. So schemes of compulsory labor—indentured servitude and chattel slavery—were instituted to support agriculture. For Dyer the slave trade and the use of slave labor violated the morality of commerce. The slave trade tainted the sanctity of commerce by employing a false contract—there was no equity in the exchange of value. "Slaves, by their tribes condemn'd, exchanging death/ For life-long servitude; severe exchange!" The use of slaves deprived enterprise of its heroic element, for the individual was not rewarded for his own vision or effort, but for the compulsory labor of others. Finally, because ill deeds beget vengeful compensations, slavery would ensure a future crisis, a societal bloodletting.

> Their sable chieftains may in future times
> Burst their frail bonds, and vengeance execute
> On cruel unrelenting pride of heart
> And av'rice. There are ills to come for crimes.
> (IV, p. 164)

Dyer, when worrying about the disturbance of commercial peace by the slave system, came closest to the perspective of British Americans. British America's georgics partook more of disturbance, more of Virgil's war with the earth, than of Young's and Kirkpatrick's peace and plenty on the seas.

"INDICO"

Given his family name and background, John Dyer well appreciated the importance of coloring cloth goods. In a century when display on the footpaths of public parks or in the boxes of the theater provided the principal means of "cutting a figure" in society, the importance of a colorful appearance was supreme. Dyes that would fix a distinctive hue in cloth without running or fading were valued extravagantly.[26] The cochineal insect that secreted an intense crimson color was valued so greatly that the Society of Arts in London, on the basis of a single specimen forwarded by Dr. Alexander Garden, offered a £600 premium for its culture in South Carolina, Bermuda, Jamaica, and Sumatra.[27] Even more desirable was indigo, the vegetable whose oil produced a blue that enjoyed prolonged fashionability because of its identification with the Knights of the Garter. "The consumption of indigo in Great-Britain, is on a medium of 13 years, viz. from 1733 to 1745, by the custom-house books, imported 681,804 lb.; but as it pays no duty, so more is often entered than is really imported; and it is presumed the real consumption is about 500,000 lb. every year; which at the usual price in time of peace, being 3 s. is £75,000, at 4 s. is £100,000 per annum, freight and charges being a trifle, it is almost all clear gain to the planter."[28] Until 1739 the bulk of this crop derived from plantations in the French West Indies. Then Eliza Lucas, after several failed experiments, successfully cultivated indigo in South Carolina.[29] It became, along with rice, the principal staple of that colony.

Much of what is now known about early Carolina indigo culture derives from the account published in *Gentlemen's Magazine* by Charles Woodmason in 1758. Woodmason, a factor possessed of facility with the pen, had contact with most of the planters of the province, and so was able to represent the current practice of planting and processing.[30] The subject's importance was great enough to warrant treatment in verse. In 1757 Woodmason published proposals for a book featuring "Indico," a georgic celebrating the creation of this "richer Dye."[31] The volume never appeared, since it failed to attract enough subscribers to pay for publication costs, and no manuscript of the collection survives. Yet 120 lines of "Indico" appeared in print as "temptation copy" in advertisements soliciting subscriptions—sufficient number to derive some idea of the poem's premises and contents.

The opening lines, a conventional invocation to heaven for aid in writing the poem, contain one distinctive thought: that providence designed the New World for agricultural production particularly.

> Kind Heav'n! whose wise and providential Care
> Has granted us another World to share,
> These happy Climes to Antients quite unknown,
> And fields more fruitful than Britannia's own;
> Who for Man's Use has blest with Herbs the Soil,
> Who crowns with Joy the weary Planter's Toil.[32]

The planters of the south had a distinctive preoccupation with the toils of agriculture. The travail of crop production dominated their thinking about the staples. Dyer when representing the wool trade showed how the farm work was integrated with manufacture and trade. A diversified economy of farmers, artisans, and merchants was supported by wool. Woodmason, while conscious of the importance of processing indigo into usable dye, emphasized the labors of axe, hoe, and plow. All the temptation copy is drawn from passages treating agricultural production.

He treats the clearing of fields:

> Being when first bleak Winter strips the Trees,
> When Herds first shudder at the Northern Breeze,
> 'Tis Time the Walnut and the Cypress tall
> And tow'ring Pride of verdant Pines to fall.
> Arm'd with destructive Steel thy Negroes bring,
> With Blows repeated let the Woodlands ring.
>
> (39–44)

The selection of soil:

> Most skilful Planters in this Judgment rest,
> That rotten Soil for INDICO's the best:
> But let not that thy Hopes of Crops impair,
> Some stiffer Soils great Droughts may better bear.
> I've seen a Crop of Weed, like Thicket grown,
> From stubborn Clay, on some Plantations mown.
> Such Lands with double exercise prepare,
> And double Harvests shall reward thy Care.
> Laborious Toil!
>
> (49–56)

Plowing and seeding:

> Let Two Feet void 'twixt every Trench remain.
> Tho' some, imprudently, their Room confine,
> Allowing half that Space to every Line.
> Give Room, one Stem as much as three full yards
> And richer far the Weed.
>
> (62–66)

Manuring:

> Yet Summer Fallows best your Crops ensure,
> And far exceed all Species of Manure.
> By this the nitrous Particles of Air
> When loose the Surface, and the Passage fair,
> With Ease descend, and to the Soil adhere.
>
> (75–80)

No doubt the remainder of the poem portrayed harvesting and the hand preparation of indigo for rendering into dye stuff. These processes receive ample treatment in Woodmason's prose account.

Poetic discussion of agricultural technique began with Hesiod's *Works and Days*, but the model that loomed in the imagination of provincial Americans was Virgil's *Georgics*. Woodmason, Grainger, and Ogilvie more closely approximated the message of Virgil than Dyer, for they more clearly apprehended the task of empire to be cultivation: that is, the forceful imposition of culture upon what is wild. Agriculture for Virgil was the quintessential imperial act, for the imposition of control upon nature, upon the newly conquered or colonized lands, was the justification of Roman power. It was a heroic activity, a war with the earth, a reformation of nature's fundamental forces to adhere to human design. The well-cultivated farm was considered the arena of human happiness, for there the human will to act, and the human instinct for industry discovered their sufficient arena.

Southern planters understood Virgil's message perfectly. Unlike their European ancestors, who like Horace enjoyed a "few paternal acres" as a resort from the cares of the world, the colonists wrested a living from primeval forest or swamp. The planters' contentment was of a different order. They were *de novo* creators, witnessing the imposition of design upon a seemingly chaotic natural profusion. They reveled in the heroism of industry, animated by that sense of discipline that comes of a pioneer's confrontation with necessity.

> Poverty is justly stiled
> Mother of Arts, Invention's call'd her Child.
> All hail, great Source of Industry! of Yore
> A Goddess deem'd, when fam'd *Fabricius* bore
> The Sway in *Rome*, and yet content to share
> But one small Field, to plant his rural Fare.
>
> (15–20)

Woodmason claims that necessity impelled Rome to world-encompassing power. It inspired Virgil, "the Mantuan Bard, who sung/ The Care of Flocks, and of their tender Young;/ Who taught the lab'ring Hind to plough and sow,/ The various Seasons of the Year to know." The desire to overcome poverty "peopled this new World." Furthermore, it compelled a resort to the slave system, for Gambians possess constitutions that "temper'd to the Heat/ By Situation of their native Soil,/ Best bear the scorching Suns, and rustic Toil."

Woodmason's poem has the virtue of directness. No other British American georgic confessed so plainly the economic compulsion behind the slave-supported staple system. Reading it, we sense the weight that the labors of cultivation placed on the minds of planters and the fear of poverty that made them resort to the Roman imperial solution—slavery. We see, too, the matter-of-fact justification of slavery not only by history, but by the design of providence. Just as God distributed commodities at different locales about the globe to encourage commerce, so too did He arrange certain races with capacities for tasks that required performance. Economic necessity was allied with the mystique of classical example in Woodmason's thought to produce a rationale that would come easily to the lips of a century of subsequent southerners. In "Indico" the "mind of the Old South" is fully formed.

"THE SUGAR-CANE"

Woodmason envisioned his primary audience to be his fellow countrymen in Carolina. "Indico" served as a record of their toils, a celebration of the material dimension of their lives. Dr. James Grainger's georgic on sugar culture, *The Sugar-Cane: a Poem. In Four Books: With Notes* (1764), was a didactic poem intended for a British audience.[33] Already a noted poet and translator before he left London for Basseterre, St. Christopher, in 1759, Grainger adjusted his georgic to metropolitan taste by returning briefly to London and inviting corrections of the manuscript from his circle of friends. The poet's literary intimates included Shenstone, Robert Dodsley, Dr. Johnson, and Bishop Percy (who included Grainger's West Indian ballad, "Bryan and Pereene," in the *Reliques*). When *The Sugar-Cane* issued from the press, it won the notice to which it aspired. Several devices contributed to Grainger's success. The narrator's persona—a sympathetic man of science—played both to the public curiosity about natural philosophy and to its sentimentalism. Writing in poetry, rather than prose, lent his descriptions an emphatic imagery, a requisite for an audience of "the curious," which he presumed to be unfamiliar with West Indian scenes. "Soon after my arrival in the *West-Indies*, I conceived the design of writing a poem on the *cultivation of the Sugar-cane*. My inducements to this arduous undertaking were, not only the importance and novelty of the subject, but more especially this consideration; that, as the face of this country was wholly different from that of *Europe*, so whatever hand copied its appearances, however rude, could not fail to enrich poetry with many new picturesque images" (v).

The problem with descriptive poetry (a fault that may be seen in the many imitations of Thomson's *Seasons*) was the tendency to employ formulas. Southern climes always suffer from "the vernal heats of meridian noon," and so forth. Grainger did not judge this difficulty to be a matter of exhausted language, but the overfamiliarity of the scenes commonly treated in descriptive verse. A new locale and subject assured a revitalized imagery. From the distance of 225 years, we see that Grainger's remedy did not wholly serve. The difficulty was apparent to the more astute of Grainger's contemporaries who wondered at the appropriateness of some passages, such as that beginning, "Now Muse, let's sing of rats."

Whereas Lucretius or Virgil could not resort to a denotative, technical language that represented physical states and processes accurately, Grainger and his contemporaries could. That "scientific" language was better suited to the task of practical instruction and description. When Grainger defended his application of "terms of art" to his didactic project by the example of Hesiod and Virgil among the ancients, or Philips and Dyer among the moderns, he begged the question. These poets subordinated instruction to celebration; Grainger made instruction his highest purpose. A reader of *The Sugar-Cane* will grasp this immediately, for the pages are freighted with lengthy explanatory footnotes. For a reader interested in the botany, material culture, or history of the West Indies, these footnotes can be fascinating reading. A lover of belles lettres sees their profusion and length as indices of verse's inadequacy to the task at hand.

Dr. Grainger set himself to the task of representing

> What soil the Cane affects; what care demands;
> Beneath what signs to plant; what ills await;
> How the hot nectar best to chrystallize;
> And Afric's sable progeny to treat:
> A Muse, that long hath wander'd in the groves
> Of myrtle-indolence, attempts to sing.
>
> (I, 1–6)

Grainger's muse wrought at these matters with prodigious energy. The result is the most informative account of a staple that survives from the colonial era, also the most curious. Its oddity arises in part from its ordering of subjects. The design begins coherently, but soon shows signs of distraction. Book I deals with soil selection and planting; also presenting the character of a good planter. Book II describes the vermin and weather that dampen a planter's success; a pathetic history in the style of Shenstone is appended. Book III treats harvest and sugar refinement; a survey of products—muscavado, white sugar, rum—is supplied. Book IV, the culminating book, is devoted to "The Genius of Africa"—that is, to a consideration of negro slavery. While the descriptions of sugar production in Books I-III employ the logic of chronology, the episodes and digressions interspersed through the descriptions and the final book reveal the tensions that disturb the heroic simplicity of the georgic mode. The poem presented no progress toward civility or triumph over the wilderness. In the culminating book, where the vision of accomplished estate should be, Grainger provided an extended discourse on the most problematic aspect of planting—slave management. Here conflicts between man of science and man of feeling became acute in the narrator's persona. The welter of cross-purposes dramatized the predicament of a progressive man, ambitious to serve as spokesman for the material improvement of mankind brought about by imperial expansion, yet compelled by economic circumstance to employ and justify slavery.

In our distaste for slavery and the pragmatism that permits Grainger to accept it, let us not misjudge the truly progressive dimensions of his thought. He saw the translation of agriculture into the New World as an opportunity to break from inefficient traditional methods of cultivation and institute the improvements wrought by Jethro Tull.

> PLANTER, improvement is the child of time;
> What your sires knew not, ye their offspring know:
> But hath your art receiv'd Perfection's stamp?
> Thou can'st not say.—Unprejudic'd, then learn
> Of ancient modes to doubt, and new to try:
> And if Philosophy, with Wisdom, deign
> Thee to enlighten with their useful lore;
> Fair Fame and riches will reward thy toil. [34]

Furthermore, he advocated experiment and technological innovation in the fining of sugar. In Book III he directs that boiling houses "should be lofty, and open at top, to the leeward," and that Bristol lime should be used as a tempering agent for the fining process; he also supplies recommendations for quickening the granulation of sugar. Here Grainger dispenses practical knowledge.

Less germane to the argument of his poem, but no less useful as information, are the many digressions and footnotes communicating botanical lore. Grainger describes the natural features in verse, then supplies their nomenclature and uses in footnotes. The artistry of the notes at times exceeds that of the verse, for invariably Grainger's remarks provide glimpses of island culture excluded from the poem by the decorums of neoclassical verse. Take, for instance, this note on soursop fruit:

> The true Indian name of this tree is Suirsaak. It grows in the barrenest places to a considerable height. Its fruit will often weigh two pounds. Its skin is green, and somewhat prickly. The pulp is not disagreeable to the palate, being cool, and having its sweetness tempered with some degree of an acid. It is one of the Anonas, as are also the custard, star, and sugar-apples. The leaves of the soursop are very shining and green. The fruit is wholesome, but seldom admitted to the tables of the elegant. The seeds are dispersed thro' the pulp like the guava. It has a peculiar flavour. It grows in the East as well as the West-Indies. The botanical name is Cuanabanus. The French call it Petit Corosol, or Coeur de Boeuf, to which the fruit bears a resemblance. The root, being reduced to a powder, and snuffed up the nose, produces the same effects as tobacco. Taken by the mouth, the Indians pretend it is a specific in the epilepsy. (40)

Grainger documents the natural object's utility among several cultures and classes of people, supplying an ethnopharmacology to supplement the results of his own experiments.

Grainger's medical knowledge is put to more dramatic use in his summary of remedies for slave maladies. The information about symptomatology and treatment far surpassed that available in *The Poor Planter's Physician*, the standard New World medical reference.[35] Long ruminations on the effects and treatment of worms, the principal affliction transported among slaves from Africa, and chegres, the principal island infestation, resulted in the relief of many an unfortunate person.

The moral neutrality of practical knowledge, indeed, of scientific description itself, may be seen in more troublesome passages—those in which Grainger prescribes the criteria by which a slave buyer chooses laborers.[36] The physician adds psychological information to his somatic knowledge to portray the purchasable African. A taxonomy of tribal dispositions is correlated with tasks on the plantation. "WHETHER to wield the hoe, or guide the plane;/ Or for domestic uses thou intend'st/ The Sunny Libyan." "Yet those from Congo's wide extended plains . . . ill bear/ the toilsome field; but boast a docile mind,/ And happiness of features. These, with care,/ Be taught each nice mechanic art: or train'd/ To household offices." "If the labours of the field demand/ Thy chief attention . . . chuse the slave, Who sails from barren climes . . . the children of the Golden Coast." "If thine own, thy children's life be dear;/ But not a Cormantee . . . They, born to freedom in their native land,/ Chuse death before dishonourable bonds:/ Or, fir'd with vengeance, at the midnight hour, / Sudden they seize thine unsuspecting watch,/ And thine own poniard bury in thy breast." "The slaves from Minnah are of stubborn breed;/ But, when the bill, or hammer, they affect;/ They soon perfection reach. But fly, with care,/ The Moconation; they themselves destroy."

Afterwards, Grainger offers a method to accustom the newly purchased African, whatever the tribe, to labor.

The poet does not escape the anxiety that the task imposes upon him. Three times during the description Grainger announces his disapproval of slavery. When he invokes the genius of Africa in Book IV, he expresses his desire for freedom.

> O attend my song.
> A muse that pities thy distressful state;
> Who sees, with grief, thy sons in fetters bound;
> Who wishes freedom to the race of man;
> Thy nod assenting craves: dread Genius, come.
> (IV, 13–17)

Grainger rejected the hierarchical subordination of Africans to a subhuman status. He was by no means one of those Europeans, who, as Montesquieu so pungently put it, "were obliged to make slaves of Africans for clearing such vast tracts of land . . . sugar would be too dear if the plants were cultivated by others than slaves . . . These creatures are all over black and with such a flat nose that they can hardly be pitied . . . It is scarcely to be believed that God, who is a wise being, should place a soul in such a black, ugly body.[37] To this prejudice, Grainger replies,

> HOWE'ER insensate some may deem their slaves,
> Nor 'bove the bestial rank; far other thoughts
> The muse, soft daughter of humanity!
> Will ever entertain. —The AEthiop knows,
> The Aethiop feels, when treated like a man.
>   (IV, 421–27)

The sympathy of the muse should, in some manner, provide recompense for the slaves' harsh fate. Yet for Grainger there is a question about the power of poetry.

> O, did the tender muse possess the power,
> Which monarchs have, and monarchs oft abuse;
> 'Twould be the fond ambition of her soul,
> To quell tyrannic sway; knock off the chains
> Of heart-debasing slavery.
>   (IV, 232–36)

In the poem Grainger was groping for some power commensurate with that of monarchs. That he did not find it was due to the restraint imposed upon his muse by that observational/scientific element of his persona. His intuition as a man of feeling came close to leading him to the historical solution. The sentimental narrative in the style of Shenstone appended to Book II indicated the way.[38] Only when the resentment of the public against the injustice of slavery was stimulated into action, only when the political passion for redress had been moved, would the "power of monarchs" be checked. Literary sentimentalism would be the means of moving the public's political passions.

The question remains whether, indeed, the power of monarchs kept slavery in force. We must pay attention to the plural here. British Americans were supremely aware that they did not introduce slavery into the New World; that Spain, with its Arabic heritage of bondage, brought captive labor into the New World. The conquistadors forced Indian tribes to labor in mines delving precious metals for their captors. Grainger, too, called before his reader the horrors of the Inca captivity:

> See them dragg'd in chains,
> By proud insulting tyrants, to the mines

Which once they call'd their own, and then despis'd!
See, in the mineral bosom of their land,
How hard they toil! how soon
Their teeth desert their sockets! and how soon
Shaking paralysis unstrings their frame!

(IV, 187–94)

When the Indians died from exhaustion, Spain resorted to the traditional source of Arabic supply, Africa.[39]

Competition made slavery a necessity in the eyes of the planters. Both Spain and France had minimized their labor costs by instituting African slavery. To maintain their share of the sugar trade, especially against the French, the British followed suit. Throughout the eighteenth century British West Indians wrote to their English compeers lamenting the use of slavery, yet declaring, "The impossibility of doing without slaves in the West Indies will always prevent this traffic being dropped. The necessity, the absolute necessity then, of carrying on must, since there is no other, be its excuse."[40] Thus it was not the monarchs who empowered the slave trade, though their legal authority gave it sanction, but the "jealousy of commerce" (to recall David Hume's disapprobrious phrase.)

It is instructive how little Grainger treats trade in his very long book. He supplies a conventional tribute to the global advantage to Britain from maritime commerce couched in an apostrophe to the Thames.[41] But the apostrophes to free enterprise one encounters in Young, Kirkpatrick, Dyer, and Oglethorpe are conspicuously absent. In their place we have praise of the commodities themselves, while the exchange value of these goods and the system they subserve have been relegated to silence. Perhaps for a humane man such as Grainger the fact that the sugar passed to New England to be distilled to rum, that the rum was sent to Africa for slaves, and that the slaves were sent to the West Indies to manufacture more sugar too blatantly revealed the complicit immorality of his existence in St. Christopher Island.[42] Perhaps he could not celebrate free trade because he recalled that the Free Company of Merchants trading into Africa, the overseers of British slave traffic, took as their motto, "Free Trade by Act of Parliament."[43] Given the possibility of freedom resulting in license, one can understand Grainger's obsessive concern with the character of the planter. Only the government of virtue held at arm's length the horrors of the mines and the transformation of the planter into a tyrant. Modanno, a model planter, proclaims the tenets of agricultural virtue.

"Be pious, be industrious, be humane;
"From proud oppression guard the labouring hind.
"Whate'er their creed, God is the Sire of man,
"His image they; then dare not thou, my son,

"To bar the gates of mercy on mankind.
"Your foes forgive, for merit must make foes;
"And in each virtue far surpass your fire.
"Your means are ample, Heaven a heart bestow!
"So health and peace shall be your portion here;
"And yon bright sky, to which my soul aspires,
"Shall bless you with eternity of joy."

(I, 631–41)

Samuel Johnson chose this passage to single out for particular praise in his review of Grainger's poem.[44] Yet one suspects Dr. Johnson appreciated its resemblance to Virgil's portrait of the virtuous farmer more than any appositeness it had to the circumstances of life in the West Indies. For the West Indian, the passage projected the possibility of a virtuous existence, despite the planter's dependence on slavery. The image of the virtuous planter proved to be the sole literary solace afforded to West Indians during the eighteenth century. When Samuel Martin composed his important defense of the West Indian slave scheme, *An Essay on Plantership*, he made the virtuous rationality of the planter central to his justification. According to Martin, the planter's task was "to become a real practical philosopher by the conquest, or government of all the human passions: for, if these are not under absolute subjection to right reason; how can the planter exert all the social virtues upon so many and great occasions, as must every day call them forth? Or how can he govern some hundreds of his dependents with ease to himself, and happiness to them, without all the influences of a good example?"[45] The problem was that in the eyes of most of the world, and indeed among themselves, West Indians exemplified all that was extravagant, arbitrary, and presumptuous in human nature. He was the tyrannical nabob; she was the capricious belle.

ISLANDS OF INIQUITY

In the geography of imperial morality no place bore so dire a reputation as the West Indies. Defoe had confirmed the islands' reputation as havens of buccaneering. Indeed, the political history of the islands was viewed by some as the consequence of Cromwell's piratical attempt to seize Spain's New World empire.

There is a Tract of Land i'th' Burning Zone,
That torn from Spain long since, was made our own
By gifted Cromwell, whose Fanatick Rage,

Imposture, rul'd the Frenzy of that Age:
Thus got by Him, Usurping Clans betimes
These settled.[46]

In the wake of the Glorious Revolution the sugar islands became the haunt of displaced Jacobites and shady adventurers. One who sought fortune there in the 1690s was Ned Ward, London's doggerel laureate, who sailed to Jamaica in hopes of setting himself up as a tavernkeeper in Kingston. He found the island to be

> The Dunghill of the Universe, the Refuge of the whole Creation, the Clippings of the Elements, a shameless Isle of Rubbish, confus'dly jumbl'd into an Emblem of the *Chaos*, neglected by Omnipotence when he form'd the World into its admirable Order. The Nursery of Heavens Judgments, where the Malignant Seeds of all Pestilence were first gather'd and scattered thro' the Regions of the Earth, to punish Mankind for their Offences. The place where *Pandora* fill'd her Box, where *Vulcan* Forg'd *Jove's* Thunder-Bolts, and that *Phaeton*, by his rash misguidance of the Sun, scorched into a Cinder. The Receptacle of Vagabonds, the Sanctuary of Bankrupts, and a Close-stool for the Purges our Prisons. As Sickly as an Hospital, as Dangerous as the Plague, as Hot as Hell, and as Wicked as the Devil.[47]

Ward's brief acquaintance with the islands and his penchant for malediction might cause us to discount his "Character of Jamaica." His sentiments, however, were echoed in the observations of less profane writers with a longer residency. Captain Thomas Walduck, who took up residence in Rupert's Fort, Barbados, in 1696, distilled his experience in 1710 to James Petiver in London:

An Acrostick upon ye Island of Barbadoes
& ye Inhabitants thereof

B	Barbadoes Isle inhabited by Slaves
A	And For one Honest man ten thousand Knaves
R	Religion to thee's a Romantick Storey
B	Barbarity and ill gott wealth thy glory
A	All sodoms Sins are Centred in thy Heart
D	Death is thy look and Dearth in every part
O	Oh Glorious Isle in Vilany Excell
S	Sin to the Height thy fate is Hell.[48]

Walduck expatiated at some length on certain charges raised in his acrostic. Concerning "ill gott wealth," for instance, he observed that the majority of estates were "gott and maintained by Charge and violence, the Governour & Lawyers fleece them every year to support their broken titles, for if an Executor or an Administrator getts into an estate here the Orphans are never

the better for what their fathers Left them (I speak of the present posses-
sions) I do not know 20 Estates in ye whole Island that are in ye hands of
their lawful Descendents." The circle of deceit described here—officials
shaking down lawyers who bilked orphans of their legacies—was com-
pressed in Jamaica, where the officials rid themselves of the middlemen and
bilked widows and orphans directly. If we are to credit the accusations of
The Groans of Jamaica (1714), Deputy Governor Rigby, Attorney General
Brodrick, and Dr. John Stuart plundered imperiled estates with im-
punity.[49]

Of "sodoms Sins" Walduck does not mean buggery so much as inhos-
pitability. He indicates that after an initial show of generosity to a stranger,
the islanders become cold and parsimonious. The first visit will be honored
with a feast, "but afterwards, you shall find nothing in their houses but Irish
beef that has been a 12 month in brine Salt fish dry Bonivess fair water or
Cowjou worse than Water."

Walduck's accusation of irreligion is the most complicated of his charges
against the planters. It is sounded at several points in his letter, but with
greatest force in his account of a West Indian wake. "As soon as the Corps
are interr'd they sit round the Liquor in the Church porch drinke to the
obsequies of the defunct, smoke & drink, untill they are as drunk as Tin-
kers, and never think of the dead afterwards, and to be sure there must be a
Hatchment sett up in the Church and a Scutchions Stuck upon ye pall, and
they out do the Dutch in Heraldry for every man assumes what Coat he
pleaseth or the fancy of ye vain Dream invent, and they are such unthinking
Devills here that if two brothers [die] ye Years one after ye other, they generally have different Coates . . . After they are buried there is no care taken of
the graves or ye Church-Yards, Hogs has routed up Children, and Dogs
carried away their bones the town people make fire of the rotten Coffins, the
Church porches is a Stable for horses, and they lye as promiscuously under
ground as they lived above." In this litany of abuses the one that stands out
is vanity. The false escutcheons erected over the corpse at the chapel well
emblematize the fanciful quests for worldly position. Recognized by no institution, not even the family of the deceased, they are solipsistic glyphs of
personal ambition. The living, besotted with indulging their own appetite,
neglect to revere these idols. The family, the usual vehicle for memorializ-
ing the departed, also appears too preoccupied to perform its duty. Consequently the dead suffer desecration. Anthropologists claim that a characteristic trait of human beings is their ritualized care for the dead. West Indians, in their carelessness about the deceased, forfeit their humanity and
become "unthinking Devills."[50]

While indifference characterized the family's attitude toward its deceased members, ill will governed its dealings with those living beings in
its control not bound by ties of kinship or amity. "In fine they are unmer-

cifully cruell to their poor Slaves by whome they get their living without a
wet finger they never give them clothes to wear or victuals to eat all days of
their lives but works them 18 hours in 24 without any intermission (It is a
common saying amgt the planters that if they give 30 £St for a Negro and
hee lives one year he payes for himself.) they shall be at 1000 times more
charge and care of their horses for their pleasure than for those poor Souls
w[i]thout whom they would be worse than the Negroes."

Reports of West Indian cruelty ballooned in the wake of the Jamaican
slave uprising of 1736. The failed rebellion brought draconian punishments: public gibbetings, torture, and mutilation. It also prompted an
anxiety that found expression in works such as *An Essay concerning Slavery,
and the Danger Jamaica is expos'd to from the too great number of Slaves, and the too
little care that is taken to manage them.* This 1746 tract confronted the planter
with the dire consequences of his carelessness. In a dialogue an English officer lectures a planter on the slaveholders' failure to perceive their obtuse-
ness.

> *Officer*: One would imagine that Planters really think the Negroes are not of the
> same Species with us, but that being of a different Mold and Nature, as well as
> Colour, they were made intirely for our Use, with Instincts proper for that Pur-
> pose, having as great a Propensity to Subjection, as we have to command, and
> loving Slavery as naturally as we do Liberty; and that there is no need of any Art
> or Discipline to subject ten Men or more, to one, no need of any Management,
> but that of themselves they will most pleasantly submit to hard Labour, hard
> Usages of all kind, Cruelties and Injustice at the Caprice of one white Man—
> such, one would imagine, is the Planter's Way of Thinking.[51]

The officer argues that a planter faces ultimate peril if his vanity blinds him
to the fact that the African slave is human and so loves liberty.

An index of how obtuse planters may have been in their assessment of
African slaves is the adamancy with which Samuel Martin argues that Africans are rational creatures. The spectacle of the most articulate West Indian
defender of slavery insisting to his fellow planters that Africans have intelli-
gence reveals the extent to which the West Indians believed them to have
been subhuman. "Rational beings they are, and ought to be treated accordingly; that is, with humanity and benevolence, as our fellow creatures, created by the same almighty hand."[52] The virtuous planter in Martin or
Grainger is not some phantom borrowed from ancient literature to lend a
classical adornment to the plantation scenery. Both see the figure as the sole
defense against the violence that will come when the "genius of Africa"
seeks its liberty. Only the master who demonstrates the worth of his authority by displaying self-government, industry by untiring effort, and humanity by his caring sympathy for his charges can avoid the resentment of the
slaves.

Grainger believed that the planter could and would manifest industry—

it served self-interest. He was less sanguine about planters cultivating a feeling for humanity that transcended self-interest. Consequently, he proposed the metropolis impose a legal restraint on the planters' scope of action by enacting the enlightened elements of the French *code noir* throughout the empire. For Grainger the empire was an imperium, an arena of command and law. He believed that the government of personal virtue, if bound to the external government of enlightened laws, might achieve an enduring rule of Wisdom. He closed *The Sugar-Cane* with a vision foreseeing the efflorescence of island civilization under Britain's "fostering smile." He prophesied that Britain will never suffer an eclipse of power, "if Wisdom guide the helm."

Grainger was prophetic in seeing that the remedy to the problem of slavery would be found in the metropolis and not in the islands. He was also foresighted in seeing poetry as a means of cultivating sympathy for the slave. Yet little did he envision the formation in the 1770s and 1780s of a school of poets whose members included William Cowper, John Marjoribanks, and Hannah More taking up his themes, arguments, and images in a campaign for the abolition of the slave trade.[53] First among the epigones was the actor, John Singleton, who memorialized his tour of the sugar islands with his blank verse relation, *A General Description of the West Indian Islands* (London, 1767).[54] Singleton and subsequent poets borrowed from Grainger a representational program: the New World African had to be seen as something more than simply a slave (thus accounts of folkways and African-American material culture are incorporated into the description); and when he was seen as a slave, an appeal had to be made to the reader's imagination to project into the circumstance of servitude. Singleton, for instance, offered the first sympathetic glimpse belles lettres affords of "the runaway," a character whose love of liberty prompts escape from bondage at great risk—a character presumably admirable to all freedom-loving Britons.

> A dreary pit there is . . .
> First found, through chance, by some delinquent slave
> Flying the lash of his revengeful lord,
> Or overseer more cruel. Once he dwelt
> A native of rich Ebo's sunny coast,
> Or Gambia's golden shore; a prince perhaps;
> By treach'rous scheme of some sea-brute entrap'd.
> When the steel-hearted sordid mariner
> Shap'd out his wat'ry course for traffic vile,
> Commuting wares for baneful dust of gold;
> Or, what is worse, made spoil of human flesh.
> Accursed method of procuring wealth!

By loading free-born limbs with servile chains,
And bart'ring for the image of his god.
Deal Christians thus, yet keep the sacred name?
Or does the diff'rence of complexion give
To man a property in man?—O! no:
Soft nature shrinks at the detested thought,
A thought which savages alone can form.

(II, 35–52)

We should not misconstrue Singleton's verse as implying that anyone less than an African prince is hardly worth the British Christian reader's sympathy. The Gambian's nobility serves a rhetorical purpose. The suffering of captured nobles in New World slavery was already a popular and powerful theme of the "Black Legend" of the Spanish conquest of Aztecs and Incas. By substituting Gambians for Incas and English slavers for conquistadors, the abolitionists adapted an effective propaganda narrative to their cause. Then too, the subliminal argument of the passage makes "prince" a resonant term. The reader is questioned as a Christian to judge whether a "prince," the image of god, may be bought by gold. The implicit analogy to the Prince of Peace being bought for thirty pieces of silver cues the reader to detest the transaction.

The tenor of the poetic indignation at West Indian slavery grew increasingly strident with the passing decades. The author of *Jamaica; a Poem, in three parts. Written in that island, in the year MDCCLXXVI* called into question the heroism of staple agriculture in the island. Sugar, the author argued, could not be viewed in Virgilian terms, as the product of a virtuous farmer's artful cultivation of nature; rather, the staple's meaning had to be read in terms of the immoral system of labor that produced it. The poet began his criticism by alluding to the conventional concerns of the georgic—indeed the very matters that absorbed Grainger:

Here could I sing what soils and seasons suit,
Inform the tap'ring arrow how to shoot;
Under what signs to plant the mother cane,
What rums and sugars bring the planter gain;
Teach stubborn oxen in the wain to toil,
And all the culture of a sugar soil:
Th' ingrateful task a British Muse disdains,
Lo! Rise on my mind, appal my tear-stain'd Eye,
Tortures, racks, whips, famine, gibbets, chains,
Attract my rage, and draw a soul-felt sigh;
I blush, I shudder at the bloody theme,
And scorn on woe to build a baseless fame. [55]

If the British empire persists in viewing itself as the New Rome, then it will risk taking Rome's fate upon itself.

Having tainted the staple by the moral contagion of its means of production, the "British muse" moves beyond the critique of the Virgilian mode to an attack on the neoclassical analogy upon which it rests. The warning is cast as an oracle:

> "Thus Rome of Old the Barb'rous nations brav'd,
> "Ev'n Indus saw his tawny sons enslav'd;
> "Far to the North she spread her proud domain,
> "And Bound ev'n Britain in a gilded chain.
> "But she who aw'd the world by arms and fame,
> "Now smoaks by slaves, now stands an empty name!
> "Fear then, like her, to meet an awful doom,
> "And let your sea-girt shores still think on Rome;
> "For your green isles, surcharg'd with bosom'd foes
> "May yield to slaves,—and feel the captive's woes."
>
> (III, 31–40)

The irony of the passage occurs in tension with the politics of sympathy found in the antislavery literature. If Britons continue to emulate Rome, they will eventually be able to understand the subjectivity of slaves, for they will be slaves themselves, made captive by those whom they oppressed.

The critical spirit of the "British Muse" was further developed in a number of metropolitan poems of the 1780s. John Marjoribanks's *Slavery: an essay in verse inscribed to planters and others concerned in the sale of negro slaves* offered a notable refutation of the economic and moral defense of the slave system found in Samuel Martin's work and William Belgrove's *Treatise on Husbandry, or Planting* (1755).[56] Hannah More's *Slavery: a poem* attacked from the perspective of Quaker spirituality the image of the virtuous planter.[57] But the rhetorical horizon of antislavery poetry is found in James Field Stanfield's *The Guinea Voyage*, published by James Phillips, the celebrated abolitionist printer, in 1789. Stanfield, who purported to be an ex-captain in the slave trade, composed a verse account of the middle passage that rivaled Wilberforce's most graphic descriptions for perfervid intensity. Every topos of the antislavery literature makes its appearance—a narrative of a conscience-troubled sailor who dies literally from the contagion of the slave vessel, the story of the thwarted love of two noble Africans, Quam'no and Abyeda, an episode in which childbirth occurs on shipboard amid the most pitiable surroundings, an address to the British ladies about same. Yet Stanfield's power is most effectively manifested in those episodes in which he projects the reader into the subjectivity of the African.

> The purchase made, in sable terrors drest,
> The ship receives each agitated guest.
> Torn as his bosom is, still wonder grows,
> As o'er the vast machine the victim goes,
> Wonder, commix'd with anguish, shakes his frame
> And the strange sight his language cannot name.
> For all that meets his eye, above, below,
> Seems but to him the instruments of woe.
> The yawning deck now opes the dreary cell;
> Hot mists exhale in many a putrid smell.
> Confin'd with chains, at length the hapless slave,
> Plung'd in the darkness of the floating cave,
> With horror sees the hatch-way close his sight—
> His last hope leaves him with the parting light[58]

Stanfield, for all the rhetorical overkill of his poem, understood how poetry could aid in the transformation of British consciousness. The poetic task was not to create a tender mood that prompted the British Christian to shed a sympathetic tear. Pity must be allied with fear. The reader must be subjected to that disorientation of being that "language cannot name." British complacency must be overcome by the estrangement of the reader's experience into that of the African captive encountering the world of the Europeans for the first time. Only when the reader discovers him or herself implicated in the horror of the unnameable will consciousness be moved beyond sympathy to action. In the opening passage of *The Guinea Voyage* Stanfield symbolized the inspiration of his verse as the "black Tornado," to be distinguished from the zephyrous breath of genteel poets.

> On the still diction of the mournful strain,
> The rising darkness should profusely reign:
> The sable cloud should wrap the sullen song,
> And in grand melancholy sweep along:
> Then, by degrees, with gathering horrour fraught,
> Tempestuous numbers, and electric thought,
> Shake the big thunder—dare th' indignant beam—
> Till the full torrent pour'd the headlong stream,
> Whelm'd ev'ry bursting breast in twofold ire,
> Grief's melting show'r—and indignation's fire.
>
> (p. 2)

The apocalyptic cleansing that Stanfield envisioned when "indignation's fire" was loosed upon society would transform the global economy. The metropolis would enjoy a moral purification, the West Indies a rehabilitation, but the greatest change would occur in Africa. There,

Science awaken'd leads the free-born strain;
And arts and commerce follow in the train.
Rear'd by protecting laws new cities rise,
And heave their turrets to the lucid skies.
Trade lifts his trident o'er the silver tide,
New harbours opens, bids his navies ride;
Sees, unpolluted by oppression's hand,
His honest wealth stream through the joyous land;
His crowded quays heap't with the guiltless toil.
Iv'ry and gold in many a burnish'd pile,
Drugs, spices, gums, in rich profusion thrown,
And all the treasures of the torrid zone.
Culture emergent o'er the damask plains
Spreads her rich vest, and gaudy Flora reigns.

(p. 36)

When imagining millennial Africa, Stanfield cannot conceive of anything beyond a free-trade paradise. Indeed, it would seem that all of the prophecies of rising glory with which British America had adorned its sense of the future have here been borrowed for the benefit of Africa: liberty ensured by law, naval potency, a trading empire on the seas, exotic resources (not manufactures), and culture stimulated by commerce, science, cities. In the oracles of the most rabid abolitionist Africans might escape the manacles of slavery, but there was no release from the ties of commerce or the dreams of the marketplace.

THE DESERTED PLANTATION

In 1776 Adam Smith wrote the economic death warrant for slavery. In a passage that became quasi-scriptural among abolitionists during the 1800s, Smith declared that "the experience of all ages and nations, I believe, demonstrates that the work done by slaves, though it appears to cost only their maintenance, is in the end the dearest of all. A person who can acquire no property, can have no other interest but to eat as much, and to labour as little as possible."[59] In one stroke Smith rendered the economic necessity of slavery doubtful. The moral impulse of Whiggery—that impulse which caused John Locke to declare that "slavery is so vile and miserable a state of man, and so directly opposite to the generous temper and courage of our nation, that it is hardly possible to be conceived that an Englishman, much less a gentleman, should plead for it"—was reasserted and correlated with the idea of market efficiency.[60] Free trade regained the untarnished luster of the good.

Unfortunately for Britain, George III and his Tory ministers lacked the ears to hear. The year in which *The Wealth of Nations* issued from the press was also the year of crisis, when the hubris of rule and a misbegotten desire to exert monopolistic control over affairs in British America prompted the rupture of the thirteen colonies. Seventeen seventy-six was also the year in which George Ogilvie composed the last of British America's georgics, *Carolina; or, the Planter*.

Written on an island in the Santee River, Ogilvie's poem described the creation of a lowland rice plantation. It also attempted to repair the disaffection between England and America. The impulse to undertake a description of the life of a rice planter came to Ogilvie in 1774, shortly after he arrived in the country. A merchant by training, he had agreed to oversee construction and cultivation of an uncle's properties in Carolina and Georgia.[61] The novelty of a rice planter's situation so struck the young Scot that he immediately formed the plan of representing it to his sister and her acquaintances in Scotland. He employed verse in his portrait because models were ready to hand and "to kill the langour of winter evening, or a sultry noon, in the solitude of those forests that surrounded my infant plantations."[62] Ogilvie's solitude was not so absolute as to insulate him from tidings of the political turmoil of his province. As he composed his georgic, he altered his scheme, injecting narratives and reflections that conveyed his hope that a rapprochement would occur between the parent nation and its American offspring. With the alteration of scheme came a change in audience. Instead of Scottish family and friends, he addressed fellow planters in Carolina—"those . . . who to their household gods,/ Raise foreign altars in these new abodes" (I, 41–42).

Ogilvie deemed the problem of disaffection to be American. It arose from the colonists' separation from ancestral modes of life and from the Old World home where "from love of birth-place patriot virtues flow,/ As from the *central point the radii* grow" (I, 63–64). Filial liberty could produce the "unfeeling man" who in his self-constituting pride held no affection for his ancestral place: "What worth entails it on *this barren spot*, / That once my parents *liv'd* where now *they rot* (I, 67–68). To dramatize the ingratitude of filial liberty Ogilvie appended a note at this juncture. "Few things strike strangers more than the little attachment generally shewn by planters to the favourite residence of their ancestors, especially when informed that those who die in the country are generally interred on their own estates, which are often sold immediately after the funeral, without any durable fence being erected to preserve the family burying ground from being rooted up by the hogs of the purchaser" (p. 10). In place of filial attachment, the American has as his principal affect the "ardent wish to augment" his material store. Ogilvie, himself having cast his fortune with the New World, did not disavow the American urge; rather he wished to restore those feelings of filial attachment that the desire for gain eclipsed. Ogilvie's means of restoring these feelings was to assert the emotional primacy of the family, in a series of symbolic narratives.

Jay Fliegelman has explored the symbolic uses of the family in the ideological conflicts of the late eighteenth century, investigating their applicability to the issue of political independence.[63] Ogilvie employed the rhetoric of filial obligation, usually associated with Tory imperial authoritarianism, at a time when many British Americans were rejecting the notion of a natural and unconditional filial debt, or rejecting entirely the applicability of the family analogy to the empire.[64] Despite the demurrals, Ogilvie plied his theme with partial success. His success resulted from his employment of the literary method usually associated with his political adversaries: the sentimental narrative.

Whig sentimentalism was a literary mode that diverted the sympathies of an audience from those traditionally possessed of power (parents, courtiers, masters, kings) to those traditionally subservient to that power (children, commoners, slaves, subjects) by asserting the latter's "authority of injured virtue." The transfer of sympathies was accomplished through narrative—sentimental tales (poetic and novelistic) that showed the immorality of those in power and the virtue of those injured by the exercise of that power. Goldsmith's *Deserted Village* is usually cited as an example par excellence of the mode.[65]

Ogilvie, in the sentimental tale of Fanny and Alexander, which forms the finale of Canto I of *Carolina; or, the Planter*, thwarts the usual working of Whig sentimental narrative. After enlisting the audience's sympathies on behalf of Fanny and her would-be lover by depicting a father who arranges his daughter's marriage for money, Ogilvie subverts the action by showing the children failing the test of righteousness by surrendering to lust. Fanny, who identifies wholly with virtue, cannot bear the fact of her sinfulness and dies. Alexander, the lover, surrenders to melancholy, and ponders the depravity of man in American exile. The poet's narrative strategy is astute. It short-circuits the demonstration of injured virtue by recalling the more fundamental truth of total depravity taught by reformed Christianity, the religious animus of Whiggery.

The tale of Fanny and Alexander is preceded by the narrative of the Santee Indian sage. Here the issue of familial disruption and generational schism is given a blatantly political coloring. The Santee Indians in 1776, as any Carolinian reader would have known, were extinct, having been extirpated in the wake of the Yemassee War in 1713. Ogilvie projects his tale back into history to a point before the tribe's extinction. Euhannih, a Santee elder "unskill'd in proud scholastic lore,/ But rich . . . in old traditioned store," is "doom'd to live in a disastrous age,/ When his lov'd country blaz'd with civil rage." Beset by faction, the Santees have been attacked by Europeans. The young men of the tribe refuse to listen to the elder's counsel until the country stands on the brink of annihilation. Then Euhannih gives his counsel in the form of a jeremiad, noting that he speaks with the authority of a father who had sacrificed his offspring—five sons and a daughter—to war. Then he traces a history of the settlement of the Santee nation in the low country—a history with marked parallels to the history of English settlement. Finally he names the transgression that caused the decline of Santee fortunes. The tribe has failed to show proper regard for the spirits of its ancestors, neglecting to perform the rite of homage to their sacred tombs.

> Succeeding generations further stray,
> And later turn the pious rites to pay;
> Until the sons, more impious than their sires,
> Nor tread the mystic dance nor light the fires,
> Forget to chant the praise of warriors dead
> Whilst weeds obscene the unswept graves o'erspread.
>
> (I, 284–89)

The sage sees but one remedy for the nation's decline: restoration of those honors due the ancestral spirits—a return to filiopiety. The efficacy of sweeping graves to stem the English onslaught might be questioned for the Santees. The application of the message to the situation of British Americans is less an offense to reason. The reconstitution of the familial bonds, the reformation of feeling, were remedies to the political situation. But George III was a wrathful father and his American offspring were prideful in their sense of injury. The symbolic bonds would not be reknit until George Washington, who like Euhannih was a childless elder, supplanted George III as the nation's father figure.

Ogilvie offered a further image of the shattered family in the second and final canto of the poem. This portrait required little symbolic interpretation. It memorialized the planter/poet Rowland Rugeley and his wife and daughter, all of whom died of disease in 1776.[66] Their deaths represented the unfulfilled promise of life in the New World. Hopes for matrimonial bliss and familial joy were thwarted. "Love too smil'd bounteous under Hymen's wings,/ And promis'd all the joy their union brings./ Promise untrue!" The reordering of nature into refined civility was forestalled, for Rugeley's influence as a model cultivator was lost.

> By Rugely taught, the Woodman's fatal steel,
> Restrains its rage, and learns from Taste to *feel*;
> Spares the gay tree with gaudy blossoms spread,
> Or sober beauties of the awful shade;
> Where the primeval Oak majestic waves.
> *Here* prudence dooms, and *yonder* genius saves.
>
> (II, 616–20)

The death of Rugeley and his family on the eve of the Revolution becomes, in the emotive argument of the poem, the occasion of civilization's passing in British America.

Ogilvie combined his concerns with the preservation of the emotional harmony of the human family and the imposition of human design on chaotic nature under the comprehending theme, humanity. "Humanity, mild pow'r! to thee belong/ The Planter's study and the Poet's song!" (I, 18–20). Following the lead of Dyer and Grainger, Ogilvie made humanity the superintending ideal of southern civilization. He cursed the master who "when his barns full teem with yellow grain,/ Unpitying hears the joyless hind complain!" (I, 27–28). He attempted to envision an ideal of private estate alternative to that of the slavemaster. The happy planter was he who built his domicile with his own effort and did not envy "him whose sickly frown can make/ A thousand sons of swarthy *Afric* shake" (I, 427–28).

Wishes that agricultural civilization could develop through the effort of an independent yeomanry were little more than fanciful. The task of wresting control of the Carolina marshes exceeded the strength of any solitary hind. To fashion a plantation on the banks of the Santee one had to "frame/ A trench, two cubits wide, its depth the same" around the perimeter of the property; form the excavated earth into a rampart to repel "each common tide"; "delve/ A ditch, full six feet deep, its wideness twelve" on either side—a horrendous task since the "tenacious roots" cannot be extracted with hoe or mattock, giving way to the "ax alone"—

> slow the ditches parts, with endless toil,
> The rooty fragments from th'adhesive soil.
> The roots, high-pil'd, await consuming fires;
> The mould to swell the rising bank retires;
> Where youths and females to recieve it stand,
> And form the sloping dike with plastic hand.
> But lo! ere half the needful depth you gain,
> Quick gushing streams o'erflow th'unfinished drain!
> No more your lab'rers see their strokes to aim;
> Chills shake their limbs, and cramps distort their frame.
>   (II, 155–64)

Ogilvie aptly conveyed the arduousness of the slaves' creative labors. When we consider that the building, cultivation, weeding, and harvesting of the plantation yet remain we can understand why the poet likened the enterprise to the great labors of ancient civilizations—the rechanneling of the Euphrates and the construction of the pyramids.

There is no reason to doubt the sincerity of Ogilvie's concern for slaves; indeed, after his exile for refusing to take the oath of allegiance to the Carolina government in 1778, the poet's chief regret was that he could not arrange for his slaves' well-being.[67] Yet slavery remained a necessary means of achieving the agricultural civilization that Ogilvie cherished. Slaves were the sole practicable vehicle for accomplishing the planter's project of will. Thus, we must conclude that for Ogilvie the second sense of "humanity"— the humanizing of nature by imposing the pattern of human will on the wilderness—possessed greater force than the imperative of fellow-feeling.

For the poet the capacity to conceive and oversee the making of a plantation vitally expressed human creativity. "Bless'd light of reason! that first led the hand / Of humanizing Man to till the land" (II, 307–8). Furthermore, it encouraged civility, for directing the human will toward nature prevented its being turned against other human beings; better the ploughshare than the sword. Fellow-feeling would follow naturally when "the ruthless *warrior* to the *ploughman* chang'd."

Ogilvie was forced to flee the country before his portrait of *Carolina; or, the Planter* had been completed. The poem lay untouched until 1789, when the urging of his friends caused him to turn to it again. The sole alteration he made to the text was to supply, as a final testament to the dream of civility that had passed away, a description of Otranto, the plantation of Dr. Alexander Garden, botanist and fellow exile.[68] The portrait codifies all the ambitions held for the British America of the empire. It displayed the morality of labor, being neat and unassuming, rather than luxurious. It showed the benefits of trade, for its gardens held the "wildings" of Carolina and the exotic flora of the globe artfully commingled. It housed the ideal citizen, the cosmopolitan scientist, who in his capacity of the physician demonstrated his feeling for his fellow man, in his library showed his respect for traditional wisdom, and in his botanical work showed his progressive desire to ameliorate knowledge and discover new sources of agricultural wealth for his province. When Ogilvie published the poem privately in 1791 he dedicated it to Garden.

The published poem closed with a prophecy that was, in fact, a retrospect of British imperial wishes: America as a cornucopia of natural resource; America as the source of a diversity of staples. The Muse

> Sees ev'ry winding Valley wave with corn,
> Sees purple Vineyards ev'ry hill adorn;
> Sees yonder Marsh, with useless reeds o'erspread,
> Give to a thousand looms the flaxen thread;
> And Hemp, from many a now neglected field,
> Its sinewy bark to future Navies yield.
> Nor shall Tobacco balk the Planter's hope,
> Who seeks its fragrance on th'irriguous slope.
> Around each field she sees the Mulb'ry grow,
> Or unctuous Olive from the frugal row;

Beholds our hills the precious Thea bear,
And all the crops of Asia flourish here.
(II, 691–702)

HEROIC AGRICULTURE

Prophecies matter only when they bear repetition or occasion fulfillment.
The New World would become an agricultural cornucopia. The Virgilian
labors of many a pioneer planter would eventually result in a Horatian landscape of cultivated estates—a countryside of Otrantos. What matters more
than the foresight of the georgic poets was their unanimity concerning the
task that must be faced in the present. Each celebrated production rather
than the trade of agricultural commodities. Each conceived of empire as the
creative extension of human design over profuse nature in a specific locality,
rather than as a global domination of material exchange. Each saw morality
to inhere in the imposition of humane reason on nature, rather than in the
equity of contract, or the intuition of a vital truth embodied in primordial
nature. These are the distinctive attributes of the British American provinces that cultivated staples. They would be the attributes of the southern
states of the republic and the British West Indies so closely tied to the
southern states.

Much has been made by historians of charting the development of regional sensibilities in early America. Polite letters here provide a means for
measuring such a development. The mind of the Old South developed as a
deviation from the mercantilist emphasis on exchange, supplanting it with
an ideology of creative production. The symbolism of this ideology borrowed heavily from the Roman imperial poets, but its animus arose from
the experience of creating agricultural estates. The labor required for the
creation of farms seemed truly heroic. Thus the Americans felt no embarrassment at presenting the business of agriculture as a matter of poetry. The
fact that impressed labor was employed to enact the planter's designs was a
matter prompting greater anxiety. Like Jefferson the georgic poets wished
for an agriculture based on the yeomanry rather than on slavery. The wish
would not be fulfilled until the Civil War broke the slave system, and would
not see its poetic fulfillment until Sidney Lanier's "Corn." Like Jefferson the
georgic poets foretold the horrendous recompense to come that only "humanity" could forestall. Southern poets repeated this augury up until the
eve of the war when Henry Timrod glimpsed crimson rivers of blood in the
whiteness of "The Cotton Boll."

PART TWO

The Paper Wars Over the Prerogative

5

The Problem of the Prerogative

Literary contention in England took on the habiliments of war during the final decades of the seventeenth century. As the body politic sundered into a complex of interests and society at large split into an aggregation of private circles, literature increasingly subserved party passion. Polemic, ridicule, satire, and parody became the ammunition of the burgeoning club and party literature. Disaffection with the ideals and methods of other parties became a superintending mood of letters. The many paper wars and battles of the books testify to the contentiousness of the period, as does the amplification of the techniques of satire from the era of Dryden and Rochester to the time of Junius and Churchill. British Americans embraced each innovation in contumely as it appeared. In their turn the works of Garth, Defoe, Swift, Pope, Trenchard, and Arbuthnot were studied as handbooks of malediction whose tropes were pillaged for use in native contests, especially in the realm of politics.

Colonial politics mirrored that of the metropolis to the extent that it, too, became a matter of organized contention. While party differences emerged on a host of issues, the critical struggle was constitutional. As in England, the colonies waged a battle concerning the proportion of royal power in the exercise of government. Since the colonies owed their legal existence to the crown's prerogative right, the issue took on peculiar weight in British America. The autarkial political organization of the empire had as its justification the power of the prerogative. Since this political arrangement enforced the metropolitan privilege in trade, economic issues quickly became political issues. Yet more important than the question whether economic advantage might be gained or lost by adhering to the imperial scheme was the question to what legal rights the colonials were entitled under the imperial constitution. The nature of the prerogative made the matter debatable.

The prerogative in British constitutional practice was that special preeminence which the sovereign, by right of regal dignity, had over all other persons and out of the course of common law. Customarily, the royal prerogative included the right of making war and peace, commissioning ambassadors, commissioning officers, appointing ministers of state, pardoning malefactors, calling or proroguing Parliament, and conferring portions of his/her own authority.[1] The establishment of overseas colonies was conducted by English subjects under the authority of the prerogative, the sovereign taking one of two actions: granting overseas fiefdoms (the ground of the proprietary colonies, New York, Pennsylvania, Maryland, New Jersey, and the Carolinas), or chartering trading corporations (the ground of Virginia, Plymouth, Massachusetts Bay, Rhode Island, Connecticut, and the West Indies). Since the exercise of prerogative rights occurred outside of common law, the issue arose whether colonies operated within the purview of that law. They did not, unless the sovereign or the proprietor who acted in the royal stead specifically endowed the colonies with English legal privileges.[2] In practice the English law became a fixture in all settled colonies, whether proprietary or chartered, and rule by exercise of prerogative right (for instance the right of imposing taxes without the representation of the taxed) became an issue only in territories annexed to the empire by conquest: New York, Jamaica, and Canada, for instance.

In one respect the prerogative had been severely limited during the seventeenth century: in the conduct of trade with the colonies. While the thirtieth chapter of Magna Carta had limited the king's right in the imposition of customs in Britain, the prerogative allowed the possibility of the royal imposition of duties in colonies not endowed with the common law. During the Commonwealth when Parliament suspended the royal prerogative, it asserted a control over customs and trade that would not be surrendered after the Restoration.[3] Parliament from 1660 until the eve of the Revolution repeatedly asserted its dominion over imperial commerce in a succession of Acts upon Trade and Navigation.

After the Glorious Revolution the sovereign, Privy Council, and Board of Trade formed a rough design to convert wherever possible the various colonial polities into royal provinces—dominions with their own legislative assemblies, a royally appointed governor, a governor's council of the colony's "great men," and a judiciary. In some instances the design succeeded, as in the transformation of New Jersey in 1702 and Carolina in 1719 from proprietary to royal provinces. In others, such as the attempts to impose an appointed executive upon the nearly sovereign states of Connecticut and Rhode Island, the efforts failed. This failure would prove costly in the course of time, for the virtual independence of Connecticut and Rhode Island would serve as a model for political nativists in Massachusetts and New York.

Most legislative assemblies in the royal provinces had one powerful

Governor Jonathan Belcher of Massachusetts. Oil painting by Moussa Ayoub after 1731? lithograph. Governor Belcher appears in the finery of a merchant enterpriser. He brandishes his commission as governor, a commission whose authority derived from the Privy Seal (conspicuously displayed) and the Massachusetts Charter of 1691. The vignette above the royal commission reveals Boston as a prosperous provincial trading center according to the conventions of the mercantilist city portrait. Reproduced by permission of The Art Museum, Princeton University.

weapon by which to gain that degree of independence enjoyed by Connecticut and Rhode Island—the power to determine the salaries of the executive. So long as the royally appointed governor was beholding to the assembly for his pay, he operated under a double bind. He ruled at the monarch's pleasure under the prerogative, he prospered on good behavior under the assembly. Often the wishes of monarch and legislature did not accord.

The crown frequently attempted to stabilize its authority by directing the provinces to establish a standing revenue and a set salary for crown officers. In provinces where substantial quit-rents stood at the crown's disposal, Virginia for instance, a civil list could be supported regardless of the wishes of the assembly. In other colonies the crown attempted to secure fixed salaries and a standing revenue by power of commissions and royal instructions, usually communicated through the governor to the provincial assemblies.[4] While commissions had a quasi-legal force, the instructions were intended as a record of the king's (or Board of Trade's) express wishes for the governor. Portions of the instructions could be communicated to the council or to the assembly as encouragement to accede to the royal will. But the legal efficacy of instructions was questionable. A nativist challenge to the attempt to secure the prerogative by fixing the executive salaries arose, and a controversial literature spawned. Paper wars over the prerogative broke out in every royal province; those in Massachusetts and New York were noteworthy for their rhetorical violence.[5]

For Massachusetts the history of the salary controversy is easily told. After the Glorious Revolution and the granting of the Charter of 1691 Governors Bellomont and Dudley both urged the royal instructions with little success. Private fortunes rendered the noncompliance of the assembly an inconvenience, not an obstacle to policy. Governor Shute repeated the attempts from 1716 to 1722 with similar results, yet his repeated testimonies against the assembly in London prompted the Board of Trade to consider providing an imperially funded salary and a revision of the Massachusetts charter. The Walpole regime, however, watered down the recommendations, so that the supplemental charter of 1725 only gave the governor the ability to negative the speaker of the lower house. Governor Burnet made the salary the defining issue of his rule. "The Assembly insisted that the Governor should be dependent, that he had no permanent interest in the colony as the King had in the realm, and might be negligent if his salary were insured."[6] Burnet's energy on behalf of the prerogative was such that he might have succeeded, but he died suddenly in 1729 before the issue was resolved. Gov. Jonathan Belcher, Burnet's successor, was instructed to insist in the prerogative demands, but surrendered to exigency and accepted temporary grants. In 1735 the Board of Trade issued a general permission allowing the governor to accept temporary grants, because the charter in its constituted form could not compel the assembly to accord to the royal instructions.

In New York the salary conflict emerged in 1710, when excise duties normally lodged with the queen's receiver-general lapsed, endangering the revenue. Governor Hunter demanded salary for a civil list. The assembly refused. Parliament began drafting bills for the securing of the revenue, but the death of Queen Anne and the success of Hunter in securing a substantial temporary grant for five years sidetracked the effort. Hunter's successors were forced to acquiesce to similar temporary payments. Governor Montgomerie in 1729 appears to have capitulated to the assembly, accepting their power over the purse strings as a fixture of political life.

One dimension of the paper wars over the prerogative is already familiar to students of colonial literary and political culture: the challenge to the prerogative posed by the creation of an opposition press. The history of James Franklin's difficulties with the Massachusetts government when publishing the *New England Courant* and John Peter Zenger's tribulations at the hand of Governor Cosby in New York have frequently been featured as "prologues" to revolution.[7] Yet the absorbing concern with the newspaper as a vehicle of cultural change has obscured the fact that both Franklin and Zenger operated in discursive arenas where manuscripts conveyed the most extreme expressions of political conviction. The rhetorical horizon of opposition to the prerogative is not inscribed in the *Courant* or the *New York Weekly Journal*, but in manuscripts and fugitive pamphlet issues of the press.

Two literary weapons enjoyed favor in the clandestine wars against the extension of executive power: pasquinade, the anonymous manuscript satire posted in a public place; and the parody speech, verse burlesque of official addresses by colonial officials. "Pump verses" were New World examples of the seditious satires perfected in London during the reign of James II. Sentiments too dangerous to be entrusted to the press passed from hand to hand in manuscript or were furtively attached to the doors of the state house, the town pump, and the lintels of the local meeting houses. In England scriptoria produced sufficient copies of satires so that Whiggish clubs and dissenting circles would be supplied. In Massachusetts and New York a similar manuscript literature sprang up among the tavern clubs after the Glorious Revolution.

The parody speech was the genre of satire developed most elaborately by the provincial wits. An official address was mocked in doggerel and supplied with ingenious "additions" lacking in the original. Royal proclamations were not parodied (perhaps because of the threat of a prosecution for treason), rather the communications of the crown's vicegerent, the governor. Official writings and speeches were rewritten to reveal the hidden agenda perceived to lie behind a governor's request. Communications between the governor and assembly were conducted according to a protocol developed for the king's official exchanges with Parliament. At the commencement of a legislative session (two sessions were commonly conducted during the course of the year), the governor would deliver an address to the legislature, delivering royal instructions, requesting legislative activity, summarizing the welfare of the province, and projecting possible threats to provincial security. The assembly would draft its response, affirming or challenging various of the governor's claims. The governor would then reply. The exchange was frequently published verbatim in the provincial paper of record. From the official accounts the satirists fashioned their parodies. The satires nearly invariably contrasted the polite mask of the executive request and the personal appetite for financial gain or power that it disguised. Thus the characteristic device of the satire was to reduce matters of state to impulses of personal appetite. This psychological reduction of executive action became a fixture of later patriot literature. The only alteration in method was that the patriot literature imputed the madness for power and greed to the king himself as well as his minions.

In the face of the satirical attack, champions of the prerogative developed their own devices. Legislators who refused to fix the governor's salary in defiance of royal instruction were caricatured as miserly obstructionists whose sense of public spirit did not exceed the ambit of their own pocketbooks. The parsimony of the legislators came in for heated attack during those not infrequent periods when the colonies were engaged in war with the French or Indians.

Because of its control over the press and post, the executive exercised a measure of influence over the spread of information. Yet the control never approximated that wished by those in power. The lapse in the licensing system in England in 1695 loosed printers from prepublication censorship. The result was an explosion of controversial material in pamphlet form and the inauguration of the great age of the newspaper.[8] Material offensive to the crown or ruling party still risked legal action for treason or libel, yet many were willing to undertake the risk.

In British America the gubernatorial commissions preserved the right to license the press after 1695. In practice there was no efficient mechanism to serve as a board of censorship for publications.[9] In 1719 Governor Shute attempted to punish an attack on the attorney general published by the lower house. Yet the council found there was no grounds for legal action. By 1723 the pretenses of licencing in Massachusetts had collapsed. Since the press had not fully engaged in the pitch of political battle until the 1710s, the duration of control was notably brief.

When the press did become the ordnance of contention, the pamphlet became the favored ammunition. This is because the pamphlet was the product of the press least tractable to government influence. Newspapers were serial publications depending upon authoritative versions of "government papers" to be of use to the merchants and tavernkeepers who were the heart of the subscription list, so they had to avoid antagonizing the governor or the assembly. Because many early publishers of newspapers often doubled as municipal postmasters using their franking privilege to distribute their product, there was additional reason not to offend authorities. Publications repugnant to the government were prohibited by law from dissemination by post. A postmaster risked losing his office if he permitted offensive material to spread. If one remained inoffensive, the government might allow the connection between press and post to be exploited. John Campbell, postmaster of Boston and publisher of the *Boston Weekly Newsletter*, made a great show of providing information "published by authority." He devised an edition of his paper "one half with News, the other half good writing Paper to write their letter on."[10] Newspapers not "published by authority" depended on distribution networks less regular and less efficient than the post. Only with a party organization as zealous and a publishing committee as talented and richly bankrolled as the James Alexander clique that produced Zenger's *New York Weekly Journal* could an opposition gazette flourish.

The earliest newspapers made their lack of contentiousness a point of commendation to their readerships. Even so bold a printer as James Franklin could feature a statement in the *New England Courant* advertising the paper as relief from partisan pamphleteering: "The press has long groaned in bringing forth an hateful but numerous brood of party pamphlets, malicious scribbles, and Billingsgate ribaldry, which have produced rancor and bitterness, and unhappily soured and leavened the tempers of persons formerly esteemed some of the most sweet and amiable" (*New England Courant*, 11 February, 1723). The pamphleteers could afford to be offensive because the number of presses in Boston made it questionable which printer was responsible for the issue. Since the title page boasted "Robinson Carusoe's Isle" as the place of publication and named no publisher, the burden of proof fell upon the authorities when tracking the malefactors or seizing the printer.

While the governors theoretically had the prerogative power to license the press, the legislatures in practice managed the the flow of information more effectively. The General Court was not shy in arresting those who challenged its authority or offended its sense of propriety.[11] Its interest in the press was reasonable, for as an elective body it served at the public pleasure. Any means of informing public opinion held the most immediate bearing on the composition and conduct of affairs.

The emergence of the public in politics during the seventeenth century complicated the conduct of affairs. The great counterforce to the prerogative in constitutional theory was the "will of the people." That will became more articulate in British America as (1) the franchise expanded during the course of the eighteenth century, and (2) as public uprisings attending the Glorious Revolution brought the will of the people into the realm of direct civil action. After 1690 the *vox populi* spoke with profounder consequence to the governors of the American provinces. The politically ambitious strove with greater force to appropriate the *vox populi* on their behalf. Governors as well as assemblymen couched their declarations in demotic forms and familiar styles. The aristocrat gave way to the common citizen, or "plain countryman," as the persona of wisdom speaking in discourses; wisdom itself transmuted from bookish expertise to common sense. And the more oral, or "conversational," the mode of expression, the more effectively it served its purpose of suggesting to the populace the thoughts it should be thinking.

Despite the expansion of the franchise by periodic naturalization acts, suffrage requirements limited the vote to the white male citizenry. Often suffrage on the provincial level differed from that of the town or locality. The town meeting granted the vote to many to whom property restrictions denied it in general elections.[12] The executive found that concentrating its political rhetoric upon the general elections in the attempt to elect a court party was more efficient than managing popular opinion between times. Opposition parties, which frequently characterized themselves as "popular" parties, would engage in rhetorical provocation of the public as issues and circumstances prompted. An ultimatum of mob action always lurked behind the popular program. At times, for instance during the destruction of the Boston market, the threat was fulfilled.

The local population was not the sole audience that the provincial writer on the affairs of state had to address. Policy also depended on the acquiescence of the crown or the lords at Whitehall. The rhetoric of petition is, of course, a more constrained and evidentiary mode of communication than party invocations of the public will. Much can be determined about the issue of public opinion when confronting the private interest of the crown by examining the writings of figures such as Lewis Morris, Sr., who addressed both the populace and Whitehall, who had served the crown, and who led an opposition.

6

The Paper Wars in Massachusetts

On May 25, 1730, the citizens of Massachusetts received "joyful News of his Majesty's unparalled Goodness and Favour to his People, in appointing Mr. Belcher to the Government of these Provinces."[1] The royal choice seemed to many a clarification by providence of New England's confused politics. A reporter for the Whiggish *Political State of Great Britain* observed that the appointment "may end in a happy Accommodation" of the people of New England with the provincial executive, "the Government here, having nominated a Governor of their own particular Body, namely Mr. BELCHER, a Person . . . fully understanding of the Constitution of that Colony, and how far their lawful Rights extends, and one who for that Reason was intrusted by the very People of New-England to manage their Affairs here, and to Sollicit in their behalf."[2]

Governor Belcher's arrival at Boston occasioned the pealing of bells and much parading. The celebration culminated on August 11 when two potentates of Boston's rival ecclesiastical establishments, Rev. Manasseh Cutler of Christ Church and Rev. Benjamin Colman, representing the associated pastors of Boston, tendered their congratulations. Cutler assured his excellency of the "Loyalty, Peaceableness and Submission" of the members of the Church of England. Colman testified with characteristic eloquence that "when we first heard of His *Majesty's* Grace and Favour to Us, in Naming *Your Excellency* our Governour, we were like Men that Dream: The Clouds that hung over us scattered in a moment, and as the *Sun* breaks out in a dark Day, so was the Face of GOD, and the Light of the KING's Countenance upon Us. We render back to the THRONE our dutiful fervent Prayers, for His MAJESTY'S long Life, and happy Reign over Us."[3]

One hopes Jonathan Belcher relished the accolade, for the unanimity of goodwill would be brief. When he presented his royal instructions in a speech to the General Assembly of Massachusetts on September 9, 1730, the anticipated announcement that the crown had dropped its demand for a fixed salary for the provincial executive was not forthcoming. Instead, the fifth paragraph of the address apologized for the prerogative and the repetition of the royal demand to regularize the governor's wages. If the salary should not "be forthwith fixed by law, his Majesty will find himself under the necessity of laying the undutiful behavior of the Province before the legislature of Great Britain, not only in this single instance, but in many others of the same nature and tendency, whereby it manifestly appears that this Assembly, for some years past, have attempted by unwarrantable practices to weaken, if not cast off, the obedience they owe to the crown, and the dependence which all colonies ought to have on their mother country."[4] Belcher's old allies in the legislative resistance to the prerogative listened in amazement at the extent of his apostasy. The dream being played out before their eyes assumed the features of a nightmare, a recurring incubus sporting the visage of every governor since Massachusetts became a royal province in 1691. In this nightmare the crown attempted to rob the assembly of its power by depriving it of its one effective check on the executive, its control over the governor's salary.

This governor's insistence that the assembly surrender its power gave the familiar nightmare a bizarre twist, for Belcher before being elevated to the executive had been commissioned as the assembly's agent to oppose the crown's demands. Belcher's predecessor, Gov. William Burnet, at his inauguration had carried royal instructions requiring the assembly to fix his salary. The assembly had balked. Belcher had been dispatched to London to plead the case against Burnet. When Burnet died suddenly and Belcher was appointed in his place, the assembly believed the issue had been resolved in its favor and its rights preserved.

Belcher's apostasy was sauced with audacity, for the governor claimed he was the savior of his colony's liberties by consenting to champion the king's desires. He declared that his appointment prevented "this, and many other Matters of dangerous Consequence to the Province, being laid before the Parliament of *Great-Britain* the last Winter."[5] Belcher implied that Parliament would have revoked the province's charter, if he had not offered assurance that Massachusetts would submit to the royal wishes.

Belcher's rhetorical art contributed to the sensation his speech caused. A graduate of Harvard whose talents ran to merchandising rather than theology, Belcher acquired a cosmopolitan polish during his frequent overseas ventures. Like many educated men of his generation, he developed a taste for letters and an appreciation of how they might be used in the service of politics. When fashioning a justification for his change of opinion, Belcher turned to Addison's "Cato," recalling to his audience the critical controversy whether Cato's suicide was aesthetically or ideologically acceptable as an expression of his political morality.

> The Fame of *Cato's* Wisdom reflected Honour on
> old Rome, while he made so brave a stand for the
> Liberty of his Country, but when *Caesar* had shut
> him up in his little *Utica*, and offer'd him Terms
> of Honour, his Murdering himself rather than submit
> to a Power he could no longer rationally Resist, has
> left a lasting Brand of Infamy on the Memory of that
> great Patriot. This, *Gentlemen*, I mention as some
> Illustration of the Dispute lately subsisting between
> his Majesty & his People of this Province.[6]

The parallel was readily grasped: Caesar was the king; Cato represented republican New England and its putative spokesman, Belcher. Suicide signified acts that would prompt cancellation of the Charter of 1691 and direct incursion of Parliament into the government of Massachusetts. The argument depended upon the audience's reformed protestant detestation of suicide and their sympathy for the objection to the conclusion of Addison's play voiced by Christian critics.

Having provoked his listeners with his parallel, Belcher immediately called it into question, reminding his audience that no Caesar had usurped New England's liberties. George II's rule was constrained by "the Excellent Constitution and Laws of his Kingdom." In short, the prerogative was no tyranny, and the only threat to the province's liberties lay in the assembly's defiance of the crown's due, a contempt that risked harsh retribution. The governor concluded by recommending that the assembly give its "most Calm and Deliberate Attention" to the salary affair, "of so nice a Consequence and now brought to a Crisis."

One citizen's calm and deliberate attention to the salary affair took the form of a poem affixed to the door of the meeting house at Roxbury where the assembly sat:

> Our Fathers crost the wide Atlantick Sea
> And blesst themselves when in the Desart Free,
> And shall their Sons, thro' Treachery or Fear,
> Give up that Freedom which has Cost so dear!
> What-e'er Pretence Our Enemies may frame,
> The Man is alter'd, but the Cause the same.
> From *Ceasar's* court should *Cato* fawning come
> Be sure that *Cato* is no friend to *Rome*.[7]

This pasquinade became immediately notorious. New Englanders copied it into their commonplace books. Outside of Massachusetts printers featured it in their newspapers. Wits parodied it repeatedly.[8] The poem's force arose from its tension between the first four lines—a psalmic testimony in the covenantal first person plural (an echo of Psalm 44 in the style of Isaac Watts?)—and the final four lines—a Juvenalian epigram. In effect, the pasquinade exploited the same tension between reformed Christian and neoclassical values that Belcher employed in his "Cato" passage, but to opposite effect.

A manuscript exposition of the poem's message and a reconstruction of its context have survived in the hand of a person suspected of having been its author, Lewis Morris, Sr. The chief justice of New York, Morris was intimately acquainted with the issues of executive power. His disquisition, entitled "On the word *that* in the Boston Poem," may be the most intensive piece of literary criticism surviving from British America. It expends seven pages on a close reading of the epigram, the bulk of the commentary glossing a single word in the final line of the poem. Morris's remarks upon the occasion of the poem introduce his exegesis.

> "The time when this was wrote is but little past, & the place Boston, the Subject matter the known dispute between our Governour and the Assembly about raising the Sallary, Directed, the intent of writing it to raise in the present generation a Generous Spirrit of liberty and resolution to leave that liberty safe & intire to their Posterity . . . I desire you to rememb[er] the first Speech made by our Governour to the Assembly here on the 9th of Septemb[er] 1730 where after he had told them that his majestie in his great goodnese had given us one more opportunity of paying a due regard to what he thought reasonable & that he had done it in the Kindest manner by placing one at the head of this government in whome we our selves placed the trust and confidence of our affairs he adds (whether in Excuse for his own conduct, or to Engage us to a complyance or for what reason I do not presume to determine) this remarkable passage [Morris paraphrases the Cato passage quoted above]; he tells the assembly that he mentioned it as some Illustration of the dispute lately subsisting between his Majestie and his province; but that he did not allow it to be a parralell and tells how it was not between his majestie and Ceasar; but letts it remaine in the light he had set it as respect to himself as like Cato reflecting honour on his country while he was an agent and made a stand for their libertie, but was not like him mad enough to cut his throat when he could no longer defend it."9

Morris willfully misconstrued the symbolic import of Cato's suicide. The issue was not whether Belcher would cut his own throat, but whether Massachusetts would act in such a way as to bring about its political self-destruction. The force of Belcher's argument could be resisted only by denying Belcher's status as representative New Englander (a difficult matter considering his Harvard education, reformed religion, and identification with political nativism); this Morris did by literalizing the identification of Cato's suicide with some purely personal impulse to self-destruction imputed to Belcher. Deliberate misrepresentation of the intentions and actions of those who championed the prerogative was a common way of stirring up popular feeling against provincial executives.

Belcher was not without his sympathizers in his wrangle with the more obtuse of his countrymen. "A Stranger passing by, and seeing several Persons read" the Boston Poem "took a piece of Chalk, and writ under-neath the Lines following, viz."

> Their Fathers crost the wide Atlantick Sea,
> To be in Desarts from their Deserts free,
> And shall their Sons with glaring Insolence
> Support a Cause so void of common Sense?
> What-e'er Pretence this stubborn People frame,
> The Case is alter'd, but the Men the same.
> From Ceasar's Court should a new Ruler come,
> Be sure they'll Starve him, as they've others done.[10]

The author spoke a sad truth. Faced with an assembly jealous of its rights, no governor had prospered or would prosper until starved into submission to the will of the legislature. Given the expansiveness of the assembly's view of its rights, no governor could submit without violating his responsibility to the crown. Belcher had witnessed several administrations languish until they expired, stuck in the constitutional impasse; his gusto in reasserting the prerogative evinced his fortitude. Belcher's doughtiness seems all the more remarkable when we consider that he knew the mettle of his chief opponent, the ur-patriot of Massachusetts, Dr. Elisha Cooke, Jr.

The contest of wills between Governor Belcher and Elisha Cooke, Jr., became the subject of a closet drama, *Belcher Apostate*, which circulated in Boston's taverns and clubs during 1731. The play, which took the "Boston Poem" as part of its prologue, portrayed the governor as a man corrupted by the blandishments of "Caesar's Court." Dr. Cooke, conversely, was the spotless champion of New England's liberties. This melodramatic dichotomy of character would rob the play of much of its aesthetic interest if the author had not captured in his characterization of Cooke something of his brilliance as a political agitator. Before we can understand the play we must learn something more of Dr. Cooke and substantially more about the evolution of the salary contest in Massachusetts.

Elisha Cooke, Jr. (1678–1737), was the son of Elisha Cooke, Sr., a politician who had led the campaign against the innovations of the Charter of 1691, and Elizabeth Leverett, daughter of Governor Leverett of Massachusetts. He was educated at the Boston Latin School and at Harvard where he studied physick. Upon graduation in 1697 he began his long political career, which burgeoned in 1714 with his leadership of the popular crusade for a Land Bank scheme. From 1714 to 1730 Cooke labored to construct a cult of personality about himself. He mastered the arts of public speaking, pamphleteering, and caucus management. He identified himself with the "popular" resistance to the prerogative and became its leader in the assembly. His premier talent was personal image making: he was the "new Elisha," come to smite the wicked Ahab. He was the "true Cato." He was the "Magna Carta man." He was the "scion of the Old Charter." A typical cult effusion was the paean nailed to the west door of the Boston Townhouse on the day after Belcher delivered his speech:

> Thou who didst well defend Thy Countrys Cause
> Continue still to merit her applause
> Resist the last attempt That will be made
> Nor be by fear or flattery betray'd
> What Thanks to Thee Elisha shall we owe
> Greater perhaps Than wee shall now bestow
> Whilst lieving Envy may Obstruct Thy praise
> Butt trust it will be known in after days
> Ages to Come shall Celebrate Thy Name
> And like the Prophet's last the Patriot's fame. [11]

Young Samuel Wentworth did not savor the sentiments and tore the poem down. Next morning another set of verses appeared in its place, excoriating Cooke, "who didst Ill defend Thy Countrys Cause/ Hast Disgar'd Relegion liberty & her laws." [12] The paper wars in Boston were characterized by direct confrontation, blow for blow.

Elisha Cooke, Jr.'s, politics constituted the extreme of political nativism in New England. He more than any other figure of the early century determined the dynamics of party struggle, for he more than any other agitated to increase local autonomy. In *Belcher Apostate* the character "Dr. Cooke" self-consciously proclaimed his vocation: "The Constitution of this Province, is what I have made my Study, And I'll never consent to any Law, that from its first Institution will render us Slaves, to the Arbitrary will of a Governour." [13] By "Constitution," Cooke did not recognize certain documents deemed constitutional by the majority of New Englanders. In particular, he did not credit the "explanatory charter of 1714," which indicated that the king's governmental appointees should be paid regular salaries. For Cooke the constitution consisted of the new Charter of 1691, the old Charter of 1629, and the Magna Carta. His special study and his special love fell upon the latter two documents.

OLD CHARTER

Just as scripture stood behind Massachusetts Bay's theological literature, so the charter stood behind its writing on the affairs of state. The charter was no mere legal instrument. For New England it stood as the foundation stone to identity, an Ebenezer to the intents of the founders. History began in Massachusetts Bay not when the Bristol fishermen made landfall, nor when the Pilgrims settled at Plymouth, but that fateful afternoon in 1630 when Winthrop delivered a copy of the charter to Endicott at Salem. What was the charter? Considered from a strictly legal viewpoint, it was a grant of autonomous authority to a corporation. A charter bore the king's name and seal, signifying that the monarch had permitted a portion of his power to devolve upon the bearer. The chartered entity received legal standing in the courts of England, the right to initiate legal proceedings, and the right to regulate itself under the authority of seals and laws. New England's colonies did not restrict themselves to the literal permissions of their charters. For them, the document warranted a demi-sovereignty: the right to establish its own form of elective government (the General Court), levy taxes, coin money, certify land titles, and raise militia. Thus Massachusetts Bay, Rhode Island, and Connecticut, while ostensibly companies, resembled commonwealths in practice. The charters came to be seen as the legal bulwarks protecting New England's theopolities. By a metonymy of cause and effect the charters came in the course of time to symbolize the "New England way."

The crisis in New England's political faith occurred in 1683 when the crown revoked the Massachusetts charter. The freemen of Boston did not surrender it willingly, arguing in the words of Japthah, "that which the Lord our God has given us, shall not we possess."[14] Yet the authority to govern had not come from the mountaintop, but from the hand of Charles I. What Charles I gave, Charles II took away.

James II, after the charters had been vacated, tried to consolidate the myriad northern polities into a unified New England. Trade could then be regulated and the crown ensured of its share of the proceeds. To promulgate his program the king commissioned Sir Edmund Andros as governor of New England. Popular discontent with the appointed executive was widespread, but did not find vent until news of the Glorious Revolution inspired a popular rising in the capital. Boston's insurrection succeeded, installing in 1689 a provisional government. Meanwhile in London, Increase Mather, who had been dispatched as agent on behalf of those injured by the Andros government, agitated for change.[15]

While purportedly in London to petition for relief from the Andros regime, Increase Mather's ambition was to promote the restitution of the old charter. The Glorious Revolution afforded Mather an unhoped-for opportunity. King William listened sympathetically to Mather's petitions, yet believed too ardently in a monarchially centered imperium to grant all that Massachusetts desired. After much negotiation, a compromise charter was formulated. The second charter granted by the crown in 1691 changed Massachusetts's polity in two fundamental respects: it invested property-owners rather than church members with the franchise, and it made the colony's governor a royal appointee rather than an elected official. "Wee doe further for Us Our Heires and Successors Will Establish and ordeyne that from henceforth for ever there shall be one Governour One Leiutenant or Deputy Governour and One Secretary of Our said Province or Territory to be from time to time appointed and Commissionated by Us Our Heires and Successors."[16]

In Massachusetts a resistance to these innovations quickly organized around Thomas Danforth and Elisha Cooke, Sr. Adherents to the primitive New England way became known as "Old Charter men." Opposing conservative zeal and promoting political pragmatism, Increase Mather counseled accommodation and suggested the advantages of the new system by engineering the appointment of Sir William Phips, New England's crusty treasure hunter and military man, as governor. Having a yankee as governor did not quiet the discontent of the Old Charter partisans. Politics in provincial Massachusetts would henceforth be articulated in the tensions between Old Charter men, New Charter men, and the Tories. The literature upon the affairs of state is intelligible only within this context.

Tensions between Old Charter men and New Charter men found immediate expression in Cotton Mather's political fables, which were "handed about" at the time of Increase Mather's agency. The fables employed the allegorical method of Dryden's "The Hind and the Panther," rather than the more general manner of the Aesopic apologue. In "The New Settlement of the Birds in New England," Mather represented the political schism of 1689–90 as a beast history. The young writer baldly symbolized the Old Charter-New Charter clash:

> Some [Old Charter Men] were of the opinion, that if Jupiter [the king] would not reinstate the birds [New Englanders] in all their ancient circumstances, they had better accept of just nothing at all, but let all things be left for the harpies [Andros Tories] to commit as much rapine as they were doing when they were ejecting every poor bird out of his nest. . . . Others were of opinion, that the birds ought rather thankfully to accept the offers [second charter] of Jupiter.[17]

Mather justified the New Charter position by reviewing the privileges that the document asserted, yet was circumspect enough to acknowledge the objection harbored by many a New England "bird." "The king's-fisher [Governor Phips] indeed was to have his negative upon the birds, but the birds were to have a negative upon the king's-fisher; and this was a privilege beyond what was enjoyed by the birds in any of the plantations, or even in Ireland itself" (note how the allegorical pretence slips).[18] It is impossible to determine from the allegory what Mather meant by the birds' negative. Was it the informal promise Increase Mather gained from the king that New England would be consulted concerning the appointment of the executive? Was it the right to control the gubernatorial salary?

Cotton Mather's assurances did not quiet the squabbling of Danforth and Cooke. Their dissension provoked another allegory, more labored and mechanical than the first. Entitled "Mercury's Negotiation," the fable barely disguised the son's contempt for those who found fault with his father.

> When Mercury [Increase Mather] returned to the sheep [people of New England], he found them strangely metamorphosed from what they were, and miserably discontented. He found that such things as the sheep would have given three quarters of the fleece on their backs to have purchased, when he first went from them, they were now scarce willing to accept of. He found that there were, (though a few,) which had the skins of sheep on them, and yet, by their claws and growls, were indeed, he knew not what. He was ready to inquire, whether no mad dogs had let fall their slaver upon the honest sheep, since he found here and there one begun to bark like them, and he feared whether these distempers might not hinder their ever being folded more. [19]

At this juncture young Mather's ire flared; he could not restrain himself from intruding upon the action. Characterizing himself as Orpheus, Cotton Mather lambasted the Old Charter critics with an extended erotema on behalf of his father's good intentions. Reading the fable, one senses that the New Charter was becoming a familial legacy of the Mathers to Massachusetts and not the grant of authority by the king. [20]

The value of Cotton Mather's fables lies not so much in their art, but in their capacity to reveal the new rhetorical situation after 1691 in New England. With a foreign, though Calvinist, monarch on the throne, an angry Louis XIV as adversary, a charter granting many, though not all, desired rights and privileges, and a politically galvanized populace, Cotton Mather realized the unsettled state of affairs. In such uncertain conditions the arts of suasion might work to greatest effect. By adopting the most popular of the demotic forms employed by the political literature of the Restoration, the fable, he hoped to seize and settle the minds of the citizens who haunted the streets and taverns of Boston. For the churchgoer and sermon reader he published a *Pillar of Gratitude* testifying to the providential mercies entailed in granting the second charter. [21]

Mather successfully consolidated a New Charter support in Massachusetts, aided by the goodwill of the people to King William and the fear that Louis XIV's minions would invade New England. [22] Governor Phips, with the blessing of the Mathers and the concurrence of the assembly, made a material demonstration of loyalty to the new regents by taking up arms on their behalf. For nine years King William's War claimed the attentions of the government, while the witchcraft trials distracted the clergy. Elisha Cooke, Sr., nonetheless attempted to keep the dream of Old Charter autonomy alive. His machinations frustrated Increase Mather's schemes for Harvard College and opposed Governor Phips in the conduct of war policy. Yet it was not until the appointment of Joseph Dudley as governor in 1702 that circumstances aligned to bring Old Charter policy into broad popular favor.

Lord Bellomont, Dudley's predecessor, avoided much of the animosity of provincial partisans by making himself scarce, by establishing good relationships with Cooke and the Mathers, and by tempering his desire to make a personal fortune from the province. When after long delay he first appeared in Massachusetts in an official capacity, Benjamin Tompson, the principal public poet of the province, tendered an affectionate greeting. Dressed as the simple cobbler of Aggawam, Tompson spoke his "rural bit" to Bellomont in Dedham as the governor made his progress towards Boston.

> Your Stamp is royal: Your Commissions Rays
> From loyal Hearts demand loud Thanks, high Praise.
> Our Senators with publick Cares so tir'd
> With chearfullness resign to you desird.[23]

The willingness of the legislature to resign business into the hand of the governor can be attributed to the backlog of business awaiting the imprint of the seal during the executive's prolonged absence. Tompson developed his greeting into a vision of New England as a potential utopia of commodity, awaiting the stimulation of trade. Bellomont with his extensive connections in British mercantile circles and his leverage with the Board of Trade promised to be a useful man in the promotion of economic prosperity. Tompson's expression of goodwill showed how closely a governor's economic influence bore on the degree of popular support he garnered.

Bellomont disappointed the expectations of the people in Massachusetts. He preferred life in New York and supported Whitehall's program for a stricter control of imperial trade. Eventually both Cooke's circle and the Mathers turned against him. At the time of the governor's death in 1701 little residue of good feeling toward the executive remained. The elevation of Joseph Dudley to the vacant office caused discontent to flourish into ill will.

THE PHARAOH OF PREROGATIVE

Joseph Dudley (1647–1720), the son of Thomas Dudley, second governor of Massachusetts, and younger brother of Anne Bradstreet, was a seventeenth-century "transatlantic man." Though educated at Harvard to be a congregationalist clergyman, he was lured by the culture of refinement developing among the Boston merchants. He took to commerce and then to politics. In popular memory he was ever associated with the darkest moment in Massachusetts history, for he bore the news of the revocation of the Old Charter from London where he had been serving as the colony's agent. With these dark tidings he carried instructions appointing him head of the interim government, enjoined to rule until Sir Edmund Andros arrived to oversee the reformation of the colonial governments into the province of New England. For his service to the Stuarts, Dudley was jailed after the 1689 rising, though his term was short.[24] Ever sensitive to the path that showed greatest promise to his fortunes, he left Massachusetts for England after his release. In London his knowledgeability brought him to the notice of the Board of Trade. Conversion to the Church of England expedited his rise. He was elected to Parliament and won the friendship of William Blathwayt, secretary for plantations. With Blathwayt, Dudley saw the necessity of restructuring the provincial governments if the empire were ever to prosper. With Edward Randolph Dudley, saw that the quickest means of accomplishing the reformation was to void the colonial charters.[25] When Blathwayt managed Dudley's appointment as successor to Bellomont, the governor assumed office intent upon extending the prerogative by vacating the New Charter.

Dudley knew who his enemies were and had studied how to exercise the prerogative against them. Because popular resentments had concentrated on matters of the pocketbook, Dudley reasoned that less resistance would attend advancing other prerogative powers, particularly appointment and veto. When Elisha Cooke, Sr., and John Saffin were elected to the Governor's Council in 1704, Dudley vetoed the result. Saffin, "a principal inhabitant of Bristol" and sometime secretary of the assembly, was stridently Old Charter in politics. He was also a poet.

Saffin's poetry has attracted the attention of commentators for its mannerist profusion of imagery and sentiment rather than for its frequent political animus.[26] His love verses in particular have won notice. Yet the political poems, too, have their interest. Their tone of personal address, their use of the persona of the righteous speaker of the *vox populi*, and their application of the techniques of Christian admonition to the task of political criticism indicate much about the rhetoric of Old Charter literature. Each verse was sent in manuscript as a private communication to the governor, who had a reputation as a "man of parts" and a lover of letters.

> Yo^r Excellence hath not fitt Measures taken;
> In the due Conduct of yor Government,
> Which has Occasiond so much discontent
> Among yor people: if you they have not hated,
> Yet to yor Self, their Love is much abated.[27]

By informing Dudley of his unpopularity, Saffin revealed no new truth. Rather, he confirmed an old enmity to lend weight to a prophecy of Dudley's imminent political downfall. The poet claimed that public disfavor had swelled because

In Church and Comon weale there's such a Chang
Made, and Endeavour'd, in so Short a Space
Which threatens all our Priviledge to Rase;
And if Accomplished would surely then:
Cause us to Cease to be Right Englishmen.
Now if you think these Hints proceed from mee
I doe assure you tis Vox Populi:
And if I miss not much in my Account
if you persist therein, 'Twill you Dismount.

(33–41)

By confronting the authority of the crown with the authority of public will,
Saffin threatened Dudley with revolution. The phrase "Church and Comon
weale" echoed the politics of the 1640s, while "all our Priviledge to Rase"
savored of the rhetoric attacking James II and his minions in New England.
The nature of the changes the *vox populi* bewailed can be adduced more precisely in a second address by Saffin to Dudley dated January 22, 1704. A
sample of New England hermeneutics, the epistle interpreted Dudley's fortuitous escape from drowning on the Charles River as a remarkable providence illustrative of divine judgment:

Sure the Most High doth by the same Intend
what you as Chief, have done amiss should mend:
not onely Privet ills, should be Bewayl'd
but as unto the Publick; you have fail'd;
And whether Inovations you han't prest,
and sought to Alter that wch God hath Blest
the People in New England . . .[28]

Saffin then particularized the governor's crime against God's chosen people:

you Designe (yor Actions don't conceale)
a Totall Change in Church, and comonweale:
is the Opinion of most Thinking men
we must Return to Egypt once agen
ah! Let it not be said that you now Dare,
To pull Down that yor Father helpt to Reare

(29–34)

Joseph Dudley's father, Thomas Dudley, had been the second governor of
Massachusetts Bay. By casting Joseph Dudley's actions as a typological re-
enactment of the biblical Joseph's binding of Israel into Egyptian captivity,
and by accusing the governor of rebellion against the designs of the New
England patriarchs, Saffin condemned Dudley's innovations with Deu-

teronomic rigor. Dudley, trained in the method of reformed Christian eristic, yet distanced from the dissenting rhetoric by his adoption of the Church of England, could well appreciate the manner of Saffin's address and its effectiveness as a vehicle of political controversy. By dressing his political criticisms in the garb of Christian admonition, Saffin could avoid the charge of sedition, for admonition required that a Christian confront a fellow with his failing; no accusation of malediction behind a magistrate's back could be made if criticisms came to him directly. (Saffin no doubt knew of Dudley's successful prosecution of John Gold of Topsfield for sedition in 1686.) Admonition also required that some indication of the course of righteous action be given to the miscreant. This, too, Saffin took care to do, asking Dudley repeatedly to cease his governmental innovations. The ingenuity of Saffin's admonitions lay in his conflation of the will of the people with the will of God.

   We do not know whether Saffin displayed his poems to other persons of like mind, nor do we know whether Dudley deigned to reply. What we do know is that the governor, if he had so chosen, could have answered Saffin's charges with a cogency and power exceeding anything that Saffin ever could have managed. Dudley's training in rhetoric and his long experience of parliamentary debate in Britain equipped him with skills of argument which few New Englanders ever possessed. Indeed, his ability to respond to accusations of sin so challenged the authority of his accusers that Dudley may be credited with severely curtailing the use of Christian personal admonition as a method of political confrontation.

   Admonition carried its greatest weight when administered by a minister of the gospel; its authority depended upon the listener or reader acknowledging the speaker as an oracle of truth. When Dudley confuted the rebukes of Increase and Cotton Mather, the most potent of New England's oracles, he broke the spell investing religious censure. The Mathers, believing Dudley to oppose their influence at Harvard College and irritated by the governor's vigorous action on behalf of the prerogative, sent a private admonition to Dudley on January 20, 1708. When Cotton Mather touched on the governor's energetic dispensation of patronage, the admonition turned to intemperate rebuke: "Sir, your snare has been that thing, the hatred whereof is most expressly required of the ruler, namely *covetousness*. . . . The main channel of that *covetousness* has been the reign of bribery which you, Sir, have set up in the land."[29] Dudley's dispassionate vindication of his conduct, expertly bolstered by scriptural citations, showed Mather that his reproofs had none of the intended effects. Dudley wrote, "I am always ready to sustain, with thankfulness, all well designed reproofs, administered with a proper bosom: But I should be stupid not to distinguish between reproaches and christian admonitions."

> I always thought that some of the laws of wise and christian reproof were, That the things reproved be as to fact notorious, and not bare matters of fears, jealousy, and evil surmisings; That these facts be evident breaches of some known laws of christianity: That the admonitions be not administered with bitterness, or vilifying ignominious language, but with a spirit of meekness. Gal. vi. I: That a superiour be treated with a respectful distance; not reviled, not stigmatized as the most profligate, but entreated as a father. Job xxxiv. 1–8. 1 Tim v. 1. That the admonition be seasonable, when the reprover as well as the reproved are in the best temper, and there is least reason to suspect him influenced by prejudice, wrath, and ill will. James 1. 20.[30]

The subversion of private admonition as an effective means of political contention marked the further redirection of controversial discourse toward a public. The Mathers, with their predeliction toward the press, published their views. Cotton Mather knew that the cultivation of ill will toward the governor in the province was ineffective as a means of checking his power. By 1708 Dudley had proved that he could operate quite well without popular acclaim. So long as Dudley prosecuted Queen Anne's war with energy and maintained good relations with his friends in the Board of Trade, he would continue in power—unless public opinion in London could be aroused against him. This Mather attempted to do, having colleagues in London's dissenting circles see two anonymous pamphlets through the press: *The deplorable state of New-England, by reason of a covetous and treacherous governour, and pusillanimous counsellors* and *A Memorial of the Present Deplorable State of New-England . . . by the Male-Administration of their Present Governor, Joseph Dudley, Esq. and his Son Paul.*[31] The pamphlets contained one charge designed to stir the dissenting interest in Britain and seize the attention: that the governor was engaged in a collusive trade with the French enemy. Unfortunately for the Mathers, this charge was unsubstantiated. Dudley's refutation, *A modest enquiry into the grounds and occasions of a late pamphlet, intituled {sic} A Memorial of the Present Deplorable State of New-England*, supplied a defense reasonable in tone and thorough in documentation.[32] The Privy Council cleared Dudley of all charges of maladministration in 1708.

Dudley's vindication in London alerts us to the fact that rhetoric had its limits as a means of bringing about political change, that the imperial constitution militated against local solutions of political problems, and that provincial complaints to the metropolis faced particular difficulties. So long as an executive was willing to risk impoverishment, he could exercise power, provided he retained the backing of the Privy Council and the Board of Trade. Armed with the ministry's vindication, Dudley displayed complacency before his critics. In 1708/09 Saffin lamented, "All sorts of Persons much Complaine/ But their bewayleings are allmost in vaine."[33] In Old Charter eyes a reliance upon powerful political connections in Whitehall became one of the chief symptoms of Toryism, along with attendance at

King's Chapel, support for strict customs jurisdiction in provincial ports, and a desire to cancel the charters.

The paradox of Dudley's reliance upon his transatlantic connections was that in the course of time his regime fell because of them. The governor's patrons went down with the general collapse of the Tories upon the death of Queen Anne. The Whig triumph and the ascension of the Hanoverian dynasty saw the end of Dudley's support in London. Consternation broke out among the Anglicans and transatlantic merchants whom Dudley had fashioned into an interest. The dashed hopes of New England's Tories are twitted in the most ingenious literary relic of 1714, a verse given to Benjamin Walker of Boston by Jonathan Stedman, Sr., of Cambridge.

> I love with all my heart. The Tory party here
> The Hanoverian part. Most hatefull doth appear
> And for That Settlement. I ever have deny'd
> My Conscience gives Consent. To be of James' side
> Most Righteous is the Cause. To fight for such a King
> To fight for Georges laws. Will Englands ruin bring
> Its my mind & heart. In this Opinion I
> Tho none will Take my part. Resolve to live & dye[34]

Read in normal scansion the poem seems a heartfelt testimony of Tory loyalty to the Stuart cause. But the text does not permit any authentic expression of Tory pathos, for the periods introduced in the midst of each line point toward another message constituted as a series of half-line couplets: "I love with all my heart. / The Hanoverian part. / And for That Settlement. / My Conscience gives Consent." Just as Tory power vanished before the instant Whig supremacy, so the Tory voice dissolved before the Whig proclamation.

THE PASSING OF THE MANTLE

The Hanoverian accession and the Whig supremacy that accompanied it in 1714 did not alleviate the constitutional tensions that had arisen in Massachusetts. George I had no desire to surrender any of the crown's prerogatives. Parliament had no inclination to abandon its oversight of imperial commerce. Furthermore, the Whig leaders, many of whom were involved in trade, acted on their determination to maintain the value of currency by repressing easy credit schemes such as land banks. They promoted hard specie as the medium of exchange. Those in the provinces who were paid salaries or who kept debt on books sympathized with the Whig policy. These persons formed the basis of the New Charter party. The Old Charter faction tended to include townsmen or country farmers, land-rich and specie-poor.[35] These men sought to enhance their credit by banking on the value of their real estate. Elisha Cooke, Jr., the son of the founder of the Old Charter faction, emerged into the political limelight in 1716 by promoting a Land Bank and attacking the tight credit policy of the New Charter merchants.

Cooke's meteoric rise to the forefront of the ranks arrayed against the prerogative may be attributed to inheritance, talent, and luck. His luck consisted in the appointment of Col. Samuel Shute, a political dullard, as governor. Shute's ignorance about imperial finance proved fortuitous to the Old Charter cause. Cooke and his allies in the assembly determined that by issuing £100,000 in bills of credit their constituents would be served by the consequent inflation reducing their debts; meanwhile taxation would be subverted, undercutting the imperial revenue. The New Charter merchants would be hurt by the inflation, for few would trade with a province whose currency was in a free fall of depreciation. With amiable condescension the governor ratified the issue of the paper money. He only realized the disaster he had authorized when the £500 he had been granted as salary sank in purchasing power to £250.[36] The governor threw off Elisha Cooke, Jr., and turned to the one voice of executive wisdom on the Governor's Council, Joseph Dudley.

Shute's reversal of policy provided Elisha Cooke, Jr., with an opportunity to ridicule the governor for weak leadership. To demonstrate the executive's impotence, Cooke, Jr., made an incursion into the royal privileges in New Hampshire, a province that possessed its own assembly, but shared Shute with Massachusetts. Cooke directed woodsmen to ignore the royal instruction that prime timberland be reserved for employment in the king's service.[37] Backcountrymen embraced the opportunity to poach on the mast trees for personal profit. Cooke furthermore claimed that the crown had no right to reserve timber in Maine, which Cooke conceived as a proprietary province of Massachusetts! Elisha purchased substantial tracts of prime forest, then offered them for sale to fee-simple purchasers, despite the royal reservation and problems of title.

The crisis came in the spring of 1720. The assembly elected Cooke its speaker. Someone made mention of this in private to Governor Shute. The governor's lack of response to the news prompted the informer to think that the executive approved the choice. "Upon this assumption the house went so far as to organize for the choice of councillors without further informing the governor it had been made. Shute then told them that no election should be held until he was informed who was chosen speaker. When a committee notified him of their choice, Shute declared that, as Cooke had treated him ill as governor, by the authority given him in the royal charter he negatived the election and desired that they would choose another person."[38] After vetoing Cooke, Shute refused the election of councilors Nathaniel Byfield and John Clarke, allies of Cooke's faction. The assembly refused to accede to Shute's veto, so the governor prorogued the session, despite the need to remedy currency and trade problems. In the recess following, a pamphlet war erupted in Boston.

The paper war of 1720 saw the rise of the second generation of partisans in the constitutional conflict. Elisha Cooke, Jr., wrote for the Old Charter view; Paul Dudley, son of Joseph Dudley, became the literary champion of the prerogative. Both writers took Defoe's prose polemics as their models. Poetry played a relatively minor role in the paper war. The literary interest of the pamphlets resides in their presentation of a cast of characters that would people the political literature of the province for years to come: the Jeremiah of liberty, the public-spirited countryman, the cosmopolitan city merchant, the venal imperial appointee.

Cooke was first to enter the public lists, by publishing in summer of 1720 *Mr. Cooke's Just and Seasonable VINDICATION: Respecting some Affairs transacted in the late General Assembly at Boston, 1720.* Elisha's *Vindication* gestured at the reformed Christian ethic of admonition, confronting the authority of the governor directly, yet it reflected the new rhetorical reality by appealing to the public for support in the coming election. Indeed, an innovation of the *Vindication* was its careful projection of the "People" as a character in the text—the role that the reader presumably would fulfill. Cooke's "People" was a body of liberty-loving commonwealthmen: "The happiness or infelicity of a People, in intirely depending upon the enjoyment or deprivation of Libertie; Its therefore highly prudent for them to inform themselves of their just Rights, that from a due sense of their inestimable Value, they may be encouraged to assert them against the Attempts of any in time to come."[39] Cooke identified the constitution as the bulwark of the People's rights. According to Cooke, the constitution consisted of the written charter—"the only Rule to direct us in the right Path"—and the procedures of British jurisprudence. If issues were not addressed in the Charter of 1691, the matter devolved to the evidence of "perpetual usage." Cooke's recourse to evidence of "perpetual usage" was the essence of Old Charter Constitutionalism, for it permitted legislators to look beyond the New Charter to the practices brought into being under the First Charter when there was no royal hand in Massachusetts government. Though Cooke himself was willing to look beyond the Second Charter, woe unto the executive who acted outside of its strict prescriptions. One deviation spelled disaster. "If the Governor can have a Negative on things transacted in the House, before they have had the Concurrence of the Board, that part of the Legislature would be in a great measure useless; which cannot be the intent or design of the Charter. . . . Had they [Old Chartermen in the Assembly] *then* given up the Cause, Ages to come would justly said, they had given a Deadly wound to the Constitution and well being of that House, and deprived the People whom they Represented of their Proper Rights."[40] The slippery slope fallacy supplied the pathos in Cooke's performance: if the governor were granted this one right, eventually the constitution would succumb.

Shortly after publication of Cooke's *Vindication* Paul Dudley, combining the method of two of Defoe's recent writings—*News from the Moon* and *Robinson Crusoe*—attacked Cooke's claims in an unsigned pamphlet entitled, *News from Robinson Cruso's Island*. Dudley supplied a continuation of Crusoe's adventures—a trip to the Island of "Insania." Insania possessed a royal charter "full of singular privileges" and a governor "that sought the good of the People, more than the People did themselves."

> There was in the Country a Man, who had rendred himself Obnoxious to the Governour, not only by base Reflections, and Abuses on his Person, but also by other Publick Offences; which procured the Censure of the Council Board upon him, the Report of which was sent home to the Court of *England*. When a Convention of the Island came together, the People were in such a strange humour, that they chose this Man to be their Prolocutor, as if it had been on purpose, to shew their Spite to the Governor, and put a Publick Affront upon him; There was not another Man in all the Island, whom the Governour wou'd have been so uneasy with. . . . The Lords of Trade & Plantations had signified under the hands, That the Governour had a Negative on the Conventions choise of their Prolocutor, and made use of it; The Convention disputed this Power, upon which he dissolved them, which no body can deny he has the power to do. And another Convention was presently called, and they now had a fair Liberty of choosing another Person for their Prolocutor, which wou'd put an end to their former disputes; when they were coming together, some rash Men willing to see the Country all in Confusion, held forth to the Country Men, that if they did not choose the same Speaker, which they had in the former Convention, they gave up their Privileges, and they had better loose all, and bring the last Degree of Slavery upon the Country, than to forbear to Insist on one trivial Point, tho' it was never so disputed an One."[41]

Dudley suspects that Cooke's hidden agenda is nothing less than the wreck of the government; that is, a situation so contentious that the New Charter would be revoked, turning the "slippery slope" argument into a self-fulfilling prophecy. Did Cooke believe the imposition of direct imperial control would recreate the situation of the Andros government in 1689? Did he anticipate a popular revolution that would establish local autonomy on Old Charter or Old Commonwealth grounds? If so, then Massachusetts was truly "Insania," for Dudley's nemesis was striving to accomplish the act—revocation of the charter—for which Dudley's father had striven unsuccessfully during his governorship.

Cooke proved troublesome to his adversaries because he was singularly apt at convincing large numbers of the "middling sort" of people to believe his claims. His flexibility as a rhetorician verged on duplicity. For instance, he could sound like the most loyal of King George's subjects, vowing "to promote and advance the Honour and Service of King GEORGE, So Glorious a Prince as our Nation, and We in these Provinces, are by the favourable Smiles of Heaven blessed with." The loyal testimony enlisted the good will of the amorphous mass of citizens who possessed friendly inclinations toward the House of Hanover. The incongruity of this testimony coming from the man whose every legislative endeavor sought to reduce the king's influence was not apparent to many. But the audacity of Cooke's promise to "Study to Abase and Behave my Self to the Powers that are Ordained over Us, as becomes every Good *English Man* to do," seemed calculated to drive adversaries to distraction.

Cooke's playful management of persona may be seen to good advantage in his unsigned reply to Dudley's pamphlet. *Reflections upon Reflections; Or, More News from Robinson Cruso's Island* took the form of a dialogue between a "Country Gentleman" and a "Boston Gentleman" troubled by the government's failure to stabilize the currency. *Country Gentleman*: "Things look Discouraging, in as much as the Times may justly be said to be *troublous*; in Regard of the Divisions and Animosities which are among us."[42] There was more than a little political craft involved in Cooke's employing a persona of a moderate hater of faction. As the arch-malcontent of the province and the chief promoter of the inflation, Cooke had stolen the rhetoric of the opposition for his own use. But the true mark of Cooke's ability lay in his subordination of the issue of the moment—monetary policy—to the larger rhetorical task, revising the country's understanding of the nature of patriotism.

Circumstances during the early 1700s conspired to tie the issue of patriotism to the person of the king of England. The Glorious Revolution had stimulated a debate upon the attributes of the patriot king; no doubt the spectacle of having a foreign prince assume the throne because he better manifested English spirit than James Stuart made the matter piquant. The installation of the Hanoverians only intensified the concern. When loyalty to the Protestant Succession became the Whig test of patriotism, the issue was only more firmly fixed to the top of the political order.[43] Cooke had no use for a patriotism that seemed some emanation of the prerogative. Thus the larger argument was that patriotism was not something measured in a country's acquiescence to the will of the king (or his appointees), but in the private citizen's love of country.

The "Boston Gentleman" apostrophized his rural friend for his public spiritedness. "From this generous Affection, so many eminent Actions have taken birth, of such HEROES as have gloriously exposed their Lives for the preservation of their Country, and laid aside their private Injuries, for fear of revenging them at the publick expence." The citizen's remark was a backhanded slap at Shute who displayed personal pique when he negatived Cooke as speaker. Yet the language was general and addressed the larger issue—the identification of the patriot with the public-spirited citizen. Of such men:

> Their Memory, which is precious, shall be transmitted to the latest Posterity, to
> their Immortal Honour: On the other Hand, with what marks of Infamy do they
> deserve to be stigmatiz'd, who (tho' Heaven has Liberally furnish'd them with
> large Abilities to benefit Mankind) are acted by a *mean, narrow, contracted spirit*,
> may be argued from what I have said: (for contraries illustrate each other.) This
> may be called *sordid Frugality* with a witness; when Men are influenc'd by private
> views, and on every Occasion sacrifice the *publick* Good to their *particular* Inter-
> ests; most certainly the memories of such shall be accurst.[44]

Just as the private citizen who exalted public benefit over private interest
was the hero of Cooke's polity, so the public man who sacrificed the common
good for private gain was the villain.

Cooke reduced matters of policy to matters of character with gusto. In
New News from Robinson Cruso's Island, after blaming the province's currency
crisis on the "covetousness," "envy," "pride," and "hypocrasy" of the rulers,
Cooke loosed as violent a volley of ad hominem invective as survives in the
writing of the period. He excoriated them for opposing the emission of
more paper money. "Is it any wonder, that a few *Muck-worms*, who have
monopoliz'd vast Hoards of Bills should oppose it; seeing they have so fair a
prospect (so they think) of raising their Estates, and bulding up their *Names*
on the *Ruins* of their Country? Tho hereby their Memory will be a Stench in
the Nostrils of Posterity. For what else can we suppose them so furiously
driving at (unless we are bound to believe their *Words*, against the *Course* and
Tenor of their *Actions*) but to *engross* all the *Estates in the Island*; and themselves being *Lords*, the rest by Consequence their *Slaves*."[45] The warnings
that New England might suffer bondage to an aristocracy were not tendered
without substantiation. Cooke had the good fortune to possess one irrefuta-
ble proof of the Tory intentions from the hand of Paul Dudley himself. A
letter dated January 12, 1703/04 contained the incriminating line: "This
Country will never be worth living in for Lawyers and Gentlemen, till the
Charter is taken away."[46]

Shute lacked the will or wit to mount an effective resistance. After a se-
ries of debacles in the legislature, the governor decamped in 1723, leaving
Massachusetts in the hands of the lieutenant governor, the native William
Dummer, and the defense of the prerogative in the hands of Paul Dudley.

The exchanges between Cooke and Paul Dudley laid down the essential
themes and methods of contention over the matter of empire. Cooke cri-
tiqued the imperial program as the means by which aristocracy, the Church
of England, and the rule of private interest would be brought into New
England. Dudley criticized the Old Charter outlook for a parochialism that
would hinder the international trade necessary for prosperity. He found
fault with the assembly's systematic attempt to invade the royal prerogative
concerning the establishment of currency, the disposition of crown property, and the jurisdiction of Chancery and other courts.

Of equal import was the method of their controversy. In Cooke's pamphlets of 1720 we find in infant form the distinctive elements of the American polemic against empire. We see policy reduced to personality. We see the personality of the imperialist portrayed as being hypocritical, disguising an appetite for wealth and power behind a facade of public concern. His hypocrisy is revealed by his own statements. Thus, in a New England that banned theatrical presentations, a literature evolved that was dialogic or at least monologic in form, featuring characters who gave voice to their opinions. At some juncture, usually in the face of the principled opposition of the Old Charter patriot, the polite surface of the imperialist's public image was rent asunder and his sordid motivations expressed. Paul Dudley stands as the first self-damning figure in a confessional literature that would in the course of time include Governor Belcher, Thomas Hutchinson, Lord North, and George III. Opposing these complex soliloquizing villains were the patriots—one-dimensional Catos forever espousing the virtue of virtue.

THE PROBLEM OF OLD SARUM'S SON

One difficulty for the Old Charter argument was that not every executive fit the paradigm. Cooke and his faction had particular difficulty painting Governor William Burnet as the epitome of vice. The governor's heritage was unimpeachable; he was the son of Bishop Burnet, "Old Sarum," champion of low church tolerance to the dissenters and savior of the protestant monarchy. No bishop of the Church of England stood higher in regard among the reformed Christian denominations. Matthew Adams (a merchant-poet best known to posterity for allowing the young Benjamin Franklin the run of his library) testified to Boston's regard for Old Sarum:

> Immortal WILLIAM sav'd the British Isle,
> Groaning in Romish Chains, and Bid it smile,
> And when th' infatuate Tribe grew mad again,
> And fain would re-assume the broken Chain:
> Great *Sarum*'s Eye Pierc'd quick the deep Designs,
> Warded the Ruin, Sapp'd the fatal Mines![47]

William Burnet's personal accomplishments, too, disposed many to look favorably upon him. Burnet's administration of New York had revealed the man to be a principled, flexible executive possessed of a marked refinement of manners. He was known to be a man of parts, capable of minting an epigram or delivering a riposte in conversation. Yet he was a man of sense rather than a wit. The undergraduates of Harvard, who were experiencing an artistic awakening, felt particularly drawn to the man. The youthful

Mather Byles hoped that the governor would transmute Cambridge, Massachusetts, into the new Athens. "By Him protected, by his Pattern led,/ Each smiling Art shall lift her beauteous Head." "In BURNET's Face our future Fame appears,/ And Arts and Graces lead his flowing Years."[48]

Along the docks and in the counting houses the New Charter merchants saw promise in the Burnet family's closeness with the Hanoverians. With the West Indies agitating for special favor in the imperial scheme of trade, the Boston merchants saw an executive with access to the King as an asset.

> Yet Great BURNET's Name,
> Swells big the Sails of Hope, as well as Fame!
> Perhaps the Trading Medium will Demand
> Some Master stroke from your Superiour Hand.
>
> . . . .
>
> The KING's high Favours bless the prosperous State;
> Whilst the KING's Friend's our powerful Advocate.
> Unnumber'd Blessings flow the Peaceful Land,
> Triumphing in your just and wise Command![49]

The merchants and the muses may have celebrated Burnet's arrival in Boston in 1728; Elisha Cooke did not. Burnet's twenty-third instruction required in terms stronger than any previous royal directive that the assembly settle an annual salary of £1,000. The assembly willingly supplied the governor with £1,700 for immediate use, but did not grant the right to a fixed income. The governor declined the offer, insisting on the fulfillment of the royal requisition. The Old Charter faction fashioned "The Advice," a historical summary of the salary controversy. "The Advice" argued that a permanent salary did not accord with perpetual usage, violated Magna Carta by depriving Englishmen of the right to appropriate public money of their own free will, disrupted the balance of constitutional power between the branches of government, and violated the provincial charter by denying the General Court the right freely to raise and dispose of all moneys. Burnet rejected the reasoning and turned down an offer by the assembly to raise a grant to £3,000, saying that acceptance would "take his Majesty's Displeasure off of you and lay it upon myself."[50]

Burnet's refusal proved a problem for Old Charter ideology, for by turning down the sweetened salary the governor put the lie to the dogma that champions of the prerogative acted only to line their own pockets. It revealed Burnet to be a true Whig, valuing the constitutional balance of powers and the principles of the New Charter over the prospect of personal gain. Old Charter flacks were forced to adjust the campaign rhetoric. In one work at least they succeeded in crafting an effective critique of policy, while excepting Burnet from personal criticism. "Election Day A New Ballad of Boston" offered the conceit that Elisha Cooke was a cook and politics a meal.

> Our Cooke prepares a wholesome feast
> Of Beef & pudding In good store
> Old English food wee like itt best
> It looks all most like days of yore
> And wou'd be quite were we not now debarr'd
> Of Custard Custard wev'e no Custard O,
>   it is Curst hard.[51]

A humorous gloss on the text indicated that Custard "in the Old Sumaritan language it means Election." The parody of scriptural glossing here playfully reminded the reader that politics was a species of New England religion. The following stanza turns on several puns; to catch the sense one must know that "Pimpernell" is another term for the English herb, burnet.

> We Hugely long for Pimpernell
> But Sallery and Penny royall
> Minced in a Sallad don't do well
> Ass men grant whov'e made the Tryall
> Old Charter dyet Sute Old Charter men
> Wee Hope Sr. & hope to taste
>   old fashion fare agen

> To taste of these we do not Choose
> Tho both (some say) are very good
> One Eat too much with wooden Shoes
> The tother's dy'd too oft in Blood
> Oh a tender Conscience does alik refuse
> To taste of Blood Sr to taste of Blood Sr
>   or ware wodden Shoe

The wearing of wooden shoes, a trait associated with the French more than the Dutch at this time, signified slavery. The allusion to blood recalls how "penny royal" (taxation) provoked the mayhem of the English civil war. Once again the threat of violence is sounded in Old Charter discourse. Yet the threat is depersonalized, being made for the sake of bluster, rather than to terrorize Burnet, whom the Old Charter types confess "they hugely long for."

The punning in "Election Day A New Ballad of Boston" updated the word-wit traditional to Puritan satire from the time of the Marprelate tracts and *The Simple Cobbler of Aggawam*.[52] What distinguished the ballad was the deftness of wordplay—there was none of the ponderousness of conceit or repetitive excess found in passages written during Cotton Mather's occasional jags of logorrhea. The wit of "Election Day" had been adjusted to the new, refined aesthetic.

A note attached to the surviving text of "Election Day" in Benjamin

Walker's diary provides a rare glimpse of how controversial writings were disseminated through the public. "I hear the above lines were put into a wheelbarrow of Bakers bread drove by Negro Frank (to supply w[i]th bread the people[)], & folded up like a letter directed to Joseph Gouch sugar Baker in Cornhill." The note suggests that the cultivation of public opinion became increasingly important in British America during the 1720s as elections became more popular in tenor. Keith in Pennsylvania, Lewis Morris, Sr., in New York, and Cooke in Boston adopted the English expedient of the campaign song to instruct public sentiment. "Election Day A New Ballad of Boston" was sung to the tune of "In the Downs."

The electorate in all the colonies constituted an elite, property and literacy commonly being the prerequisites for the franchise. As the literate populace of British America became increasingly enamored with the refinements of belles lettres in the years after 1700, the importance of literary performance in politics increased. The utility of the campaign song may be readily understood. More elaborate forms also served. Robert Hunter's witty conquest of his opponents with the satirical play, *Androboros*, accomplished what no force or bribe could accomplish in New York. One of Hunter's collaborators in *Androboros*, Lewis Morris, Sr., may have composed—if J. A. Leo Lemay's hypothesis concerning authorship is correct—*Belcher Apostate*.[53] Morris's experiences in New York struggling against the prerogative gave him an ideological perspective analogous to that of the Cooke faction. The play displays a circumspection, an objective sense of the pattern of political interaction, that bespeaks a perspective somewhat distant from the heat of the engagement.

Whoever the author, he took pains to represent all the ingredients of Boston's political stew—the mob, the ministers, and the political cronies of the principals. A similar attention was paid to the crucial institutions of New England politics—the council, the assembly, the town meeting. A prologue supplied the ideals by which the actions of the characters were to be judged:

> In Antient Rome, the Tribunes kept them free
> And were the Guardians of their liberty,
> The Spartans by their Ephori took care
> To hinder Tyranny from entring there
> And Brittain, by her Parliaments, hath Shown
> That She'll keep Kings, to what they've Justly Sworn
> And Surely it can ne're be taken ill, if we
> By the Same methods keep our liberty.[54]

The action begins with Dr. Cooke and his circle discussing the news of Burnet's appointment and tidings that he carries "very positive Instructions" for the fixing of his salary. Jonathan Belcher, a member of Cooke's circle, remarks, "The King has given such Instrucionns to the Governour thats' coming, which if we give into, New England from that time may date its Slavery." Cooke identifies the province's predicament as "the Consequence of accepting of the Explanatory Charter." Belcher concurs, proclaiming a favorite nostrum of Old Charter politics, "the Sooner we reject the Explanatory Charter, the better." Oedipus-like, Belcher pronounces the rule of consistency that will later condemn his own governship: "I lay this down as a certain Rule, from which I'll never deviate, that which is not Just, is not lawfull, And that which is not lawfull, ought not to be obeyed. And no Instruction can bind a free people, Except by their own consent." Cooke, a cautious strategist, suggests that such a course of defiance may prove difficult, because of Burnet's character. "This Gentleman has been long Governor of a province, which, I beleive has made his Circumstances to differ pretty much from those, who undergo a tedious Solicitation at Court they will be glad to take money any how or way to [aggrandize] themselves, which is not this Gentleman's caise, And I much fear he will insist Strenuously, upon the letter of his Instructions."

Burnet's first encounter with Cooke proves a trial, for when the governor proffers his instructions to the doctor to be read, he discovers the heat of the patriot's political passion when Cooke denies that royal instructions possess the binding force of law. Burnet remarks that "such a Speech may well enough become a Member of the house of Commons but Savours too much of Rebellion in a Member of an American assembly, to whom the Kings Instructions are Laws." Cooke replies, "The Kings will can be no Law or binding upon any persons, Except in a Conquer'd Country, which this is not."

The assembly resolves that instructions are not laws, and that "the liberty of a people is the gift of God and Nature." Burnet responds by proroguing the government. Afterwards he soliloquizes, "Hard is my fate, if I comply with the Kings Instructions, I must want; If I give them up, I shall loose the Government, Oh could I retire, and Spend the remainder of my Days free from Contention, I should then know what happiness is, which the hurry of my life has hitherto made me a Stranger to." Burnet's somber reflection sets off the turbulence of sentiment at the town meeting in the following scene; private composure contrasts with public tumult. The meeting itself is politically suggestive—an analogue to the committees of safety that took over the task of government during the 1689 rebellion.[55] It opens with prayer (showing the proximity of religious rhetoric to political expression). After the Amen the meeting erupts in a welter of voices revealing the various desires of the mob. The author's designation of the people as a mob, a word that came into popular parlance during the street contentions between the Tory and Whig tavern clubs during the reign of Anne, locates the meeting in the context of the new popular urban politics.

The mob's various inclinations resolve into the desire to appoint Belcher moderator; they chant his name in unison. He assumes control, announcing that "the Design of the Meeting is to appoint a proper person to be your Agent in England, That your affairs may be well represented to the King." The intention: to inform the king how "arbitrary" his instructions are.

Belcher riles the mob with descriptions of subsequent royal instructions for increasing amounts of money, raising the prospect of times when the royal demands would be so great that citizens would be compelled to sell their estates "to support the Pride and Arrogance of a Governour, and Send our Children beyond Sea, to begg their Bread." That Belcher's imagined threat contradicts the letter of the royal instruction "to fix" the gubernatorial salary at the annual rate of £1,000 is beside the point; the issue is the legal status of royal decrees. If the assembly concedes the authority of this instruction, there would be no grounds upon which to interdict the authority of subsequent instructions repealing, increasing, or compounding executive salaries. The author, too, wished to communicate something of Belcher's demagoguery—his willingness to serve as vehicle for the mob's passion. His remark about children begging bread beyond the sea plays upon the fondest element of New England self-understanding: that the "Fathers crossed the wide Atlantick sea" to escape beggary. Should the children return under the compulsion of a poverty created by royal decree?

The hyperbole of Old Charter political fantasy derived from that distinctive extremity of reformed Christian conscience which viewed any fault as fraught with the direst consequence. There was no such thing as a modest sin; any human error made one liable to absolute damnation. One slip of the foot sent one tumbling down the slippery slope to the eternal fire. Any adjustment of the political constitution led to beggary and abject slavery "unto the fourth generation." The political Torah for New England marking the path of righteousness from the slippery slope was the Magna Carta. When the mob proposes Belcher to be agent, a speaker commends the choice on the grounds that "he is a Magna Charta man, and will defend our Charter."

Commissioned by the people and instructed by Cooke, Belcher departs for England where Burnet has already gone to lay matters before the Board of Trade. His parting sentiments: "I thank God I am above want but should I be reduced, An honest beggar I think is to be preferr'd to one that raises himself to riches and honour upon the ruins of his Country."

"BELCHER APOSTATE"

The dialogue between governor and assembly over the issue of salary took place in public according to a long-established rite. The addresses of the king to Parliament and Parliament's reply at the commencement of a legislative session provided the model. These addresses, published in the public gazettes, had become the focus of public debate since the reign of Charles II. By the era of the Georges the performances had become highly ritualized. The king's addresses were composed by sympathetic ministers of the Whig supremacy in Parliament; the reply crafted by one of the principal representatives in Commons. Because the German-speaking Georges delegated much authority to trusted ministers, the clash between prerogative and parliamentary right was diminished greatly. While the colonial governments followed the form, they rarely evinced the harmonious tone of British governmental intercourse during the Whig supremacy. Governor Belcher when presenting his program before the General Court knew that his insistence on fulfillment of the royal instructions regarding salary would be a matter of exquisite controversy. Consequently, he crafted other portions of his addresses so as to satisfy as many special interests as possible. Belcher never confined his sense of audience to the walls of the assembly chamber. He recognized that the clergy and the Boston merchants would serve as powerful allies against the Old Charter clique. A congregationalist and graduate of Harvard, Belcher promised a renovated piety in government and an elevation of the college in governmental regard. His appeal won immediate sympathy from Rev. Samuel Mather, heir of the dynasty, who published a poetic *Country Treat* celebrating those paragraphs of Belcher's speech promising restoration of religion to the civic life of Massachusetts.

> Your Speech is thus, You're serious,
>   we doubt it not at all,
> For to Revive You do Contrive
>   Religion in us All.
> Good Laws therefore You would have more
>   that Vice may be suppress'd,
> Religion Thrive, Grow and Revive,
>   this will be fore the best.
> Legislature should now be sure
>   true GOD to Honour, and
> His only Son and Him alone
>   Obey at His Command.[56]

Publication of *A Country Treat* announced the allegiance of the mainstream clergy to Belcher. The divorce of the clergy from Old Charter politics had been long brewing. The inflationary issues of paper money engineered by Cooke's party had depreciated the pay of every clergyman on fixed salary in Massachusetts. The Mathers had long resented Cooke's zeal in rebuking those ministers who would preach on civil affairs. On more than one occasion the Mathers felt the zealot's lash. Other ministers of Boston

grew to resent Cooke's highhandedness for his part in the controversial re-
settlement of Rev. Peter Thacher in Old North. Against the counsel of every
minister in the city, the Old Charter contingent in the church engineered
Thacher's placement in the pulpit.[57]

In the final lines of *A Country Treat* Samuel Mather anointed Belcher as
the head of the chosen people.

> His Excellence return'd from whence
>   over the Atlantick Sea,
> Here He Arriv'd and us Reviv'd
>   our *Moses* now we see.
> *Aaron* and He how kind they be
>   each other Kiss and Greet,
> In *Israel* it was full well
>   when these two Brothers met.
> An Angel Light let BELCHER bright
>   our Lovely JONATHAN
> GOD Wisdom give and let Him Live
>   Rule well His People then.
>   (76–87)

One can read Samuel Mather's benediction as a typological rewrite of the
Old Charter epigram, "Our Fathers crossed that great Atlantick sea."
Belcher would repay the support of the clergy with policies to curb inflation, a program of legislation for the suppression of vice, regular attendance
at Sunday services, and assistance to Harvard College. Belcher drew a generation of ministers into the New Charter camp. These men would be the Old
Light ministry against whom the enthusiasts of the Great Awakening
would turn. It would be among the New Lights that the Old Charter vision
would enjoy renewed vigor.

Belcher cultivated a second interest, the merchants in the port cities.
Born into this group, Belcher sympathized strongly with mercantile concerns for stable currency, equitable trade policies, and mitigation of customs duties. Belcher won much credit for his spirited opposition to the
Sugar Acts, which would have endowed the West Indies with disproportionate advantages in the transatlantic trade. But the merchants understood
too well how self-interest guided the governor's actions. There was a cynical
"appreciation" of Belcher's expediency in espousing the king's prerogative.
When the governor eventually accepted his salary as a grant of assembly,
rather than a fixed income, the merchants saw his acquiescence as another
instance of his flexibility.

The most astonishing evidence of Belcher's adminstrative flexibility was
his appointment of Elisha Cooke to a judicial post. Despite the offense to
the prerogative that would be seen in the appointment by New Charter and

Tory champions of the crown, Belcher put through the appointment. His daring was rewarded by the spectacle of seeing Cooke shorn of all popular support when he accepted. Cooke let fall the mantle of Cato.[58]

Belcher's actions may have belied his insistence upon principles, but it was no great matter: his backers, the merchants, understood that business often needs to be done wearing a false face. Parliament might restrict trade between Boston and the West Indies, yet the demand by planters for New England rum and the desire by Boston factors for sugarcane commended commerce despite the prohibition. Boston became a center of occult trade. It is appropriate that the wittiest appreciator of Governor Belcher would be a Harvard-trained rum-distiller, Joseph Green.[59] Harvard supplied the ideals that indicated what a governor and government "should be"; the wharves and distilleries provided the experience about what men "would be."

To reduce Joseph Green's thought to an ideology would be to perform an injustice. New England's greatest satirist was one of a handful of writers (Nathaniel Gardner, Sr., James Franklin, and Jeremiah Gridley were others) whose sense of things ranged beyond party dogmas. Though a merchant and belonging to the network of clubs dominated by New Charter beliefs, he understood the benefits of paper money for the common people of Massachusetts; when the hard-money policies of the New Charter party triumphed and Old Tenor was replaced by specie-backed bills, he composed a lament upon the death of Old Tenor.[60] Though many Boston tradesmen grew enamored of Freemasonry, joining Governor Belcher in the St. John's Lodge, Green demurred, making Masonic antics a target of his wit.[61] The governor's self-importance rankled Green as much as the parsimony and parochialism of the assembly. When Green applied his wit to the political dance between governor and assembly, Moses and Cato were nowhere to be seen. The contestants were stripped of all biblical or classical finery and stood revealed as what they seemed to all circumspect persons: an ex-merchant corrupted by power, an assembly distempered by small-mindedness.

Green's satires take the form of a parody exchange between Belcher and the Assembly of New Hampshire. The legislature of the northern province exceeded that of Massachusetts in its jealousy over money. Parsimony was combined with a suspicion that Belcher, because of real estate holdings in territories disputed between Massachusetts and New Hampshire, wished to see the northern province injured in any boundary settlement. The legislative conversation took place in 1733. Green's parody was dispatched to Capt. Samuel Pollard (known to New England folklore as the "man who kissed the pope's toe") of Portsmouth for circulation at the merchants club.[62] "Govr. Belchers Speach to Assembly N:Hampshire in Verse" commences with the governor raising the threat of imminent war, a ploy to pry dollars out of the assembly for upgrading Fort William and Mary.

By Letters which from London were sent
I hear the World is in a Ferment.
The French King has declared War
Against the German Emperor
Whom his Britannick Majesty
Is Bound to treat as an Ally.
And how far this unhappy Breach
May o'er the Rest of Europe reach
Uncertain is.—A fair Alarm
It is, howe'er for us to arm.
This Province is, you understand,
Expos'd by Sea and eke by Land
The Fort, at River's Entrance standing,
To keep the Enemey from landing,
You know is for Defence unable,
And in Condition miserable.
Nor can you, Friends, be ignorant
How much I wanted, and do want
To have this *Fortress* in Repair,
Which I've press'd on th' assemblies here.
'Tis true there's Forty Cannon planted,
Yet Men to shoot 'em off are wanted.[63]

Green's doggerel reduction of Belcher's warning renders it awkward and
artificial—an effect intensified by its being followed by a plea for the repair
of the jail. The speech ends with a discussion of the boundary issue.

Last *April* I th' Assembly met
Of Province of *Massachusett*,
And told the pitiful Condition
Of those by the *Line of Partition*,
Whose Br[ea]ch, unless some Stay they found
Betwixt two Stools must come to ground.
Earnest I press'd them to be brief,
In finding Means for their Relief,
That they would lay their Case to Heart
And do, as you had done, their Part.
But *Fleet* or *Draper* or *Bat. Green*
Whose weekly Works, I trust you've seen,
In Publick Print have made it plain
How much I urg'd, but urg'd in vain.
                            (55–68)

The governor's confession of failure to resolve the issue was generally
deemed temporizing. When the assembly supplies "The Answer" to Belcher's address, its words prove blunt.

As what you Say of War Declard
Twixt French and Germans we're not Scar'd
And to be plain we'll tell you why—
We're apt to think you tell a lie.
Wee should indeed have tho't it True,
Had we but heard it, not from you.
But be it True, we do not Care
We only say, *Fight Dog, Fight Beare.*

(8–15)

In Green's epistle to Pollard framing the poems, the satirist entertained the conceit that the governor's speech was found in "a little Spanish Book" and that the reply was kept from publication by the governor's oppression and found in manuscript. Green also observed, elaborating his pretense that the poems were taken from the history of one "Gov. Lanco," that the history informs us, "That after he came to his government, he soon lost all Credit with the people, by breaking his promises, and by his mismanagement of public affairs, and his unpopular behaviour gained general Displeasure and resentment."[65]

The culmination of the governmental exchange occurred with Belcher/Lanco's "In Answer to Your Answer." Here the governor's facade of public-spiritedness was ripped off in a savage tirade. The poem merits quotation in full because it is a prime example of the genre of mock speech so favored in British American belles lettres upon political matters.

In Answer to your Answer Sirs
I think you all a Pack of Currs,
Indecent Scoundrels void of Grace;
For tell me pray, with w. a Face
Can any of you all pretend,
'Gainst Royal Power to contend
and your own Properties defend.
Pray Sirs consider who I am
I represent the very Man
Whose loud mouth'd Canons roar like Thunder
And fill the frightened Sea with Wonder.
In me alone you may descry
The Head of British Monarchy
My honest Council bear a part
And fitly figure out the Heart
Whilst You but barely represent
Th' indecent Arse or Fundament
Now tell me how it can be said
The Tail should ever Rule the Head
With what Propriety of Speech

The Heart be subject to the Breach
For th' by fatal proof I know
The Head is Honoured from below
The Tail does oft the Brow adorn
And very high exalt the Morn
Yet still 'tis plain the Head is all
The only true Original
And all the Powers beneath are small
They serve to fill up empty Spaces
To cover Blunders hid[e] Disgraces
For what is wisely done or said
Is still the Product of the Head.
But once if Humane Nature fail,
The Heart's corrupt, the flesh is frail
And all is father'd on the Tail
But not to condescend to Argue
I think you every One too hardy
For know you every One in me
Insult His Royal Majesty.
Your so insisting on your Right
Appears to me like downright Spite
It hurts my Honour, what is worse
It nearly does concern my Purse.
But let it be for this or that
Sic Volo 'tis no matter what
I've order[ed] honest Sec. to send you
Each to his Home, the D----l mend you
Nor care I five pence how you grumble
For till I finde you prove more humble
I will prorogue, Dissolve, & Damn you
Ther's not a Rogue alive will blame me.[66]

The interest of Green's satire does not lie in its procedure of reducing policy to the secret motives of a politician; this is a convention from which the satire proceeds. Rather, the interest resides in the audacity of the confessed matter. More than a villain's soliloquy of his evil intentions to the audience, Belcher's proclamation of his designs astonishes with its candor. His willingness to boast his authority, his greed, his contempt for popular opinion in the face of his opponents regardless of consequence transforms the political world so thoroughly into the Hobbesian arena of willful appetite that civilization itself seems prorogued at the end of the speech.

Lest we mistakenly identify civilization and the mitigation of appetite with the assembly, Green provided an additional poem illustrating that he possessed none of Elisha Cooke's respect for legislatures. "An Acct How the Nuptials of the Prince of Orange was Celebrated at Portsmo[uth] in Verse"

depicts the New Hampshire legislature's response to the executive order of
June, 1734, to celebrate the marriage that would ensure the continuance of
the protestant succession in Britain.

> The Chief, to whose extended sway
> Two provinces obedience pay,
> As soon as he receiv'd the News
> Of Brittain's Princess takeing Spouse,
> A Messanger, with Orders, sent
> Unto *his other Government*,
> To Keepe a day with pomp & State
> To drink and eke illuminate;
> As soon as the August Command
> Which he had sent, should come to hand.[67]

The provincial council—"No disobedient factious Blades"—convenes to
debate the manner of celebration.

> Here there Arose a small debate
> About the Charges and all that,
> But they Resolved to wave dispute
> B[elcher] Commands & they must do't
> All things in readiness were Got
> A Drum a Pistol and what not,
> For though a Great Gun Goes off Louder
> A Pistol takes but little powder,
> Nay if they could have made it do
> They wou'd have had a Trumpet too,
> But in it's stead, were forc'd to Chuse
> The horn which Post in rideing use
>   (19–30)

The celebrants retire to a tavern and drink themselves to illness in toasts to
"all the Royall Race."

> Punch, as Philosophy maintains,
> Has a Sure effect on the Brains;
> And, as Experience can tell ye
> Some Peoples Brains are in the Belly,
> Hence when drink Gripes, 'tis a sad Omen
> The Brains are lodg'd in the abdomen
>   (65–70)

The stomach having supplanted the brain in New Hampshire, appetite pre-
vails over reason. The megalomaniacal desire of the governor competes with

the appetites of the council and assembly. The Hobbesian dissensus indicates that New Hampshire is the state of nature.

Shaftesbury as the thesis of his *Sensus Communis* argued that wit founded a
community of "shared laughter." Green, by rendering the New Hampshire
dissensus ludicrous, established a community in opposition. This community roughly coincided with the network of private societies formed by merchants and tradesmen throughout New England. The clubs were arenas of
wit offering a liberty of expression that the public arena did not afford.

Though the pragmatic Belcher surrendered principle on the salary issue,
harmony was not forthcoming in the affairs of Massachussetts. His following—the Old Light ministers and the hard-money merchants—would
both face critical challenges in the 1730s, the former by the outbreak of the
New Light ministry during the Great Awakening, the latter by a revival of
the Land Bank scheme. Belcher had little hand in spiritual affairs, but his
efforts bore heavily on the outcome of the monetary crises in Massachusetts.
Royal instructions restricted the issuance of bills of credit. Belcher abided
by the instructions, and consequently the currency of Massachusetts dried
up, money eventually becoming sufficiently scarce to disturb the conduct of
commerce. The situation encouraged a revival of John Colman's Land Bank
scheme to popular acclaim. Belcher's opposition resulted in widespread alienation among the landholding and debtor classes—opposition great
enough to imperil his authority. His unpopularity was increased when the
findings of the boundary commission gave New Hampshire more of the disputed territory than it had claimed. Ridicule was heaped upon the Massachusetts government for its role in the setting of the boundary. A Boston
wag (Green?) composed, in Irish patois, "An Account of the Procession of
the General Court into Salisbury, in the Year 1737. when the Affair of the
Boundary Line was debated between the two Provinces of the Massachusetts
and New-Hampshire." The "Account" suggests that the "fixing of the line"
is somehow an execution.

> My *dear joy, ye* did never behold this fine sight,
> As yesterday *morning* was seen *before night*;
> Oh! I fear it means no good to your *neck*, nor mine,
> For they say 'tis to *fix a right place* for the *line*.
> You in all your *born days* saw, *nor I did not neither*,
> So many fine *horses* and men *ride* together.
> At the *head* the *low'r* house trotted *two* in a *row*,
> Then all th' higher house pranc'd *up* after the *low*.
> Then the governor's coach *gallop'd* on like the *wind*.
> And the *last* that came *foremost* was troopers *behind*.[68]

After the Board of Trade confirmed the boundary against Belcher in 1740 it could be said that all the king's horses and all the king's men couldn't prop up the governor again. In 1742 William Shirley was appointed in his place. It was Shirley who slew the dreaded Land Bank while Belcher languished in Scotland, then later took over the governorship of New Jersey from Lewis Morris, Sr. The succession of Morris to Belcher is not without its ironies, for Morris is reputed to have been one of the earliest literary detractors of Belcher's rule; and certainly he was responsible for "the spread of Boston principles" to New York and New Jersey.

7

The Spread of Boston Principles

New York with its polyglot population of Dutch, German, French, and English presented great obstacles to efficient governance. Yet under the leadership of Col. Robert Hunter it developed the most effective administration in North America during the first decades of the eighteenth century. Governor Hunter's governmental consensus was hard won, taking four years— 1710–14—to establish. Once consolidated, it lasted through the end of his term in 1719 and through much of the term of his hand-picked successor, William Burnet.

When William Burnet departed New York for his brief, troubled stewardship of Massachusetts, he left a province that had enjoyed more than a decade of political stability to rule over a colony notorious for its contrariness. His travails with the Old Charter men did not prompt any envy of his successors in New York. Governors James Montgomerie and William Cosby had in a few short months of rule squandered popular respect for the executive and governmental harmony. New York politics in the 1730s quickly degenerated into turmoil, with Cosby damning his many critics as bedlamites infected by the spread of "Boston principles."[1] While Cosby was correct in noting a Boston style to the rhetoric of his opponents, his accusation does not explain why the public spirit dissolved with his administration. Effective government, as the Dudley regime in Massachusetts showed, can withstand the rhetorical assault of an antagonistic ideology.

The doleful path from political stability to the Zenger debacle is clearly marked by a series of literary productions, works composed by the principal actors in New York politics. The politicians believed (as many Englishmen did during the reign of Queen Anne), that ability with the pen constituted a form of power. Verse operated as a mode of suasion in elite circles and the inspirer of political passion in the wider public. Governor Hunter's success arose partly from an ability to instruct popular feeling in his favor. The failure of Governor Cosby's regime stemmed from its inability to evoke public sympathy. The will of the people, if unified and well instructed, could overbalance even the strongest political backing in Britain. Cosby's complaints about "the spread of Boston principles" really objected to the reemergence of political tensions predating Hunter's regime. Old libertarian yearnings, desires that dated from the 1680s, found new voice, a "Boston" voice refined by training in the techniques of belles lettres. Cosby's assertive exercise of the prerogative lacked eloquent defenders to compete with the circle led by James Alexander and Lewis Morris, Sr., that supplied Zenger with copy.

To understand the collapse of the imperial consensus during the Cosby regime, we should consider the political situation predating 1714 when that consensus was formed. In particular we must turn to Governor Hunter's play, *Androboros*, fashioned as a weapon to overcome those persons and forces who opposed the creation of an effective government.

THE KEEPER

On September 9, 1709, the crown appointed Col. Robert Hunter governor of New York, the long-awaited reward for his good service as an officer under Marlborough in the War of the Spanish Succession. Shortly thereafter Richard Steele, Hunter's friend, congratulated the new appointee in the *Tatler*. "[I]t was no small Delight to me to receive Advice from Felicia. That Eboracensis [Hunter] was appointed a Governor of one of their Plantations. As I am a great lover of Mankind, I took Part in the Happiness of that People who were to be govern'd by one of so great Humanity, Justice, and Honour. Eboracensis had read all the Schemes which Writers have form'd of Government and Order, and been long conversant with Men who have the Reins in their Hands; so he can very well distinguish between chimaerical and Practical Politicks."[2] Hunter would need every scintilla of his practical experience to extend the benefits of Felicia (Mother England) to New York. The disarray of New York politics during the two decades following the Glorious Revolution made rule a task of great magnitude.

When the hangman cut Jacob Leisler from the gallows on May 16, 1691, those in attendance little realized that the dead man's ghost would haunt the halls of government for twenty years. Leisler's coup and his twenty-one months of rule after the flight of Lt. Gov. Francis Nicholson galvanized the political ambitions of the middling merchants and the restless Dutch. Leisler's favoritism towards his constituency and his persecution of Tories and large landholders stimulated a resistance that eventually caused his downfall and execution.[3] Directed by Gov. William Fletcher, Tory vengeance took economic as well as political form. The power of the river barons increased enormously as Governor Fletcher granted huge tracts of Hudson Valley land to a small circle of planters. The injustices that had

Army Proceedings or the *Conjunct Expedition,* Concordia Discors, 1741. Depicting the debacle of the English invasion of Cartegena, this print identifies the failure of the expedition to be the cross purposes of Vernon's naval forces and the Army. Reproduced courtesy of the trustees of the British Museum.

prompted Leisler's rebellion increased, rather than diminished. When the earl of Bellomont took over the executive, he checked the power of the rich landlords by seeking allies in the Leislerian circles. Roles reversed, and the cycle of vengeance was repeated. Anti-Leislerians, such as Robert Livingston, author of "A Satyr Upon the Times," found themselves cursing the executive.

> Twas gold (that curst Tempter) that did bribe
> The grand Ringleader of this hellish Tribe
> great by his Title Vile in every action
> He's gon but has entailed a Curse on's faction.[4]

The curses and the deeds of vengeance would be repeated with each change of government until Hunter interrupted the pattern of retribution.

The method by which Hunter broke the cycle of vengeance has been well treated in a number of books, most notably Patricia U. Bonomi's *A Factious People: Politics and Society in Colonial New York* and Mary Lou Lustig's *Robert Hunter 1666–1734: New York's Augustan Statesman*.[5] My interest is the important aid that polite letters lent Governor Hunter in overpowering those who resisted him. Hunter of all the British American belletrists had the most direct relation with the brilliant constellation of writers who enlivened life during the reign of Queen Anne.[6] A friend of Swift, collaborator with Steele and Addison, Hunter shared their profound belief that literature could be a vehicle of political power.

Governor Hunter's *Androboros* inaugurated America's tradition of dramatic composition in English. Because of its primacy it has attracted attention in the surveys of American theater history. Yet it is a curious piece with which to commence a consideration of American theater, for it was never intended for the stage, despite the inclusion of effective bits of dramaturgy in certain scenes. *Androboros* was a political closet drama intended for manuscript distribution among the political factions of New York; William Smith, Jr., the historian, testified that the piece proved quite successful as a political tool, for it "so humorously exposed" Hunter's enemies "that the laugh was turned upon them in all companies and from this laughing humour the people began to be in a good humour with their Governour."[7]

Hunter identified the play as "A Biographical Farce in Three Acts, VIZ, The Senate, The Consistory, and The Apotheosis."[8] By "biographical" he meant that the farce should be approached as a reflection upon actual personalities rather than the misadventures of human types. Hunter does not discard the type conventions of farce, rather he adjusts them to his parodic ends. Only Tom of Bedlam, the popular hero of street balladry, operates as a pure type character, serving in the conventional capacity of the fool voicing truths too uncomfortable for any sane person to speak. The remaining characters represent identifiable persons. Hunter, for instance, invests David Jamison, his closest personal friend, with the character of Aesop, the ancient fabulist and philosopher who enjoyed renewed popularity in the 1690s as the protagonist of a number of farces.[9] Aesop/Jamison functions as the moral center of the play. There are three butts of the satire. The first is the clownish legislators— Doodlesack, the burgher (Abraham Lakerman); Babilard, the officious man (Samuel Bayard); Coxcomb, the presuming fop (Daniel Coxe); Mulligrub, the malcontent (Samuel Mulford); and Cobus, the Dutch bumpkin (Jacobus Van Cortlandt).[10] Their antics are featured in "Act I, the Senate." Second, and more pernicious than these political bumblers, are Fizle (Rev. William Vesey) and Flip (Adolph Philipse), who plot to depose The Keeper (Governor Hunter) and put in his place Androboros, "the man eater." Androboros is the butt of butts of the satire. The misdeeds of Fizle and Flip make up Acts II and III.

Androboros is supposed to symbolize Francis Nicholson, ex-governor, ex-general of the failed expedition of 1711 against French Canada. Nicholson during his long career in colonial service manifested extraordinary energy on behalf of the crown in a variety of posts, including the governorships of South Carolina, Virginia, and Maryland.[11] His dynamism, when channeled toward constructive ends, animated much good; his contributions to the erection of Williamsburg earned an extended panegyric in poet John Fox's *The Wanderer*.[12] When the man's energy was thwarted, however, the result was mania. Cadwallader Colden observed of Nicholson that "[h]e was subject to excessive fits of passion so far as to lose the use of his reason. After he had been in one of these fits while he had the command of the army [in 1711], an Indian said to one of the officers, 'The general is drunk.' 'No,' answered the officers, 'he never drinks any strong liquor.' The Indian replied, 'I do not mean that he is drunk with rum. He was born drunk.' "[13]

The Tory government empaneled during Queen Anne's last years commissioned Nicholson, an ardent Tory, to range the American colonies, monitoring and correcting whatever governmental improprieties he discovered. His arrival in New York was awaited with exquisite anticipation by Tories and churchmen, foremost among them the Rev. William Vesey of Trinity Church.[14] Hunter, a Whig and a secularist with a Scots tolerance for Presbyterianism, had little reason to savor the appearance in his precincts of Nicholson, since rumor asserted that Nicholson would topple Hunter from power.

Given the threat Nicholson posed to Hunter, the governor's cavalier literary treatment of the general might seem astonishing. At the commencement of Act III, for instance, The Keeper/Hunter regards the arrival of Androboros as a diversion: "My Superiors, as I am inform'd, have Cloath'd him with Sham-Powers meerly to get rid of his Noise and Trouble" (29). Tom of Bedlam, the play's resident madman, recognizes Androboros as a fellow lunatic. "His Imagination is very ductile when 'tis heated, and by a Long Practice upon't, he has made it as susceptible of Impressions from Without, as it has been of these from Within." Androboros's mental ductility invites manipulation. The Keeper and his allies engineer a scheme in which they convince the man-eater that he has died. How is it that the figure viewed as the hope of Hunter's enemies, a man bearing a commission from the Tory government in London, can be treated as "Old Nick-Nack," a chimera? The answer may lie on the title page of the printed play text. There we discover that the piece has been "Printed at Moropolis since 1st August, 1714." On August 1, 1714, Queen Anne died. Shortly before expiring she passed the white rod of authority to a Whig minister, ensuring the protestant succession and the elevation of the elector of Hanover to the throne of Britain. Tory plans to restore the House of Stuart collapsed and with them the Tory government of Bolingbroke—the government that had commissioned Nicholson. The Whig triumph in Britain rendered the man-eater toothless and provided Hunter with the support that he had lacked for some years. Indeed the conceit of the final act—that Androboros is the walking dead—makes sense only in terms of the state of affairs post August 1. Only then could Hunter be so sure of his authority that he would compose the audacious portrait of his nemesis found in the climax of the play. Androboros—deluded, blinded by snuff, raging that he'll "have the Villain Hang'd; Dog, Raskal, Rogue, Scoundrel"—enters the audience room for his presentation to the Assembly.

> *Aesop*: By my Life, it is the General making his Entry; It seems he has got no Herald for this Triumph, that he thus Proclaims his own Titles. (39)

Hunter inverted the "apotheosis" announced in the Act title. Instead of the glorification that Fizle, Flip, and Androboros anticipate, they all suffer a bathetic fall. Snuff-blinded Androboros blusters blindly into the Chair of State which Fizle and Flip have boobytrapped, intending that the Keeper fall into a pit. Seeing that their hero totters on the brink, the plotters rush to assist him, only to be grabbed and pulled into their own trap. The play closes with Solemn (Lewis Morris) observing that

> In former Ages virtuous Deeds
> > Rais'd Mortals to the blest Abodes,
> But Hero's of the Mode[r]n Breed
> > And Saints go downward to the Gods. (39)

That Nicholson should drag Reverend Vesey and Adolphe Philipse with him on his descent into the nether regions is appropriate, for the men had conspired as early as 1711 against Hunter. Vesey in particular became anathema to the governor. It may be that the falling out that took place between Nicholson and Hunter in the wake of the failed Canadian campaign was greatly encouraged by Vesey's rumor-mongering. What is certain is that Vesey organized the principal opposition to Hunter from the governor's arrival. [15]

William Vesey, the man "largely responsible for what would otherwise seem to be the pathological fear of Episcopacy in New England and Pennsylvania," was the first rector of Trinity Church, New York. [16] Born in New England, son of a Jacobite, educated at Harvard, he shed that college's congregationalist principles. At the invitation of Governor Fletcher of New York, Vesey commenced his career in the Trinity pulpit on March 13, 1697/98. He quickly distinguished himself as an articulate champion of anti-Leislerian aristocracy and a tireless asserter of the privileges of the Church of England in New York. His Tory inclinations attracted General Nicholson, a man with a violent attachment to the established church, endowing its missionary and collegiate schemes and joining the Society for the Propagation of the Gospel, the foremost agency for advancing Episcopacy in North America. Nicholson credited insinuations that a Scots convert to the Church of England was little better than an occasional conformist.

The accusations Vesey and Nicholson directed at Hunter did not hold water. Hunter was no enemy to the Church of England. He was a friend of Henry Compton, bishop of London; he belonged to the Society for the Propagation of the Gospel; and he took active part in the effort to seat a bishop in North America. Indeed, he purchased a residence for such a bishop in Burlington. Hunter's criminal neglect of the church in Vesey's eyes lay in his unwillingness to coerce Presbyterians into submission to ministers and taxes they considered anathema. Hunter's Whig tolerance for dissent fired Tory enmity. His willingness to balance the claims of competing interests in the province offended Vesey's absolute convictions concerning the privileged status of the Church of England. [17]

Vesey's partisan spirit manifested itself before the governor's arrival. He organized an opposition in the assembly in an attempt to starve Hunter out of office by depriving his administration of revenue and him of salary. Hunter responded to Vesey's animosity with ingenuity. The governor directed that the soldiery worship at the garrison chapel rather than Trinity, depriving Vesey of a salaried group of parishioners. Hunter, too, interfered with Vesey's attempt to quash the autonomy of a congregation of Presbyterians on Long Island. The "Poyer" incident revealed to all Reformed Christians in America the willingness of Churchmen to impose by force their order of worship and their ecclesiastical authority on a community. [18] This ecclesiastical tyranny stimulated much of the antiestablishmentarianism that raged in Pennsylvania and New England during succeeding decades. Only John Checkley in Boston would stand in as exalted a position in the demonology of New England congregationalism. [19] Checkley could be dismissed as an import from Britain, a log from the decaying Old World ripe for the burning. Vesey, however, was native timber.

Vesey directed a cannonade of petitions against Hunter to the civil authorities in Great Britain. The fusillade reached a pitch of intensity in February, 1714, after vandals desecrated Trinity Church, smearing dung on prayer books and vestments. Despite Hunter's being in Burlington at the time, Vesey laid the blame upon him. At the same time the priest floated a rumor that the governor practiced adultery. As Mary Lou Lustig has argued, the desecration serves as the context of the second Act of *Androboros*.[20] Here we see Flip and Fizle conspire to bring the Keeper down by smearing shit on their vestments and blaming the action on him. The scatology of the notorious prologue addressed to Vesey derived from this incident.

> And it was a most Masterly stroke of Art
>   To give Fizle Room to Act his part;
> For a Fizle restrain'd will bounce like a F---t,
>   Which no Body can Deny, Deny,
>   Which no Body can Deny.
> But when it Escapes from Canonical Hose
>   And fly's in your Face, as it's odds it does,
> That a Man should be hang'd for stopping his Nose,
>   That I flatly and boldly Deny, Deny;
>   That I flatly and boldly Deny.
> Long kept under Hatches, 'twill force a Vent
>   In the Shape of a Turd, with its Size and Scent
> And perhaps in its way may beshit a Vestement,
>   Which no body can Deny, Deny;
>   Which no body can Deny.
> But However 'tis Dignify'd or Disguis'd,
>   That it should be for that the higher Priz'd,
> And either Don Commis'd or Canoniz'd,
>   That I flatly and boldly Deny, Deny,
>   That I flatly and boldly Deny.
>
>   (7)

The final stanza of prologue alluded to the appointment of Vesey as commissary of New York, leader of New York's Churchmen in 1713. This appointment by John Robinson, bishop of London and successor to Hunter's friend, Henry Compton, coincided with the rise of a frenzy of high church Toryism. Hunter's observation that Vesey after his appointment "enter'd New York in Triumph like his friend Sacheverel" aptly conveys the political spirit of the moment.[21] It was the high church mystique of 1714 that *Androboros* dissolved. It was the power of the consistory, that Tory cabal governing the church (and operating, we are led to believe, as an alternative government, something like the town meeting in *Belcher Apostate*), that was ridiculed.

That a Tory shadow government had come to power is explicable only in light of the first Act. There we witness the chaos of proceedings in the assembly, a chaos controlled only by the prorogation of the government by The Keeper. Their frenzy is "big with Expectation of some mighty Deliverance"—the arrival of Androboros. Coxcomb announces the house's credo: "That neither this House, or they whom we Represent are bound by any Laws, Rules or Customs, any Law, Rule or Custom to the Contrary Notwithstanding" (12). This credo is adumbrated into a principle of absolute rule by Mulligrub, "That this House disclaims all Powers, Preheminencies or Authoritys, except it's own" (12). Babilarb extends the doctrine further, "That this House has an Inherent and Undoubted Right to the Undoubted Property of those we Represent" (12).

Hunter's caricature of the assembly as a chaotic gathering of grotesques besotted with power has the harshness of one speaking more from injury than circumspection. The portrait of unanimous self-gratulation and peculation glosses over fascinating contradictions in the opposition to Hunter during his first years in office. In one regard—the issue of property—Hunter struck home in his assessment. The common hope of those who opposed him, from the crypto-New Englander, Samuel Mulford (Mulligrub), to the Tory landbaron Adolphe Philipse (Flip), was the hope that no imposition would be made upon property, whether for reasons of revenue or defense. To this end city merchants, large landlords, and Long Island freeholders conspired to frustrate schemes of taxation. Because of huge debts incurred by an attempt to establish Palatine refugees in the manufacturing of ship stores, Hunter suffered at the assembly's repeated restriction of salary.[22] Eventually Hunter decided that the conflict between landholders and merchants could be exploited to his advantage, so he proposed trade duties rather than property taxes as a means to bolster the revenue. Politically this was an astute decision, for the growth areas of New York lay on the frontier. The number of freeholders expanded while the number of merchants remained stable. Hunter took care to ensure that the growth of the merchant community would be controlled, enlisting the city factors' own greed in his behalf by having them support a trade monopoly. The attempts by Long Islanders to open another port were quashed, much to the disgust of Samuel Mulford. Having limited the growth of the merchant population and identified them as the prospective source of revenue, Hunter moved against them at the polls. In the 1713 election Hunter wrested six seats in the legislature from the opposition. With the aid of Lewis Morris, Sr., the governor exploited the advantage. So effective were his efforts that Samuel Mulford exploded in rage on the assembly floor, delivering a rambling jeremiad that he was imprudent enough to put into print.[23] This speech, a monument of anti-imperial rhetoric in New York, is parodied in Mulligrub's speech in Act I of Hunter's play.

> Gentlemen, The ill Measures that have been taken, and the Foundation that hath been laid within this Tenement, to make the Tenants thereof, Tenants therein, is the Cause which causeth me to make this Speech. Our Grievances being innumberable, I shal Enumerate them. The first I shal mention, is this, That tho' the Tenement be large, the Mansions many, and the Inhabitants Numerous, There is but One Kitchin, and one Cellar, by which means we are kept from Eating and drinking What we please, When we please, and as Much as we please, which is our Birth-Right Priviledge by the Laws of God and Nature, settled upon us by Act of Parliment; for which cause I humbly [inquire of the] House Whether it may not be more Convenient that each Mansion have its proper Kitchin and Cellar under the special Direction of the respective Tenants? (10–11)

If reading this we hear a garbled echo of Puritan allegory—the tedious working of a conceit that we have encountered already in Cotton Mather's fables of 1690—we hear acutely. Hunter identified Mulford with the contentious New Englanders with whom he traded (avoiding customs duties) across the sound. In a later passage of his oration, Mulligrub justifies his illegal trade, because

> we of the East End of the Tenement suffer most, for by reason of our distance from the Kitchin, our Porrige is cold before it comes to our Hands. To Remedy this, we fell upon a private Intercourse with the Bethlemites on the other side of Moor-fields, who by virtue of their Charter run at large, by which we broke the Laws pretty Comfortably for a season; but this same subtle Fellows of the Kitchin found it out, and put a stop to't, to the Great Prejudice of the Freedom of the Subject, and the direct Discouragement of our indirect Commerce (11).

Connecticut's charter, which granted the colony virtual autonomy, seemed to the Whig imperialist a warrant to lawless indulgence. The Connecticut traders' cavalier attitude toward customs duties and the Articles of Trade is mirrored in Mulford.

Mulford's justification of his right resides in the same airy talk about "Freedom of the Subject" that came so easily to the unsophisticated opponents of prerogative. We also see the Old Charter inclination to disregard royal instructions and imperial legislation in the name of fundamental rights—"Our Birth-Right Parliamentary Rights, settled upon us by the Ten Commandments." Hunter's parody renders the characteristic rhetoric of Old Charter libertarianism mumbo jumbo—a salmagundi of legal and biblical chatter. Hunter did not rest content with showing Mulford's ideology to be inarticulate nonsense; he arraigned the Long Islander for publishing his seditious speech and had him expelled from the assembly.

In *Androboros* Hunter contrasts the nonsense of Mulford, hypocrisy of Vesey, and delusion of Nicholson with the commonsensical wisdom of

Aesop/Jamison. Each Act of the play contains at least one Aesopic apologue
supplying the standards by which we should judge the miscreants. For instance, the assembly's love of the blustering, saber-rattling Nicholson is rebuked in the fable of the bees.

> The *Bees* so fam'd for Feats of War,
>   And Arts of Peace, were once, of Sense
> As void as other Insects are,
>   'Till time and late Experience
>   The only Schoolmaster of Fools,
>   Taught them the use of Laws and Rules.
>
> In that wild state they were Assail'd
>   By th' Wasps, oft routed and Opprest;
> Not that their Hearts or Hands had fail'd,
>   But that their Head was none o'th' best,
>   The *Drone* being, by the Commons Voice,
>   Chose for the Greatness of his Noise.
>
> Thus ill they sped in every Battle;
>   For tho' the Chief was in Request
> At home, for's Fools Coat and his Rattle,
>   Abroad he was the Common Jest.
>   The *Wasps* in all Ingagements, held—
>   His Folly more then half the Field.
>
> Grown Wiser by repeated Woes,
>   The Bees thought fit to change their Chief,
> It was a *Humble Bee* they Chose,
>   Whose Conduct brought them quick Relief;
>   And ever since that Race has led 'em,
>   The *Drones* are Drums, as Nature made 'em.
>   (16)

We can see the care with which the fable has been designed. The central
actors, the Bees, have been chosen to ensure maximum positive identification for the readership, while permitting a discrimination to be made between the industrious commonality of bees and the larger, blustering
drone. The war of the bees and wasps symbolized the contest between British America and French Canada. The Drone's failures in the conduct of the
war recall Nicholson's failure in the campaign of 1711. The moral argument of the fable is that prudence commends the choice of modest though
substantial leadership over bluster.

The clear common sense of Aesop's fables supplies a counterpart to the
destructive malediction that constitutes much of *Androboros*. Since the fable
enjoyed intense vogue as a vehicle of political discourse in British America

during the eighteenth century, it deserves critical scrutiny. Because of the genre's identification with the *sensus communis*, it raises provocative questions concerning both the articulation of the commonality's political understanding and the formation of popular sentiment from above.

THE POWER OF FABLE

The power of persuasion is a political power, and the forms of persuasion are the weapons of politics. Of the traditional forms of discourse, the fable enjoys a singular advantage: it can seize popular imagination and hold it enthralled. At the end of the seventeenth century, on the verge of the era when the populace would reassert its will in western politics, Jean de La Fontaine reflected on "The Power of Fable." In an apologue he asked, "Can Excellencies stoop from their high places/ To listen while an old wives' tale is told?" They can, the fable concluded.

"The Power of Fable" tells of an Athenian orator who urged his countrymen against approaching danger. Despite employing the most exalted devices of rhetoric, the orator failed to capture the assembly's ear. In desperation he resorted to fable:

> Ceres . . . walked abroad one day
> Companion'd by the swallow and the eel.
> A river barred their path. The eel by swimming
> The swallow o'er the water skimming,
> Were soon across . . . "And what did Ceres do?"
> Cried the assembly with one voice.
> "I'll tell you what she did—she flew
> Into a proper rage with you,
> To find the people of her choice
> Paying more notice to a children's tale
> Than to the fast approaching ruin
> At which the rest of Greece turns pale.

What power does the fable possess? To seize the attention of "the many-headed, bladder-headed beast." To capture the popular imagination, as Aristotle noted in Book II of the *Rhetoric*, with invention. And furthermore, to render a disagreeable truth agreeable by dressing it in a fanciful disguise. The most ancient of Roman orations, recalled by Joseph Addison in the *Spectator*, featured the fable of the belly and the limbs; it quelled a popular mutiny against taxation and saved the nation. Though a lover of fact, Addison commended the invention of fable for its political utility; the Roman's employment of it "was indeed very proper to gain the attention of an incensed rabble, at a time when perhaps they would have torn to pieces any man who had preached the same doctrine to them in an open and direct manner."[24] In politics truths must often be disguised; the fable excels in presenting a harsh thought in agreeable dress. Antoine Houdar de La Motte aptly summarized critical thought concerning the fable when he in 1719 observed, "The Fable is disguised philosophy, which does not banter except to instruct, and which always instructs more than it amuses."[25]

In early America we find disguised instruction appearing just at that juncture in history when the popular will moved against dominion from above—during the agitations that preceded and attended the Glorious Revolution in 1689. We have seen Cotton Mather in "Mercury's Negotiation" and other fables enlisting the support of the Boston mob. These fables-cum-allegories merely gestured at disguise. As rhetorical vehicles they are dissatisfying, lacking sufficient aesthetic distance from their subjects to be pleasing and lacking sufficient generality in their circumstances to be philosophical. The same criticisms might be leveled at other fable/allegories—Spenser's "Mother Huberd's Tale" or Dryden's "The Hind and the Panther"—which represent symbolically the complexities of a specific political situation. To be effective a fable should possess sufficient generality to be applicable to a variety of analogous political situations. Of the fables Mather penned only his updating of Melanchthon's "The Dogs and the Wolves" satisfied this requirement.[26] It alone possessed sufficient generality to appear commonsensical. Its generality also invited credence in another way; when a message must be decoded by departing some distance from literal circumstance, the reader's imagination is enlisted in the endeavor. As Thomas Noel, the historian of fables, has observed, "The fable functions obliquely, allowing the reader himself to search for truth; and the sense of personal discovery impels him to believe it."[27]

In colonial America a tradition of effective political fabulation emerged only after the fable/allegory was rejected in favor of the more general Aesopic apologue; that is, when Dryden's "The Hind and the Panther" was supplanted as the model for emulation. This shift in taste occurred in conjunction with the rise of belletrism. It is seen fully accomplished in *Androboros*.

The political situation of the colonies during the 1710s encouraged a resort to the Aesopic form. The almost ritual contention between royally appointed executives and native assemblies over issues of taxation and salary for governmental officers had become a popular issue. The development of a literary tavern culture in the 1700s and the proliferation of newspapers in the 1720s and 1730s were responsible for the increased public discourse on affairs of state; so was the expansion of the franchise in several of the provinces. (Governor Hunter sponsored one of the more important extensions of the franchise in 1714, legislating a naturalization act that conferred citizenship on protestants of foreign birth resident in New York since the Glorious Revolution.)[28] A simpler and more generally intelligible mode of commentary was called for in the effort to enjoin popular opinion. The more generalized form, too, was safer for a publisher to print, for when publishers made their criticisms too pointed they ran the risk of suffering the fate experienced by James Franklin or John Peter Zenger. If criticism was to be published, a prudent critic of the local powers made certain that his reflections were circumspect.

This is not to say that the Aesopic fable lacked power in its critical task. The more general speaking of a fable lent it the moral authority of philosophy; thus the rebukes a fable delivered could possess greater moral weight than the strident particularities of a fable/allegory. Certainly the surviving early American examples support this proposition. John Hughes's long beast allegory on Pennsylvania politics, "Utopia," printed in his almanac for 1726, seems ill-tempered in the length and detail of its castigations.[29] Yet Franklin's Aesopic reflection on the Belcher salary dispute in Massachusetts, "The Rats and the Cheese," satisfies with its pungency and dispassionate perspective. It told of a mighty Cheshire cheese obtained by a prince so that "his Ministers of State, Might live in Plenty and grow Great."

> A powerful Party straight combin'd,
> And their united Forces join'd
> To bring their Measures into play,
> For none so loyal were as they;
> And none such Patriots to support,
> As well the Country as the Court.
> No sooner were those Dons admitted,
> But (all those wondrous Virtues quitted)
> Regardless of their Prince, and those
> They artfully led by the Nose;
> They all the speediest Means devise
> To raise themselves and Families.
> Another Party well observing
> These pamper'd were, while they were starving;
> Their Ministry brought in Disgrace,
> Expell'd them, and *supply'd their Place*:
> These on just Principles were known,
> The true Supporters of the Throne;
> And for the Subject's Liberty,
> They'd (marry would they) freely dye,
> But being well fix'd in their Station,
> Regardless of their Prince or Nation
> *Just like the others*, all their Skill
> Was how they might their Paunches fill.[30]

Franklin's moral: politics is farce, politicians' virtues are "mine Arse." Their "Contentions are but these, / Whose Art shall best secure the *CHEESE*." Franklin does not bother to tailor the fable to the complex contours of the

Belcher case. Rather his point is more general: in any political circumstance the contending parties will cloak self-interest in whatever virtuous guise they deem most effective. The moral is not only useful to Massachusetts readers, but to those in Franklin's Philadelphia, for Pennsylvania suffered from similar disputes between the party allied to the Penn family and the party led by Andrew Hamilton. The test of a good fable is its applicability to more than one situation or occasion. One may contrast Franklin's satire to those Joseph Green directed at Belcher throughout the 1730s. Green's jibes were so pointed and so tied to the occasion they were never printed, let alone reprinted. "The Rats and the Cheese" on the other hand appeared so appropriate to the New York faction fights of 1751 that the editor of the *New York Gazette* reprinted it in full in his issue for December 23.

We see how the Aesopic fable permits those with lesser power to reflect on those with greater, and we can surmise how popular opinion might be enlisted against the high-handed activities of the powerful; yet it would be a mistake to see the fable as a form of *Tendenzdichtung* necessarily serving the revolutionary aspirations of the people. The *Virginia Gazette* records a paper war in which an ex-governor, Col. Alexander Spotswood, stifles the criticisms of a disgruntled underling by fable. The underling's name was Edwin Conway. He complained that during Spotswood's term as governor power was exercised arbitrarily and public funds were misused. (In order to circumvent the burgesses' periodic restrictions on salary, Spotswood diverted monies appropriated for the purchase of arms for Brunswick into an interest-bearing account; the interest supplied him operating expenses.) Rather than dignify the charges with a serious rejoinder, Spotswood published the following piece, purportedly composed by his schoolboy son.

> Mr. Parks:
> I Have learnt my Book so far, as to be able to read plain *English* when printed in your Papers; and finding in one of them my Papa's Name often mentioned by a scolding Man, called *Edwin Conway*, I asked my Papa, Whether he did not design to answer him? But he reply'd, *No Child, this is a fitter Contest for you, that are a School-boy, for it will not become me to answer every Fool in his Folly; as the Lesson you learnt the other Day, of the Lion and the Ass, may teach you.* This Hint being given Me, I copied out the said Lesson, and now send you the same, for my Answer to Mr. Conway's Hint, from
>
> Sir, Your Humble Servant,
John Spotswood.
>
> Fab. lo. A Lion and an Ass.
>
> An Ass was so hardy once, as to fall a Mopping and Braying at a Lion. The Lion began at first to shew his Teeth, and to stomach the Affront: But, upon second Thoughts, *Well*, (says he,) *Jeer on, and be an Ass still*; take Notice only by the Way, that it is the Baseness of your Character, that has saved your Carcass.[31]

To refute Conway's complaints would grant them too great a measure of credence. To dismiss them without refutation for reasons *ad hominem* would be equally risky, for such a rejection would smack of aristocratic high-handedness. Yet such a dismissal might be palatable to the public if Spotswood himself did not seem to make it—if it was couched as the anonymous wisdom of *sensus communis*, as a fable that every schoolboy knew. The fable, not Spotswood, would assign Conway the role of ass, and the fable would condemn Conway's complaints as braying. Spotswood is the lion; he displays the nobility of the lion in his disinclination to bare his teeth. Using the fable, Spotswood makes it seem an act of wisdom to dismiss a critic *ad hominem*.

The Spotswood case is instructive because it shows the method by which members of elites could harness the power of the *sensus communis* on behalf of the old aristocratic order. Spotswood has made the fable the tool to keep "excellencies" in "their high places." He does so by exploiting two devices: adopting a persona (his schoolboy son) in the frame to the fable, so that he is both inferior (boy) and superior (lion) simultaneously in the writing; and recalling the traditional hierarchical image of the animal kingdom. The former enables him to dismiss his opponent *ad hominem* without appearing high-handed; the latter accommodates the popular reader to the hierarchical status quo by suggesting that nature itself warrants social gradations of worth.

La Fontaine may have seen the exalted forced to condescend by the power of fable, but as we examine its employment in British America what compels attention is the fable's repeated and effective use by the exalted to advance a policy, form public sentiment, or chastise an opponent. Just as the Roman ur-fable, the belly and the limbs, forced the disgruntled populace to accept an unwanted tax, the Hunter fables reformed the public mind to the service of executive power. By mastering the fable form, the form rhetorically best suited to the common understanding, Hunter stole the thunder of Mulford and other rhetoricians plying the retrograde allegorical mode of popular argument. The crowning touch of Hunter's wit is his assignment of the fables to Aesop/Jamison rather than himself. Here Hunter avoids the envy and resentment that attach to the moral instructor, though the fables are literally his.

Hunter's choice of Aesop as the agent of his wisdom has more than a surface appropriateness. The legendary biography of Aesop, which became a matter of acute theatrical interest in the 1690s, tells of a man who began as slave, yet by wit elevated himself to kingship.[32] Aesop employed fable both to raise himself to high station, and to consolidate and maintain his authority once in power. Both dynamics of the power of fable were expressed in Aesop's life. Both had applications to Hunter's situation. He belonged to that circle of obscurely born men—Swift, Addison, Steele—who rose to high station by force of wit. Once in power he knew how to rebuke and instruct his constituents with an *Androboros*. Hunter's example was not lost on those whom he left behind in 1719. Curiously, of The Keeper's two allies, it was not Aesop/Jamison who would buckle on Hunter's literary armaments, but Solemn/Lewis Morris, Sr. Morris would turn the fable and the epigram against one of Hunter's successors, Governor William Cosby. In the attack upon Cosby, Morris would use the fable as a means of revitalizing "New England" principles and suiting them to other political climes. Why did Morris, the collaborator of the Whig imperialist Hunter, become the great antagonist of a later imperialist?

"THE MOCK MONARCHY OR KINGDOM OF APES"

Lewis Morris, Sr., (1671–1746) possessed a zest for politics. His absorption in the play of power, his understanding of the competing ideologies, and his grasp of the motives of the leading personalities were impressive. The nephew and ward of Colonel Lewis Morris, the crusty Quaker manufacturer and statesman of New Jersey, young Lewis learned law and statecraft at the knee of a master.[33] He studied polite letters with George Keith, reputedly the most brilliant man resident in the Delaware Valley during the seventeenth century. Lewis became a judge of the Court of Sessions in East New Jersey at age twenty, a member of the Governing Council of East New Jersey at twenty-one, and president of the Governing Council of East New Jersey shortly thereafter. As a young politician, he was fearless in the promulgation of his policies, being suspended from the Governor's Council of New York four times during the regimes of Bellomont and Cornbury. In 1702 he traversed the Atlantic and successfully petitioned Queen Anne concerning the consolidation of the two Jerseys, winning appointment as governor. The appointment was quickly rescinded and the post, combined with the governorship of New York, given to Lord Cornbury, the Queen's dissolute cousin. In 1720 when Governor Hunter arrived in New York, he recognized the man's ability immediately, appointing him head of the Governing Council of New York. Shortly thereafter the governor appointed Morris chief justice of New York, a post he would hold until deposed by Cosby two decades later. Morris's political career culminated with his appointment as governor of New Jersey in 1738.[34]

Throughout Lewis Morris, Sr.'s, political career, despite his shifts from the opposition to alliance, then back to opposition, he maintained several important principles: he esteemed real property above cash and thus valued landowners more than merchants; he entertained a Whiggish respect for the rule of law, yet saw the dangerous consequences arising from any unthinking imposition of British legal institutions upon the different circumstances of the colonies; he had a healthy skepticism concerning the pretensions of American planters to aristocracy. These attitudes he brought to bear on the thinking of the Country (or River) party, the circle of landowners in the Hudson Valley who constituted Hunter's strongest support in the colony.

The Country party crossed cudgels with the merchant group, organized around Adolphe Philipse, already familiar to us in the character of Flip, the second of the conspirators whom Androboros drags with him into the pit. By 1725 the merchants had organized their interest and refined their election rhetoric sufficiently to wrest control of the electorate from Morris and the Country party. Philipse exacted a price for passage of Governor Burnet's revenue bill: exemption of key articles of trade from taxation. Burnet was forced to turn to his supporters for the lost revenue, much to their disgust.[35] At this juncture Lewis Morris, Sr., composed his "Dialogue Concerning Trade," the inaugural work in a paper war that would climax in the trial of John Peter Zenger a decade later.[36]

When Philipse seized control of the assembly, the merchant interest determined that it would do business with any governor who would promote trade. Burnet would not, but successors Montgomerie and Cosby would. Montgomerie and Cosby received their salaries; in return, the Merchant party (or Court party as it came to be known) received preferment. The situation so disgusted Morris that he composed "The Mock Monarchy or Kingdom of the Apes" satirizing it.[37] The poem takes the form of a mock philosophical myth, a parody of those fictions employed by Hobbes, Locke, and others to explain the origins of institutions. The myth explains how the assembly came to tyrannize the New York government.

The gist of the humor in "The Mock Monarchy" is that the monarchial pretention of the governor is a charade; the Apes (creatures of the assembly) rule the kingdom. The satire goes to the heart of the constitutional debate in New York. Where did authority rest? Did the people of New York have a right to participate in legislative power? Was the assembly the wise substitute for parliamentary representation? Or did authority reside, as the governors frequently held, in the "grace and will of the crown?"[38] Morris, a Whig, believed that a balance between the governor, council, and assembly was the constitutional form of government. As an astute politician, however, he realized that power had devolved to the assembly.

"The Mock Monarchy" commences with an echo of that most famous of all poems dealing with the historical shifts in the British political scene during the late seventeenth century, "The Vicar of Bray." Morris presents a picture of a golden age, "when men attempted honest ways" and "publick Spirit was itself." Yet that time when merchants were enterprising, country squires honest, priests politically disinterested, and physicians devoid of quackery was quintessentially expressed in the New World where the grandfathers sought and found "the certain garden Spot." In the New World the enterprising and just settlers nurtured morality by following "mother Natures light."

Portraits of the golden age are primarily useful in satire for setting up protests about the declension in morals that circumstances have effected.

"The Mock Monarchy" does not stray from model. News of New York's Eden attracts the flotsam and jetsam of Europe

> from Danes, from Hollander, and Swede,
> from Wales and from the north of Tweed
> our first Supply's came o'er,
> from franse a band of refugees,
> and from fair Ireland rapperees,
> came crowding to this Shore.
> A mungrell brood of canting Saints,
> that filled all Europe with complaints
> came here to fix their Stakes
> and such another shyning gang,
> that rather chose to move than hang,
> came from the land of cakes
> the germans send a numerous train,
> And Some from England cross the main,
> who were none of the best
> from the low country came a crue
> whose parents were the Lord knows who
> the Jayles Supplyed the rest.
>
> (85–102)

Morris's roll of immigrants is as clear-eyed and as arch as that contained in any of the anticolonization tracts Tories distributed in the Old World. Given the heterogeneous composition of New York, the lawless liberties of eden were quickly supplanted. "Reason Suggested use of Law,/ to keep this motley crown in aw" (ll. 106–7). "To punnish and reward," a governor was installed to administer the law. As an aid in government the executive chose "out of the mob" those who possessed superior acumen to serve as "the councill board."

Morris, though he long served on provincial councils, did not harbor any illusions concerning the institution's origins, activities, or aspirations. Its membership—"Each man a leather apron Lord" (note the oxymoron)—was middle class; indeed many were failures or nonentities "on tother Side the lake/ when here, were metamorphos'd Streight/ into great ministers of State" (ll. 130–32). From the conquest of New York by Richard Nicholls in 1664 until the administration of the capable Colonel Dongan, the government consisted solely of governor and council; the institution of popular government with the founding of an elective assembly by Dongan presented something of a constitutional redundancy, for unlike Britain, where the House of Lords preserved the interest of the landed aristocracy, and the House of Commons the interest of the untitled, no such distinction inhered.[39] Rather, both council and assembly came from the same untitled welter of humanity, the former being appointed by the executive while the latter were elected by the people. Since tenure of a council seat depended upon gubernatorial appointment, there is little wonder that the governor's "will, was to his Councill Law," or that the governor's pretention to monarchial authority and his "dreaming on mines of ore" should be mirrored in the demand among councilmen that they "would need be Peeres."

Several passages of "The Mock Monarchy" concern the rise of the assembly. The "commons" of New York petition "his Highness." "Since they paid the bill of fare," they ask that "they might have a parliament/ and tast of Libertie." Morris takes pains to show that the claim for governmental authority on behalf of "commons" arose from a principle of self-government, as most champions of the assembly claimed and most governors disclaimed; yet Morris also indicates that "the Royal bounty did bestow" the favor. He refers to King William's grant of a charter in 1691 permitting the establishment of a representative legislature.

The problem of popular government was that the electorate chose not the best qualified but the most unprepossessing candidate. The ignorant, therefore, were selected over the literate, "for if a man could write or read,/ they all were in a mighty dread,/ he would destroy their Charter" (ll. 247–8). In effect, the distinction between membership to the council and membership to the assembly was not property so much as learning. The governor, following the specifications of the charter, chose capable and learned men. The people chose whom they chose. To dramatize the point, Morris provides as vignette an election where bumpkins select bumpkins and the lawyer carrying an emblematic inkhorn meets rejection.

We understand at this juncture the constitution of New York government. It consists of a British placeholder who masquerades as a monarch while serving as governor, a council of somewhat capable men who pretend to be peers, and an assembly of ignorant mechanicals besotted with the sense of their own authority. The ingredients constitute no recipe for a love feast. Morris does not spare his reader the resolution of the *conjunctio oppositorum*. A governor comes, he requests financial support and in return offers consent for whatever laws they decided. The upper and lower houses debate "of piggs and fowl/ what bigness Stallions out to Strou'l?" These considerations give way to the crucial issue, "that grand one of giving Cash."

> betwixt them and the Peeres
> and spite of all the caution us'd
> the terms each offer'd, and refused
> they fell to't by the Eares,
> the Peeres to alter did pretend;
> the commons, would not let them mend.
>
> (316–21)

The contest over the right to the purse strings here discussed took place in 1713, during the most difficult moments of Robert Hunter's administration. The council held that it could amend money bills; the assembly insisted otherwise. Morris, having been excluded by the assembly shortly before, witnessed the resulting impasse from the sidelines,

> till arguments on both Sides failing,
> they those declin'd, and fell to railing,
> to make each other yield.
> the Peeres did to the commons Say,
> they upstarts were of Yesterday,
> a vile mechanick race,
> who did reply, they should not huff
> Since both were form'd of forreign Stuff
> and differ'd not an ace.

> (368–73)

Caught up in a frenzy of name calling, both houses of the legislature refuse to do business. Meanwhile the governor goes without salary. Though naturally inclined to the council, the chief realized that the money would have to be obtained from the assembly.

> the peeres might clamour loud, and prate,
> about prerogative, and State,
> and consequences dread:
> but he, was no such ninny Oaf,
> as nott to know, that half a loaf,
> was better than no bread.

The technique of starving a governor forced the executive into a constitutional concession, depriving forever the council of significant authority. Morris brings the story up to date by noting that few succeeding governors have been willing to risk disaffecting the institution that masters the purse strings. Morris concludes the poem with a long analysis of the goal of the assembly, which he concludes to be the formation of "a true onocracy/ [so they] themselves might rule alone."

The danger of an "onocracy" was the lack of any check to inclinations of the assembly. So long as "cash was in their hand" the legislators controlled the government, for "money doth all things command." This command became truly pernicious when the governor determined that collusion with the legislature might be profitable. This situation arose in 1732 with the coming of Cosby. The danger lay in the fact that a governor's support of legislation had great weight with the authorities in Great Britain who held veto power over all laws. The transatlantic check could be rendered worthless by a governor's acquiescence to the assembly. It is worth noting that the surviving copy of Morris's poem identifies the author as "A gentlemen of New Jersey in America." The poem is intended for an English audience, perhaps for the eyes of those who sat in judgment on the provincial laws. Given such an audience, which would be thinking in a broad sense about prerogative and government, we can appreciate the poet's decision to generalize rather than particularize the issues at hand. One wonders, however, how potent the argument would have been, since the Whigs enjoyed a virtual "onocracy" in Britain.

BESTIAL RIDDLES

For political historians, 1726–36 remains the most fascinating period in the history of provincial New York. For literary historians, too, 1726–36 possesses great attractions. We see a constellation of talented politicians armed with literary ability in the Country party—Cadwallader Colden, William Smith, James Alexander, as well as Morris. This group undertook a systematic attempt to coopt popular opinion on its behalf against Philipse, the Merchant party, and Governor Cosby. The Country party's principal weapons were the pen and the press. The merchant (or court) faction had few capable writers, indeed only one, Francis Harrison.[40] When Morris and James Alexander unleashed Zenger and the *New York Weekly Journal* upon Cosby, the *New York Gazette* found itself quickly overmastered. Losing the battle for the hearts and minds of New Yorkers, Cosby resorted to force, jailing Zenger. The incarceration had long been anticipated by Morris and circle. Zenger behind bars proved ostensibly the Country party's contention that Cosby was oppressing the liberties of freeborn citizens. One can, perhaps, sympathize with Cosby in his anger at Zenger, for the paper made the most of its liberty; indeed, reading the writings of Morris and his circle, one understands the meaning of the phrase "taking liberties."

One of Zenger's liberties was to print libelous prose caricatures of the Philipse-Cosby circle. Each of the major figures was assigned a beast identity and subjected to satirical advertisements or verses. Francis Harrison, the laureate of the Court party, appeared as a lap dog: "A Large Spaneil, of about Five Foot Five Inches High, has lately stray'd from his Kennell with his Mouth full of fulsom Panegericks, and in his Ramble dropt them in the NEW YORK GAZETTE." Stephen Delancy, the principal Indian trader of the province, was caricatured as a baboon: "The Baboon is of a redish colour, chatters extreamly, and no Person is in Danger of being bit by him, for he has lost his fore Teeth: He is fond of Indian Corn, and generally in the Summer Time keeps in the Corn Fields."[41]

Most maligned of the Court party was Adolphe Philipse, Esquire, whose initials A. P. E. suggested to his tormenters his figure in the menagerie. "A Monkey of the larger Sort, about four Foot high, has lately broke his Chain, and run into the Country, where he has playd many a Monkey Trick: Amongst the rest, he having by some Means or other got a Warr Saddle, Pistols and Sword, this Whimsical Creature fancied himself a General."[42] James Alexander was largely responsible for creating the figure of the ape, using the imagery in polemical pamphlets as early as 1728.[43]

The beast symbolism coalesced fully into Aesopic fable with the arrival of the weak but rapacious lion, Governor Cosby. The governor wasted little time choosing his allies in the colony. Ape and Baboon controlled the Merchant party, which controlled the assembly and consequently the distribution of salaries. With few qualms the governor surrendered to his bestial appetite for wealth, striking a deal with the mercantile menagerie. After securing with little opposition five years of salary, he requested an additional £1,000 bonus for his assistance to the province while in Britain. The assembly saw fit to grant him only £750. According to Cadwallader Colden, the governor then invited "some of the members who had voted agt the £1,000 to dine with him that day After Dinner he Damn'd them & askt them why they did not make the Present in pounds shillings & Pences upon which the Assembly next day alter'd their Minute & put on thousand pounds in place of £750. The Members of the Assembly submitting so meanly to this insulting language it probably incouraged him to pursue afterwards the like insulting Measure with all ther were under his Govertment as the shortest & easiest way to carry his point."[44] This incident inspired the following fable in the *New York Weekly Journal*:

I Have Read in Esop's Fables, that the Lyon the King of all four footed Beasts, thro Sickness was grown so infirm that he could not follow much less overtake his Prey, and thereby reduced to a perishing Condition, for want of Food. He thought on a Stratagem, which was to keep his Den, and make a friendly Invitation to those several Kinds of Creatures he formerly used to Prey on to come to his Den, which he accordingly put in Execution, by Reynard the Fox. I suppose the Reason he gave to perswade them to receive Restitution for the Evil he had formerly done them. They all came, some in hopes Perhaps of the promised Restitution, others in hopes of Preferment, all Rejoycing to see so great a Reformation. When they came to the Den he saluted them in a friendly Manner. But, they being too forward, he took an Opportunity to get between the Entrance and them, and mustering all his Strength, he tore a great many of them to Pieces, and by devouring their Flesh he recovered his former Strength and Capacity to follow his old Course, which he did accordingly. Now had they left him his Den by himself, he would have Perished, and they would have been freed from the Mischiefs he did them afterwards.[45]

Here we encounter the hyperbolic warning of peril to the commonweal and the thoroughgoing antipathy to a powerful imperial executive that we encountered among the Old Charter faction in Massachusetts. The writer wished to make this association too, so signed himself "a Long-Island Man," the code designation of anyone holding Boston principles in New York. The interest of this identification lies in the fact that New England principles have been fitted in a well-tailored belletristic costume—no longer the ponderous conceit or the over-wrought typology.

William Cosby was an avaricious man, who like many a colonial governor saw his office as a means of establishing a fortune. No one, of course, expected a governor to absorb himself in unremunerated and altruistic service to the crown. A desire for property and fortune was the common motive of every person in the public sphere. Yet Cosby's hunger for land and gold was so bald and his public spirit so undeveloped that he inspired the passionate hatred of his opponents. The governor's character is best assayed by the dispassionate Colden:

> Coll. Wm Cosby Govr of New York was of an English Family in Ireland When he was Young he travel'd to Italy where drawing at once a considerable sum of Money from a Gaming Table he bought a small Equipage & went into the Army in Spain under the Command of General Stanhope & gain'd a Commission. But it is most probably that his rise was chiefly owing to his Marrying the Earl of Halifax's sister who was likewise nearly related to the D of New Castle & several other Noble Families & by their Interest got a Regiment. He was sent Lt Governor to Minorca where he govern'd in a very Arbitrary manner & acted as if he thought no measures unlawful or dishonorable that could serve to make his Fortune.[46]

Among Cosby's first acts as governor of New York was to demand half the salary that Councilman Rip Van Dam had earned as interim governor after the death of Governor Montgomerie in 1731. Invoking an "irregularly observed custom," Cosby took Van Dam to court when the councilman refused to pay. "Unwilling to trust his chances with a jury of New Yorkers, Cosby turned instead to the New York Supreme Court in December, 1732, asking that it sit as a court of exchequer in order to try the case on the equity side."[47] Long-simmering fears concerning the arbitrary powers of equity courts were brought to a boil. Lewis Morris, Sr., the chief justice of the Supreme Court, had served as acting governor of New Jersey before Cosby's arrival. "Assuming that Cosby might also demand one-half of Morris's interim salary, as indeed he did in February, 1733, Morris in a sense was being asked to render a judgment contrary to his own interests."[48] This Morris did not do. Indeed when the case came before the court, Morris argued that the Supreme Court could not and would not function as a court of exchequer, refusing to hear the case over the objections of justices James Delancy (son of Stephen/Baboon) and Frederick Philipse (nephew of Adolphe/Ape). Morris wrote up and published his opinion. Cosby could not abide this challenge to his authority; he dropped the Van Dam case, but suspended Morris from the court.

Deprived of his post, Morris went on the warpath. He sought and won election to the assembly in the Westchester by-election of 1733, he sponsored the founding of Zenger's *New York Weekly Journal*, and he liberally dipped his quill into venomous ink. The story of Zenger's arraignment and trial for printing has become one of the set pieces of colonial American history. When the invocations of the sanctity of press freedom are recited, Zenger's totemic name sounds with potent originality. Yet as Stanley Katz and others have argued, Zenger and the Morris circle conceived of the newspaper as an experiment in the limits of libel.[49] From the first Zenger's inclusion of essays on press freedom and British libel sought to purchase as much ground for party invective as could be had. The invective when it appeared did not scruple.

> Why don't we keep in with Serpents, and Wolves . . . Animals much more innocent, and less mischievous to the Public than some Governors have proved. Will not the very same Argument be as conclusive to justify the keeping in with Pyrates, Robbers, and Enemies; or lastly with Indians to keep in with the Devil and worship him, as they are said to do, for Fear: He is as powerful as any Plantation Governour, and as un-comeatable; tho' perhaps not quite so pertinatious in his Pursuits as some of them have been; because if you *resist him, he will fly*. And whether his Servants will have more Courage is a Question.
>
> A Governour turns Rogue, does a Thousand Things for which a small Rogue would have deserved a Halter: And because it is difficult, if not impracticable, to obtain Relief against him; therefore it is prudent to keep in with him and joyn in the Roguery, and that on the Principle of Self Preservation.[50]

By saying "a governour" the critic hardly disguised which governor he deemed worthy of the halter. After suffering a year of insult, Cosby responded, ordering issues 7, 47, 48, and 49 of the *New York Weekly Journal* burned by the hangman at the pillory. These newspaper essays, their contents and methods, have frequently been subjects of analysis. Recently an edition of the offending items was issued by Stephen Botein and the American Antiquarian Society.[51] Neglected in the republication are the other writings ordered to be burned by the public hangman: two street ballads excoriating Cosby. Chief Justice Delancy remarked that "sometimes heavy, half-witted men get a knack of rhyming, but it is time to break them of it, when they grow abusive, insolent, and mischievous with it."[52] The "heavy, half-witted" man who wrote the first of the ballads was none other than Lewis Morris, the chief justice whom Delancy supplanted. The printed ballads burned at the pillory were merely the most widely distributed of a series of songs with which the Country party flooded the countryside. Like the

fable, the song became a powerful literary device for forming public sentiment. The Court party once again failed to garner popular sympathy because they lacked the wit and condescension to wage the ballad war.

BALLAD WAR

Political ballads had been staples of popular culture in the British-speaking
world at least since the arrest of balladeer John Hogon for sedition in 1537.
Because many ballads were simply narratives of events—in effect news—
authors who wished to color the public's understanding of events exploited
the form from the first. The fall of Thomas Cromwell in 1540 occasioned
the first ballad war, pitting Catholic critics against protestant defenders of
Henry VIII's chief minister.[53] Because of the political utility of the form,
the literary elite periodically borrowed it from the tavern poets and catch-
penny singers. The literary exploiters of the form characteristically fit their
words to one of the fund of traditional songs known on the streets. This
permitted the sentiments to gain the quickest possible currency and eased
the task of creation, for it was a difficult matter to fashion both tune and
verse.

British America mirrored Britain in its employment of the ballad, producing both common balladeers and "court" satirists. The taverns housed a
breed of ballad poets tailoring verses to suit the popular ear. Tom Law of
Massachusetts earned a reputation as the great writer of verse to fit all occasions in New England. Pennsylvania boasted the talents of John Dommett,
a wine-bibbing failed schoolteacher, of whom an elegist wrote,

> His Style and Sense were never known to vary.
> He was good natur'd, for when Dulness prest
> To be admitted, 'twas a welcome Guest;
> And should a tuneless Rhyme accost his Ear,
> He'd say, my Friend here's Room enough, sit here.
> Oft' would low Nonsense on his Pen impose;
> But he would seldom one kind Offer lose:
> So much Civility, so little Pride,
> Had never Poet, else he would them hide.[54]

New York had its street songsters. Zenger's *New York Weekly Journal* in 1738
announced the inauguration of the career of "Non Ignotus," who prefaced
his "Masque of Life" with a brief autobiography. "I Have for these 14 or 15
Years resided in *America*, and followed most Callings that depended least
upon Labour, for to that I have a natural aversion, and could never attain to
be rich. Now I am returning to my native Land, but at a Loss what Employ-

ment to follow when I get there; I have a Project in my Head, which if it meets with your Approval, I think to put in Execution, that is to turn Ballad Singer; I have already provided a Jointstool, and in order to save Shoe Leather and many a weary step to Grubstreet, I intend to compose for myself."[55]

Exploiting the rough doggerel of the pothouse bards, educated American poets fashioned "court ballads," satirical songs designed to sway public opinion. The Country party in New York knew full well the potency of the form: how Matthew Prior's "The Orange" and Thomas Wharton's "Lilli burlero" chased James II out of England. Bishop Burnet observed that the latter of these songs "made an impression on the army that cannot be imaged by those who saw it not. The whole army and at last the people, both in city and country, were singing it perpetually."[56] Hunter had already demonstrated the power of fable; Morris and the Country party had merely to apply the lesson of 1688 by adding the ballad to their literary arsenal.

Two songs were printed in broadside and distributed by the jointstool singers throughout New York City. The printed version lacked a title, but Morris's holograph supplies both title and occasion: "A Song made upon the Election of the New magistrates for this Citty to the Tune of to you fair Ladies now at Land &c." As the text indicates, the song encourages party solidarity in the wake of a successful electoral challenge to the Court party in New York.

> To you Good Ladds that Dare oppose
> All Lawless power and might.
> You are the Theme that we have Chose,
> And to your praise we write.
> You Dar'd to Show your Faces Brave
> In Spight of E'ery abject slave; with a fal &c
>
> Your Votes you Gave for Those Brave men
> Who Feasting Did Dispise,
> And Never prostituted Pen,
> to Certifie Their yes.
> That were Drawn Up, to put in Chains
> As well our Nymphs, as Happy Swains. fal &c.
>
> And tho' the Great ones frown at this
> What Need have you to Care,
> Still Let them fret & Talk amiss
> You'll shew you Boldly Dare
> Stand up to Save your Country Dear
> In Spight of Usquebaugh & Beer—Ec[a]
>
> They Beg'd and pray'd for One Year more
> But it was all in Vain

> No wollawants You'd have you Swore
> By Jove You made it plain
> So Sent them Home to Take their Rest
> And Hear's Health Unto the Best &c[57]

The reasons Cosby had the broadside burned by the public hangman are apparent: he is being accused of arbitrary rule ("Lawless power and might"), the charge laid against both Charles I and James II; his followers are characterized as an aristocratic cabal intent upon subverting the electoral process with booze, food, and propaganda. Those who follow Cosby's direction are characterized as abject slaves. In Britain these slanders would have been actionable under the authority of the licensing law. For this reason the majority of the court ballads circulated in manuscript among networks of correspondents. Morris's willingness to resort to print in both the *New York Weekly Journal* and the broadside demonstrate a willingness to confront the administration in the most conspicuous arenas where popular opinion would have greatest effect.

Mention of the "prostituted pen" in Morris's song might suggest that the Court party, too, resorted to popular ballads to coopt popular feeling. Evidence, however, suggests that this was not the case. Francis Harrison, the penman of the Court cause, composed rejoinders, asking

> Why should the dareing Press be thus allow'd
> To Midwife Scandal in the Brainless Crowd,
> Who to the worst Misconstrue every Hint,
> And will believe what e'er they read in print,
> Especially if levell'd at the Great,
> Or impudently meant to abuse the State?
> Whole Sheets of Weekly Filth are sent about
> To Cozen and Inflame the giddy Rout.[58]

Given the superciliousness of this verse, it is little wonder that Morris and his collaborators managed to enlist popular opinion. What citizen wished to be called "brainless" or "giddy"? What virtue inheres in being "Great" if the great are so distempered by their critics? What wit resides in highhanded rebukes?

With Zenger in jail, Morris and Alexander set the taverns abuzz with manuscript reflections upon the governor's extension of the prerogative to control of the press.[59] Manuscript circulation symbolized the argument that the writings made—that the Cosby regime exercised a tyrannical control over the press, depriving the public of its liberties. James Alexander composed some of these pieces, including a ballad with a title so archly unspecific that it defied prosecution: "A mournfull Elegy on the funeral pile & Execution of [the] ballad or ballads burnt by publick authority before [a

great crowd] in a small town in a certain Country under the Northern
hemesp[here on a] certain day since the year 1600." The analogy between
the ballad burning and a public execution was also exploited in "The last
words and testament of the song on the election condemn'd to be burnt by
the C----t partie," which ended with an old cliche given an ironic twist:

> my death I pray you not lament
> but mind the golden story
> dulce et jucundum es
> pro patria thus to mori.

David Humphreys of Albany Manor, a minor figure affiliated with the
Country party, composed the most effective of the execution songs. Its success derived from Humphrey's decision to avoid the jocularity of Alexander's parodies and treat the execution as a subject worthy of an audience's
sympathy. The poem bore the grandiloquently lachrymose title, "The Lamentable Story of two Fatherless & Motherless Twins which Lately Appeared in ye City of N-w-Y-k who for their Prophetick Cries where Condemn'd to be burnt by ye Common Hangman which was Accordingly Executed &c." Sung to the Tune of "Great William Our Renowned King," the
ballad must surely be the earliest native instance of that most inciting of
literary modes, Whig sentimentalism. The heart of the narrative is as fol-
lows:

> 'Twas in ye Streets of York we hear
> Two pretty Babies did Appear   10
> No Parent Careing them to Own
> For Reasons to themselves best known
>   As through ye Streets they run forlorn
> Naked and bare as they were born
> 'Gainst Arbitrary Power they Cried   15
> 'Gainst Knaves & Sychophants Inveigh'd
>   They Sang ye Downfall of ye fate
> Of wicked Ministers of ye State
> Who against Law and Common Right
> Did in most wicked Schemes Delight   20
> . . . .
>   But when ye Great Men Came to hear
> The Cries they made begun to fear   30
> Least that ye Vulgar Charmed thereby
> Would make them Rise their Villany
>   Wherefore in haste they did Convene
> A Certain Number of true Men
> And Strict Terms Commanded these   35
> To tell from which these twins Arose

But when these Good men Could not find
The Parent they ye babes did bind
And brought to a hall where Sate
The Judges in Great Pomp & State   40
    Who without pity o[r] Remorse
O Cruel Arbitrary Course
Instead of Singing Lullaby
Condemn'd those babes in flames to fry
    The hour then appointed was   45
When these two twins must Die Alas,
At whose Sweet harmless Innoscence
Since none but Brutes Could take Offence
    But thus it is Great Mens Decree
Just or Unjust Obey'd must be   50
For only warbling Tuneful Lays
These babes in flames must end their Days
    Without regard to Tender Years
Or the Beholders Cries or Tears
They by ye Hangmans hands were press'd   55
In to ye fire O God be Bless'd
    But just Expiring thus did Cry
Behold we here Unjustly Dye
A Sacrifice to Great Mens Ire
We perrish in this Scorching fire   60
    But ah Dear friends whose hearts do Ake
To See our fates do not Mistake
This fire does only Purifie
Our better parts Shall Never Die
    The Gentle Breeses Kind and Soft   65
About This Town our Dust Shall waft
Inspiring every Blooming youth
To Liberty & Love of Truth
    In due time they'l Revenge our Cause
Defend their Country and their Laws   70
From Arbitrary power & Might
Pull down ye wrong Set up ye Right.[60]

The martyrdom of the orphan twins for their "Prophetick Cries" against political tyranny plays upon the popular mind at several levels. The orphans' crime—prophesying the truth—shows them to be grandchildren of the worthies martyred in Foxe's famous *Book of Martyrs*. We are reminded of the Reformed Christian animus of Whiggery. That the tyranny practiced by the great is political rather than religious merely reflects the extent to which politics has subsumed religion in Britain and the empire after Cromwell's rule and the rise of the party system. That the victims are orphans brings us to a crucial feature of Whig literary method—sentimentalism. Whiggery transmuted Reformed Christian pietism into a love of civic virtue. This love of civic virtue might be called the ruling passion of Whiggery. The literature of Whiggery became a literature of moral passion. Borrowing the allegorical mode of Bunyan, whereby virtues were represented by personalities, Whig writers began to formulate narratives designed to enlist popular sympathy for "injured virtue." The vulnerability of the political good, the fragility of rights and liberties, were dramatized by representing them as children, maidens, or imperiled youths.[61] To enlist the greatest sympathy the writer did not stint at depicting the murder, rape, or execution of the victims. Whig sentimentalism inspired violent indignation at the perpetrators of political affliction—"the Great" and the powerful. Addison's tragedy depicting the martyrdom of Cato at the hands of Caesar is often cited as the great master-piece of Whig sentimentalism, and we have seen its influence on Old Charter rhetoric in Massachusetts. An earlier play, however, was just as influential in determining the imagery and method of Whig sentimentalism—Otway's *The Orphan*. Otway stands behind the verses we are considering here.

Otway's tragedy has fallen into neglect among literary historians because its plot was reiterated to the point of inanity in the melodramas of the early nineteenth century. At the end of the seventeenth century, however, the tale of a guardian's secret exploitation of an orphaned heir and his seizure of a fortune at the cost of his ward's life stimulated a great catharsis. The peril arising from the loss of familial love as the guarantor of personal security and property is rendered graphically. The play is in effect a demonstration of the truth that familial trust is the ground of social integrity. When a surro-gate parent permits the love of gold to usurp care for the child in his heart, more than the child's fate and fortune is at stake. Social integrity itself is challenged—the rights of property and the imperatives of fellow feeling. The morality of the play made it the favorite inaugural production in Brit-ish American theaters, a potent weapon against those who railed at the im-morality of the theater. Thomas Dale of Charleston, Archibald Home of New York, and John Barrell of Boston all made the point of the moral worth of the audience's grief at the orphan's fate.[62] Lewis Morris, Sr., too, had reason to attest to the play's moral force. In 1690/91 Morris contested the doctored will of his uncle, Col. Lewis Morris. He proved that William Bickley, the executor, had purchased a copy of *The Orphan* at the time the will was being drawn up and had borrowed the stratagem of deceit to bilk young Lewis Morris of his inheritance![63] The court found in the heir's favor.

So as the orphans' ashes rise from the bonfires of New York to spread about the city and resurrect the love of liberty, we sense that a new era in political discourse has begun in America, an era during which the urge to spread popular discontent against the prerogative had found an adequate vehicle to accomplish its ends: the sentimental narrative. So long as the crown's guardians in the provinces exalted the love of coin over the love of

Britannia's offspring, "prophetick cries" would be heard in the streets and sobering ballads sung in the taverns.

THE RIDDLE

Popular discontent was never enough to check the power of the prerogative in British America during the early eighteenth century. Despite the public demonstrations against Cosby, despite the governor's humiliation with the acquittal of Zenger, despite the regime's failure to consolidate power in the assembly, Cosby ruled. So long as Whitehall backed the governor, Cosby could withstand the turmoil in the provinces. The assemblies throughout British America resorted to a system of agency whereby the legislative interest was maintained by a hired representative dealing with the branches of British bureaucracy. Mercantile circles also enlisted trading partners in Liverpool, Bristol, and London to speak on behalf of the colonies when transatlantic trade came into jeopardy. Despite the political leverage these vehicles afforded, the governor wielded disproportionate influence at the Board of Trade, provided he maintained political backing in ministerial circles. Dissidents time after time were forced to rely upon the remedy of last resort, direct petition to the crown. In 1735–36 the deposed chief justice of New York journeyed to London with his son, Robert Hunter Morris, to convey his charges against Cosby's government.[64] The expedition proved a nightmare. No restoration of office was granted; Cosby remained in force, suffering only a mild verbal reprimand; and Morris himself came in for sharp criticism for publishing his sentiments regarding the power of courts in New York. The ministry insisted that government be a privy matter of officials and legislators, not a matter of popular concern.[65] While Morris may have solved the problem of obtaining popular backing in New York, his methods were frustrated in Great Britain. Not until Franklin enlisted the radical Whig literati and publishers in England as effective allies in his propaganda assaults on the ministry during his agency in the 1760s did ballad, fable, and satire work their ways in Britain.

Morris's disillusionment with transatlantic government found bitter expression in "The Dream; a Riddle." Composed in 1737, the poem is a transparent allegory, a riddle requiring no effort to answer. The vision tells of the dreamer's voyage across a wide sea "to get misrule redressed." In particular, the dreamer hopes the officials when apprised of the ruler's misdeeds

> will command the actors home,
> And make them such examples for their crimes
> As may prevent the like in future times,
> On this I can assuredly depend.[66]

Like an eighteenth-century Mr. Deeds, the provincial dreamer radiates faith in the ability of the imperial government to correct the errors of its servants. He is disabused of his fond notions by a lawyer approached to assist in the petition. Complaints, according to the counselor, are "not encourag'd in the courts of Kings," for "t' accuse your Chief, they'll construe to be meant/ a side reflection on the Government: and Senders will defend the Sent." In a scabrous expose of imperial *Real politik*, the lawyer rehearses the conventional objections that the ministers of trade and privy councilors will make to the petition. They will

> either hide his conduct from the State,
> or, what they can't deny, will palliate.
> will call you factious, turbulent, & Say
> You stirr'd the People up to disobey:
> that if such men as You be heard, there's none
> henceforth will undertake to serve the crown.
> they'l to his acts wrong appellations give
> and call abuse of Power, Prerogative.
> And if at hand convincing proofs You have,
> to shew your Chief no better than a Knave;
> They'l not be heard, but put from day to day
> They'l tire your patience out with long delay;
> And when You've spent your little all in vain,
> You may, if You think fitt, go back again,
> and truly shew tis bootless to complain.
>   (114–28)

Lest the dreamer think that corruption is restricted to the political sphere, the lawyer commences a systematic critique of all the professions, showing how luxury, enthusiasm, and greed have perverted the whole of society.

> Virtue, and Conscience, here, are words of course,
> that on mens conduct have but little force.
> Place and preferment yield substantial joys:
> these are obtain'd by parting with such toys.
>   (287–90)

The criticisms are much the same as those made by the great Tory satirists in Britain, Swift and Pope. What marks Morris's brandishing of the lash is his resolutely historical explanation of Britain's moral declension. Whiggery in Britain may have had a progressive view of history, simple-mindedly so at times; but American Whigs had a more circumspect view of the flow of events. The sensitivity to declension inculcated by generations of jeremiads, the attunement to the biblical view of history which envisioned human affairs in terms of cycles of vicissitudes, and a distanced view of a century of political discontinuities in Britain prevented the American Whig from being entirely sanguine regarding the course of empire. The final third of Morris's dream presented an allegorical history of Britain, that nation "greatly fam'd for Love of liberty," from Cromwell's rule through the Glorious Revolution. The lawyer's speech finishes with a celebration of King William's virtues. The balance of governmental powers is celebrated.

> Their Senate, formerly in deep distress,
> how well their liberty's presserv'd confess:
> how much they're free'd from terrors of ye crown
> wch can't encroach unless the fault's their own.
>   (623–26)

In such a state the prince will detest tyranny and the legislature preserve liberty. The glories of the Glorious Revolution become the hollow pieties used to cloak the corruption of the government under Walpole. The lawyer's final irony is his observation that

> Your Pilot took this for some other shore.
> If bound unto that land of Liberty
> I just describ'd! then know it is not night;
> but lyes far distant from this place some where.
>   (657–60)

Shocked by the lawyer's remark, the dreamer wakes, posing the riddle of where he arrived in his travel. The answer, of course, is London of 1736.

When a New World Whig of Morris's ilk looked upon a Walpole Whig, he found much empty verbiage and an open palm. New World intellectuals came to think of themselves as the saving remnant of political morality as well as the refuge of the church. The doctrines of America's rising glory, the *translatio studii*, are the flip side of the coin of Tory satire. A political morality that permitted Walpole to buy off the empire's enemies did not sit well with the righteous in British America.

Political life under Walpole and Newcastle had the advantage of flexibility. The lack of ideological fixations permitted the ministry to strike deals and change directions. The disappointed Morris of 1737 became upon the death of Crosby the first independent governor of New Jersey in 1741.(There he experienced the travails of executive rule firsthand, attempting to quell popular agitations for land reform.) Because money and personal influence had such effect in Whitehall, the colonial agents, the great merchants, and the petitioners learned to play the game so their favored policies were inaugurated. The lack of system in the imperial scheme practically permitted sufficient liberty that colonial animosities never achieved critical weight until the great colonial reorganization begun in the wake of the Seven Years' War. Then when corruption was being extirpated from Whitehall and imperial rigor imposed from on top, the tensions of transatlantic government became unbearable.

In one regard Walpole's policy of peace at a price did not sit well with colonials: British Americans could not abide the territorial incursions of the French in the American interior and the interruptions of trade by the Spanish. Much of the literary comment on affairs of state in the latter 1730s agitated against Britain's sufferance of her traditional enemies. Indeed by 1737 the issue began to eclipse the debate over prerogative. The tensions between British American shippers and their Spanish competitors grew perilous. The War of Jenkins' Ear doomed Walpole's peace and, eventually, his career.

PART THREE

The Rhetoric of Imperial Animosity

8

Empire of Evil

Great Britain assured itself of the righteousness of its imperial mission by the myth of the *translatio imperii* and the humanist belief that trade engendered the "arts of peace." It also understood its righteousness in contrast to the depravity of its imperial rival, Spain. Spanish depravity, like English righteousness, formed part of a larger mythic construct. "La leyenda negra," the Black Legend of Spanish imperial cruelty, proved to be a long-lived and potent myth. Emerging in Italy and the Netherlands—Spanish imperial dominions—during the sixteenth century,[1] the legend blossomed with the accretion of narratives telling of the conquistadors' demonic cruelty in the New World. Bartolomé de Las Casas gave the legend great impetus with his *Brevísima relación de la destrucción de las Indias* (1551), paraphrased in English as *The Spanish Colonies, or Brief Chronicle of the Actes and Gestes of the Spaniards in the West Indies* (1583). The telling of the Black Legend was not restricted to a single text, but emerged in many narratives of the Spanish conquest. The writings of Antonio Perez, onetime secretary to King Philip II, proved particularly damning.[2]

The myth generated three long-lived traditions of employment: among Spanish critics of the conduct of colonization; among protestant rivals for world empire; among South American opponents of colonialism and its historical legacies. The second of these traditions most concerns us here, because it supplied the anti-Hispanic rhetoric suffusing the literature of the First British Empire. Indeed, the protestant version of the Black Legend so dominated literary representation of the Spanish colonial enterprise that some might claim that a factual, historical consideration of that enterprise never saw print in British America or, indeed, ever enjoyed much influence subsequently. Among historians of the Spanish empire, the resistance of the myth to factual historical memory has proved frustrating; but this resistance reveals the authentic mythical character of the Black Legend. "Myth neither requires nor includes any possible verification outside of itself."[3]

Slavery, 1738-39. A "Patriot" print, the engraving shows the merchants of Britain being driven by a Spanish overseer. In the background, Captain Jenkins loses his ear to a Spanish *guarda costa* while a British merchantman is molested by a Spanish police vessel. Critical of the Walpole "Peace," this print incites the British lion to throw off his subservience to Spanish force. Reproduced courtesy of the Trustees of the British Museum.

The Black Legend tells of how agents of the greatest power in the Old World, Spain, came into the New World and found a people living in paradisiacal innocence. The land that these people inhabited was a place of wonders blessed with luxuriant flora, astonishing animals, gorgeous minerals. The people apportioned the materials of this world with "orden y concierto" (order and harmony), governing themselves with simple justice. Though the Spaniards justified their dealings with the people of the New World as expanding the dominion of the Book and the Cross, their actions proved that their true god was gold and their task the enslavement of the native population to serve in the mines. The lives of the Indians were sacrificed to serve the Spaniards' depraved appetite. In sum, the Black Legend tells of the conquest of innocence and simplicity by evil and hypocrisy. The potency of the Black Legend may lie in its representation of the blatancy of the conquistadors' evil. Few crimes known to ancient history are excluded from Spain's conquest. Genocide, infanticide, rape, idolatry, the murder of people for sport, and incest all figure in the tale. A characteristic passage from Las Casas reveals the extent of Spanish depravity.

"They layed wagers with such as with one thrust of a sword could paunch or bowel a man in the middest, or with one blow of the sword should most readily and deliverly cut off his head, or that would best pierce his entrails at one stroke. They took little souls by the heels, ramping them from their mother's dugs, and crushing their heads against the cliffs. Others they cast into the river laughing and mocking, and when they tumbled in the water they said, now shift for thyself, such a one's corpse."[4] The deeds were so vicious that no crueler hidden agenda, no deeper depravity could be conceived.

With the conflation of sinful wish and sinful action, with viciousness made absolute in action, we confront evil in its theological extremity. In England after the armada, one did not have to be a Puritan to see Spanish designs as infernal. Marlowe's *Tragical History of Doctor Faustus* (1590s) speaks of Satan's particular oversight of Spanish enterprises; indeed, Faustus desires control over one of these, commissioning his devils to take "from America the golden fleece/ That yearly stuffs old Philip's treasury." Yet among the Puritans the conception of Spanish depravity became particularly elaborate. Reformed Christians understood man as a creature who attempted to hide his sinfulness. The secret sin "cherished in the heart" revealed man's depravity as being framed in duplicity. The Black Legend presented the conquistadors as persons who did not hide appetite or passion; for this reason their deeds are "inhuman" or "devilish." Thus we can understand how the Black Legend became for British and British American critics a narrative of the demonic invasion of a New World Eden.

Calvinists did not believe that anyone, no matter how isolated from the vices of the Old World, possessed innocence; natural man was sinful man.

The myth of the paradisiacal innocence of the natives arose in Christian humanist circles in Italy and Spain as a refraction of the Renaissance myth of the golden age. The symbol of the New World Eden emerged in the first generation of comment and fixed itself into the myth before the assessment of the Indian capacity for moral renovation darkened later in the sixteenth century.[5] In the Black Legend this vision of the New World Eden is always seen in retrospect, as an opportunity squandered. The Dominican Las Casas tied this lost opportunity to Spain's failure to disavow appetite for material goods. "Over against the acquisitive instinct, which had been sharply stimulated among Europeans by the sudden availability of silver and gold, this great medieval mendicant is setting the simple virtues of a society free from greed."[6] In the Calvinist interpretation of the Black Legend beginning with the commentaries of Urbain Chauveton upon Girolamo Benzoni's *Historia del mondo nuovo* (1594–97), the contrast was given different emphasis. The victimization of the Indians exculpated their sinfulness. Compared to the absolute depravity of the Spaniards, the Indians were comparatively free from blame.[7]

In the story of demonic invasion that the protestants told, the "poor" and "simple" Indian is forcibly deprived of his opportunity for salvation by the forces of the Antichrist. The violence of the conquistadors is conflated with the evangelism of the Catholic church in a "religion of the sword": "Long has the Furious Priest assay'd in Vain, / With Sword and Faggot, Infidels to gain.[8] By resistance to the violent dominion of "Catholic Spain" (always conceived as a monolithic entity despite the testimonies of Catholic evangelists like Las Casas against colonial policies), the Indians reveal a nobility that precludes any judgment that the conquest was divine punishment for their unredeemed condition. All Catholic Spaniards share an identical depravity: a satanic pride (the self-confessed yearning for *reputación*) that prompts them to idolize the objects of their own appetites—gold and power—and justify the exercise of violence and cruelty in their acquisition.

The literary consequences of this understanding of the Black Legend are patently visible in a host of British and British American texts. Spaniards are often not differentiated in character; when they do possess differences, they tend to function as one-dimensional allegories of vicious human impulses. Often no motive is supplied for the actions of Spanish characters, as though like devils the will to do evil exists *a priori* in their nature. Just as devils seek to bind souls to sin, so Spaniards enslave souls to their evil will.

This portraiture was not limited to polite letters. It was the operative political understanding of most English dissenters. When Cromwell harangued Parliament for support in his ill-fated attempt to conquer the West Indies, his rhetoric consisted of little more than a representation of the demonic Spaniard. "Why truly, your great Enemy is the Spaniard. He is. He is a natural enemy. He is naturally so through-out, by reason of that enmity that is in him against whatsoever is of God."9 John Milton, the Latin secretary, then imbued the verbal caricature with Roman eloquence in his 1655 declaration on Cromwell's crusade.

While the representation of Spaniards remained constant among British reproclaimers of the Black Legend through the seventeenth and eighteenth centuries, images of the Indians changed. The transformation of the legend of the golden age into the polemic myth of the noble savage in humanist circles would eventually influence the protestant interpretation. Though signs of the assimilation of the noble savage mythology can be seen in the writings of Francis Bacon and John Smith, the synthesis of the Calvinist and humanist interpretations did not occur until the eighteenth century, and only then in tension with Whig mythologies of self-understanding. The most ambitious writer that British America produced during the provincial period, James Ralph of Philadelphia, contributed to this synthesis. He revitalized the neoclassical epic by infusing it with an American fable.

"Zeuma; or, The Love of Liberty" (1729)

James Ralph's epic of the Indian resistance to the Spanish conquest of Chile reminds us that the animus of the Black Legend was to inspire resentment of the Spanish. Published in 1729 when Walpole's peace and the myth of trade held particular power in the discursive world of British America, *Zeuma; or, The Love of Liberty* challenged the mystique of mercantilism by asserting that accommodation to Spanish tyranny invariably meant the death of liberty. In effect, Ralph's epic must be approached as an incitement to war with Spain and an expression of an emerging spirit of Whig militancy that would fire the War of Jenkins' Ear, the rhetoric of Pitt, and eventually the rhetoric of American revolutionaries.

A brief survey of Ralph's career will attune our reading to the political context of his poetry. Ralph (1695?–1762) grew to maturity in Philadelphia, a town that had suffered periodic outbreaks of invasion anxiety during the first decades of the eighteenth century because the Quaker-controlled legislature refused upon religious grounds to appropriate money for defense. (Ralph's closest friend, Benjamin Franklin, would eventually attempt to assuage this anxiety by organizing a private militia.) When, in the company of Franklin, Ralph emigrated to England in 1724, he immediately sought patronage from the "Patriots"—the loose circle of militants including Chesterfield, the Duke of Bedford, and the elder Pitt—who opposed Walpole's administration.10 Ralph in a satire entitled *Sawney* made the error of setting himself against Alexander Pope, whose hegemony over the world of wit and the interest of the booksellers brooked no challenge. Pope unleashed a witty hue and cry against Ralph in the 1728 edition of the

Dunciad, which effectively scotched the Philadelphian's attempt to become an eminence in the world of letters as a poet of the natural sublime. Publication of *Zeuma* in 1729 marked the emergence of a political program in Ralph's writing. The remainder of his lengthy and prolific career saw his pen in the service of party. After a rather unsuccessful foray at play writing and managing at the opposition Haymarket Theater, Ralph discovered his metier: pamphleteering. He became, during the rule of the Pelhams, the most consistently troublesome controversialist plying the political press— so powerful an opponent that he had to be pensioned off. His final years were devoted to history and criticism which he executed with diligence, if not genius.[11]

Because of Pope's critical malediction and because of the longstanding prejudice against the first generation of professional authors ("grubstreeters"), historians have not bothered to determine whether Ralph's poetry was organized by an aesthetic program of any merit. There is reason to question the valuation put on it by Pope and his army of witty ephebes, for their condemnations reiterate a blanket prejudice against the poetry of sense, the principal literary aesthetic against which the wits contended. Pope's dismissive couplet upon Ralph's *Night* (1728)—"Silence ye wolves, while Ralph to Cynthia howls / And makes night hideous, answer him ye owls"—speaks of the two camps: the wolves of the sublime address night in its terrifying aspect, baying at the moon with howls of Longinian terror; the witty owls address night with the voice of wisdom. The contest between the poets of sublime sense and the wits dated from the turn of the century when Sir Richard Blackmore and John Dennis rebuked Garth and Dryden for the degeneracy of wit. A paper war raged until the emergence of Pope occasioned wit's ascendancy. In 1726, however, the publication of James Thomson's *Winter* marked a powerful renovation of the sublime. Ralph's first major poems, *The Tempest, or the Terrors of Death* (1727) and *Night* advertised their affiliation with Thomson's project of naturalizing the sublime. When Ralph made the mistake of adopting Pope's own mode in *Sawney* (1728) to attack *The Dunciad*, the wits seized the occasion to launch an attack on the rival aesthetic. Note that Pope did not comment on Ralph's ability or disability at satire; the real claim Ralph made to attention lay in his Thomsonian verses. By drowning out Ralph's nocturnal howling, Pope hoped to suppress other members of the wolf pack of the sublime as well. The attack succeeded in undermining the demand for Ralph's books among the London reading public, but failed to eradicate the school of sense. Edward Young, who manifested a remarkably similar descriptive sensibility to Ralph, would soon publish his enormously successful *Night Thoughts* (1743–46). After Pope's death in 1744 the Whartons would make the "graveyard manner" so popular that it would eclipse the productions of the later wits.

Zeuma; or The Love of Liberty (1729) was Ralph's final poetic gesture at fame. Aesthetically, it marked an advance over his earlier poems, for it worked through the artistic consequences of his encounter with *The Dunciad*. In particular, it emerged out of a consideration of the problem of the epic in English letters. Pope's *Dunciad* argued the exhaustion of the form: the declension of manners and letters had advanced to such an extent that the classic form could only be applied to contemporary circumstance as a form of mockery. Ralph acceded to the fact of the exhaustion of the epic, but conceived of the problem as the overfamiliarity of the element of fable.

> There is scarce any known story among the ancient *Greeks*, or *Romans*, but what is already exhausted, either in prose, or verse; consequently another entertainment of the same nature, would have wanted it's due relish; and any obscure one, even among them, would be as liable to exception as this. Beside, 'tis to be presum'd that an *Indian* history may prove as effectual to fix the reader's attention, as any other; to awaken, and confirm his *Love of Liberty*, even better, when 'tis consider'd that those whom we esteem *Savages* could dye in it's defense; and divert by the novelty of it's scenes. [12]

The possibility that the epic might serve to advance the "Love of Liberty" shows that Ralph did not abide by the Tory myth of declension undergirding Pope's sense of history and literature. Ralph's sense of literary history developed from the myth of progress traditional to Whig patriots. Thus, the historical circumstance that presents the problem is the exhaustion of the vehicle, not the message to be conveyed. The repetition of classical imagery in countless epics had deprived the great myth of the war between civic virtue and vice in the advance of civilization of its relish. A recourse to "Indian history" for the fable would supply the novelty to compel a reader's attention.

Attempts to renovate the epic had, of course, been made before Ralph's experiment of 1729. Of some pertinence to Ralph's *Zeuma* was the cycle of epics upon English heroes fashioned by Richard Blackmore—*Prince Arthur* (1695), *King Arthur* (1697), *Eliza* (1705), and *Alfred* (1723). English legendary history provided the novelty that would overcome the exhaustion of classical fable in the epic. Yet Blackmore's epics could not overcome the suggestion that political greatness can only be experienced retrospectively in English life. The celebration of Whig political virtues—liberty, justice, industry, and enterprising vision—lacked immediacy. The represented actions seemed inapplicable to the present moment. The myth of progress operated in too rhetorical a fashion.

The political debate between Walpole and the Patriots over the British relationship with Spain lent Ralph's epic of Spanish conquest an interest that none of Blackmore's managed to generate. Ralph's means to his political end was to intensify the love of liberty by narrating a history of its oppression. The Black Legend of Spanish tyranny would be the fable of the English patriotic epic.

Ralph's epic, while gesturing at the history of the conquest of the Incas, was essentially fabulous. Zeuma, the Chilean prince who served as the hero of the poem, was Ralph's invention, as was his betrothed, the Princess Zirene. The battles, too, were imaginary exercises in sublime description having no discernible connection with the historical record. The poet did supply a historical digression in Book II reviewing the events of the Spanish invasion, yet his own narrative depended solely upon two general circumstances: that the Spanish invaded Chile successfully; and that the invasion was led by Diego de Almagro. Almagro's expedition into Chile was a minor dimension of the conquest of the Incan empire, notable to commentators primarily for the arduousness of the invasion's passage over the snow-covered mountain passes to the south. Why then did Ralph choose to feature this marginal transaction of the Inca conquest as his epic? Several answers are plausible. The paucity of historical comment about the Chilean invasion permitted him to avoid comparisons with the magisterial literary representations of the Spanish chroniclers, especially Garcilaso de la Vega, El Inca's *Royal Commentaries of the Incas and General History of Peru*.[13] The history of the conquest of the Incas in Peru also presented difficulties for an artist who wished to portray the Indians in terms of the noble savage myth. Pizarro had succeeded in his invasion because Atahualpa and Huascar, the rival claimants to the Inca throne, were engaged in a civil war of Machiavellian complexity. Ralph's artistic end was to manipulate the anti-Hispanic argument of the poem to inspire maximum antipathy. The success of this project depended upon the contrast between the evil hubris of the conquistadors and the simple virtue of the Indians. The portrait of the conquistadors could not be altered greatly because the Black Legend already presented them as manifestations of an absolute. Thus Almagro and his troops are identical in motive and action.

> Fir'd by *Ambition*, and desire of *Gold*,
> Th' *Iberian* squadrons, rang'd in meet array,
> Begin their march along the trembling green,
> And tow'rds the *River*, slowly moving, bent
> Their dreadful progress, pleas'd with *Arms* and *Blood*.
> *Almagro* at their head, with gloomy pride,
> And savage, surly glance, portending dire
> Destructions to his foes, rode haughty on
> And, like his troops, with barb'rous joy revolv'd
> Th' ensuing slaughters that must drench the plains.
> (Book I, 23–24)

Ralph's repeated use of the adjective "barb'rous" throughout the poem to characterize the Spanish points to the paradox around which the epic revolves: that the "Christian" conquerers are the brutes whose society manifests the violence and oppression of Hobbesian natural man, while the Chilean Indians, the putative savages, are the truly civilized beings. Ralph's manipulation of the argument entailed fashioning the Indian protagonists to inspire the greatest sympathy in British and British American readers. "I have taken the freedom to deviate a little from the simplicity of manners, which the *Indians* are so remarkable for; because every one knows such a people, without some improvement, would make but a very indifferent figure in poetry" (Preface, v). One "improvement" Ralph undertook was to attribute the traditional traits of the noble savage to his imaginary Chilean prince:

> There *Zeuma* reign'd,
> A prince, who in the opening bloome of youth,
> Prefer'd his country's welfare to his own;
> Who, night and day, with an unwearied care,
> Employ'd his hours to benefit mankind,
> And study their content; who drew the sword
> With a reluctant hand; and, tho' 'twas just,
> With years, bewail'd the miseries of war;
> Who liv'd his country's darling and defence,
> The boast of human nature, and the joy
> Of nations that rever'd his growing worth,
> And idoliz'd his name.
>   (Book I, 7)

Ralph did not rest content with making his epic a tale of the unjust conquest of the noble savage as patriot king. In order to amplify the pathos of his narrative, he introduced a romantic interest. Thus the "simplicity" of a tribal culture whose hereditary aristocracy was generated by a system of royal concubinage was improved in Ralph's narrative into monogamy. By testing Zeuma's heroic public spirit by Almagro's lustful demand to surrender Princess Zirene, the prince's bride-to-be, at the moment of their wedding in return for peace, Ralph could inspire the sympathy of a reading public increasingly enamored of a sentimentalism based on the tribulations of the nuclear family. (The sacrifice of the integrity of the family for civic welfare is related to the choices made by Nathaniel Lee's "Junius Lucius Brutus" or Addison's "Cato.") Ralph's sentimentalism exploited the vulnerability of Zirene, dramatizing her injuries at the hands of the conquistador, to incite the audience's resentment at the persecution of the weak. In the end the Black Legend has been "improved" into a Whig sentimentalist tale about a demonic attack on the nuclear family.

Before we dismiss *Zeuma* as a fanciful melodrama, we should recognize the compelling power for philosophical cosmopolites of the sorts of revisions Ralph undertook in the Black Legend. The vogue for Indian melodrama probably began with Sir Robert Howard and John Dryden's *The Indian Queen* (1663/64). Voltaire explored many of same issues in his tragedy, *Alzire ou Les Americains* (1737), as did Frederick the Great in his libretto for Graun's opera, *Montezuma* (1756). If the Indians operated in the same realm of affections as did Europeans, a realm where the emotional interactions operated most powerfully in the structure of the family, then an imaginative emplacement into the situation of this other people was possible. The wish of many Europeans to be the other—not only for the refreshment of a strange point of view or for the opportunity to occupy a different perspective from which to judge the European self (the task of *The Persian Letters* and *Citizen of the World*)—but to assert the power of the European psyche to subsume and encompass all other subjectivities was the Enlightenment's particular addition to imperialism. To the extent that the alien subjectivity was subsumable, the alien was mentally and spiritually redeemable. The possibility of a psychospiritual conversion stood against the Spanish Catholic religion of the sword, which forced behavioral compliance with the dictates of viceroy and priest. The final book of Ralph's epic is a revelation supplied by Zeuma's "guardian-genius" of "a future state of rewards and punishments" where justice will be served. Ralph's blissful realm of future justice is a Deist paradise ruled by Virtue.

> Virtue . . . at length,
> You see, rewards the troubles of her *Sons*;
> In these delightful haunts she reigns on high,
> And pours down *Pleasures*, with profusive hand,
> Grateful as evening showers to sun-burnt fields,
> Or pearly dew-drops in the morning ray.
> (Book III, 115)

Ralph envisioned Zeuma converting from stoic fatalism to an optimistic faith that the exercise of virtuous action will result in the millennial rule of justice. In Book II the "guardian-genius" had revealed that the only virtuous and reasonable course of action in dealing with the Spaniards was total war.

Ralph fashioned his epic as a call to war with Spain. Military annihilation of the Chileans depicted in the text anticipates the war of vengeance to be undertaken later by those who cherish liberty. *Zeuma; or the Love of Liberty* testified that the war of retribution was already commenced in a contest of ideals. Since the Indian patriot prince and his followers suffered obliteration at the poem's end, the overthrow of the demonic horde would have to be undertaken by Zeuma's sympathizers, the readers.

Though Ralph's epic seems an anticipation of the War of Jenkins' Ear, we should not view it simply as the tocsin for 1737. The themes impelling Ralph's pen—the possibilities of a Pan-American empire born of the overthrow of "Spanish evils"—would motivate writers of the American republic as well. Joel Barlow's elaborate reimagining of the career of the Incan king Manco Capac in *The Vision of Columbus* (1787) took up the theme of the common civility of the Indians and North American republicans to extrapolate from it the possibility of a global political harmony under the aegis of reason, arts, and science. [14] A generation later Simon Bolivar would make the most determinative reproclamation of the millennial reversal of the Black Legend when he attempted to inaugurate the era of Pan-American liberty.

The War of Jenkins' Ear

Spain's empire in America overlapped with Britain's in a semitropical expanse of marsh and pine forest south of the Savannah River, which the Spanish called "Guale" and the British "Azilia." Because mineral wealth did not abound in this region and because opportunity for *reputación* and material betterment seemed more promising in other regions of the New World, Spanish colonists settled elsewhere. Guale did not share in the mystique of "la Florída." Until 1733 Great Britain had as little success enticing enterprisers into the region, despite the lavish promotion of Azilia as "the Most delightful Country of the Universe." Then Oglethorpe with his promises of the material redemption of England's debtors and Europe's religious refugees enlisted a sufficient company of settlers to plant Georgia in 1733. Oglethorpe from the first grasped the provocative nature of his enterprise to Spanish interests. During Walpole's peace the occupation of disputed lands could be a means of territorial aggrandizement as effective as conquest. A prudent military man, Oglethorpe did not leave his settlements undefended. With astonishing rapidity Oglethorpe's "utopia" became a network of fortifications and armed camps. When Spain's allies in the region, the lower Creek Indians, began welcoming the blandishments of the openhanded English general, the anxieties and resentments of the Spaniards in St. Augustine first prompted them to diplomatic force, then, in 1735, to the thought of war.

A desire for war also developed among the British planters and merchants of the West Indies where the empire of the sea was being challenged by the Spanish *guarda costa*. Spain's maritime police included a goodly number of freebooters who did not bother with the usual pretexts when seizing British trading vessels. The West Indian writer "Britannicus" (Samuel Martin of Antigua?) catalogued the depredations in poetic mock confession by the Spanish agent in London, Don Thomas Geraldino:

> *Iberia*'s Sons, grown bold by Length of Peace,
> Rov'd, unchastiz'd, upon the trading Seas;
> Secure they ravag'd on, despising Power,

Nor saw the coming of a fatal Hour;
With lawless Force, and yet pretended Right,
They search'd, seiz'd, plunder'd, and condemn'd at Sight:
The wretched TRADER's, doom'd to endless Fears
Of plunder'd Treasure, and the Loss of Ears. [15]

In the face of mounting pressures for war, Walpole exercised the full extent of his political craft to preserve the peace. He signed a convention with Spain authorizing periodic meetings of commissioners to negotiate Floridian border disputes and West Indian commercial difficulties. With increasing acrimony Walpole's enemies, the Patriots, called for the talk to halt and the war to begin. In 1738 Captain Robert Jenkins brandishing his mummified ear made his theatrical testimony to the House of Commons. Ralph and other Patriot grubstreeters flooded the metropolis with ballads and satirical cartoons. Typical was "The Negotiators. Or, Don Diego brought to Reason," which contained the most pungent of the mock panygerics addressed to Walpole.

How happy is *Britain* such Heroes to breed,
To stand by the Nation in Cases of Need!
What a Great Man is he! who his Enemies beats,
Without the Assistance of Armies or Fleets?
        He can quell ev'ry Foe,
        Without striking a Blow,
        And can conquer *as far as the Money will go*:
And when he at last has exhausted your Store,
On his Personal Credit he'll borrow you more. [16]

The negotiations with Spain ceased. "Then, breathing Vengeance, *Britain*'s Genius rose." [17]

The War of Jenkins' Ear commenced brilliantly for Britain with a successful naval conquest of Porto Bello, the Spanish trade terminal in Central America. The conquerer, Admiral Edward Vernon, was one of the more acerbic of Walpole's critics and was prone to military bluster. He had vowed he could reduce the fortress port with six ships; this he did. The quick reduction of the Spanish port lent luster to the tarnished Cromwellian dream of wresting the Spanish empire in America into English hands. It also loosed the "genius" of a host of bellicose bards chastising "tedious Treaties and the Wiles of Courts." One of these, a Bostonian, composed an ode "On the taking Porto-Bello by Admiral Vernon," which won some popularity. Several of the ideas in the verse compel attention: George's Peace has been transformed into "GEORGE's Cause," a cause that forces the "haughty Spaniard" to reveal his cowardice in the face of Britain's righteous might.

To stop proud Rapine's foul felonious Course,
Our gracious Monarch sends a Naval Force:
Our thundering Navy bold Ambition checks,
And bears chastizing Vengeance on her Decks;
Those dreadful Bulwarks wear great GEORGE's Cause,
Of Honour, Justice, Property and Laws.
Methinks I see each gallant warlike Boat,
Ride on the Waves, and triumph as they float:
All uncontroul'd they lord it o'er the Main,
Nor heed the puny Rage of haughty *Spain*;
Their Pirate *Guarda Costas*, Authors of our Jarrs,
Sculk and abscond when *Britain*'s Flag appears:
Their Port of War, vain-pompous, empty Name,
At once surrender'd when great VERNON came.[18]

The caricature of the Spaniards as cowardly bullies may be so crudely and obtrusively drawn as to distract a reader from the most historically telling aspect of the Bostonian's ode: the wholehearted identification of Britain with the spirit of war. The cultivation of the figure of "the genius of Britain" in the Whig Patriot rhetoric of the 1730s deserves some brief notice. While the notion that a corporate spirit presides over the destiny of a nation is a feature of archaic mythologies, its rehabilitation by Pitt's faction during Walpole's peace had a specifically political animus. First, it reasserted a British "unity of being" in the face of the party divisions of the body politic, discovering that unity in the restitution of a primitive simplicity of action. This atavistic "genius" revealed the alien character of recent complexities of policy. Walpole thus was rendered un-British, somehow tainted with the foreignness of those nations with whom he repeatedly parleyed. (The presence in London of the Spanish agent, Geraldino, was a conspicuous symptom of the foreign contagion for Patriot commentators and was obsessively noticed in the Patriot press of the late 1730s.) Against Walpole, the Patriots discovered in their own militant zeal for the British ethic of "Honour, Justice, Property, and Laws" a sign of their manifestation of "the genius of Britain." A willingness to fight for "Honour, Justice, Property, and Laws" became the index of true Britishness in 1738.[19]

A second element of "the genius of Britain" was its instantiation in the untutored, uncomplicated man of action rather than the refined and court-wise man of policy. The Tory writers recognized the tendency and burlesqued it in the character of John Bull, only to see their creation embraced and glorified by the opposition. The Whig hero was a man of indifferent background—one of the mass who, under the influence of his place of nativity and aided by his innate talents, concentrated the national spirit into his being. The force of his genius is such that despite lack of schooling he bursts onto the public stage. "Great VERNON," the plain-spoken sea dog, with his half-dozen ships besting the bully Spaniards at Porto Bello, had to be jimmied to fit the paradigm, since he was the son of a secretary of state. But his coarse boasts and "salt" allowed one to forget his refined background. Magazine laureates vied to serve in the glorification of Vernon: "to raise thy fame/ Beyond victorious *Churchill's* deathless name."[20]

The Patriots had galvanized an empire to arms and had made Vernon a hero; they could not, however, unseat Walpole. With a home government at odds with the intuitions of its admiral, the ingredients of debacle were in place. Vernon's strategy was to dominate the shipping lanes—to militarize the empire of the seas.[21] His quick success at Porto Bello, however, set several powerful lords in the ministry dreaming of an English "reconquista" that would wrest Panama, Mexico, Guatemala, New Granada, and finally Peru from the enemy. The breach point chosen for the invasion was the port of Cartagena, under the command of Admiral Don Blas de Lezo. Yet the expedition was long in getting under way, delayed by a plan to employ land troops with naval artillery, by the difficulties of provisioning, and by the appearance of a French fleet in the West Indies. When Vernon and Wentworth finally attacked on March 9, 1741, they met with initial success, taking the fortifications at the mouth of the harbor. From this point onward the invasion degenerated. Vernon could not harmonize his strategy or his views with his counterpart General Wentworth. Wentworth's troops were inexperienced, ridden with yellow fever, and disorganized in their attempt to storm the fort of San Lazaro protecting the city. The invasion failed, and the expedition withdrew from Cartagena on May 8 much to Vernon's disgust. The failed attempt to win the Spanish empire became a matter of literary soul-searching. William Davidson's *Carthegena, a new poem, containing a true and particular relation of every thing material in that fatal expedition* (Edinburgh, 1741) is typical of the retrospective scrutiny of events, attempting to discover what went wrong. The answers were various. Tobias Smollett, who participated as a seaman, blamed Vernon: "He ought to have sacrificed private pique to the interest of his country; that where the lives of so many brave fellow citizens were concerned, he ought to have concurred with the general, without being sollicited or even desired, towards their preservation and advantage."[22] Most considered the admiral a hero hobbled by the interference of a ministry confused about its conduct of the war. The most amusing American commentaries on the war were concocted by members of the Mather Byles literary circle, perhaps by Joseph Green or Byles himself. The commentaries versified the rumors and unsubstantiated reports that circulated through British America during May and June, 1741, when fantasies about the invasion of Spanish America became most extravagant. The first piece, *Some Excellent Verses on Admiral Vernon's taking the Forts and Castles of Carthagena, in the Month of March. 1742, 3*, employed a method usual to

Green's satire, parodying a vulgar genre for burlesque ends.[23] The mocked genre, the news ballad, was a species of writing identified in New England with the productions of Tom Law.

The burlesque begins with a balladic "come all ye," calling upon "all the nations round about, / who dwell on ev'ry shore" to attend to the tale, invoking a global audience for the account of Britain's escapade at Cartagena.[24] (Here the rhetoric of Britain's global empire of the seas comes back humorously to suggest the expanded scope of British embarrassment.) The mock balladeer, true to the technique of burlesque, accepts the claim that Vernon is a hero deserving of fame. By trumpeting the admiral's fame in tawdry doggerel, the true value of his heroism is suggested.

> I sound great VERNON's spreading fame,
>   sound heav'ns expanded arch;
> Who thund'ring on the Spaniards came
>   on the last ninth of March.
>
> Four ships against two forts sail'd on,
>   And took them as they stood;
> Tho' both the forts were built with stone
>   and th' ships were made of wood.
>   (5–12)

In the battle of Cartagena Don Blas de Lezo had abandoned the forts at the harbor mouth, staging a strategic retreat into the heavily armed central fortification in the city. To inhibit seaward approaches he scuttled several ships in the harbor. The mock ballad views this strategic movement through the exaggeratedly self-glorifying attitude of a Briton who believes that his own righteous might is annihilating the Spaniard by fear. The tone is borrowed from that of the letters from Jamaica about the invasion published in the *Boston Evening Post* of May 18, 1741. (The double edge of the satire here is that Vernon's heroism in conquering the outer forts consisted of overcoming an enemy who wasn't there.)

> The *Spaniards* star'd at the loud ring,
>   as at a rod stares dunce;
> Like frighted pidgeons they took wing,
>   and vanish'd all at once.
>
> Castle *Legrand* to guard the boom,
>   stood threat'ning far and wide;
> Two men of war did boldly come
>   and pour'd a whole broad-side.

> But, gen'rous, give the foes their due,
> there was no sign of fear;
> VERNON *fire on, a fig for you!*
> for not a man was there.
> (17–28)

Having likened the Spanish to dunces and pigeons, the mock balladeer strains to find other similes to represent the Spanish troop movements.

> So a young lady in new stays
> tail-nestling keeps a rout;
> And so a maggot in a cheese
> rolls wriggling round about.
> (37–40)

One finds the humor of these similes in their contrast to the dreadfully serious depictions of demon-Spaniards in works employing the Black Legend. Here the balladeer twits the extremity of the serious representations in the extravagance of his own imaginings. The parody is intensified when the balladeer offers his own version of a set scene of the Black Legend literature, a bearded conquistador raving in a fit of barbaric rage. Here the Spanish admiral throws a tantrum at the sight of the British advance.

> Don *Blass* beheld, he sob'd and whin'd,
> his huge black whiskers tore;
> And had he not fear'd to be fin'd,
> he would have curs'd and swore.
> (53–57)

Fear of the inquisition might temper the rage of a bilious Spaniard, but when the inquisition itself has declined in dreadfulness to being a monitor of politeness imposing penny penalties on curse words, then the myth of Spanish evil has been robbed of much of its potency, and the grounds of anti-Hispanic passion undermined.

Some Excellent Verses ends with Wentworth arrayed before Cartagena at night, his troops moved to terror by the nocturnal scene. The balladeer abruptly interrupts the sublime moment with a cheerful interjection.

> As ghost stalks on by moon-light gleam
> still terrible to nurse,
> So frightful did each soldier seem
> that went away from us.
>
> Our picture shows all this with art,
> (was ever work so pretty!)

And soon you'l see the second part,
when we have took the city.
(69–76)

"Carthegena's Downfall," an iambic tetrameter narrative of Wentworth's attack on the city, abandoned the ballad form of *Some Excellent Verses*. Its tone and technique suggest it may have been written by Thomas Kilby, a witty correspondent of the Byles circle, living at Canso.[25] The poem presents the imaginings of the British infantrymen as they broach the town. These imaginings see Cartagena as the land of Cockaigne, a place where mundane objects seem to have been gilded in fantasy gold. From a letter dispatched from the invasion fleet in March and published in the *Boston Evening Post* of May 15, 1741, we learn that these imaginings fed upon rumors of treasure rife among the troops: "*Don Blas*, Governour of Carthegena, has caused all the Plate and other rich Merchandize that was on the Man of War and other Ships that were in the Harbour, to be lodged in Carthegena and that he has prevented the inhabitants of that Place from carrying their Money and Goods out of Town, intending thereby to induce them to stay there, and help defend the Place and their own Goods and Riches in the Town of Carthegena, [which] greatly animates the Sailors and Land Forces to be within the Walls of the Same."

Nearer our men, and nearer creep,
Each takes his prospect glass to peep.
And O! what riches here were seen,
In ev'ry alley, street, and lane!
In ev'ry corner mingling rays
Of silver, gold, and diamonds blaze.
All the tin pots were silver fine,
And silver wire was us'd for twine.
The land-bank bills were yellow mould,
And all the gridirons made of gold.
The spits and skewers of ev'ry skullion,
And wooden cans were solid bullion.
Each bed was velvet sew'd together,
Stuff'd with leaf-gold without a feather.
Each cup-board groan'd beneath its weight,
For all the earthen ware was plate.
What endless wealth spread o'er the ground!
What storms of guineas rain'd around!
Each soldier at a distance views,
Hope fills his pockets, sleeves and shoes;
Each heart beats fast, assur'd to come
Loaded with bags of money home.[26]

The British infantryman's fantasy has a peculiarly domestic cast. "Home" is the imagined destination of the loot viewed through the perspective glass. The object to be pillaged is also a home—Jack Spaniard's. The perspective glass does not gaze fancifully at the public treasury or the gilded cathedral, but into the kitchen and bedroom of a commoner of the other side. The equipment of a townsperson's domestic life, his pots, pans, and gridirons, are transformed into imaginary precious metals. The infantryman's perception of these objects is shown to be delusive by a series of antimetaphors. Example: "all the earthen ware was plate." If the dishes were plate, they could not first be identified as earthenware. The consequence of the British delusions is general mayhem, in which destruction eradicates the distinction between Jack Tar and Jack Spaniard in its indiscriminate ravages.

> Hark then! and see! trumpets and drums,
> Cannons and muskets, shouts and bombs;
> Masts cracking, tumbling city walls,
> Steeples o'erturn'd by iron balls;
> Ten thousand dangers, deaths and harms,
> And shower of heads, trunks, legs and arms.
> Whole magazines blown up on high,
> And soldiers flying thro the sky.
>
> (33–40)

According to an authoritative account of the failed battle, Wentworth's charge against the fort failed because the scaling ladders were eight to ten feet too short, preventing the possibility of knocking out the artillery on the walls. One-third of the infantry died in the assault. Vernon's supply of bombs was exhausted. The fort stood (*Boston Evening Post*, June 29, 1741).

During the early weeks of June as hints of disaster were making their way to Boston, a rumor floated by a certain Captain Hubbert ran through the town "that Carthegena had surrendered, and had ransomed the Town for Nine Millions." Nine million pounds, though a formidable sum, was believed to be only a portion of the treasure contained in the city. Thus the report was met with some indignation as an instance of Walpolism—cash payment substituting for the true penalties inflicted (and potential rewards to be seized) in order to keep the status quo intact. Kilby—if the poem is indeed by him—closes his account of "Carthegena's Downfall" by pretending that the rumor is true.

> lest they should be all o'erthrown,
> The Spaniards sent to buy the town.
> Just as we seiz'd all to our use,
> Out comes a paltry flag of truce,

And after a short modest parl'ing
Only paid down nine millions sterling.
(41–46)

The irony of the resentment—the pique that only nine million had been
wrenched from the Spaniards—took on particular sharpness in 1743 when
the expenses accrued by the failed expedition were tallied.

The Boston satires assume their greatest pungency when read in tension
with the Black Legend. The demonic Spaniard of legend has meta-
morphosed in the satires into Jack Spaniard, a figure whose character and
motives are familiar to the Briton because they are shared by him. The distinction between the ethical Briton and the wicked Hidalgo hardly pertains
when we see British infantry infected with a gold fever as virulent as that of
the conquistadors seeking El Dorado. Greed and senseless slaughter have
become the fruits borne by the militant "genius of Britain."

Paradoxically, the failure of Vernon's invasion preserved the myth of the
ethical empire. Within a decade after Vernon's failure, Provost William
Smith was rehashing the imperial myths with the gusto of a true believer.[27]
As radical Whig moralists observed, if Britain had wrested control of Spanish America—her land, mineral wealth, and Indian work force—luxury
would have vitiated British industry and the exercise of dominion caused
the neglect of liberty. Thus, the failure of the invasion could be viewed as a
providential preservation of the empire in the paths of righteousness. Parliament chose to view it as a failure of the Walpole ministry.

The War of Jenkins' Ear did not cease with the recall of Vernon and
Wentworth to face a board of inquiry in Britain. In the wilds of Georgia a
Spanish invasion was repulsed by General Oglethorpe at Bloody Marsh on
St. Simons Island in 1742. By force of arms the general had resolved once
and for all the British claim to the disputed region south of the Savannah.
The victory recouped Oglethorpe's reputation, which had tarnished upon
the failure of his attack on St. Augustine.[28] It set American pens scribbling
once more about the contest of imperial good and evil. "Philanthropos"
would have the last poetic word on the war. His panegyric to Oglethorpe
offers little new in the way of praise, but much about the atmosphere of
contention that now enveloped Oglethorpe's enterprise and the war with
the Spanish. "Philanthropos" marks the inhabitants of South Carolina as
nemesis.

He bravely fought: Whilst you supinely lay,
And in inglorious sloth Slept fame away;
Untouch'd with wrongs like these great *Georgias* cause
Of Honour, Justice, Property or Laws,
Carless of these as of your Countrys Fate,

In sullen sloth supinely proud you sate,
When lo! e'en every better hope was past,
And every Danger seem'd the last;
Or to be *Slaves* or *Free*, a like prepar'd,
Ingloriously you unconcerned hear,
Your Country's Wrongs; your valiant Chief complains;
And let him fight, unequal to maintain. [29]

Thus the "genius of Britain" must outface enemies within the empire as well as adversaries without.

The contentions concerning the worth of the War of Jenkins' Ear were rendered moot when the conflict was swallowed up by the European struggles occasioned by the death of the Austrian emperor in 1741. The War of the Austrian Succession displaced Spain as the imperial adversary with France. Concomitantly, the anti-Hispanic rhetoric engendered by the Black Legend gave way to the discourse of "Gallic Perfidy."

9

Gallic Perfidy

If the Spaniard was the gross devil of Patriot fantasy, then the Frenchman was the subtle Satan. The simple viciousness of the Hidalgo was supplanted by the duplicity of the Chevalier. Because of the "craft," "cleverness," "guile," and "policy" of the French, they posed a greater danger to the British than did the Spanish. The special quality of the Gallic threat was comprehended by the term *perfidy*, a word that took on great rhetorical weight when employed by English pamphleteers and British American poets.[1] It meant calculated faithlessness—programmatic dissimulation toward malevolent ends. The term assimilated to itself a wealth of significances. The faithlessness of perfidy came to mean both the Catholic apostasy from primitive Christianity and a Gallic proclivity to break treaties and contracts. An element of secrecy attached to the term, which recalled the Jesuit assassinations of King Henry IV of France and William I of Orange, the plotting of the St. Bartholomew's Day Massacre, and the secret treaties between Louis XIV and the Stuarts concerning the restoration of the Roman Church in England. Because the surface of French policy was understood to conceal a depth, Whig expositors of Gallic perfidy made much of decoding signs. When properly decoded these signs told of French treachery against British liberty, property, religion, and government. Expositors warned that no appearance of peaceableness or submission could be trusted. A thousand anti-Papist tracts and the testimonies of hundreds of injured Huguenots fueled the enmity. The fulminations of the Sun King, especially when asserting the Pretender's right to the British throne, whipped the patriotic blazes into a crown fire. Not even the phlegmatic ministrations of Robert Walpole could damp the ardor of Britain's "tongues of flame."

Repeatedly, hot words ignited into action. From the Glorious Revolution to the American Revolution, Britain was more often at war with France than not. King William's War (1688–1697) gave way to the War of the Spanish Succession (1702–1713); the peace mandated by the Treaty of

Utrecht was punctuated by a series of clashes; the War of the Austrian Succession (1744–1748) produced an uneasy peace that collapsed with the Seven Years' War (1756–1763). The colonies were invariably actors in these conflicts.

British America participated as well in the rhetorical war against the French. The distinctive contribution of the American literature was its linkage of Gallic perfidy with "Indian Barbarism," to compose the formula of imperial peril. The personal testimonies in New England's many Indian captivity narratives imbued this peril with a peculiar intimacy. Poetry was occasionally employed to give these testimonies greater memorability. John Williams's brief protest about the fate of the residents of Deerfield (1707) presented French and Indian treachery in pathetic terms calculated to provoke indigation:

> Many, both Old and Young were slain out-right;
> Some in a bitter Season take their Flight;
> Some burnt to Death; and others stifled were;
> The Enemy, no Age or Sex would spare.
> The tender Children with their Parents sad,
> Are carry'd forth as Captives. Some unclad,
> Some Murdered in the Way, unburied left;
> And some thro' Family, were of Life bereft.
> After a tedious Journey, some are sold,
> Some left in *Heathen* Hands, all from Christ's Fold
> By *Popish Rage*, and *Heath'nish* Crueltie,
> Are banished. Yea some compell'd to be
> Present at *Mass*. Young Children parted are
> From Parents, and such as Instructors were.
> Crafty Designs are us'd by *Papists* all,
> In Ignorance of Truth, them to inthrall. [2]

The captivity narrative invariably presented the danger of the French and Indians in terms of physical travail and spiritual seduction. The former was inflicted by the "barb'rous Heathen," the latter by the "Crafty Papist." But few narratives meditated on the question of how the Heathen and the Papist should have entered into their collusion; nor did the captivity tales offer much insight into the goal of "Romish Plots" other than the securing of a few additional souls to the service of the Antichrist. We must look elsewhere for interpretations of the design of Gallic perfidy.

In British America at the end of the seventeenth century anti-French prejudice found its most articulate literary exploiters not among the native-born, but among that circle of refugees who had left England during "the Stuart Revenge"—from the Rye House plot in 1683 through James II's reign. Charles II's treaty with Louis XIV and the prospect of the Catholic

The Rebel's reward: or, *English Courage Display'd.* Boston, 1724. The crude woodcut serves as a stylistic correlative to Tom Law's bumptious ballad. The illustration does not suggest that the attack took place at night, though the extent of the slaughter is aptly conveyed. Reproduced by permission of The Huntington Library, San Marino, California.

duke of York assuming the crown infuriated dissenters. The Gunpowder Plot sparked anti-Catholic resentment into a frenzy of accusations and persecutions, which bred the Stuart reaction when the plot of the Whig Rye House lords to murder the king was uncovered in June, 1683. Among the volatile Whig penmen who entered the propaganda fray against the Stuarts were Richard Steere and Benjamin Harris, both of whom emigrated to New England rather than face the probability of seizure in London. In New England they continued where they had left off in the Old Country, albeit to an audience of the already converted.

As Donald P. Wharton has shown, Richard Steere's career as a poet began in the desire to vindicate Shaftesbury, the arch-Whig, from Tory calumny, particularly that of Dryden's *Absalom and Achitophel*.[3] Steere's riposte, *The History of the Babylonish Cabal*, inaugurated a series of theopolitical polemics—*A Message from Tory-Land to the Whig-Makers of Albian* (1682) and *Romes Thunder-Bolt, or, Antichrist displaid*—conflating Romanism, Tory politics, and French policy. Steere's denunciations were no more strident than those of a host of his dissenting brethren. The Book of Revelation was opened to discover the Whore of Babylon wearing Romish garb and the Antichrist propped up by Peter's throne. "And by *Implisset* faith the people grope / After the blind Directions of the *Pope*, / And his black tribe of *Locust* which devour / And eat the labour of the Labourer."[4] After the repression of the Whig press in July 1683 and the arrest of Steere's printer, a specialist in controversial imprints, Steere decamped for Connecticut. There he witnessed the tumults of the native country from afar and wondered at the remarkable turn of providence that drove the Catholic James into exile. His exultation at the Glorious Revolution was such that he took up a copy of his *Antichrist displaid* and revised it, adding lines justifying the exclusion of the apostate king from the British throne and the installation of William and Mary:

> Such crowds of Locusts, from th' infernal shade
> Come crawling forth, in Roman Masquerade;
> *Britains*'s Priviledges to Invade.
> This was beheld by the All-seeing Eye,
> Who in great mercy found a Remedy;
> Sends Royal *William*; who, as with a Broom
> Swept all into the pit, from whence they come.
> Illustrious *William*; with his Royal Queen,
> Dispell'd th' impending storm, & drew the scaene,
> Whom Heav'n Preserve—[5]

The metaphor of Catholic influence as a plague of vermin cleansed by William's broom gave sweeping governmental change a reassuringly domestic cast. No doubt the Dutch mystique of cleanliness offered the broom as the instrument by which the regent performed his clean-up; the sword was not the tool of the Glorious Revolution. The peaceableness of William and Mary's preservation of Britain's privileges contrasted with the violence of the Whore of Babylon's "Prodigious Rage: / Both in the Antique and this modern Age."

Steere's revised version of *Antichrist Display'd* was printed in his 1713 collection, *The Daniel Catcher. The Life of the Prophet Daniel: In a Poem*. The title poem of the collection aspired to more than biblical paraphrase. Daniel's career as the advisor to rulers lent itself to typological applications to the political situation of the 1680s and 1690s, particularly to the situation of those men who wished to explicate God's designs to the Stuarts. Steere's narrative is garnished with several meditations on political topics, including a thinly veiled attack on the desire for royal absolutism with which Louis XIV had infected Charles II and James II.

> Those Tributes due to Caesar, I will pay,
> But who makes man a God, doth man betray;
> Those Honours and Prerogatives, which be
> The proper Rights of Earthly Majesty,
> I, in Obedience to my *God* will bring
> And pay, as due unto my Sov'reign *King*.
> But those, who *Kings* Exalt to that degree,
> As they did *Herod*, by their Flattery,
> Are none of *Caesars* Friends, for *God* Above
> Now for his Honour is oblig'd to move,
> And with his flaming darts, and Arrows keen,
> Make mortal *Kings* to know they are but men.[6]

The sword may not have been the instrument of the Glorious Revolution, but "flaming darts, and Arrows keen" were the rewards providence reserved for those who presumed upon divine prerogative. Louis XIV, the modern Darius, would suffer war as the bitter fruit of his ambition.

American responses to the Glorious Revolution possessed little of the prescience of violence found in the writings of the refugees. Instead of predicting the punishments and trials that would eventuate from Louis XIV's frustration at William and Mary's accession, native poets memorialized the event as a thing unto itself—a *factum brutum* of providential history—a remarkable deliverance. Consider John Saffin's "A Thankfull Memoriall October 6th 1704":

> Next James the 2. did the Throne Advance
> He came in Smoothly, and with great Applause
> But soon Eclipst Our Libertys, and Lawes
> Strove to reduct us to French Slavery

And us Subject unto the Roman See.
Untill the Belgick Glorious Star arose
And did his Arbitrary power Oppose
Which made him (like a Coward) leave the State
His Crown and his three kingdoms Abdicate.[7]

The generality of Saffin's remarks revealed the distance from which the New Englander observed events in England. The identification of French slavery with the arbitrary subversion of laws and liberties, particularly the liberty of worship, was conventional to the point of being formulaic. Only those who had experienced the political turmoils in London at close range possessed a sophisticated grasp of the various interests at work in deposing James II, or the perils that arose from his installation by Louis XIV at Saint-Germain-en-Laye. One depends on ex-Londoners such as Steere and Harris for the large picture of imperial conflict, rather than Saffin or Benjamin Tompson. Harris, as a printer and bookseller, possessed a particularly sure grasp of the French peril. Using the "advice to a painter" device popularized by Waller and Marvell in the 1660s, Harris limned a historical panorama of the Glorious Revolution striking in design and color.

GO call a careful *Painter* let him show
The Poor in Pain, the *Tyrant's* Overthrow:
[Dr]aw the *Oppress'd*, their *Suff'rings* and their *Fears*;
[On]e *King in sorrow*, while the other *swears*.
[Show] how the *Priests*, in spite of *Sex* and *Age*,
[Fi]r'd up the Fury of most *Christian Rage*.
[Tim]ely Stroaks let his just Pencil tell
[How] the *Reform'd*, by those *Reformers* fell.
[In de]ep-dy'd Red, shew their fresh *bleeding Wounds*;
[*There*]'s bloody Mercy by St. *Ruth's Dragoons*.
[Show] how the *Tyrant* with the *Churches Rod*
[*Marty*]r'd the *Protestants* to please his *God*.
[Then] shew the *Plagues* that by *Gods Laws are due*,
[And b]y just Merit *murd'ring Kings pursue*:
[A *Mur*]*dring Court*, a *Tyrant King* undone;
[And] *Nuns* and *Priests* in curst Confusion run.
[Now Ki]ng-scorn'd *Slaves* and *Subjects* do their part,
[Draw] their own *Swords*, their *own just Rights* assert
[So tha]t thou may'st the Just again restore,
[Oh let] there be one *Abdication* more.[8]

Harris ordered his details in a pictorial organization mimicking the historical scheme of consequences. Thus a double emphasis was given each image in the argument. This standard effect of the "advice to a painter" genre conveyed the "advisor's" political adamance.[9] Besides this conventional employment of the form, Harris arranged a series of contrasting historical vignettes, each actor being seen in proximity to his victim(s). While the inevitable kings and priests appeared prominently, Harris recognized new figures on the political scene—"St. Ruth's Dragoons." St. Ruth was the French general directing the Jacobite army in Northern Ireland. By a poetic transmutation the Jacobite became the British equivalent of the Catholic soldier who enacted the slaughters of St. Bartholomew's Day. The creation of a new army of persecutors darkened the celebration of James II's abdication, for they would endure to work the monarch's will despite protestant hopes that one vacated throne would prompt the evacuation of a second.

Having added the Jacobite to the Jesuit and the Chevalier in the demonology of British American anti-Gallicism, the writers of the seventeenth century transformed their traditional anxiety at the native population into a horror at the possibility of a French and Indian coalescence on the frontier. No longer simply the servants of Satan, the native populations seemed puppets of French imperial policy.

ANTICHRIST IN THE WILDERNESS

The success of New England's arms in King Philip's War ended the threat to the English colonies posed by tribes residing in Massachusetts and Connecticut. Peril relocated to the periphery—to Maine, the upper reaches of New Hampshire, the northern territory of New York, and especially to Canada. The Abenakis and the Huron belonged to the French trading sphere, and many individuals converted to the Roman Catholic Church. As a demonstration of their loyalty, the northern tribes took up arms when King Louis launched his assault against King William and his allies. The War of the League of Augsburg commenced in 1689, shortly after Parliament ratified the claim of William and Mary to the throne. On August 9, 1689, the war spilled over into America when French and Indian troops torched Pemaquid, Maine. One of the American captives, John Gyles, late in his life composed a captivity memoir notable for the artful circumspection of its argument.

Memoirs of Odd Adventures, Strange Deliverances, etc. in the Captivity of John Gyles, Esq; (Boston, 1736) narrated a history containing something more than "popish rage and heathenish cruelty."[10] (In the mythology of empire the paired agents of Satanic policy, the French Jesuit and the cruel Indian, could be considered the antitypes of the material saint, Oglethorpe, and the noble savage, Tomochichi.) Gyles did not accept the pairing at face value; instead, his narrative prompted readers to consider the psychological reasons why the two should have entered into any compact.

A great conundrum for New England's theological and political establishments was the relative success of the French Catholics in converting natives to their faith. How could it be that providence meted greater success to the apostate Jesuits than upon the spiritual heirs of John Eliot, the "apostle to the Indians"? New England counted modest enlistments to the role of the saints, such as the Mashpees and the surviving Narragansetts, while the French weaned whole nations in the north and west to the religion of Rome. The Church of England determined in the first decade of the eighteenth century that the conversion of the Indians stood prominently on the roll of actions that would strengthen the interest of the church in America and founded the Society for the Propagation of the Gospel in America. New England congregationalists then took to interpreting their own lack of success in the endeavor. They found the problem in their projected converts and not in themselves. Gyles's portraits of the Abenaki who burned Pemaquid presented them as monsters (that is, creatures of secularized inhumanity) rather than devils, for to assign them so inveterate an opposition to New England's God would suggest that the saints' long-avowed mission to the Indians was an exercise in futility. [11] Rather, the Indians suffered a constitutional inclination toward superstition.

Gyles's consideration "of Their Familiarity with and Frights from the Devil" appeared in his narrative only after he had established his captors as "monsters of cruelty." Their monstrosity consisted in an inhumanity that distinguished them from their French allies. "Not one of the Indians showed the least compassion, but I saw the tears run down plentifully the cheeks of a Frenchman that sat behind, which did not alleviate the tortures that poor James and I were forced to endure for the most part of this tedious day."[12] The barbarity of the Indians was such that a Franciscan priest, "a gentleman of a humane, generous disposition," delivered a warning of providential retribution if the natives persisted in their unfeeling torments. When Gyles finally turned to his consideration of Indian superstition, he showed how the unfeeling Indian was moved to terror by an *ignis fatuus*:

> An Indian being some miles from his wigwam and . . . was going home but had not passed far before he saw a light like a blaze at a little distance before him, and darting his spear at it, it disappeared; then on the bank of the river he heard a loud laughter with a noise like a rattling in a man's throat. The Indian railed at the demon whom he supposed made the noise, calling it a rotten spirit of no substance, etc. He continued to hear the noise and see the light till he came into the wigwam, which he entered in his hunting habit, with snowshoes all on, so frightened that it was some time before he could speak to relate what had happened.[13]

One could imagine the inferences that Cotton Mather would have drawn from this incident. Gyles did not freight his experience with theological reflection and application. As a recent editor of his narrative has noted, Gyles, despite his collaboration with Rev. Joseph Seccombe in the narra-

tive's preparation, employed no biblical citations, interlarding his text instead with quotations from Pope's Homer, Dryden, and William King.[14] A
consequence was that theological prejudice never prevented observational
curiosity or an openness to experience. Alone of the major captivity narratives it suspended the narration of events to offer horticultural and eth-
nographic observations in the spirit of a Royal Society "transactioneer." The
ethos of inquiry was used to greatest effect when Gyles turned his attention
to the actions of a Jesuit visitor to the French family that had purchased him
from the Indians:

> The gentleman whom I lived with had a fine field of wheat which great numbers
> of black birds visited and destroyed much of. But the French said a Jesuit would
> come and banish them, who came at length and all things were prepared, viz. a
> basin of what they call holy water, a staff with a little brush to sprinkle withal,
> and the Jesuit's white robe which he put on. I asked several prisoners who had
> lately been taken by privateers and brought hither, viz. Mr. Woodbury, Cocks,
> and Morgan, whether they would go and see the ceremony. mr. Woodberry
> asked me whether I designed to go. I told him that I did. He said that I was then
> as bad a papist as they and a damned fool. I told him that I believed as little of it
> as they did, but I inclined to see the ceremony that I might rehearse it to the
> English. They entered the field and walked through the wheat in procession, a
> young lad going before the Jesuit with a basin of their holy water, then the Jesuit
> with his brush, dipping it into the basin and sprinkling the field on each side of
> him, next him a little bell tingling and about thirty men following in order,
> singing with the Jesuit, *Ora pro nobis*. At the end of the field they wheeled to the
> left about and returned. Thus they went through the field of wheat, the birds
> rising before them and lighting behind them. At their return I said to a French
> lad [that] the friar hath done no service; he had better take a gun and shoot the
> birds. The lad left me awhile (I thought to ask the Jesuit what to say) and when
> he returned he said the sins of the people were so great that the friar could not
> prevail against those creatures. The same Jesuit as vainly attempted to banish
> the mosquitoes from Signecto, for the sins of that people were so great also that
> he could not prevail against them but rather drew more as the French informed
> me.[15]

Gyles's findings concerning the Jesuit exorcism courted the reader's trust,
for they were presented as observations of the curious, not the condemnations of the already convinced. The author's rejection of anti-Papist prejudice secured his credit, and his bemusement at the proceedings maintained
the regard of the *sensus communis* with the play of modest wit. Without explicitly stating the parallel, Gyles showed the shared proclivity for superstition by native and Jesuit, while revealing the groundlessness of their
respective beliefs. Exorcising crows and and pow-wowwing for game became roughly equivalent in their challenge to credulity.
     Gyles, who attempted an understanding of the French and Indian en-
emies, reveals the extent of the alienation of the New Englander from his

foes. Though not objects of prejudicial hatred, the French and Indians remained objects nonetheless. The captive's curiosity never resulted in intersubjectivity—not even an identification-with-the-captor syndrome. Gyles, in the end, substituted for the Puritan stereotype of twin devils the enlightenment stereotype of twin dupes of superstition. In sum, Gyles simply altered the categories of disapprobation.

THE VIOLENCE OF POPULAR FEELING

In the abundant literature of calumny against the French and Indians there developed by the 1720s a distinction between the polite and popular styles. The polite style generalized the offenses of the malefactors with metaphor, myth, and abstracted description; the popular style specified crimes and cast accounts of retributions. The polite style is seen to advantage in Mather Byles's "To Pollio, on his preparing for the Press a Treatise against the Romish Church":

> Long had the *Romish* Darkness mock'd the Eyes,
> And Smoke and Locusts hover'd round the Skies;
> Like some dire Plague th' infectious Errors run,
> They stalk'd thro' Midnight, and devour'd at Noon.
> Confederate Schools secur'd the dark Retreats,
> With sacred Lies, and consecrated Cheats;
> Amazing Change! Obedient to the Priest,
> Bread leaps to Flesh and omnipresent Paste!
> To fill their Coffers all their Fancies team;
> Ev'n Purgatory proves a golden Dream;
> All Merchandise thro' their wide Market rolls,
> From rotten Carcasses, to humane Souls. [16]

Heeding the belletristic dictum that satire must not be reduced to a sole occasion, Byles presented a universalized catalogue of charges against the Catholics. These familiar slanders were poeticized by coloring them with images of corrupt carnality. The passage that begins with the metaphor of Catholic doctrine being a disease ends with the image of decaying carcasses bought and sold in the market/church. Even when Byles treated an occasion, as in his elegy, "To the Memory of a young Commander slain in a Battle with the Indians, 1724," the nature of the victim, crime, and perpetrator were unspecified. Consider the climax of the verse when elegiac praise gives way to narration:

> Now on the Waves in the small Bark he stood,
> And ting'd the Billows with th' Opposers Blood;

Now, daring, on the thickest War he bore,
Broke thro' the Ranks, and gain'd the distant Shore.
His Sword, like Light'ning, glitter'd from above,
When dreadful on, th' undaunted Hero drove,
And with such Sounds destructive Thunder roars,
As his swift Lead impetuous onward pours.
Now on the Left he bent, now to the Right
The youthful Warriour led along the Fight.
You Pagan Troops, could scarce his Rage sustain,
Tho' your dire Numbers blacken'd all the Plain,
Till feeling in his Breast the fiery Wound,
The sinking Youth drop'd fainting to the Ground;
In quick short pants ebb'd out his quiv'ring Breath,
While o'er his Eye-lids hung the Shades of Death. [17]

One cannot tell who the subject was, where he was slain, whether he died in his bark or on the shore, or who his attackers were. The lack of specificity might be explained by the fact that the poet was not present to witness the events, so must supply the productions of his own fancy in place of experience. Yet accounts of the death of Captain Josiah Winslow (Harvard, 1721) at St. George's circulated aplenty in Boston to provide detail for an elegist. [18] Byles abstracted the incident to suggest the timeless character of the heroic struggle against "Pagan Troops." In effect, the sacrifice of the "young Commander" was a rite in the cyclical conflict between civility and barbarism that has gone on since the rise of the ancient empires.

Samuel Penhallow, the provincial historian whose account of Winslow's death became canonical, made use of the legendary war between civility and barbarism to frame his narrative of the Indian wars on the northern perimeter. "I might with Orosius very justly entitle this History *De miseria hominum*, being no other than a Narrative of *Tragical Incursions* perpetrated by Bloody Pagans, who are Monsters of such Cruelty, that the words of Virgil may not unaptly be apply'd to them: *Tristius haud illis monstrum, nec Saevior ulla Pestis et ira Deum*." [19] Thus, the French and pagan Indians manifested a universal principle of enmity to civilization and humanity. The coalescence of the French and the Indians in "Paganism" entailed an exchange of symbolic attributes. The French assumed new depths of cruelty, while the Indians adopted perfidy. Penhallow delighted in tracing the psychic genealogy of French and Indian barbarism, finding its ultimate ancestry in the arbitrary violence of the Roman stadium: "No Courtesy will ever oblige them to gratitude; for their greatest Benefactors have frequently fall'n as Victims to their Fury. The *Roman Spectacles* of old were very lively in them repeated." [20]

In Penhallow and in Byles one sees little of the identification of the New Englander with the native that certain commentators have seen in their readings of the literature of the captivities. The myth of the war between civility and barbarism entailed no topos of exchange. As the political manifestation of the theological myth of the war between good and evil, the war between civility and barbarism preserved the theological interdiction of "the other." When good was touched by evil, the stain polluted it entirely. Thus, when the myth was invoked, the identity of "the civilized" was maintained sacrosanctly. The task of the intellectual historian is to determine which myth determined the representations in a text, and then to judge the prevalence of individual myths in discourse at large. While this is not too difficult a task when evaluating the literary productions of the elite, the interpretation of popular writings presents a greater difficulty. Public feeling did not find apt expression in the myth and generalization of the polite style; prejudice was not articulated as myth.

During the border wars of the 1720s the commonality produced its own poet, Tom Law, who sated the hunger for news and comment upon the French and Indian depredations in a series of popular ballads. The ethic of these compositions was Old Testament, expending stanza after stanza casting up accounts, eye for eye, tooth for tooth. (Indeed a Boston wit satirizing Tom Law had the balladeer proclaim, "Thus cypher, Sirs, you see I can, / and eke make poetry."[21]) The ballad on "Lovewell's Fight" has long captured the attention of folklorists and balladeers. Yet it says little of Gallic perfidy, and must be passed over in favor of his other major composition, "The Rebels Reward: or, English Courage Display'd."[22] This ballad recounted the famous Norridgewock Fight of 1724, when a band of New England militia surprised the Abenakis on the Kennebec River, routing them and killing their Jesuit missionary, Sebastien Rale.[23]

The Kennebec marked the border between French Canada and Maine. The French, in order to consolidate influence on the perimeter, established a Jesuit mission to which Rale fell heir. An energetic man, whose mastery of the Abenaki tongue and skill as a physician earned him a strong native following, Rale operated as the advance man of French imperial policy. He encouraged the anti-British sentiments of the Abenaki when New Englanders began settling the lower reaches of the Kennebec. When Gov. Samuel Shute bullied the tribe into a treaty in 1717, Rale turned the sentiment of many natives against the document. In 1721 he frustrated Samuel Penhallow's parley to consolidate the peace at Georgetown. The meeting disintegrated into an armed disorder. The arms brandished by the Abenaki had been secured out of Rale's royal pension of six thousand livres a year. After 1721 New Englanders considered the Abenaki in a state of rebellion. An unsuccessful attempt was made to seize the Jesuit; only his papers fell into New England hands. These convinced colonial authorities of a French plot to control Maine. In 1724 a second attempt to capture Rale was undertaken by Captain Harmon and four companies of men. In August they surprised the sleeping settlement of Norridgewock. The militia routed the unprepared Indians and slew man, woman, and child.

Tom Law supplied "A full and true Account of the Victory obtain'd over the Indians of Norrigiwock, on the Twelfth of August last, by the English Forces under Command of Capt. Johnson Harmon" set to the tune of "All you that love Good Fellows."

> He march'd, and gave the Rebels
>   a sad and fearful shock
> Full Sixty fighting Indians,
>   with Rallee their old Priest,
> And Women and Papooses
>   five Score there was at least.
> These all were come together
>   to make their horrid Dins,
> Whenas their Priest pretended
>   to pardon all their Sins.
> But you shall be informed
>   how they were forc'd to fly;
> For tho' their sins were pardon'd,
>   full loth they were to die. 24

The old protestant censure of Catholic pardons here operates to humorous effect because the Indians, instructed in the ways of perfidy, betrayed their faith. Their betrayal called into question the potency of Rale's promises while revealing Indian cowardice. Explaining the murder of Rale, especially since the troops carried specific orders for his capture, required the transformation of a sixty-seven-year-old man into a prodigy of violence:

> But I must not pass over
>   old Fryar *Rallee*'s Fate,
> Who staid it out most firmly;
>   and fought with cruel Hate.
> A Lad that was his Prisoner
>   he shot and wounded sore,
> Likewise Lieutenant *Dimmick*,
>   and also one Man more.
> They entred then his dwelling
>   and shot him in the thigh;
> Yet he refused Quarter,
>   and for his Gun did try.
> But still he cry'd, I'm ruin'd,
>   alas, I'm ruined;
> At which an English Soldier
>   did shoot him thro' the Head.
>   (81–96)

With similar bluntness Law narrated the "Reward" of the other major rebels. As for the "Reward" of Harmon's troops,

> Our Men got store of Plunder,
>   both Guns and Blankets too,
> And drank the Fryars Brandy
>   which was their Honest due;
> Good Powder took and Kettle;
>   which they had long enjoy'd;
> Their Houses they were burned,
>   and their Canoes destroy'd.
> They brought away a Squaw
>   and likewise Children three
> Which only were preserved
>   our Bond Slaves for to be.
>   (185–96)

Law's relish for plunder, slaughter, and slavery did not promulgate a higher morality; nonetheless, his title announced that his concern was precisely the suitability of crimes to punishments. In the grim world of the borders where war was a fact of life, the scheme of justice had been reduced to the righteous violence of the Israelites against the philistines. Levitical justice rather than the beatitudes was the theonomy embodied in Law's "cyphering."

Given Law's frank accounting of the militia's plunder, it is curious that the most valuable reward won at Norridgewock passed unremarked: the land secured for settlement. The silence portended something of importance. Because the acquisition of land was the dearest desire of the backcountryman, the forceful seizure of land—"grabbing"—was the most cherished and secret of "heart sins." Though Tom Law and his militia might have been loath to acknowledge the occult motive firing their zeal, the wits in Boston and many legislators in neighboring provinces had little trouble adducing where the hearts of the borderers lay. New Charter wags treated the declarations of patriotic or religious zeal issuing from the ballad bards with suspicion. The violence and the pretence of the border wars were lampooned in "A full and true Account of how the lamentable wicked French and Indian Pirates were taken by the valient English Men" (1724?):

> The *English* made their party good,
>   each was a jolly lad:
> The Indians run away for blood,
>   and strove to hide like mad.
>
> Three of the fellows in a fright,
>   (that is to say in fears)

Leaping *into* the sea *out-right*,
    sows'd over head and ears.

They on the waves in woful wise,
    to swim did make a strife,
(So in a pond a kitten cries,
    and dabbles for his life;

While boys about the border feud,
    with brick-bats and with stones;
Still dowse him deeper in the mud;
    and break his little bones.)

What came of them we cannot tell,
    though many things are said:
But this, besure, we know full well,
    if they were drown'd, they're dead.

Our men did neither cry nor squeek;
    but fought like any sprites:
And this I to the honour speak
    of them, the valiant wights![25]

Here the heroic violence of the militiaman became the gratuitous destruction of brutal boys. Ballad archaisms—"woful wise," "valient wights"—heightened the ludicrousness by dressing the action in the affectations of the Spenserian revival. (The English Neo-Spenserians attempted to infuse contemporary literature with the heroic spirit of the past by cultivating the language and symbolism of the poetry of the Elizabethan court.)[26] The duplicity of the borders' heroic posing apparently lacked the craft or finesse to rate as perfidy. They killed to grab; they grabbed to satisfy their childish appetites.

While all the French were suspect in the eyes of good Whigs and Patriots, not all Indians were rated as barbarians and enemies. The Mohawk Confederacy, because of its power and its organization, inspired many fantasies among British imperialists. If it could be solidified in its antagonism to the French; if it could be rendered truly subservient to the English crown; if it could be employed to dominate the peltries of Canada and the West, then the provinces would have less to fear from Gallic plots.

"Indian Songs of Peace"

Just as the Reformed Christian hoped that the Indian would become a convert to scriptural religion, the imperialist hoped that he would become an obedient subject of the crown. Behind the hope that the Indian would become a useful subject of the king lay the anthropological assumption that "the principal Difference between one People and another proceeds only from the Different Opportunities of Improvement."[27] Environment, not inheritance, dictated the differences between races. Therefore, the task of those who would incorporate the Indian into the empire was education—"improvement"—not conquest. For most thinkers (Oglethorpe, Spotswood, Lewis, Penn) improvement meant Christianization, and integration into the networks of trade. William Byrd commended "the Care Colo Spotswood took to tincture the Indian Children with Christianity," but suggested that miscegenation would be the surest means of acculturation. Doubting that the planters would intermarry with the natives, Byrd resigned himself to the hope that Spotswood's school could accomplish the metamorphosis from woodland hunter-gatherer to British citizen:

> With fairer Hopes he forms the Indian Youth
> To early Manners, Probity and Truth.
> The Lyon's whelp thus on the Lybian Shore
> Is tam'd and Gentled by the Artful Moor,
> Not the Grim Sire, inured to Blood before.[28]

The protestant attempted a reformation of the Indian heart by instilling Christian teachings in Indian youth. Virginia, like New England, had its academy for training promising Indian males—a building was constructed on the grounds of the College of William and Mary for this purpose. The Book rather than the sword would become the vehicle of "irresistible grace." The "Natural Dignity" and "Bright Talents" that Byrd saw beneath the Indian's dark surface would be refined in the ways of religion and civilization.

British Americans attached their greatest hopes as well as their greatest ambitions to the cultivation of the Five Nations in western New York. This powerful confederacy of the Mohawk, Oneydo, Onondaga, Cayuga, and Seneca tribes during the 1740s and 1750s controlled the peace from Virginia to Canada and New England. Cadwallader Colden, the New York politician and scientist who wrote a *History of the Five Indian Nations*, saw the confederacy as a league of imperial republics: "They strictly follow one Maxim, formerly used by the Romans to increase their Strength, that is, they encourage the People of other Nations to incorporate with them."[29] Colden's analogy between the Indians and the ancients served an argument: The vaunted cruelty of the Indians in war merely evinced an early stage in cultural development. "Whoever reads the History of the so famed ancient Heroes, will find them, I'm afraid, not much better in this Respect" (I, xxii). If the Five Nations could be extended the ameliorating influence of civilization, their primitive manners would be refined. "It is wonderful, how Custom and Education are able to soften the most horrid Actions, even among a polite and learned People" (I, xxii). Colden's *History* inspired a poet who envisioned himself to have been the agent of "Custom and Education" in New York—William Smith. Smith's *Indian Songs of Peace* (1752) elaborated a program by which the Five Nations would be culturally absorbed into Britain's imperium.

The avowed purpose of Smith's writings was to convince the New York Assembly to erect Indian schools. The assembly had scheduled a meeting of a committee to investigate the state of the Indian nations, since the province wished to preserve and strengthen its alliance with the Five Nations. Smith proposed (as generations of Virginians and New Englanders had proposed) that the Indians be schooled under British imperial auspices. Smith's *Indian Songs of Peace* provided a foretaste of those adornments of civility which would grace the Indian's thought when untutored genius was refined by Old World learning. They were also an appeal to colonists' sense of fellow-feeling. Smith invoked "that Love of Liberty and Honour;—that *Roman*,—that *British* Spirit:—They seem naturally akin to us,—beside our Alliance,—let us help our Brethren. If the rough Gem throws out some Sparks of Light, how will it shine when polish'd."[30]

The songs themselves purport to be translations of Indian originals: an ode entitled "The Tree of Peace" composed by an Indian bard, Maratho, and a soliloquy, spoken by a virtuous maid, Yariza. There are several reasons why Smith chose to render the songs as the expressions of Indians, rather than to compose lyrics about them. Because the protestant religion required personal testimony to the experience of God, the soliloquy was a preferred form when speaking of divine matters. The psalmist may be heard (Isaac Watts, too) in Maratho's invocation to

> The Great Spirit, Lord of all,
> He, who bids the Thunder roll,
> Who commanded the Sun's Birth,
> Who sends Showers to water th' Earth.
>
> (15)

Then, too, there was the matter of Indian eloquence. From the earliest era of settlement, Europeans had noted the Indian love of declamation on ceremonial and political occasions. Because transcripts of the sachems' speeches were included as essential matter in treaty documents, examples of Indian oratory had come into the hands of men of letters. By the 1740s Indian eloquence had become a fashionable concern of European and American belletrists, particularly in connection with speculations concerning the sublime rhetoric of the Bible and the early oratory of the Greeks and Romans. The emerging cult of aesthetic primitivism in Britain—a cult that would flower with the publication of Ferguson's *Ossian*—found an enlivening genius in native oratory. Colden's remarks on Indian eloquence argued its merits with admirable concision:

> The People of the Five Nations are much given to Speech-making, ever the natural Consequence of a perfect Republican Government: Where no Single Person has a Power to compel, the Arts of Persuasion alone must prevail.
>
> I am inform'd, that they are very nice in the Turn of their Expressions, and that few of themselves are so far Masters of their Language, as never to offend the Ears of their Indian Auditory, by an unpolite Expression. They have, it seems, a certain *Urbanitas*, or Atticism, in their language, of which the common Ears are ever sensible, though only their great Speakers attain it.
>
> They have some Kind of Elegancy in varying and compounding their Words, to which, not many of themselves attain, and this principally distinguishes their best Speakers. (I, xxii)

Of all the features of Indian discourse, Smith emphasized its employment of figurative speech. Borrowing images drawn from the transcripts of native orations included in Colden's history, Smith had Maratho the bard admonish his brethren to

> Plant and bless the sacred Tree,
> Prosper'rous may its Shadow be!
> Fast lay hold of Earth its Roots!
> Be the Fruits of Peace its Fruits!
> (13)

The natural imagery allows Smith to introduce a religious dimension to the call for peace.

> Lofty let its Top arise,
> And be favour'd by the Skies!
> Spirits good, from High who view,
> Water it with heav'nly Dew!
> (13)

The goddess Peace appears to instruct the young men of the tribe to "view to make the Field, / More abundant Bread to yield." Having read Colden's history, Smith knew that this oracle entailed the reformation of the native economy. Cultivation of crops was work relegated to female hands; males applied themselves to hunting and forest craft. Peace required that "where now the Wood-Land stands, / Shew well cultivated Lands" (15). To live in conformity with British civilization, the Indians would cease being hunter-warriors and commence life as agrarians. Maratho announces the end of the life as hunter-warriors by telling the tribe to bury a symbolic ax in the earth, "the Grave of War" (14).

Maratho bids that the entire nation bind itself by "Concord's Chain" in a unified resolve to cultivate the arts of peace. In the final stanzas the Indian nation voices its desire for instruction from New York in these arts. The bard petitions Governor Clinton to

> Send, *Corlaer* [Gov. Clinton], more good Men here,
> Who such Words may more endear,
> And our Knowledge more increase,
> From the House and Book of Peace.
>
> (15)

After this petition Smith inserted a passage on the imperial hierarchy, reminding readers that "The high *Sachem*", George II, had planted the "tree of Peace,/ Th' Earth, and the great Lake to grace" (16). Furthermore, the reader was assured that the royal sachem's care for the tree was "giv'n in Charge to the *Corlaer*," Governor Clinton. Smith closed Maratho's rhapsody with a chorus to be sung by the Indian nations:

> Heav'n preserve the *British* State!
> And the *British* Chief, and Race,
> And these Lands,—and bless the Peace.
>
> (17)

If Maratho's declarations of fellow-feeling and praise for New Yorkers did not move the assembly to sympathy, William Smith offered a second song, spoken by the virtuous maid, Yariza, and intended for the ladies of New York.

> Tree of Paradise! grow high!
> Let thy Top ascend the Sky!
> And thy Boughs spread more and more,
> Till the Earth they cover o'er!
>
> Ever Bird of sweetest Voice,
> Come and in this Shade rejoice;
> In the Song of Peace combine,
> Come and tune your Notes to mine.
>
> Come ye Younglings with your Dams,
> Come the little gentle Lambs!
> Bounding as ye come along,
> As if Dancing to the Song.
>
> (19)

Abiding by the convention of pastoral verse, Yariza's song seeks the restoration of a primordial, natural harmony. Animal and vegetable nature moves in concert with the song of peace. Cruel elements are kept at bay: "far hence Savage Beast,/ That delights in laying Waste" (20). Thoughts turn to the improvement of nature—"Now our Hands shall grace this Shade."

Yariza's notions of how native hands would improve nature sound curiously similar to the dreams of arts and industry we have heard from the lips of those who would diversify colonial trade.

> Wool and Flax, shall by our Care,
> Turn to Habits fine and fair;
> Can't our Wheels as well go round?
> Or can't Looms for us be found?
> (20)

Textiles produced by cheap Indian labor could, perhaps, compete with inexpensive German linens on the world market; but Smith's mind is more captivated by the prospect that Indian lace-making might find global approbation. Smith envisioned Yariza taking a lace to present to the queen.

Yariza's song concluded with an enthusiastic apostrophe to heaven. Smith explained that the maiden acts "as a Sybil, or rather a Prophetess in a divine Transport," when in a visionary trace she delivers a benediction upon the King and nations.

> And thy *British* Servant bless,
> Yet with Years of happy Peace,
> And the *Britons* of all Lands,
> Where so e'er that People stands.
>
> Bless us, also, Pow'r Divine!
> Form'd by thee, we too are thine;
> Make us yet more clearly see
> The sure Path, which leads to thee.—
> (22)

The oracle reminds us of the colonial tendency to make religion a means of furthering empire. If the Five Nations become protestant, their flirtations with the Catholic French would cease. Or as Smith says, "It is becoming . . . to advance the Cause of Christianity; and it not unworthy . . . to promote, by all proper Means, the Maintaining the Balance of Power in *America*, as well as in other Parts of the World" (10).

William Smith concocted the *Indian Songs* for a New York readership. Their rhetoric has nothing to do with Indians—indeed, the suggestion that the Five Nations become subjects of George II would have offended the Iroquois love of liberty. The citizens of New York were being persuaded that the possibility existed of a permanent pacification of the frontier through means other than conquest. If rifles were exchanged for ploughshares, the chase for agriculture, an assimilation would be accomplished that would establish British sovereignty over the native population permanently. New

York's lucrative trade in furs might be subverted; but this would serve imperial ends by breaking the influence of the Dutch traders in Albany and their allies in New York City. Since the Indian population, which was not large, would derive its wealth from the fruits of the soil, they would not require vast hunting tracts of land. The excess could serve the unquenchable thirst for land of settlers on the frontier.

Smith's poems were expressions of imperial wishes. As wishes, they lacked the substance of practical policy. (It would take the "Lord of the Mohocks," Sir William Johnson, to forge a practicable method of assimilation in his Johnstown community.) As wishes, too, they looked toward a future, rather than recognizing the present circumstance of American-Indian relations. Closer attention to the present circumstance would have prompted Smith to reconsider his understanding of that critical symbol of Indian oratory—the covenant chain. The symbol was explained by Canassatego, a sachem, to the governor of Maryland in 1744 at the conference at Lancaster courthouse, as Colden records:

> "It is true, that above One Hundred Years ago the Dutch came here in a Ship, and brought with them several Goods; such as Awls, Knives, Hatchets, Guns. . . . we were so well pleased with them, that we tied the Ship to the Bushes on the Shore; and afterwards liking them still better. . . and thinking the Bushes too slender, we removed the Rope, and tied it to the Trees; and as the Trees were liable to be blown down by high Winds . . . again removed the Rope and tied it to a strong and big Rock (here the Interpreter said, They mean the Oneida Country)." Afterwards the British came and took the place of the Dutch. The English governor "found the Rope which tied the Ship to the great Mountain was only fastened with Wampum, which was liable to break and rot, and to perish in the Course of Years; he therefore told us, he would give us a Silver Chain, which would be much stronger, and would last for ever. This we accepted, and fasted the Ship with it, and it has lasted ever since."
> (I, 139–40).

The covenant of the chain was economic. The Indians gave land to secure the benefits of trade. The rewards of trade with the Dutch, characterized by a rope fastening, were strengthened by the greater rewards of British trade, characterized by the silver chain. Smith misrepresented the chain as a symbol of concord binding the Indian people in a harmony and peace founded upon agrarian competence. The Five Nations understood it as the bond of self-interest connecting two sovereign peoples in a trade that encouraged the traditional life of hunting and fighting.

THE CONQUEST OF LOUISBOURG

While ballads of the border fights and visions of Mohawk settlement revealed an increasingly territorial view of empire, the writings generated by the most successful imperial adventure of the era, the expedition against Cape Breton, displayed the unalloyed spirit of mercantilism. Governor William Shirley's scheme of a concerted land and naval strike against Vauban's great fortress, Louisbourg, was inspired by the need to secure the coastal shipping lanes in the wake of France's surprise invasion of Canso, Nova Scotia, in 1744. The fall of Annapolis Royal and all of Nova Scotia was feared. Prompted by reports of Canadian malaise brought back by exchanged prisoners who had been held at Louisbourg, Shirley promulgated his plan to attack the citadel guarding the mouth of the St. Lawrence at a secret meeting of the Massachusetts General Court in 1745. Shirley believed that "the coasting trade . . . will be now in danger of being quite destroyed and lost to the enemy."[31] But the legislature balked, fearing the expense and the weakness of the province, until Shirley linked a promise of territorial expansion to his demand to protect trade. "[Canada] may be reckoned a more valuable territory to Great Britain than what any Kingdom . . . in Europe has."[32] The legislators did not doubt which British subjects were most conveniently situated to exploit the value of the lands. The General Court voted to fund the enterprise.

While the governor may have had to resort to the rhetoric of "grabbing" to move the assembly to favor, there was little doubt among the members of the expeditionary force about the purpose of the campaign. Samuel Niles, laureate of the reduction of Louisbourg, has the New England victors announce the justice of the cause on the ramparts of the vanquished at the moment of victory.

> It's not from thirst of Blood, nor for your Lives
> O! you Besieged, your Children, nor your Wives,
> That we 'gainst you this formal Siege Commence.
> But Country's Freedom, from Praeeminence,
> Which you assume, in these our Northern Seas,
> Obstruct both Im-, and Export of Supplies.
> You for long time, by your usurped Measures,
> Robb'd some of Life, and many, of their Treasures.
> Combining, likewise with the *Heathen* Tribes,
> Delusive, Popish Doctrines, and with Bribes:
> By these Incentives they do us Annoy,
> Whose Cruelties, give you, with them much Joy.
> Which moves us thus, our Weapons, to Employ.[33]

Niles did not equivocate in assigning blame; Admiral Warren's English fleet and General Pepperel's New England foot soldiers were engaged in a war of retribution, punishing the French for the usurpation of "our northern seas." The French disruption of trade—"both Im,- and Export of Supplies"—threatened the life of the British colonies. Theft of life and treasure was crowned by the perversion of the native population, binding it in heathenism and violence.

Niles's *A brief and plain essay on God's wonder-working Providence for New-England, in the reduction of Louisburg* disavowed an attempt to address "Polite" or "refined Tast," offering instead a narrative "design'd for Common Use." That is, it narrated for a middling audience the events of the expedition, in light of a common "providential" interpretation of New England affairs. Though Niles's introduction announced that his poetic essay intended "to give the World, an adequate Report," and though he proclaimed that the combatants "as loyal Subjects of the *British* Crown, / Their lives, their fortunes, & their *all* lay down," it was clear that the author meant New England when he said they fight to secure "the Country's Peace, her Liberties and Laws," and that he envisioned Americans as the principal readers of his account of the defense of "our Land."

The parochial tone of Niles's essay sounded clearly when he digressed from the narration of events to a discourse "on the Modes of Devotion, among the *French*, when thus Distrest and in great Fear":

> Saints Statues they adore, Im'ges numberless,
> And Beads, tell o're, the greater with the less.
> They mortifie their Flesh, with lashings manifold
> As *Heathens*, cut themselves in days of old.
> Profound Confessions, Pennances renew,
> Devoutly strict, much Sanctity, in shew.
> . . . .
> These meritorious Acts, as they pretend,
> Challenge Rewards, from GOD *Almighty*'s Hand.
> Denying Scripture use to' the Vulgar sort,
> Is to *Romes* Clergy, as a mighty Fort:
> It's falsly said, the Mother of Devotion,
> ----Is Ignorance,----
> But, Maxim true, of *Papacies* Subjection.
>
>   (15)

The familiar charge of a perfidious plot to alienate the common people from God is bolstered by the traditional charges leveled since the Reformation. In short, "th' implicit Faith, that Sons of *Rome* profess, / Is faithless Fraud."

New England, encouraged by the pronouncements of many of its Reformed prophets, had dressed the expedition in the rhetoric of a crusade. George Whitfield's motto, "Nil desperandum Christo duce," a host of militant sermons, and typological exercises such as "Moses Pleading with God for Israel . . . With a Word to our Brethren gone and going out on the present Expedition against Cape-Breton, 1745" commissioned the soldiery to become a vessel for God's wrath. "Destroy proud Antichrist, O Lord, /

And quite consume the Whore."[34] Yet the curious consequence of the success of the venture was not the glorification of "wonder-working providence," but the creation of provincial pride.

The conquest of Louisbourg was a collaborative venture of English naval force and New England soldiery. The relationship between Admiral Warren and General Pepperel had its uneasy moments during the course of the siege, particularly when Warren bridled at the disorder of the New England force.[35] But the keys of the fortress were surrendered to the New Englanders. The success of the venture suggested that in military valor, no metropolitan advantage existed, and that the provincial was the equal of the English Jack Tar: "Rough *English* virtue gives your deeds to fame. / And o'er the *Old* exalts *New England's* name."[36] On the heels of the debacle at Cartagena, the success of an enterprise conceived by a colonial governor and prosecuted as much by colonial forces as the vaunted navy inspired some to see the genius of old Britain newly emerged in New England.

> BRITANIA strove a *Cathegene* to gain,
> While Numbers perisht on the Wat'ry Main;
> And Wentworth's Forces languish'd ev'ry Day,
> 'Till Rum and Fevers swept whole Hosts away:
> The Spaniards smiling at the ill-laid Scheme,
> Were sure it was concerted in a Dream.
> When Christian *Lewis* comes to hear what's done
> With his strong Fortress on the Isle *Breton*,
> He'll swear the Valour of the British Breed,
> In Western Climes, their Grandsires far exceed;
> And that New England Schemes the Old so pass,
> As much as solid Gold does tinkling Brass.[37]

The order of praise in many a provincial paean reflected the valuation of worth. "The grand Promoter should begin the Verse: / Of noble SHIRLEY, then my Muse shall sing."[38] "A PEPP'REL and a WARREN's Name, / May vie with MARLB'ROUGH and a BLAKE for Fame."[39] With the provincial pride came a little righteous resentment, for the condescension of the British regular service toward the New England militia was not forgotten after the victory. In the siege camps a military balladry developed during the expedition, and in it the tensions of the Yankee and the Englishman emerged.[40] After the success of the campaign some of these burlesques were refashioned to form the kernel of a song that would haunt the British at the moment of their humiliation at Yorktown—"Yankee Doodle."

> Brother Ephraim sold his Cow
>   and bought him a Commission
> And then he went to Canada
>   to fight for the Nation

> But when Ephraim he came home
> he prov'd an arrant Coward
> He wou'dn't fight the Frenchmen there
> for fear of being devour'd.
>
> Aminadab is just come Home,
> His Eyes all greas'd with Bacon
> And all the news that he cou'd tell
> Is Cape Breton is taken.[41]

The greatest wonder of wonder-working providence, according to the British prejudice burlesqued here, was that Jehovah should permit so rude a creature so astonishing a victory.

While the tension between Yankee and Briton could be diffused in humor or submerged in the knowledge of their common contribution to the victory, the fact of a disparity between provincial and imperial understandings could not be evaded. The disparity became particularly troublesome in connection with the understanding of the enemy. With each decade the cosmopolitan imperialist became increasingly secular in his interpretation of the French threat. In 1747 the cosmopolite could offer the following "Directions to the French King's Painter."

> Swoln with ambition, let the tyrant stand,
> With Pride and Treach'ry plac'd on either hand:
> In scraps let broken treaties strew the ground,
> Here Vice exulting, and there Justice bound:
> Fill his throng'd levee with a wretched crowd,
> Mean sneaking slaves, of fancied blessings proud,
> A dull, tame race whom nothing can provoke,
> Fond of the chains that bind them to the yoke.
> Stript by his laws present the country bare,
> And ruin'd commerce sinking in despair.[42]

The perfidy of King Louis here has diminished from the "implicit faith . . . of faithless Fraud" to diplomatic untrustworthiness. The slavery he imposed upon his subjects was simply political subjugation, not the bondage of body and soul. Men of good faith did not strike deals with the Antichrist. But with politicians, no matter how untrustworthy, agreements might be made. When the lords of Whitehall returned Louisbourg to France as part of the settlement of the Treaty of Aix-la-Chapelle in 1748, New Englanders saw how little the metropolis regarded the depth of French depravity and the righteousness of New England's crusade; at the same time they learned how the imperial mind might revise its assessment of the worth of trade with certain provinces. No amount of hard specie paid in compensation for New England's efforts could buy off the conviction that Whitehall had disregarded American interests and devalued New England's sacrifices:

> Vanquish'd by Peace, that Heros like withstood,
> Loud thund'ring Cannons, mix'd with Streams of Blood.
> The Gallics triumph—their Recess so short
> Joyful return, to the late conquer'd Fort,
> Where Monuments of English Arms will shew,
> When Time may serve, ye shall our Claims renew,
> New England's Fate insult! The Day is Yours,
> Constrain'd we yield that Conquest that was ours. [43]

When the British attempted to enlist aid a decade later to take Louisbourg again, the irony of the entreaty did not escape those who had stood on the battlements in June, 1745. The sense that the metropolis formed policy without regard for the wishes of the provincials became increasingly common. The conduct of the Seven Years' War did little to allay the disquiet.

10

The Tenuousness of Imperial Identity

Of all the successes attending the expedition against Cape Breton, the most notable may have been the union of the several New England colonies in a federated military enterprise. Even in the face of an aggressive French and Indian advance against the borders of the British provinces, concerted action was difficult to achieve in the colonies. Provincial militias insisted upon their own regulations and officers when combining with other colonial forces; provincial assemblies proved parsimonious when funding military exercises. The habitual recalcitrance of Rhode Islanders, and Quakers in New Jersey and Pennsylvania, to fund any military enterprise, and the periodic reluctance of assemblies in other provinces to contribute to campaigns in distant regions frustrated Americans who saw the general threat posed by the French and Indians. Dr. Adam Thomson, a literate Scot, operated as a literary gadfly in Pennsylvania, publishing verses designed to counteract Quaker pacifism. "An Ode, In Honour of New-England, (on their important Conquest of Cape-Breton from the French,) of ever glorious Memory" petitioned that "ancient Valour well approv'd" be "Rever'd with one Accord."[1] When Franklin organized a private military company, evading the legislature's ban on funding a militia, Thomson supplied "An Ode, humbly inscribed to the Associators of Pennsylvania," asking of the citizenry,

> shall we, like a spurious Race,
> Our glorious Ancestors disgrace?
> Sit tamely still, a Prey to Knaves,
> And turn the Back to abject Slaves?
> Oh Shame! forbid it all ye Powers
> That guard *Britannia's* lofty Towers.[2]

Even New York, which had suffered greatly from Indian incursions over a long period, had difficulty composing its will against the threat. While assemblies often gave lip service to the need for defense, they were reluctant to levy taxes to fund the troops. In New York the Long Island delegates proved so closefisted that Lewis Morris, Jr., distributed a parody of a rural representative's letter to his constituents:

> My friends your letter came Safe To my hand
> Now To Make a Full answer I am at a Stand
> To begin with our selves our Tax is but Small
> but New York's To pay the Devill and All
> I must tell you Ive got full fifty pound
> On praetence of keeping our Indians sound
> Hold Them besides The Ohio Lay neer
> And Turned up my Eyes with an [ ] sneer
> being put To the vote I gaind my point
> Tho some broken Noses were put out of Joynt
> The bills we have passed are but very few
> but They are full Long give The Devil his Due
> The Lottery bill contains Sixty pages
> which I could not read in Twenty Ages
> It is to bring in by way of a chance
> Money to oppose The power of france
> As I am Told if Ere They pretend
> To attack The city before the war End
> The Next is a bill To Make us all fight
> and Like a soldier To Exercise Right
> There Some Part Declares a man that shall run
> at The head of his Troop Shall Dye by a Gun
> but I hope The french will never come here
> and then the cowards have nothing To fear
> The bill of bills is the Ten thousand pound
> which is Laid on funds [ ] sound
> but To make all things go down with great Ease
> The citys to pay as much as we please
> They sure can afford what on them we Lay
> for all people chide They have money To Pay. [3]

The self-interest and parochialism displayed here constituted a fundamental danger to British America in the eyes of cosmopolitan Americans. When Benjamin Franklin in 1754 presented his plan for a colonial union to the Albany Congress, the rationale for the federation was "Security and defense."[4] The occasion for the Congress was the French advance into the western lands claimed by Virginia. According to Franklin, the circumstances recommending a plan of union were

the difficulties that have always attended the most necessary general measures for the common defence, or for the annoyance of the enemy, when they were to be carried through the several particular assemblies of all the colonies; some assemblies being before at variance with the governors or councils, and the several branches of the government not on terms of doing business with each other; others taking the opportunity, when their concurrence is wanted, to push for favourite laws, powers, or points that they think could not at other times be obtained, and so *creating* disputes and quarrels; one assembly waiting to see what another will do, being afraid of doing more than its share, or desirous of doing less; or refusing to do any thing, because its country is not at present so much exposed as others, or because another will reap more immediate advantage.[5]

The fate of the Albany Plan illustrated the difficulties. Provincial assemblies rejected it as an incursion into their rights, and the crown disallowed it as an invasion of prerogative. These results were, perhaps, forecast in the conduct of the Albany Congress itself: the West Indian governments, Georgia, and Nova Scotia did not receive invitations to attend. Virginia and New Jersey chose to absent themselves from the proceedings. Without an institution about which to consolidate a federated American political identity, British American imperialism would remain piecemeal, a politics constituted more in the relations of individual provinces with the metropolis than in terms of British America.

The magnitude of the French threat during the 1750s, and the prospect of the loss of the transappalachian territory "now well known both to the English and French, to be one of the finest in North America, for the extreme richness and fertility of the land"[6] could not force the provinces into federation; nonetheless, the empire asserted itself in America during the 1750s as the metropolis dispatched troops to fight the Seven Years' War. Imperial mythology enjoyed a reinfusion of life because of the war. The presence of vast numbers of British regular troops in the New World attested to the metropolis's concern for America. The contest with the French and Indians enjoyed near-universal approbation in the colonies. Yet the bards who arose to celebrate the empire during the 1750s—Jonathan Beveridge, Benjamin Young Prime, John Maylem, George Cockings, and John Duncombe—identified the benefit of empire so completely with the triumphs of arms that the commercial mythology of mercantilism disappeared.[7] Maylem's pseudonym, "Philo-Bellum," suggested the martial character of the muse of empire during the 1750s. His *Gallic Perfidy* inspired resentment at the French and Indian foes, while his *Conquest of Louisburg* praised the empire's exercise of "glitt'ring Arms" in the 1758 retaking of the fortress.[8]

George Cockings alone of the celebrants of the Seven Years' War apprehended the peril entailed in identifying war as the spirit of empire. After the successful global conquest of the Catholic powers, the demonic Hidalgo and the scheming Chevaliar were laid to rest. The success of arms obviated the principal imagined benefit of empire, protection. As a sequel to his *War;*

an Heroic Poem, Cockings attempted to revive the empire's commercial mythology in *Arts, Manufactures, and Commerce*. The poem argued that

> ARTS, and COMMERCE, in Britannia's Isle;
> To distant Isles, with Hearts benevolent,
> And North America's wide Continent,
> Shou'd stretch their Hands, replete with friendly Aid,
> To planting Schemes, and beneficial Trade.[9]

The agency for the transfer of arts and technology to America would be private bodies, such as the Society for the Encouragement of Arts, Manufactures, and Commerce. The result would be a revision of the imperial contract, for America would enjoy the industrial development that metropolitan privilege had prohibited under the Acts upon Trade and Navigation. Cockings saw danger in the maintenance of the status quo; he intuited the potential violence at metropolitan imposts in the provinces, wishing that

> th' Americans for ever prove
> Obedient Children, and deserve the Love
> Of an indulgent Parent, always pleas'd,
> Whene'er her Sons of just Complaints are eas'd;
> Tho' distant far remov'd o'er Oceans wide,
> May FILIAL DUTY all their Actions guide:
> May they more tractable, more placid grow,
> Be wise betimes, and their true Int'rest know;
> Nor in her Bosom fix, by Tumults rude,
> The poignant Stings of black INGRATITUDE!
> (3)

Even while extending the promise of a greater commercial equitability, the spokesman of the metropolis reasserted England's privilege. The threat of parental lashings as compensation for the "stings" of filial ingratitude lurked behind the good wishes and benedictions.

THE SUM OF ALL PROPHECIES

Mercantilism, for all its debilities as a political program, had at least the commendation that its ministers paid attention to the balance sheet of costs and revenues. One cannot imagine Walpole undertaking a global conflict such as the Seven Years' War, or amassing so extravagant a debt as that contracted by William Pitt. Since it was the debt accrued in the great victory that prompted the several attempts of Parliament to tax the colonies and eventually led to the rebellion, one could argue that the shift from mercantilism to territorial imperialism in the 1750s contributed directly to the collapse of the First British Empire. In the colonies certain presumptions survived from the time of Walpole and the Pelhams that were ill suited to Pitt's imperialism. Foremost among these was the provincial belief that British military protection was compensation for the metropolitan privilege of economic arrangements. Though Parliament never acknowledged the linkage, there is little doubt that the colonial assemblies believed a tacit contract was in force, and for this reason did not display alacrity at funding supplies for the military though self-defense was at stake. With the promulgation of a territorial model of empire, however, the metropolis lost whatever sympathy it had for the colonial disinclination to contribute to the support of the army. Since the fruits of victory were territories that would be enjoyed by colonials, Whitehall believed that Britons were underwriting an enterprise whose benefits fell mainly to Americans.

During the 1750s the debate over empire became so greatly ramified that the literature of the Seven Years' War and its aftermath requires investigation by itself. In my discussion in chapter 4 of the historical shift in the southern colonies from a concern with the exchange value of commodites in the 1720s and 1730s to emphasis on agricultural production of staples in the 1750s and 1760s, I have touched upon an issue that must be confronted at greater length in subsequent histories: the efflorescence of the "land interest" in America. The "mystique of land" had been an element of imperial discourse since the era of first settlement. Mention has already been made of various of its manifestations: the "grabbing" of the frontier settlers, the abundant colonial literature dealing with boundaries, the attempts to render real property into a form of credit in the various Land Bank schemes. In the 1750s, the literature of land changed fundamentally. The "mystique of land" found philosophical justification in the doctrines of agrarianism, pragmatic expression in Pitt's seizure of Canada, and economic impetus in an agricultural production boom. Trade became an appendage to the enormous productive capacity of the American countryside. It is by no means clear what the ideological consequences were in the tipping of the balance from trade to land. But the writings of the 1750s and 1760s displayed the tensions and their effects quite prominently—in the literature of the Regulator Revolts, the pamphlet war caused by the Paxton rebellion in Pennsylvania, and the beginning of the extensive New England protest against land companies and "speculation." The effects in more benign dress may be seen in the vogue for letters and tracts by Americans who characterized themselves as farmers.

Before literature's preoccupation with the issue of land and its degeneration into martial effusion in the 1750s, the poetry of British empire in America promulgated a commercial mythology, a legal mystique, an autarkial politics, and an imperial demonology. None of these components of imperial discourse survived the Revolution intact in the literature of the United States. While trade had its celebrants, poems such as Freneau's "The Village Merchant" attacked the commercial ethos of the early republic. [10] An agrarian ethic, typified in John Searson's *Mount Vernon*, informed a competing poetic vision of economic competence. The glorification of trade became an ideological component of federalism, but shorn of mercantilist notions of restraint on free exchange. Embargos, tariffs, and monopolies became the political devices of the Jeffersonians.

In the early republic the British legal mystique was also transmuted. Its two components—the gospel of contract, and the cult of liberty—suffered something of a divorce, the former becoming the animus of federalist legalism, the latter the political antinomianism of the democratic republicans and their elevation of rights over laws. The experience of Shays's Rebellion shaped federalism's legal conservatism. Jonathan Trumbull's *The Anarchiad*, Royall Tyler's "The Contrast," and Richard Alsop's *The Echo* all present, as the Whig imperialists did, law as a vehicle of instantiating public virtue. [11] Freneau, on the other hand, elevated "Liberty" over the British legal heritage: "A curse would on your efforts wait, / Old British laws to reinstate." [12]

Autarky disappeared completely from the poetic discourse of the republic. The notion of metropolitan privilege, the metaphor of the empire as a political family in which patriarchal authority is exercised over offspring teritories, the image of the virtuous monarch, all vanished in the United States. It was preserved in the work of the Loyalists poets in Halifax, particularly in Jacob Baily's "America." [13] It may also be found in the work of West Indian poets—in Bryan Edwards's *Poems, Written Chiefly In the West Indies* (1792) and in "A native of the West Indies," *Poems on subjects arising in England and the West Indies* (1783). [14] But it remained most vital in the work of Tory poets in the metropolis. During the course of the Revolution, the "loyal" poets in Britain worked the traditional tropes with great energy: Joseph Peart's *A Continuation of Hudibras in Two Cantos* (1778), Thomas Hasting's "A New Song" (1778), John Cole's *The American War* (1779), Thomas Maurice's "Verses Written in the Year 1774" (1779), the anonymous author of *Spirit and Unanimity* (1779), John Farrer's *America A Poem* (1780), the author of *Rebellion and Opposition* (1780), Edward Greene's *The Prophecy of Andree* (1782), Jeremiah Davies's *An Epilogue to the Late Peace* (1783), Miles Parkin's *Columba, A Poetical Epistle* (1783), and the works of a host of other minor writers. [15]

The success at arms of the British forces in 1763 mitigated American fears of the French and Spanish. Indeed, the patriotic alliance with France revealed the extent to which traditional fears had dissolved. Only with news of the horrors of the French Revolution and the appearance of Citizen Genet did the rhetoric of Gallic perfidy emerge again, supplied with a veneer of

Jacobinism, in the writings of the federalists. The Spanish ceased to haunt the American imagination, though the Black Legend was dusted off whenever convenient for "diplomatic" reasons: during Bolivar's campaign of liberation, during the Mexican American War, during the Spanish American War. "Heathen Indians" alone of the original figures of the imperial demonology retained the onus of evil.

The oracles of empire were garbled when repeated as prophecies of the rising glory of the United States. Yet they were not entirely forgotten or thoroughly transmuted. A prophecy's repetition, however, was not the sole means by which an oracle's meaningfulness could be attested. The Hebraic law laid out a standard by which true prophecy was discriminated from false: "If what a prophet proclaims in the name of the LORD does not take place or come true, that is a message the LORD has not spoken" (Deu. 18:22). When we consider the oracles of empire in light of this rule, a further appreciation of their value may be gained. Were the prophecies fulfilled? Different traditions of exegesis supply different answers. Did a global network of trade enrich America? It did; but the commercial imperialism that the United States embraced entailed costs whose extent and consequence are matters of intense debate. Did trade bring into being the "Arts of Peace"—science, fine arts, education? They did; but the "commercial spirit" also spawned a countervailing anti-intellectualism, which denigrated such pursuits as useless. Did the progress of liberty bless the country with order and instill in its citizenry virtue and a love of law? Perhaps the question can best be answered by observing that the need for justice is recognized as a crucial issue of American civic life: no millennium of peace and order has yet been inaugurated, nor has the collapse into libertinism and selfishness prophesied in the jeremiads of generations of critics been accomplished. Did the righteous empire maintain its enmity against its evil and perfidious rivals? It did; though its recognition of which power constituted "the heathen," "the treaty-breaker," "the deceiver," and "the evil empire" has shifted with time, and the violence exercised against its foes has at times been questioned as being inspired by the phantasms of a superstitious civil religion.

Assessing the predictive power of the imperial oracles for the United States does not comprehend their meaning, for the prophecies have other applications that affect their significance. These other prophetic traditions inhibit me from asserting the necessary and exclusive connection between the literature of British America and that of the United States. The fullness of the oracles cannot be known until other connections have been charted and other questions answered. How did the imperial oracles bear on the self-understanding of Canada? What was the legacy of the imperial mythology on nineteenth- and twentieth-century West Indian writings? How did the literature of the Second British Empire take up or revise the promise of the Old Empire? How did the imperial mythos of British America compare with those of the rival powers in the New World? For example, what accounts for the profound similarities between the southern georgics and Rafael Landivar's *Rusticatio Mexicana*, or what circumstances explain the ideological disparity of Kirkpatrick's *The Sea-Piece* and Francisco Ruiz de Leon's contemporaneous imperial epic, *Hernandia*? These questions lead to other histories—histories in which the worth of Britain's imperial oracles might finally be judged, both in their character as auguries and as works of political art. One value of this book is its assistance in enablng these questions to be framed. Moreover, it clears ground for a question that has not yet been posed properly: What are the imperial legacies in the self-understanding of the United States?

Notes

INTRODUCTION

1. Benjamin Tompson, "New Englands Crisis," *Benjamin Tompson Colonial Bard: A Critical Edition*, ed. Peter White (University Park: Pennsylvania State University Press, 1980), 84. Tompson, sometime schoolmaster in Boston, Charlestown, and Braintree, was a polymath, capable of "performing physick," preaching, and preparing legal documents. When master of the Latin School in Boston, he introduced Cotton Mather to the study of literature.

2. See Hugh Adam's verse against wigs and hoop coats, "March 20, 1722," *Proceedings of the Massachusetts Historical Society*, 1st ser., 3, 326; *The Origin of the Whale bone-petticoat. A Satyr. Boston, August 2d, 1714* (Boston, 1714).

3. William Bradford, "Of Boston in New England," *Seventeenth-Century American Poetry*, ed. Harrison Meserole (New York: Anchor Books, Doubleday, 1968), 388. (This anthology is hereafter referred to as *SCAP*.) A striking contrast, illustrating the commercial muse of the late seventeenth century, is Benjamin Lynde, "Lines Descriptive of Thomson's Island", *SCAP*, 491–94. Thomson's island is located in Boston harbor.

4. White, *Benjamin Tompson*, 157. This fascinating poem was apparently delivered in person to Governor Bellomont by Tompson dressed as a shoemaker. Neil T. Eckstein, "The Pastoral and the Primitive in Benjamin Tompson's 'Address to Lord Bellamont,'" *Early American Literature*, 8 (February, 1973), 111–16. The shoemaker served as an icon of New England political nativism from Nathaniel Ward's *Simple Cobbler* to Samuel Adams's "Salem Shoemaker" columns in the *Independent Advertiser* during 1748–49. There is a distinctive ambiguity found in most New England complaints. The discommodities of the land are represented as being at one and the same time annoyances and challenges to spiritual resilience. See J. A. Leo Lemay, *"New England's Annoyances": America's First Folk Song* (Newark: University of Delaware Press, 1985), 79–81.

5. Consider John Saffin's "New England's Lamentation of her present S[t]ate &c":

> The Inhabitants of Boston, they Complaine
> for want of Trade, sufficient to mainetaine
> their familys; and many Lately Broken
> are of their poverty a certaine Token;
> Behold New England! how throughout the Land,
> Thy Chiefest gainefull Trade, is at a Stand;
> Thy Mercuries, by whose Industrious care
> They brought into the Land, both Money & ware,
> Even they, begin to [Sink] for want of Trade;

> Yet of the Publick Charge they most, are made
> To Beare; wch with their frequent loss at Sea
> By Shipwreck, Stormes, and by the Enemie,
> they'r much Disabl'd, and Discourag'd to,
> they know not where to send, nor what to do[.]
> (5–18)

John Saffin His Book 1665–1708, ed. Caroline Hazard (New York: Harbor Press, 1928), 98. My correction from examination of manuscript, line 13: "Sink" for "Smile."

6. David S. Shields, "Then Shall Religion to America Flee; Herbert and Colonial American Poetry," *Like Season'd Timber: New Essays on George Herbert*, ed. Edmund Miller and Robert DiYanni (New York: Peter Lang, 1987), 281–85.

7. Margaret Anne Doody, *The Daring Muse: Augustan Poetry Reconsidered* (Cambridge: Cambridge University Press, 1985), 5–29.

8. "Poems on affairs of state" were topical political verses, often satirical, that first appeared with frequency during the Restoration. Often gathered by enterprising publishers into miscellanies bearing such names as *State Poems* or *Poems on Affairs of State*, they "illuminate the political, cultural and literary evolution of England." George deF. Lord, Introduction, *Poems on Affairs of State; Augustan Satirical Verse, 1660–1714*, 8 vols. (New Haven: Yale University Press, 1963), vol. 1, xxv–lvi. Unfortunately, no equivalent collection of British American poetry exists.

9. Samuel Johnson, *Lives of the English Poets*, ed. George Birkbeck Hill, 3 vols. (New York: Octagon Books, 1967; reprint 1905), vol. 2, 393.

10. Rusk attempted to catalogue every printed American verse in book, magazine, or newspaper published during the eighteenth century. The catalogue was never completed and has languished unused in the special collections of the Columbia University Library. Wroth's many contributions to early American bibliography are so familiar they need no description. His critical essays deserve close attention: "The Maryland Muse by Ebenezer Cooke," *Proceedings of the American Antiquarian Society*, 44 (1934), 267–308; "John Maylem: Poet and Warrior," *Publications of The Colonial Society of Massachusetts, 1934–37*, 32 (Boston, 1937), 87–118; "James Sterling: Poet, Priest, and Prophet of Empire," *Proceedings of the American Antiquarian Society*, 41 (1931), 25–76.

11. Ernest Lee Tuveson, *Redeemer Nation: The Idea of America's Millennial Role* (Chicago: University of Chicago Press, 1968). For an assessment of the status of recent investigation into early American literature, see Philip F. Gura, "The Study of Colonial American Literature, 1966–1986: A Vade Mecum," *William and Mary Quarterly*, 3rd ser., 45 (April, 1988), 305–41.

12. William Spengemann, "Discovering the Literature of British America," *Early American Literature*, 8 (1983), 3–16. Spengemann's provocative ruminations on American literature have been collected as *A Mirror for Americanists: Reflections on the Idea of American Literature* (Hanover: University Press of New England, 1989).

13. J. A. Leo Lemay, "Richard Lewis and Augustan American Poetry," *Publications of the Modern Language Association*, 83 (March, 1968), 80–101.

14. J. A. Leo Lemay, *Men of Letters in Colonial Maryland* (Knoxville: University of Tennessee Press, 1972).

15. "Governor Bellomont Describes Factionalism, 1698," *The Glorious Revolution in America*, ed. Michael G. Hall, Lawrence H. Leder, and Michael G. Kammen (Chapel Hill: University of North Carolina Press, Institute of Early American History and Culture, 1964), 129.

16. Isaiah Thomas, *The History of Printing in America with a Biography of Printers & an Account of Newspapers*, ed. Marcus A. McCorison (New York: Weathervane Books, 1970), 131–33.

17. Jerome J. McGann, *The Beauty of Inflections: Literary Investigations in Historical Method and Theory* (Oxford: Clarendon Press, 1985), 82–83.

18. There is, of course, danger in viewing pragmatic affairs as consequences of literature. Yet the writings upon the affairs of state by early eighteenth-century authors, such as Swift, Defoe, Addison, and Steele, lend themselves to interpretation by viewing their reception in terms of political acts and changes of policy. Since those acts and policies invariably became textualized in an apologetic literature, influences can be mapped by a historian's intertextual readings.

1. THE LITERARY TOPOLOGY OF MERCANTALISM

1. Xavier Flores, ed., *Le "Peso Politico de Todo el Mundo" par Antony Sherly* (Paris, 1963), 70–74.

2. E[phraim] Lipson, *The Economic History of England*, 3 vols. (London: Adam and Charles Black, 1943), vol. 3, 13–196.

3. Joyce O. Appleby, *Economic Thought and Ideology in Seventeenth-Century England* (Princeton: Princeton University Press, 1978).

4. John J. McCusker and Russell R. Menard, *The Economy of British America 1607–1789* (Chapel Hill: University of North Carolina Press, Institute of Early American History and Culture, 1985), 35–39.

5. Adam Smith, *An Inquiry into the Nature and Causes of the Wealth of Nations (1776)*, ed. R. H. Campbell, A. S. Skinner, and W. B. Todd, 2 vols. (Oxford: Oxford University Press, 1976), vol. 1, 440–543.

6. Doody, *The Daring Muse*, 11–14.

7. For a recent study of the graphic dimension of the iconology, see Wayne Craven, *Early American Portraits* (Cambridge, U.K.: Cambridge University Press, 1986), 38–54.

8. Joan Thirsk and J. P. Cooper, eds., "John Keymer's Observations Touching Trade and Commerce, 1618–1620," *Seventeenth-Century Economic Documents* (Oxford: Clarendon Press, 1972), 464–71.

9. Francis Bacon, *Advancement of Learning and Novum Organum* (New York: Colonial Press, 1899), 281.

10. John Harvard Ellis, ed., *The Works of Anne Bradstreet in Prose and Verse* (Gloucester: Peter Smith, 1962), 73.

11. The thesis that early modern and modern imperial enterprise entailed atavistic ambitions over and above economic motives was broached by J. A. Schumpeter in his landmark essay, "Zur Soziologie der Imperialismen" (1919). Schumpeter's picture of imperialism, devised to identify precapitalist legacies in early twentieth-century imperial enterprises, has the merit of recognizing the economic program *and* ideological compulsions animating such enterprises. Schumpeter's notion of atavism seems particularly apposite for a commercial empire that cloaked its colonial efforts in Roman trappings. *Imperialism and Social Classes*, ed. Paul M. Sweezy (Oxford: Blackwell, 1951).

12. William D. Andrews, "The *Translatio Studii* as a Theme in Eighteenth-Century American Writing," Ph.D. diss., University of Pennsylvania, 1971.

13. Thomas Dale, Letter "December 19, 1736," Thomas Birch manuscripts, British Library.

14. The issue of the place of the various tribes of Amerindians in the imperial scheme is so complex and the literature so vast that it demands monographic treatment by itself. I glance at the matter incidentally at several places in this volume, particularly in my treatment of "Gallic perfidy," but do not scrutinize it with the profound attention it deserves.

15. [William Smith], *Indian Songs of Peace: with A Proposal, in a prefatory Epistle, for erecting Indian Schools* (New York: Parker and Wayman, 1753).

16. [James Sterling], *An Epistle to the Hon. Arthur Dobbs, Esq; In Europe. From a Clergyman in America* (Dublin: J. Smith, 1752), I, ll. 371–74.

17. Eusey D. Domar, "The Causes of Slavery or Serfdom: A Hypothesis," *Journal of Economic History*, 30 (1970), 18–32. Oscar and Mary F. Handlin have argued that the colonial experience determined the development of the legal doctrine of slavery in perpetuity ("Origins of the Southern Labor System," *Colonial America: Essays in Politics and Social Development*, ed. Stanley N. Katz and John M. Murrin [New York: Knopf, 1983; 3rd ed.], 230–49.)

18. According to Herbert, after sin domineers in France and England,

> Then shall Religion to *America* flee:
> They have their times of Gospel, ev'n as we.
> My God, Thou dost prepare for them a way,
> By carrying first their gold from them away:
> For gold and grace did never yet agree:
> Religion alwaies sides with povertie.
> We think we rob them, but we think amisse:
> We are more poore, and they more rich by this.
> Thou wilt revenge their quarrell, making grace
> To pay our debts, and leave our ancient place
> To go to them, while that which now their nation
> But lends to us shall be our desolation.
> Yet as the Church shall thither westward flie,
> So Sinne shall trace and dog her instantly.
> ("The Church Militant," ll. 237–56)

19. See, for instance, James Reid's "The Religion of the Bible and Religion of K[ing] W[illiam] County Compared," in Richard Beale Davis, "The Colonial Virginia Satirist," *Transactions of the American Philosophical Society*, new ser. 57, 1 (1967), 43–71. William Eddis, *Letters from America*, ed. Aubrey C. Land (Cambridge, Mass.: Belknap Press, Harvard University Press, 1969), 35–46. Hector St. John de Crevecoeur, "Letter IX; Description of Charles Town; Thoughts on Slavery; On Physical Evil; A Melancholy Scene," *Letters From an American Farmer* (New York: Signet Classics, 1963), 150–73. For a general history of the critique of slavery in America, see Roger Bruns, *Am I Not A Man and A Brother: The Anti-Slavery Crusade of Revolutionary America, 1688–1788* (New York: Chelsea House Publishers, 1977).

20. Roger Wolcott, "A Brief Account of the Agency of the Honourable John Winthrop, Esq; in the Court of King Charles the Second, Anno Dom 1662," *Poetical Meditations* (New London, 1725), 22–24.

21. McCusker and Menard, *The Economy of British America*, 119–27, 158–60, 177–78.

22. George A. Billias, *The Massachusetts Land Bankers of 1740*, University of Maine Studies, 2nd ser., 74 (Orono, Maine: University of Maine, 1959).

23. John R. Dunbar, *The Paxton Papers* (The Hague: M. Nijhoff, 1957); William S. Powell, *The Regulators in North Carolina: a documentary history, 1759–1776* (Raleigh: North Carolina State Department of Archives & History, 1971); J. A. Leo Lemay, "Robert Bolling and the Bailment of Colonel Chiswell," *Early American Literature*, 4, 2 (Fall 1971), 99–142.

2. THE TIDE OF EMPIRE

1. John Winthrop IV, "Ad Regem," *Boston Weekly News-Letter* (22 August, 1723); [Matthew Adams], "A Poetical Lamentation, occasioned by the Death of His Late Majesty King George the First," *New England Weekly Journal* (12 February, 1727/28); "The Introduction," *The Loyal American's Almanack For the Year 1715* (Boston, 1715). Recently a Pennsylvania broadside attesting to the Hanoverian mystique has surfaced: [Joseph Breintnall], *The Death*

of King George Lamented in Pennsylvania; Being Part of a Letter to the Author's Country Friend ([Philadelphia: Keimer?], 1728). It is presently in the collection of the Library Company of Philadelphia.

2. The son of Joseph Byles and nephew of Cotton Mather, Mather Byles was tutored in verse at Harvard by John Adams. The Adams-Byles circle embraced the aesthetic of the religious sublime and the example of Isaac Watts. Alexander Pope's moral poetry also exerted an influence upon the group. For a period of time in the late 1720s the circle made up the editorial board of the *New England Weekly Journal*. It used the newspaper as a medium for ameliorating the public's taste. Byles married into the Belcher family, so found himself in proximity to official circles. During the 1730s he served as an unofficial laureate to the province. Appointed as pastor of the Hollis Street Church, Byles earned a reputation as a sermonizer in the polite style. The single competent biographical sketch is Clifford Shipton's in Sibley, *Biographical Sketches of Those Who Attended Harvard College*, 17 vols. (Boston: Harvard University, 1933–75), vol. 7, 464–93. Edward Griffen is preparing a book-length study of Byles's career. For the mythography of Augustan poetry and an account of its attenuation, see Howard D. Weinbrot, *Augustus Caesar in "Augustan" England: The Decline of a Classical Norm* (Princeton: Princeton University Press, 1977).

3. [Mather Byles], "A Poem on the Death of King George I, and Accession of King George II," *New England Weekly Journal* (4 September, 1727), ll. 19–26. The poet's first public success, the verse was reprinted with minor corrections in pamphlet form: [Mather] Byles, *A Poem on the Death of His late Majesty King George, Of glorious Memory: And the Accession of our present Sovereign King George II. To the British Throne* ([Boston, 1727]). The text of the corrected pamphlet is quoted. A facsimile collection of the poetry has been published as *Mather Byles Works*, ed. Benjamin Franklin V (Delmar, N.Y.: Scholars' Facsimiles & Reprints, 1978).

4. For a cogent contemporary review of the variety of governments subsumed in the British empire, see James Abercromby, "An Examination of the Acts of Parliament Relative To the Trade and Government of our American Colonies (1752)," *Magna Carta for America*, Memoirs of the American Philosophical Society, 165, ed. Jack P. Greene, Charles F. Mullett, and Edward C. Papenfuse, Jr. (Philadelphia: American Philosophical Society, 1986), 47–62.

5. Edward Young, "Imperium Pelagi. A Naval Lyric. Written in Imitation of Pindar's Spirit. Occasioned by His Majesty's Return, September 10th, 1729 and the Succeeding Peace: The Merchant. Ode the First. On the British Trade and Navigation," Strain I, stanza 4, *The Complete Works Poetry and Prose*, ed. James Nichols (Hildesheim: George Olms Verlagsbuchhandlung, 1968). All citations will be by canto and stanza from this edition.

6. George Lichtheim, *Imperialism* (New York: Praeger, 1971), 44.

7. Ibid., 32.

8. "The woolcomber and the poet appear to me such discordant natures, that an attempt to bring them together is to 'couple the serpent with the fowl'." Samuel Johnson, "John Dyer," *Lives of the English Poets*, vol. 3, 344. Though Johnson in the "Life of Savage" avowed an interest in the enterprise of colonization, his conception of ethical imperialism was bound to the Virgilian model, or to the notion of the occupation of vacant lands; he had little use for the "shopkeeper empire" of mercantilism.

9. Thomas Makin, "A Discription of Pennsylvania [1728]," *Pennsylvania Magazine of History and Biography*, 32 (1913), 372.

10. Sterling, *Epistle to Dobbs*, 8–9 (Part I, ll. 111–14).

11. While Eric Williams's famous thesis that profits from slave-based colonial agriculture supplied the investment capital for the industrial revolution has been challenged thoroughly, a new case for the importance of the colonial trade to metropolitan prosperity has been made by Jacob M. Price, "Colonial Trade and British Economic Development, 1660–1775," *Lex et Scientia: The International Journal of Law and Science*, 14 (1978), 101–26.

12. James Kirkpatrick, *The Sea-Piece; A narrative, philosophical and descriptive Poem. In Five cantos* (London: Cooper and Buckland, 1750). All extensive passages will be cited by canto designation and line numbers.

13. Joseph Ioor Waring, "James Killpatrick and Smallpox Inoculation in Charlestown," *Annals of Medical History* (1938), 301–8.

14. James Killpatrick, *A Full and Clear Reply to Doct. Thomas Dale* (Charleston: Peter Timothy, 1739). Dale published two pamphlets attacking Killpatrick, *The Case of Miss Mary Roche* (Charleston: Timothy, 1738) and *The Puff; or, A Proper Reply to Skimmington's last Crudities* (Charleston: Timothy, 1739). Neither of these works has survived.

15. J[ames] Kirkpatrick, *The Analysis of Inoculation: comprizing the History, Theory, and Practice of it: With an occasional Consideration of the Most Remarkable Appearances in the Small Pox* (London: Millan, Buckland, and Griffiths, 1754).

16. Desmond Clarke, *Arthur Dobbs Esquire 1689–1765* (Chapel Hill: University of North Carolina Press, 1958), 21–25; Caroline Robbins, "The Case of Ireland," *The Eighteenth-Century Commonwealthman* (Cambridge, Mass.: Harvard University Press, 1961), 149–53.

17. Kirkpatrick's association of businessmen with "grimace" may be borrowed from Richard Steele, *The Tatler*, 38 (1709), 8. For a general discussion of the issue of the morality of trade in Whig discourse, see J. G. A. Pocock, "Virtue and Commerce in the Eighteenth Century," *Journal of Interdisciplinary History*, 3 (1972–73), 125–34.

18. Emory Elliot, *Revolutionary Writers; Literature and Authority in the New Republic, 1725–1810* (New York and Oxford: Oxford University Press, 1982), 79.

19. Judge Nevill was the moving force behind the publication of the *New American Magazine*. His career and the history of his periodical are told in Lyon Richardson, *A History of Early American Magazines 1741–1789* (New York: Thomas Nelson, 1931), 123–35. Nevill's life of Columbus is found in vol. 1 (January, 1758).

20. Kenneth Silverman, ed., *Colonial American Poetry* (New York: Hafner, 1976), 424.

21. Philip Freneau, "The Pictures of Columbus," *The Poems of Philip Freneau Poet of the American Revolution*, 3 vols., ed. Fred Lewis Pattee (Princeton: Princeton University Library, 1902), vol. 1, 99. Pattee used the 1788 version as copy text. Some later versions of the poem eliminated these lines, since they repeated the sense of the first picture.

22. [Edward Kimber], "A Letter From a Son, in a distant Part of the World, March 2, 1743," ll. 45–50, *The London Magazine*, 13 (July, August, 1744), 355–57, 405–06. Kimber, the son of the publisher of *The London Magazine*, was attached to the expeditionary forces under Oglethorpe.

23. Martius Scriblerus [Alexander Martin], "An Ode," *New American Magazine* (November, 1759), 690–91.

24. Richard Walser, "Alexander Martin, Poet," *Early American Literature*, 6 (Spring, 1971), 55–62.

3. THE MATERIAL REDEEMERS

1. Richard S. Dunn, *Sugar and Slaves: The Rise of the Planter Class in the English West Indies, 1624–73* (Chapel Hill: University of North Carolina Press, Institute of Early American History and Culture, 1972), 81–83; also, "The English Sugar Islands and the Founding of South Carolina," *South Carolina Historical Magazine*, 72 (1971), 81–93. J. M. Sosin, *English America and the Restoration Monarchy of Charles II: Transatlantic Politics, Commerce, and Kinship* (Lincoln: University of Nebraska Press, 1980).

2. [William Penn], *The Excellent Priviledge of Liberty and Property* (Philadelphia, 1687). It was the first work by the proprietor published in the colony.

3. J. William Frost, "William Penn's Experiment in the Wilderness: Promise and Legend," *Pennsylvania Magazine of History and Biography*, 107 (October, 1983), 581–84.

4. Richard Frame, *A Short Description of Pennsilvania. Or, A Relation What things are Known, enjoyed, and like to be discovered in the said Province* (Philadelphia: William Bradford, 1692).

5. John Holme, "A True Relation of the Flourishing State of Pennsylvania, 1686," *Bulletin of the Historical Society of Pennsylvania* (1845), 161–80.

6. T. M.[Thomas Makin], "On the Arrival of the Honourable Thomas Penn, Esq; one of the Proprietors of the Province of Pennsylvania," *American Weekly Mercury*, 659 (17 August, 1732). Lemay's speculative attribution must be affirmed on the basis of internal evidence.

7. "Congratulatory Verses, wrote at the Arrival of our Honourable Proprietary," *Pennsylvania Gazette* (21 August, 1732). Lemay's speculative attribution of the verse to Richard Lewis of Annapolis seems unlikely. Rev. William Becket of Lewes (author of a later ode to Thomas Penn) seems a more plausible candidate.

8. Sir William Keith's literary skills were formidable; their contribution to his political success in Pennsylvania has been evaluated in Thomas Wendel, "The Life and Writings of Sir William Keith, Lieutenant-Governor of Pennsylvania and the Three Lower Counties, 1717–1726," Ph.D. diss., University of Washington, 1964. See also Wendel, "The Keith-Lloyd Alliance: Factional and Coalition Politics in Colonial Pennsylvania," *Pennsylvania Magazine of History and Biography*, 92 (1968), 289–305.

9. Oxf. Schol. Exit. [George Webb], ["A Memorial to William Penn"], ll. 37–48, *The Genuine Leeds Almanack For the Year of Christian Account, 1730* (Philadelphia: David Harry, 1730).

10. [William Penn], *The New Charter of Privileges to the Province, granted October 28, 1701* (Philadelphia: Kiemer, 1725). Though it is probable that the charter was printed at the time of issue, this is the first native edition that survives.

11. William Penn, "The Benefit of Plantations, or Colonies," *The Most Delightful Country of the Universe*, ed. Trevor R. Reese (Savannah: The Beehive Press, 1972), 100–104.

12. [George Webb], ["The New Athens"], ll. 39–43, *American Weekly Mercury*, 495 (3 July, 1729). For the basis of the attribution, see my "Wits and Poets of Pennsylvania: New Light on the Rise of Belles Lettres in Provincial Pennsylvania, 1720–1740," *Pennsylvania Magazine of History and Biography*, 109 (April, 1985), 122–33.

13. A member of the first generation of belletrists born in British America, Taylor began publishing almanacs in Pennsylvania in 1698. An avid student of the astronomical writings of Flamsteed, Taylor quickly gained a reputation for the accuracy of his ephemeris. As filler for his pages he inserted poems of his own composition, usually modeled on the verse of Cowley and Withers. From 1706 to 1736 Taylor served as the surveyor general of the province. He belonged to the belletristic circle gathered around Aquila Rose during the 1720s. In 1736 he retired to his nephew's plantation in Chester County and devoted his declining years to verse and almanac making. Franklin viewed Taylor's publication as the principal local model for *Poor Richard's Almanac*. The best biography of Taylor is a typescript pasted onto the front binding of vol. 1, Jacob Taylor Surveys, Manuscripts, Historical Society of Pennsylvania.

14. Enroblos [Jacob Taylor], ["Pennsylvania,"], ll. 43–50, *American Weekly Mercury*, 1051, 1052 (19, 26 February, 1739/40). For my attribution, see "Wits and Poets," 121.

15. Missionary of the Society for the Propagation of the Gospel in Foreign Parts, Griffith Hughes resided at Radnor, Pennsylvania, from 1733 to 1736. A student at St. Johns College, Oxford, he undertook his mission before receiving his degree. Difficulties with health and payment troubled his tenure at St. David's, Radnor. He left in 1736 to assume a more lucrative post as rector of St. Lucy's Parish, Barbados. He composed a widely distributed three-volume *Natural History of Barbadoes* in 1750, which earned him election to the Royal Society.

16. "Ruris Amator" [Griffith Hughes?], "From Chester County in the Province of Penn-

sylvania. To a Friend at Oxford," ll. 43–50, *American Weekly Mercury*, 794 (20 March, 1734/35). My speculative attribution; Lemay concurs in the probability.

17. [William Smith], *A Poem on Visiting the Academy of Philadelphia, June 1753* (Philadelphia: [Franklin & Hall], 1753).

18. [Joseph Breintnall], "To the Memory of Aquila Rose, Deceas'd," *Poems on several Occasions, by Aquila Rose: To which are prefixed, Some other Pieces writ to him, and to his Memory after his Decease* (Philadelphia: [B. Franklin], 1740), 3–13; for my attribution see "Wits and Poets," 105.

19. *Benjamin Franklin's Autobiography*, ed. J. A. Leo Lemay and P. M. Zall (New York: W. W. Norton, 1986), 42–43, 220.

20. [George Webb], ["A Prospect of Philadelphia"], *Pennsylvania Gazette*, 125 (8 April, 1731).

21. Queen Caroline enjoyed remarkable repute as a positive influence upon the king. She was an ardent supporter of Walpole, who bestowed upon her the largest jointure ever granted any queen. A capable and intelligent person, Caroline gave trusted counsel to the king on affairs of state. Her death in 1737 provoked three British American elegies, the most elaborate of which was Mather Byles, *On the Death of the Queen. A Poem. Inscribed to His Excellency Governour Belcher* (Boston: Draper and Henchman, 1738).

22. Thomson in 1727 had dedicated *A Poem Sacred to the Memory of Sir Isaac Newton* to Walpole. Shortly thereafter, perhaps because of Walpole's disinclination to war during the Spanish aggression of that year, Thomson became critical of Walpole. His *Britannia* (1729) expressed his disapprobation of the peace policy.

23. Nicholas B. Wainwright, ed., "Nicholas Scull's Junto' Verses," *The Library* (January, 1949), 82–84.

24. William Becket, "Fragment From an Ancient Poet, Ap. 4. 1738; Dedicated to the Hon. Thomas Penn, Esq.," ll. 1–18, Notices and Letters Concerning Incidents at Lewes Town 1727–1744. Manuscript Am. .0165. Historical Society of Pennsylvania. Born in Over Peover, Cheshire, Becket (1697–1743), was appointed as the second missionary of the Society for the Propagation of the Gospel in Foreign Parts to Sussex in the Lower Counties of Pennsylvania in 1721. He settled in Lewes and became the close friend of politician and poet Henry Brooke. An admirer of Swift and of Church of England prerogatives, he exercised much of his literary ability in polemics against dissenters. The pointed allusion to the military heritage of the Penn family suggests Becket's sympathy for the anti-Quaker political faction.

25. Kenneth Coleman, "The Founding of Georgia," *Forty Years of Diversity: Essays on Colonial Georgia*, ed. Harvey H. Jackson and Phinizy Spalding, Wormsloe Foundation Publications, 16 (Athens: University of Georgia Press, 1984), 6–10.

26. Robert Mountgomery, *A Discourse Concerning the design'd Establishment of a New Colony to the South of Carolina, in the Most delightful Country of the Universe, 1717*, in *The Most Delightful Country of the Universe*, ed. Trevor Reese (Savannah: Beehive Press, 1972), 11, 24–28.

27. Verner W. Crane, "Dr. Thomas Bray and the Charitable Colony Project, 1730," *William and Mary Quarterly*, 3rd ser., 19 (1962), 49–63.

28. [Benjamin Martyn], *Some Account of the Designs of the Trustees for establishing the Colony of Georgia in America* (London, 1732). *Reasons for Establishing the Colony of Georgia, With Regard to the Trade of Great Britain, The Increase of our People, and the Employment and Support it will afford to great Numbers of our own Poor, as well as foreign persecuted Protestants* (London: W. Meadows, 1733).

29. "A muse from India's savage plain" [James Kirkpatrick?], "An Address to James Oglethorpe, Esq; on his settling the colony in Georgia," *South Carolina Gazette* (10 February, 1732/33). Reprinted, "Two Colonial Poems on the Settling of Georgia," ed. Hennig Cohen, *Georgia Historical Quarterly*, 37 (1953), 131–34. My speculation about authorship derives

from the similarity of the poem's descriptions of the commodities of Georgia to passages on the fruits of New World development in *The Sea-Piece*; also Kirkpatrick appears to have been the one man of letters in Charleston not ill-disposed to the Georgia project.

30. [Moses Browne?], "To the honourable James Oglethorpe, Esq, On his Return from Georgia," *Gentleman's Magazine*, 4 (September, 1734), 505. Attribution, Richard C. Boys, "General Oglethorpe and the Muses," *Georgia Historical Quarterly*, 31 (1947), 25.

31. Phinizy Spalding, *Oglethorpe in America* (Athens: Brown Thrasher Books, University of Georgia Press, 1987), 76–97.

32. [Thomas Fitzgerald], "Tomo Chachi, an Ode," ll. 53–60, *Georgia, And Two Other Occasional Poems on the Founding of the Colony, 1736*, ed. John Calhoun Stephens, Jr., Emory University Publications, Sources & Reprints, ser. 6, 2 (Atlanta: The Library, Emory University, 1950), 12–16.

33. Milton L. Ready, "Philanthropy and the Origins of Georgia," *Forty Years of Diversity*, 46–59.

34. Ibid., 49.

35. "A Rapsody, occasioned by a Review of the Common Misery of Human Kind, especially in that Part of the World called Great-Britain," *Virginia Gazette* (10 December, 1736), ll. 9–16.

36. "To James Oglethorpe Esq; on His late Arrival from Georgia (London, October 5)," *Pennsylvania Gazette*, 327 (20 March, 1735).

37. James Thomson, *The Prospect: Being the Fifth Part of Liberty. A Poem* (London, 1736), V, ll. 639–44.

38. Martyn, *Reasons for Establishing the Colony of Georgia*, in *The Most Delightful Country of the Universe*, 181.

39. For the importance of the workhouse as a model for Georgia's scheme of labor, see Ready, "Philanthropy and the Origins of Georgia," 47–49.

40. Colonial projectors thought in terms of global analogies from the beginning of English settlement. Thomas Hariot in his 1588 *A briefe and true report of the new found land of Virginia* (Frankfort: DeBry, 1590) began his fantasy that marshgrass might be converted to silk with the observation, "The like groweth in Persia, which is in the selfe same climate as Virginia, of which very many of the silke workes that come from thence into Europe are made. Here of if it be planted and ordered as in Persia, it cannot in reason be otherwise, but that there will rise in shorte time great profite to the dealers therein" (7).

41. James Oglethorpe, *A New and Accurate Account of the Provinces of South-Carolina and Georgia*, in *The Most Delightful Country of the Universe*, 144.

42. [Samuel Wesley], "Georgia, A Poem," *Georgia, and Two Other Occasional Poems on the Founding of the Colony, 1736*, 10.

43. William Stephens, *A Journal of the Proceedings in Georgia, Beginning October 20, 1737*, 2 vols. (London: Meadows, 1742), vol. 1, 182, 233, 238. The various publications of the malcontents are collected in *The Clamorous Malcontents; Criticisms and Defenses of the Colony of Georgia, 1741–1743*, ed. Trevor Reese (Savannah: The Beehive Press, 1973). The best assessment of their ideology may be found in Milton L. Ready, "The Georgia Trustees and the Malcontents: The Politics of Philanthropy," *Georgia Historical Quarterly*, 60 (1976), 264–81.

44. Patrick Tailfer, Hugh Anderson, and David Douglas, *A True and Historical Narrative Of the Colony of Georgia In America* in *The Clamorous Malcontents*, 34.

45. *A True and Historical Narrative of the Colony of Georgia by Pat. Tailfer and Others With Comments by The Earl of Egmont*, ed. Clarence L. Ver Steeg (Athens: University of Georgia Press; Wormsloe Foundation Publications, 4, 1960), 14.

46. *The Deserted Village*, ll. 344–51, *The Collected Works of Oliver Goldsmith*, ed. Arthur Friedman, 4 vols. (Oxford: Oxford University Press, 1966), vol. 4, 300.

4. STAPLES

1. Aubry C. Land has devoted much of his career to elucidating the interests of Maryland's planter class. See in particular "The Planters of Colonial Maryland," *The Maryland Historical Magazine*, 68 (1972), 109–28.

2. William Byrd, *Histories of the Dividing Line betwixt Virginia and North Carolina*, ed. William K. Boyd (New York: Dover Publications, 1967), 2.

3. The text of "The New Metamorphosis" appears as an appendix to David S. Shields, "Henry Brooke and the Situation of the First Belletrists in British America," *Early American Literature*, 23 (Spring, 1988), 20–24. Ebenezer Cooke, *The Sot-Weed Factor: or, A Voyage to Maryland* (London, 1708).

4. "Tobacco, mortal Pest," Nathan Fiske notebook, American Antiquarian Society [ca. 1752]. The closest approximation to a georgic on tobacco production is the central section of "Verses Occasioned by the Success of the British Arms in the Year 1759," *The Maryland Gazette*, 765 (3 January, 1760).

5. *A Description of the Golden Islands* (London: Morphew, 1720). Reprinted in *The Most Delightful Country of the Universe*, 35.

6. Lawrence A. Harper, *The English Navigation Laws: A Seventeenth-Century Experiment in Social Engineering* (New York, 1939); Charles M. Andrews, *New England's Commercial and Colonial Policy*, vol. 4 of *The Colonial Period of American History* (New Haven: Yale University Press, 1936).

7. Oglethorpe, *A New and Accurate Account of the Provinces of South-Carolina and Georgia*, 151–52.

8. Amos Aschbach Ettinger, *James Edward Oglethorpe Imperial Idealist* (Oxford: Clarendon Press, 1936), 102.

9. While the calculation of the worth to the metropolis of the various staples has been the subject of much contention because of the inability to measure accurately occult trade and proceeds from resale, recent research has provided a rather detailed picture of the tobacco trade. See McCusker and Menard, *The Economy of British America, 1607–1789*, 117–43. See also Jacob M. Price, *France and the Chesapeake: A History of the French Tobacco Monopoly, 1674–1791, and of Its Relationship to the British and American Tobacco Trades* (Ann Arbor: University of Michigan Press, 1973).

10. E. C. Gent. [Ebenezer Cooke], *Sotweed Redivivus: Or the Planters Looking-Glass. In Burlesque Verse. Calculated for the Meridian of Maryland*, ll. 46–48 (Annapolis: [Parks], 1730), 3, See Lemay, *Men of Letters in Colonial Maryland*, 97–100.

11. Richard Lewis (1700?–1734), the Latin master at Annapolis, may have been born in Montgomeryshire, Wales. It is presumed that he was the Richard Lewis who studied three terms at Balliol College, Oxford, in 1718. Shortly thereafter he emigrated to Maryland and quickly distinguished himself as the premier poet of the colony. Conscious of his pioneering role in the refinement of taste and the introduction of belles lettres into the province, Lewis took pains to see that his works were printed and that his friends used their influence to have them reprinted in neighboring colonies and in Great Britain. He is generally deemed the most accomplished neoclassical poet working in British America. J. A. Leo Lemay, "Richard Lewis and Augustan American Poetry," *Publications of the Modern Language Association*, 83 (March, 1968), 80–101; C. Lennart Carlson, "Richard Lewis and the Reception of His Work in England," *American Literature*, 9 (November, 1937), 301–16.

12. Paul G. I. Clemens, *The Atlantic Economy and Colonial Maryland's Eastern Shore: From Tobacco to Grain* (Ithaca: Cornell University Press, 1980), 170–74.

13. Richard Lewis, "To His Excellency Benedict Leonard Calvert, Governour, and Commander in Chief, in and over the Province of Maryland," *The Mouse-Trap, or the Battle of the Cambrians and Mice. A Poem. Translated into English* (Annapolis: W. Parks, 1728), vii-viii.

14. Charles Calvert, fifth Baron Baltimore, arrived in British America on November 14, 1732, and remained until July 10, 1733. He was the only proprietor to visit Maryland, doing so on the centenary of the grant of the Maryland charter to his ancestor, perhaps as a means of consolidating the political dominion of the family over the province at a time when sentiment in Whitehall ran against proprietary governments.

15. Benedict Calvert reported to Charles Calvert, "When all is done, our tobacco sent home, it is perchance the most uncertain commodity that comes to market, and the management of it, there, is of such a nature and method, that it seems to be of all other, the most liable and subject to frauds, in prejudice to the poor planters. Tobacco merchants, who deal in consignments, get great estates, run no risk, and labor only with the pen; the planter can scarce get a living, runs all the risks, attendant upon trade, both as to his Negroes and tobacco, and must work in a variety of labor" (26 October, 1729). In Charles A. Barker, *The Background of the Revolution in Maryland* (New Haven: Yale University Press, 1940), 71.

16. Richard Lewis, *Carmen Seculare, for the year, M,DCC,XXXII* ([Annapolis: Parks], 1732); reprinted in two installments as "A Description of Maryland, extracted from a Poem, entitled, Carmen Seculare, addressed to Ld Baltimore, Proprietor of that Province, now there," *Gentleman's Magazine*, 3 (April, 1733), 209–21; (May 1733), 264. The cited passage is drawn from the latter text.

17. *A Poem by John Markland of Virginia*, ed. J. A. Leo Lemay (Williamsburg: The William Parks Club, 1965), 16.

18. Vertrees J. Wyckoff, *Tobacco Regulation in Colonial Maryland* (Baltimore: Johns Hopkins University Press; University Studies in Historical and Political Science, extra vols., 22, 1936).

19. While in London in 1662 Winthrop delivered on September 24 a paper to the Royal Society "Concerning the Building of Shipps in New England." Register Book of the Royal Society, II, 292–305; "Extracts," Royal Society Journals, Add. Mss. 4447, fol. 36, British Library.

20. Joseph A. Goldenberg, *Shipbuilding in Colonial America* (Charlottesville: University of Virginia Press, 1976), is the sole study; it has not met with general critical approbation.

21. [Richard Lewis], "To Mr. Samuel Hastings, (Ship-wright of Philadelphia) on his launching the Maryland-Merchant, a large ship built by him at Annapolis," *Pennsylvania Gazette*, 61 (13 January, 1729/30), 1–2. For attribution, see A. Owen Aldridge, "Benjamin Franklin and the *Maryland Gazette*," *Maryland Historical Magazine*, 44 (1949), 186–89.

22. Basil Williams, *The Whig Supremacy 1714–1760* (Oxford: Clarendon Press, 1949 edn.), 105–7. It must be pointed out, however, that from the 1730s onward the consumption of wool suffered periods of stagnation. Phyllis Deane, "The Output of the Woolen Industry in the Eighteenth Century," *Journal of Economic History*, 17, 1 (1957), 208–22.

23. John Dyer (1700?–1758) was born the second son of an attorney in Carmarthenshire. Educated at the Westminster School, Dyer resisted attempts to train him to the bar, opting instead for the fine arts. He studied to be a landscape painter in Rome, yet won reputation as the poet of *Ruins of Rome*. Returning to England, he took holy orders, settling in Warwickshire. Shortly thereafter he secured the patronage of Philip Yorke, earl of Hardwicke, in Kerkby, Lincolnshire. There he died of tuberculosis.

24. Of Philip's *Cider* Dr. Johnson observed "that it is . . . at once a book of entertainment and of science." Before Dyer's publication of *The Fleece* (London, 1757) several attempts were made to bind economic information to poetry: Miles Aston, *An Heroick Poem on the Weaving Trade setting forth its Antiquity and Use* (Dublin: Gowan, [1734]); John Brailsford, *Derby Silk-Mill. A Poem* (Nottingham: Ayscough, 1739); Cornelius Arnold, *Commerce* (London, 1751). None of these compositions earned critical notice.

25. John Dyer, "The Fleece," *Poems by John Dyer, L. L. B.* (London: R. and J. Dodsley, 1761), 117–18.

26. The West Indies, besides providing indigo and cochineal, supplied logwood (a dye giving a rich brown color), fustic (yellow), and brazilwood (red). The development of new natural dyes drawn from American sources fueled the rage for fashionable display.

27. Edmund and Dorothy Smith Berkeley, *Dr. Alexander Garden of Charles Town* (Chapel Hill: University of North Carolina Press, 1969), 113–14.

28. C. W. [Charles Woodmason], [Indigo Culture in South Carolina], *Gentleman's Magazine*, 25 (May, 1755), 201–3; (June, 1755), 156–59.

29. *The Letterbook of Eliza Lucas Pinckney 1739–1762*, ed. Elise Pinckney (Chapel Hill: University of North Carolina Press, 1972),

30. Charles Woodmason (1720?–1775?) may have been born in Portsmouth; he appears to have lived in London before emigrating to South Carolina in 1752, leaving a wife and son behind. He became a planter in the Peedee River region, supplementing his income by being a vendor of stores. In 1762 he left for England, returning to Carolina the next year and settling in Charleston. There he entered a civic career whose success was balked in 1765 by his attempt to become a stamp distributor. He returned to England to take holy orders and became a frontier missionary for the Church of England. Roaming the backcountry of Carolina, Woodmason strove to proselytize a population of dissenters and nonbelievers. He composed many of the important tracts for the Regulators during their rising. He left South Carolina in 1771 for Virginia. Charles Woodmason, *The Carolina Backcountry on the Eve of the Revolution*, ed. Richard J. Hooker (Chapel Hill: University of North Carolina Press, Institute of Early American History and Culture, 1953), xi–xxxix.

31. *South Carolina Gazette*, 1200 (25 August, 1757).

32. Hennig Cohen, "A Colonial Poem on Indigo Culture," ll. 1–6, *Agricultural History*, 30 (1956), 42–43.

33. James Grainger, *The Sugar-Cane: A Poem. In Four Books: With Notes* (London:[R. and J. Dodsley], 1764). Grainger (1721?–1766) was trained in medicine at the University of Edinburgh where in 1757 he presented a dissertation on "de modo excitandi ptyalisum et morbis inde pendentibus." He resided briefly in London and won a reputation as a classical scholar with his *A poetical translation of the elegies of Tibullus; and of the poems of Sulpicia* (London: Millar, 1759). While resident in the city he became a familiar of Dr. Johnson. He removed to St. Christopher Island shortly thereafter, composing *The Sugar-Cane* and tracts on agriculture and medicine.

34. I, ll. 278–85. Dr. Johnson, reviewing Grainger's poem, remarked that the poet extends "the bounds of natural history, while he seems only to address the imagination." A friend of Grainger, Johnson claimed great merit for him: "we have been destitute till now of an American poet, that could bear any degree of competition." *Critical Review* (October, 1764), 170.

35. [John Tennent], *Every Man his own Doctor or, the Poor Planter's Physician* (Williamsburg: Parks, 1734). The work was frequently reprinted during the eighteenth century.

36. Grainger wrote the standard medical treatise for the islands, *An essay on the more common West-India diseases; and the remedies which that country itself produces: to which added, some hints on the management, etc. of Negroes* (London: Becket & DeHondt, 1764).

37. Quoted in Noel Deerr, *The History of Sugar*, 2 vols. (London: Chapman and Hall, 1950), vol. 2, 295.

38. William Shenstone (1714–1763) transformed the pastoral mode by making it a vehicle for his ideology. Lyrical forms were infused with narrative to increase their sentimentality. The suffering of simple folk enjoyed a peculiar prominence in his works. Later West Indian poets made their debt to Shenstone equally explicit: the Jamaican poems in manuscript m–3814, Perkins Library, Duke University (attributed incorrectly to John Steward); Philip Freneau's "The Island Field Negro" and "A native of the West Indies," *Poems on subjects arising in England and the West Indies* (London: Faulder, 1783).

39. There are two important histories of the rise of the slave trade in the sugar islands: Richard S. Dunn, *Sugar and Slaves: The Rise of the Planter Class in the English West Indies* (Chapel Hill: University of North Carolina Press, 1972), and Richard B. Sheridan, *Sugar and Slavery: An Economic History of the British West Indies, 1623–1775* (St. Lawrence, Barbados, 1974).

40. John Hippisley (1764), quoted in Deerr, *The History of Sugar*, vol. 2, 290.

41. The prototype for this address and all apostrophes to the empire's great trading rivers appears in John Denham, *Cooper's Hill* (London, 1642). Particularly,

> Nor are his blessings to his banks confined,
> But free and common as the sea or wind;
> When he to boast, or to disperse his stores,
> Full of the tributes of his grateful shores,
> Visits the world, and in his flying towers
> Brings home to us, and makes the Indies ours:
> Finds wealth where 'tis, bestows it where it wants,
> Cities in deserts, woods in cities plants,
> So that to us no thing, no place is strange,
> While his fair bosom is the world's exchange.
>   (179–88)

42. Rum itself is celebrated in Grainger's poem. Yet it enjoyed something of a bad press among colonial poets. Consider Joseph Dumbleton's "A Rhapsody on Rum," *Gentleman's Magazine*, 19 (September, 1749), 424; Lemay 942—a longer version of the poem appeared in several colonial gazettes. Philip Freneau, "The Jug of Rum," *Daily Advertiser* (11 February, 1791), continues the tradition.

43. Deerr, *The History of Sugar*, vol. 2, 269.

44. "The character of a good planter is beautifully described." *Critical Review* (October, 1764), 170, 270–77.

45. Samuel Martin, Sr., *An Essay on Plantership* (London: T. Cadell, 1773; 5th edn. with "A Preface Upon the Slavery of Negroes in the British Colonies), xiv.

46. [A. Wagstaffe], *The Politicks and Patriots of Jamaica A Poem* (London: T. Warner, 1718), ll. 5–10.

47. [Edward "Ned" Ward], "A Trip to Jamaica," *The Second Volume of the Writings of the Author of the London-Spy* (London: J. How, 1704), 161.

48. Thomas Walduck, Letter of Thomas Walduck to James Petiver, 12 November, 1710. Sloane MS 2302, British Library. The Walduck correspondence to Petiver from 1710 to 1712 is of extraordinary interest, reflecting upon aspects of culture, commerce, history, and natural philosophy in the West Indies. Dunn prints the text of the acrostic, *Sugar and Slaves*, 340.

49. *The Groans of Jamaica express'd in a Letter from a Gentleman residing there, to his Friend in London* (London, 1714), 13, 17.

50. One token of the development of a humanitarian attitude toward African slaves among poetic commentators on the West Indies is the concern manifested in recording slave burial customs. See, for instance, the extraordinary verse description of a negro funeral in John Singleton, *A General Description of the West Indian Islands* (London, 1767); Book III, ll. 524–77. One can recognize the antecedents of the New Orleans funeral customs in Singleton's description.

51. *An Essay concerning Slavery, and the Danger Jamaica is expos'd to from the too great number of Slaves, and the too little care that is taken to manage them* (London: Charles Corbett [1746]), 19.

52. Martin, *An Essay on Plantership*, 2.

53. No adequate literary history of the abolitionist poets exists, and to write one would be a worthy effort. Besides the poets named, such a study should include research into the

work of William Roscoe, author of the *Wrongs of Africa* (London, 1788); Edward Rushton, whose *West Indian Eclogues* (London: W. Lowndes & J. Philips, 1787) includes some of the most lurid scenes of the punishment of runaways; also the author of "The Field Negroe; or the effect of Civilization" (*Poems, On Subjects arising in England and the West Indies*).

54. Singleton, a player with Hallam's company, composed his descriptive poem during a tour of the islands and included accounts of his visits to planters in the "British, Dutch, and Danish Governments." Book II contains an apostrophe to Grainger.

55. *Jamaica, a poem, in three parts. Written in that island, in the year MDCCLXXVI*, Part I, ll. 180–91 (London: William Nicoll, 1777), 18. The author also wrote "A Poetical Epistle, from the Island of Jamaica, to a Gentleman of the Middle-Temple."

56. The particular interest of this book is its attempt to convince the West Indian planters on the grounds of economic doctrine that the slave system did not perform as well as they believed it did. By combining a critique of the economic efficacy of the slave system with a moral condemnation, the author was the most thoroughgoing of the abolitionist poets. John Marjoribanks, *Slavery: an essay in verse inscribed to planters and others concerned in the sale of negro slaves* (Edinburgh, 1792).

57. Hannah More, *Slavery: a poem* (London, 1788).

58. James Field Stanfield, *The Guinea voyage: a poem, in three books* (London: James Phillips, 1789), 18.

59. Adam Smith, *An Inquiry into the Nature and Causes of the Wealth of Nations (1776)*, ed. R[oy] H. Campbell, A[ndrew] S. Skinner, and W[illiam] B. Todd (Oxford: Oxford University Press, 1976).

60. John Locke, *Two Treatises of Government* (London, 1689), 1.

61. The Ogilvie-Forbes family papers are held by the Queens Library, University of Aberdeen. Permission to quote from them has been granted by M. F. Ogilvie-Forbes of Boyndlie House. A brief biographical sketch of Ogilvie prepared by a descendent is found in the microfilm collection, manuscript department, South Caroliniana Library.

62. This and all other citations are drawn from my edition of George Ogilvie, *Carolina; or, the Planter (1776), Southern Literary Journal*, special issue (1986), which presents the privately printed 1791 text of the poem in facsimile as well as the text of letters written during Ogilvie's residence in South Carolina.

63. Jay Fliegelman, *Prodigals & Pilgrims: The American Revolution against Patriarchal Authority 1750–1800* (Cambridge: Cambridge University Press, 1982), 113–22.

64. Explicit rejections of the familial metaphor begin as early as George Mason's June 6, 1766, letter "To the Committee of Merchants in Lond," *The Papers of George Mason, 1725–1792*, ed. Robert A. Rutland (Chapel Hill: University of North Carolina Press, 1970), vol. 1, 65–73. It is repeatedly attacked in Thomas Paine's various writings.

65. Kenneth Silverman, *A Cultural History of the American Revolution* (New York: Crowell, 1976), 82–85.

66. Rowland Rugeley and his brother Henry came to Carolina in 1769. Rowland was appointed register of the colony; Henry served as the American agent of their father's cloth-shipping business in St. Ives. Both set themselves up as planters in the Camden area. Having published *Miscellaneous Poems and Translations from LaFontaine and Others* (Cambridge, 1763) before arriving in Carolina, Rowland established himself quickly among the literati of the province. The poet and his family died in 1776, the estate falling to Henry, who became a notorious loyalist militia captain. The Rugeley family papers, including materials of Rowland and Henry, are on deposit as manuscripts X 311/1–242, Bedfordshire County Record Office.

67. "I fear they must all be subjected to the most humiliating circumstance of human nature—that of being *sold like the Brutes that perrish*; and when deprived of the little indulgences I allowd them, will they now have reason to curse me for having taught them wants they might else have never known? not that I would insinuate that my slaves are used

better than any others—some Masters I know & I hope there are many who treat theirs with the utmost humanity—and If I do sell mine, I shall certainly endeavour to find such Masters for them and not let them go, as many do, to the highest bidders, without regarding any other consideration." Letter of George Ogilvie to Alexander Ogilvie, 25 April, 1778, *Southern Literary Journal*, special issue (1986), 129.

68. On July 24, 1789, Garden wrote Ogilvie a letter containing an extensive description of Otranto. *Southern Literary Journal*, special issue (1986), 132–34. The plantation house still stands. The grounds have been converted into a housing development.

5. THE PROBLEM OF THE PREROGATIVE

1. D. E. C. Yale, ed., *Sir Matthew Hale's The Prerogatives of the King*, Publications of the Selden Society, 92 (London: Selden Society, 1976).

2. A. Berriedale Keith, *Constitutional History of the First British Empire* (Oxford: Clarendon Press, 1930), 9–17.

3. David Lindsay Keir, *The Constitutional History of Modern Britain since 1485* (Princeton, N.J.: Van Nostrand, 1960), 347–49.

4. Leonard W. Labaree, *Royal Instructions to the British Colonial Governors 1670–1776*, 2 vols. (New York: Appleton-Century, 1935), vol. 1, 239–82.

5. Keith, *Constitutional History*, 202.

6. Stephen Botien, "Printers and the American Revolution," *The Press and the American Revolution*, ed. Bernard Bailyn and John B. Hench (Worcester: American Antiquarian Society, 1980), 16–23.

7. Michael Harris, "Print and Politics in the Age of Walpole," *Britain in the Age of Walpole*, ed. Jeremy Black (New York: St. Martin's Press, 1984), 189–93.

8. Richard Buel, Jr., "Freedom of the Press in Revolutionary America," *The Press and the Revolution*, 68–76.

9. The Governor's Council could not serve as the censorship board, for it was not in session during much of the year when items issued from the press.

10. *Boston Weekly News-Letter* (11 January, 1721).

11. See for instance Isaiah Thomas's account of the arrest of Daniel Fowle for printing *The Monster of Monsters*, an anti-assembly satire, *The History of Printing in America* (New York: Weathervane Books, 1970), 126–33.

12. Keith, *Constitutional History*, 237. The figures have long been matters of debate. Robert E. Brown has argued for much higher percentages of adult males exercising the franchise. *Middle-Class Democracy and the Revolution in Massachusetts, 1691–1780* (Ithaca: Cornell University Press, 1955), 50. Yet Brown's figures, in turn, have been questioned. What seems incontrovertible, however, is the expansion of the franchise over the course of the eighteenth century and the increasing consolidation of power in the lower house of Assemblies. These tendencies were not restricted to New England and New York. See Jack P. Greene, *The Quest for Power: The Lower Houses of Assembly in the Southern Royal Colonies, 1689–1776* (Chapel Hill: University of North Carolina Press, 1963). The role of literature in the "democratization" in colonies other than Massachusetts and New York could be written. Samuel Keimer, ed., *Caribbeana*, 2 vols. (London: Osborne, 1741) collects many of the most eloquent controversial writings composed in the West-Indies, particularly Barbados. Most of these polemics are in prose. What is striking about the controversial literature in Massachusetts and New York is the high incidence of poetic compositions, signifying the survival of the genre of poems on the affairs of state in the New World.

6. THE PAPER WARS IN MASSACHUSETTS

1. [Letter from London Merchant dated 6 February, 1729/30], *Boston Gazette*, 546 (25 May, 1730).

2. Extracted, *Boston Gazette*, 544 (11 May, 1730).

3. *Boston Gazette*, 558 (17 August, 1730).

4. "The Speech of His Excellency Jonathan Belcher, Esq; Captain General & Governour in Chief, to and over His Majesty's Province of the Massachusetts-Bay in New-England," *Boston Gazette*, 562 (14 September, 1730).

5. The "other Matters of dangerous Consequence" to which Belcher alludes were the assembly's issuance of bills of credit without a term of redemption and the disinclination to fund repairs on frontier forts.

6. Belcher may have been recalling the lines of George Granville, Baron Landsdowne, concerning Cato's suicide:

> The Honest man who Strives and is undone,
> Not fortune but his Virtue Keeps him down.
> Had Cato bent beneath the Conquering Cause
> He might have liv'd to give new Senates laws:
> But on Vile terms, Disdaining to be great,
> He perisht by his choice and not his fate.

7. "Lines put over the Door of the General Court," *New York Gazette* (2 November, 1730). Manuscript copies survive in the John Smibert notebook and the Benjamin Walker Diary, Massachusetts Historical Society. The Walker text notes, "1730 I hear That when our assembly sat at Roxbury a paper Containing the within lines was put on the Roxbury meeting house door where our assembly was then sitting (& one at The house where the Governor & Concill sat [)]." A smallpox outbreak in Boston had caused the relocation of the government.

8. The tradition of imitations is discussed in Kenneth Scott, " 'Rattling' Verses on Royal Prerogative," *New York Folklore Quarterly*, 13 (1957), 195–203.

9. [Lewis Morris, Sr.], "On the word *that* in the Boston Poem," Robert Morris Manuscripts, Rutgers University Library.

10. *New York Gazette* (2 November, 1730).

11. "The above lines, whare written on a piece of paper That some person had fixt to the west door of the Town house (I & several others see them There Early in ye morn some time after I see Mr. Samll Wentworth a young man that lives at Mr. H. Dering Tare down[)]," Benjamin Walker Diary, vol. 1, loose papers, Massachusetts Historical Society. Walker lived on Corn Hill in Boston. His diary is an invaluable source of information on the 1730s and 1740s. I thank Barbara Ward of the Essex Institute for calling it to my attention. A copy of this poem is also found in the Smibert notebook.

12. "1730 Boston Sept ye 11 The above lines I hear ware Taken down from the Town house door, In the morn by one of Mr. Dll Henchman's lads So Mr. H. Adams Told me & shew'd me the Original paper himself that I Took the above Coppy from," Benjamin Walker Diary, vol. 1, loose papers, Massachusetts Historical Society.

13. Robert E. Moody, ed., "Boston's First Play," *Proceedings of the Massachusetts History Society* (1980) 111–40. A second manuscript copy of the play, a nineteenth-century transcription, not noted by Moody, survives in the Bancroft collection, New York Public Library. It supplies the play's name, *Belcher Apostate*. This manuscript was discovered by J. A. Leo Lemay.

14. Michael G. Hall, ed., "The Autobiography of Increase Mather," *Proceedings of the American Antiquarian Society*, 71, 2 (1962), 307–8.

15. David Lovejoy, *The Glorious Revolution in America* (1972; rept., Middletown, Conn.: Wesleyan University Press, 1987) is the standard history of the unrest.

16. "The Massachusetts Charter of 1691," *The Glorious Revolution in America: Documents on the Colonial Crisis of 1689*, ed. Michael G. Hall, Lawrence H. Leder, and Michael G. Kammen (Chapel Hill: University of North Carolina Press, Institute of Early American History and Culture, 1964), 76–79.

17. "Political Fables by Cotton Mather," *The Andros Tracts*, Publications of the Prince Society (Boston: Prince Society, 2 1869), 326–27. Robert Calef, in his attack on the Mathers in *More Wonders of the Invisible World*, rather archly observed that "tho' this Paper was judged not convenient to be printed, yet some Copies were taken, the Author having shewn a variety of *Heathen* Learning in it" (Salem, Mass.: Carlton, 1796), 151.

18. On the Mathers' imperial ideology, see Philip S. Haffenden, *New England in the English Nation 1689–1713* (Oxford: Clarendon Press, 1974), 52–64.

19. Calef observed of the fable, "His Father under the Name of *Mercurius* and himself under the Name of *Orpheus* are extoll'd, and the great actions of *Mercurius* magnified. . . . And indeed the whole Country are compared to no better than Beasts, except *Mercurius* and *Orpheus*, and the Governour himself must not escape being termed an Elephant," *More Wonders*, 151.

20. This suggestion arises as an implication in Jeremiah Dummer's *A Defence of the New-England Charters* (Boston: Kneeland, 1721).

21. Cotton Mather, *A Pillar of Gratitude* (Boston, 1700).

22. Haffenden, *New England in the English Nation*, 72–97.

23. Benjamin Tompson, "To Lord Bellamont when entering Governour of the Massachustts," *Benjamin Tompson Colonial Bard*, 157.

24. Everett Kimball, *The Public Life of Joseph Dudley: A Study of the Colonial Policy of the Stuarts in New England 1660–1715* (New York: Longmans, Green, & Co., 1911), 39–56.

25. Haffenden, *New England in the English Nation*, 190–95.

26. Kathryn Zabelle Derounian, "'Mutual sweet Content': The Love Poetry of John Saffin," *Puritan Poets and Poetics; Seventeenth-Century American Poetry in Theory and Practice*, ed. Peter White (University Park: Pennsylvania State University Press, 1985), 175–85. The standard discussion of Saffin's literary career is Alyce E. Sands, "John Saffin: Seventeenth-Century American Citizen and Poet," Ph.D. diss., The Pennsylvania State University, 1965.

27. "To his Excellency Joseph Dudley Eqr Gover: &c." *John Saffin His Book, 1665–1708*, ed. Caroline Hazard (New York: Harbor Press, 1928). Since there are occasional transcription errors in Hazard's texts, I've checked all cited passages against the Saffin manuscript collection in the Rhode Island Historical Society.

28. John Saffin, "Bristol 22th January 1704 To his Excellency Joseph Dudley Esqr Govr: &c," ll. 19–25, *John Saffin His Book*, 80. In a marginal gloss Saffin notes, "This Letter was written to his Excellency upon the Occasion of the Newes that his Excellency was on the [ ] of January 1704 goeing over Charles River upon the Ice with a sley, and four horses with his Wife and Daughters, the ice suddenly broke, and all the horses falling into the River the two hindermost Horses were Drowned, and His Excellency and His, hardly Escaped but were Wonderfully preserved Laus Deo."

29. Kenneth Silverman, *Selected Letters of Cotton Mather* (Baton Rouge: Louisiana State University Press, 1971), 77–82.

30. Joseph Dudley, [Letter to Increase and Cotton Mather], *Massachusetts Historical Society Collections*, 1st ser., 3 (1794), 135–37.

31. There has been some debate whether Cotton Mather wrote these tracts; there is little doubt that the attack against Dudley, however, was instigated by the Mathers. *Massachusettes Historical Society Collections*, 5th ser., 6 (1879), 96–131.

32. The grounds for believing that Joseph Dudley or his son Paul wrote *A Modest Inquiry* are much stronger than those for the Mather authorship of the two London pamphlets. *Massachusetts Historical Society Collections*, 5th ser., 6 (1879), 65–95.

33. John Saffin, "New England's Lamentation of her present S[t]ate &c," *John Saffin His Book*, 164–67.

34. Benjamin Walker Diary, loose papers, Massachusetts History Society. Isaiah Thomas

located a manuscript of this poem some sixty years after its original circulation and printed it in *Royal American Magazine*, 1 (October, 1774), 392.

35. Robert E. Brown, *Middle Class Democracy and the Revolution in Massachusetts*, 120–49. Richard Bushman prefers to employ the English designation, Country Party, for the Old Charter faction, *King and People in Provincial Massachusetts* (Chapel Hill: University of North Carolina Press, Institute of Early American History and Culture, 1985), 253–267. Yet the opposition of Country and Court does not fit the more complicated allignments in Massachusetts.

36. Herbert Osgood, *The American Colonies in the Eighteenth Century*, 4 vols. (Gloucester, Mass.: Peter Smith, 1957), vol. 3, 153.

37. Joseph J. Malone, *Pine Trees and Politics, 1691–1775* (Madison: University of Wisconsin Press, 1964).

38. Osgood, *The American Colonies in the Eighteenth Century*, vol. 3, 155.

39. Elisha Cooke, [Jr.], *Mr. Cook's Just and Seasonable Vindication: Respecting some Affairs transacted in the late General Assembly at Boston, 1720* ([Boston], [1720]), 14.

40. Ibid., 11.

41. *Boston Gazette* (11 July, 1720), 3.

42. War, of course, also proved a problem for the Old Charter ideology, for the hatred of French Catholics and the hunger for Indian-held territory inclined the Old Charter faction to favor imperial contests. Yet the structure of military authority, the taxes to support martial enterprises, and the level of expenses accrued all became matters of complaint.

43. [Paul Dudley], *News from Robinson Cruso's Island: With an Appendix relating to Mr. Cook's late Pamphlet* ([Boston], 1720), 2–3. My attribution.

44. [Elisha Cooke, Jr.], *Reflections upon Reflections: Or, More News from Robinson Cruso's Island in a Dialogue between a Country Representative and a Boston Gentleman, July 12, 1720* (Cruso's Island [Boston], 1720), 2.

45. The words *loyalty* and *patriotism* have a peculiar history from the Glorious Revolution to the American Revolution. The Jacobites employed *loyalty* to signify a personal attachment to the Stuart monarchy. The Whigs adopted the term as a more general attachment to the monarchy; thus when the Hanoverian settlement occurred, American Whigs, both Old Charter and New, published "loyal" testimonies (see *The Loyal American's Almanac*). The term *patriot* became associated with Marlborough's interest during the reign of Queen Anne; during Walpole's regime it came to denominate the militant faction of the Whigs (and several attached Tories) who opposed the commercial peace of the 1730s.

46. [Elisha Cooke, Jr.?], *New News from Robinson Cruso's Island, in a Letter to a Gentleman at Portsmouth* ([Boston], 1720]), 5–6.

47. [Matthew Adams], "A Gratulatory Poem received from a Friend the Day after the Arrival of His Excellency Governour Burnet," ll. 1–6, *Boston Weekly News-Letter*, 91 (25 July, 1728), 1–2.

48. Burnet's accomplishments are the theme of an elegy by a New York poet, "An Eleagy upon His Excellency William Burnet, Esq; who departed this Life Sept. 7th 1729 AEtat 42," *New York Gazette*, 206 (13 October, 1729). The poet might be Francis Harrison. "Ye fairer Souls whom the gay Nine inspire, / Mourn him who tun'd your Tongues and fed your Fire." Mather Byles, *A Poem Presented To His Excellency William Burnet, Esq; On his Arrival at Boston, July 19. 1728* ([Boston]: By Order of his Excellency the Governour, 1728), 3.

49. [Matthew Adams], "A Gratulatory Poem," ll. 31–34, 39–43.

50. Osgood, *The American Colonies in the Eighteenth Century*, vol. 3, 203.

51. "Election Day A New Ballad of Boston May the 18, 1729," Benjamin Walker Diary, loose papers, Massachusetts Historical Society. Walker addendum: "Boston in N.E. June the 9:1729. This taken from a coppy Taken from Mr. Joseph Gouches."

52. James Egan, "Nathaniel Ward and the Marprelate Tradition," *Early American Literature*, 15 (1980), 59–71.

53. Lemay, private conversation with the author, December, 1986. Lemay points to Morris's several compositions in play form, the provenance of both surviving manuscripts from New York, the Bancroft collection copy from the Morris family, and the similarity of ideology found in the play and in the anti-Cosby material of the 1730s.

54. Moody, ed., "Boston's First Play," 114.

55. Though the franchise was limited, the commonality participated in the play of politics in the town meeting. Thus the glimpse of the operation of this democratic institution is of more than usual historical interest. Michael Zuckerman, "The Social Context of Democracy in Massachusetts," *Colonial America: Essays in Politics and Social Development*, ed. Stanley N. Katz and John M. Murrin (New York: Alfred A. Knopf, 1983), 380–93.

56. S. M. [Samuel Mather], *A Country Treat Upon the Second Paragraph in His Excellency's Speech, Decemb. 17. 1730*, ll. 5–16 ([Boston], 1730), broadside.

57. See *A Letter To An Eminent Clergy-Man in the Massachusett's Bay. Containing some Just Remarks, and necessary Cautions, relating to Publick Affairs in that Province* (Boston, 1720).

58. Clifford Shipton, "Elisha Cooke," *Sibley's Harvard Graduates*, vol. 4, 354–55. Bushman, *King and People*, 77.

59. Clifford Shipton, *Sibley's Harvard Graduates*, vol. 8, 42–53. Also Thomas V. Duggan, "Joseph Green—The Boston Butler," Master's thesis, Columbia University, 1941.

60. Joseph Green, *A Mournfull Lamentation for the Sad and Deplorable Death of Mr. Old Tenor* (Boston, [1750]).

61. David S. Shields, "Clio Mocks the Masons: Joseph Green's Anti-Masonic Satires," *Deism, Masonry, and the Enlightenment; Essays Honoring Alfred Owen Aldridge*, ed. J. A. Leo Lemay (Newark: University of Delaware Press, 1987), 109–26.

62. Pollard visited Rome and had a ring blessed by the pope. In satires by Thomas Kilby and John Barrell, he is designated the man who kissed the pope's toe.

63. Joseph Green, "Govr. Belchers Speach to Assembly N:Hampshire in Verse," Smith Townsend manuscripts, Massachusetts Historical Society; another copy, F. L. Gay Papers, Box 1 1374–1823, Massachusetts Historical Society.

64. Joseph Green, "Answer to ye Govr Speach to ye Assembly New Hamp in Verse," ll. 1–22, 27 January, 1733/34. Smith-Carter Papers, Massachusetts Historical Society; another copy, F. L. Gay Papers, Box 1 1374–1823, Massachusetts Historical Society.

65. This prefatory statement is found only in the copy in the Smith-Carter Papers.

66. G——[Joseph Green], "Belchers Answer to an Answer of the House of Representatives of N H in Verse," ll. 1–51, Smith-Carter Papers, Massachusetts Historical Society.

67. [Joseph Green], "A True & Impartial Accot. of the Celebration of the Prince of Orange's Nuptials at P--------," ll. 1–10, 3 June, 1734, Smith-Carter manuscripts, Massachusetts Historical Society.

68. "An Account of the Procession of the General Court into Salisbury, in the Year 1736. when the Affair of the Boundary Line was debated between the two Provinces of the Massachusetts and New-Hampshire," ll. 1–10, *A Collection of Poems. By several Hands* (Boston: Green & Gookin, 1744), 54–55.

7. THE SPREAD OF BOSTON PRINCIPLES

1. William Smith, Jr., *The History of the Province of New York* 2 vols., ed. Michael Kammen (Cambridge, Mass.: Belknap Press, The John Harvard Library, 1972), vol. 2, 9.

2. Richard Steele, *The Tatler* (17 September 17, 1709); cited in Mary Lou Lustig, *Robert Hunter 1666–1743: New York's Augustan Statesman* (Syracuse: Syracuse University Press, 1983), 59.

3. Lovejoy, *The Glorious Revolution in America,* 255–57 Lovejoy justifies much of Leisler's action on legal grounds.

4. Robert Livingston, "A Satyr Upon the Times," ll. 25–28, *The Glorious Revolution in America: Documents,* 132–33. See Lawrence H. Leder, *Robert Livingston 1654–1728, and the*

Politics of Colonial New York (Chapel Hill: University of North Carolina Press, 1961), 171. The satire was circulated as a manuscript among the Hudson Valley landowners.

5. Patricia U. Bonomi, *A Factious People: Politics and Society in Colonial New York* (New York: Columbia University Press, 1971).

6. Lustig, *Robert Hunter*, 50–58.

7. Cadwallader Colden, Letter 12, Colden to Alexander Colden, 15 October, 1759, Appendix B, William Smith, Jr., *The History of the Province of New-York*, vol. 1, 306.

8. Robert Hunter, "Androboros A Biographical Farce in Three Acts, VIZ. The Senate, The Consistory, and The Apotheosis By Governor Hunter," *Satiric Comedies: America's Lost Plays*, ed. Walter J. Meserve and William Reardon, vol. 21 (Bloomington: Indiana University Press, 1969). All quotations will be drawn from this edition. See also Lawrence H. Leder, "Androboros, A Biographical Farce in Three Acts," *Bulletin of the New York Public Library*, 68 (1964), 153–60.

9. Thomas Noel, *Theories of the Fable in the Eighteenth Century* (New York: Columbia University Press, 1975), 31.

10. The sole surviving copy of the printed play in the collection of the Huntington Library contains Hunter's inked-in identifications of the characters.

11. Stephen Saunders Webb, "The Strange Career of Francis Nicholson," *William and Mary Quarterly*, 3d ser., 23 (1966), 513–48.

12. John Fox, "The Publick Spirit," *The Wanderer* (London, 1718); for an assessment of his career, see Kenneth Murdock, "William Byrd and the Virginian Author of *The Wanderer*," *Harvard Studies & Notes in Philology and Literature*, 17 (1935), 129–36.

13. Colden, Letter 12, *The History of the Province of New-York*, vol. 1, 306.

14. Clifford K. Shipton, "William Vesey," *New England Life in the 18th Century: Representative Biographies from Sibley's Harvard Graduates* (Cambridge, Mass.: Belknap Press, 1963), 12–19. For Hunter's official assessment of Vesey, see Letter 665, 10 November, 1715, *Colonial Papers: America and West Indies*, 333.

15. *Documents Relating to the History of Colonial New York*, ed. E. B. O'Callaghan, 15 vols. (Albany: State of New York, 1856–1887), vol. 5, 311.

16. Shipton, *New England Life*, 12.

17. Lustig, *Robert Hunter*, 106–12.

18. [Poyer letters, 3 December, 1710, 3 May, 1711]. *Ecclesiastical Records of New York*, vol. 3, 1875–79.

19. An Oxford graduate, John Checkley (1680–1754) matched an ugly countenance with a polemical spirit. His visage was celebrated in an epigram on Smibert's portrait of Checkley by Joseph Green, which grew so famous that it became the wit's autograph piece, supplied to correspondents who wrote requesting a piece from the poet's pen:

> John had thy Sickness snatch'd thee from our sight
> And sent thee to the realms of Endless Night
> Posterity perhaps had never known
> Thine Eye by beard, thy Cowl and shavin Crown
> But now thy fate by Smyberts matchless hand
> Secure of immortality shall stand
> When Nature into Ruin shall be hurld
> And the last Conflagration burn the world
> This piece shall still survive the General Evil
> For flames we know can ne'er consume the Devil

Text: Benjamin Lynde [Jr.] Poetry Collection, Oliver Papers, Massachusetts Historical Society. Checkley's attacks on dissenting theology and church polity are contained in *Choice Dialogues Concerning Election and Predestination* (Boston, 1720), and *A Modest Proof of the Order and Government Settled by Christ and His Apostles in the Church* (Boston: Fleet for Eliot, 1723).

20. Lustig, *Robert Hunter*, 138–39.

21. In 1705 the House of Commons had approved a resolution stating that "whoever goes about to suggest . . . that the Church is in danger . . . is an Enemy to the Queen, the Church, and the Kingdom." On November 5, 1709, the arch-champion of the Church of England, Dr. Henry Sacheverell, preached a sermon at St. Paul's cathedral excoriating dissenters and low church partisans as threats to the church. The Tory party printed and distributed some forty thousand copies of the piece. Sacheverell was put on trial. When the trial began on February 27, 1710/11, the London mob staged a massive demonstration on his behalf and took to burning Presbyterian pulpits in town. Sachaverell was impeached by a seven to six vote of the clergy. But to the disgust of ardent Whigs, Parliament determined upon a mild punishment.

22. Lustig, *Robert Hunter*, 84–90.

23. *Samuel Mulford's Speech to the Assembly at New-York* (New York: [Bradford], 1714).

24. Joseph Addison, *Spectator*, 183 (29 September, 1711).

25. Antoine Houdar de La Motte, *Fables nouvelles* (Paris, 1719), xiii. Cited in Noel, *Theories of the Fable*, 40.

26. Cotton Mather, "Political Fables," 328–29.

27. Noel, *Theories of the Fable*, 8–10.

28. John D. Runcie, "The Problem of Anglo-American Politics in Bellomont's New York," *William and Mary Quarterly*, 3d ser., 25 (1969), 191–217.

29. John Hughes, "Utopia," *An Ephemeris for the Year . . . 1726* (Philadelphia: A. Bradford, [1725]). A Church of England partisan and ally of Lieutenant Governor Keith, Hughes was one of the most able controversial poets of early Pennsylvania. He published much of his verse in his almanacs, which were issued in Philadelphia until 1735, though none survive for years after 1728.

30. [Benjamin Franklin?], "The Rats and the Cheese, a Fable," *Pennsylvania Gazette* (24 September, 1730). Regarding attribution, see J. A. Leo Lemay, *The Canon of Benjamin Franklin, 1722–1776: New Attributions and Reconsiderations* (Newark: University of Delaware Press, 1986), 46–47.

31. [Alexander Spotswood], Letter and fable signed John Spotswood, *Virginia Gazette* (17 June, 1737).

32. Herodotus, Aristophanes, and Plato all cite details of Aesop's legendary biography. Most scholars believe that a fifth century B.C. life, now lost, circulated with a copy of the fables. The version of the biography that has come down is a fanciful construct and was debunked by Bentley in his famous critique inaugurating the battle between the ancients and the moderns.

33. Samuel Stelle Smith, *Lewis Morris Anglo-American Statesman ca. 1613–1691* (Atlantic Highlands, N.J.: Humanities Press, 1983), 90–93.

34. The standard biography is Eugene R. Sheridan, *Lewis Morris, 1671–1746: A Study in Early American Politics* (Syracuse, N.Y.: Syracuse University Press, 1981).

35. Edmond Dale Daniel, "'Dialogue Concerning Trade': A Satirical View of New York in 1726," *New York History* (1974), 199–229. Morris's predilection for the dialogue form may reflect his view of politics as a clash of interests.

36. Morris as a political polemicist preferred to circulate his poetry and dialogues in manuscript; his prose was published. The surviving Morris manuscripts are scattered in several collections: the New York Public Library, The New-York Historical Society, the Massachusetts Historical Society. The bulk of the literary work, however, is preserved among the Robert Morris Papers, Rutgers University Library. Eugene Sheridan is currently preparing an edition of these writings.

37. "By a gentleman of New Jersey in America," [verso: Governour Lewis Morris], "The Mock Monarchy or the Kingdom of Apes A Poem," Robert Morris Papers, Special Collections and Archives, Rutgers University Libraries.

38. William Smith, Jr., *The History of the Province of New-York*, vol. 1, 256–57.

39. Charles M. Andrews, *The Colonial Period of American History*, 4 vols. (New Haven, Conn.: Yale University Press, 1934), vol. 3, 116–21.

40. Councilor Francis Harrison (1690?–1739?) of New York was the principal literary voice in favor of the prerogative during the paper war in New York during the term of Governor Cosby. An opportunist who in 1730 switched political affiliation from the River party to the Court party to profit from the "oblong grant" land transfer between New York and Connecticut, he earned the particular hatred of James Alexander, William Smith, and Lewis Morris, Sr. When Cosby came to power in 1732, Harrison became the laureate of the executive, supplying panegyrics to the *New York Gazette* to counter the libels and satires appearing in Zenger's *New York Weekly Journal*. He became the center of controversy concerning a forged threat in 1734 and later lost his reputation when it was learned he used his position to conduct vindictive suits against innocent figures. In 1735 he was dispatched (some believe he fled) to England to testify on behalf of Cosby in the hearing of Lewis Morris's complaint. Cosby's death left him bereft of fortune and patronage. He died shortly afterwards in poverty.

41. *New York Weekly Journal*, 8 (24 December, 1733).

42. *New York Weekly Journal*, 6 (10 December, 1733).

43. Bonomi, *A Factious People*, 98.

44. Cadwallader Colden, "History of Gov. William Cosby's Administration and of Lt. Gov. George Clarke's Administration through 1737," *Collections of the New York Historical Society*, 68 (1935), 288.

45. *New York Weekly Journal*, 11 (14 January, 1733/34).

46. Colden, "History of Gov. William Cosby's Administration," 283.

47. Ibid.

48. Bonomi, *A Factious People*, 108.

49. Stanly N. Katz, ed. *A Brief Narrative of the Case and Trial of John Peter Zenger, Printer of The New York Weekly Journal, by James Alexander* (Cambridge, Mass.: Belknap Press, Harvard University Press, 1963), 1–35.

50. *New York Weekly Journal*, 12 (21 January, 1733/34).

51. Stephen Botein, ed., *Mr. Zenger's Malice & Falshood: Six Issues of the "New York Weekly Journal," 1733–34* (Charlottesville: University of Virginia, American Antiquarian Society, 1985).

52. William Smith, Jr., *The History of the Province of New-York*, vol. 2, 14–15.

53. Leslie Shepard, *The Broadside Ballad: A Study in Origins and Meaning* (Wakefield, U.K.: EP Publishers, 1962), 32.

54. [Joseph Breintnall?], "To the Memory of John Dommett, the unborn Poet, lately deceased," *Pennsylvania Gazette*, 556 (9 August, 1739).

55. Non Ignotus, "The Masque of Life," *New York Weekly Journal*, 243 (10 July, 1738).

56. Gilbert Burnet, *Bishop Burnet's History of His Own Time*, 2 vols. (London, 1724, 1734), vol. 1, 792.

57. [Lewis Morris, Sr.], *A Song made upon the Election of the New magistrates for this Citty to the Tune of to you fair Ladies now at Land &c.* ([New York, broadside, 1734]). Manuscript texts: Lewis Morris holograph, Robert Morris Papers, Special Collections and Archives, Rutgers University Libraries; Miscellaneous Papers Songs (Cosby 22), Manuscript Division, New York Public Library.

58. [Francis Harrison], ["Concerning the Purveyors of Scandal in New York"], *New York Gazette*, 442 (15 April, 1734).

59. A collection of songs, several in the hand of James Alexander, survives: Miscellaneous Papers Songs (Cosby 19, 20, 21, 23, 24), Manuscripts, New York Public Library. Cosby 19: "of a merry sing song burnt by sound of ding dong," twelve lines, also "A mournfull Elegy on the funeral pile & Execution of [the] ballad or ballads burnt by publick authority before a

grea[t crowd in] a small town in a certain Country under the Northern hemesp[here on a] certain day since the year 1600," thirteen numbered quatrains; also "The last words and testament of the song on the election condemn'd to be burnt by the C---t partie," three unnumbered quatrains. Cosby 20: "Poor Toby's Fate or a farewell to Courtiers To the Tune of Daphny our Dearest bitch ohone ohone" [Satire upon Francis Harrison], forty-five lines plus refrain, published *New York Weekly Journal*, 119 (16 February 1735/36,) under pseudonym "Thos. Right." Cosby 21: (see footnote 60). Cosby 23: [Untitled Horatian Imitation], epigraph: justum et tenacem propositie virum, non avium ardor prava jubentium, not vultus instantis tyranni mentes quatit volida," thirty lines, first line: "Assist O! god my muse with rage divine." Cosby 24: [Untitled Verse Epistle rebuking the Court party], twenty-two lines, first line: "I've read with care the c------ls letter ore."

60. D[avi]d H[u]m[phre]ys, "The Lamentable Story of two Fatherless & Motherless Twins which Lately Appeared in ye City of N-w-Y-k who for their Prophetick Cries where Condemn'd to be burnt by ye Common Hangman which was Accordingly Executed &c." Two manuscript copies survive. The text reproduces the version found in the Cadwallader Colden Papers, [unsigned, undated ms of 1734], Courtesy of The New-York Historical Society; this was published by Alex J. Wall, ed., "Verses on the Burning of Two Songs in New York City November, 1734," *Cadwallader Colden Papers: Additional Papers 1715–1748*, 8 vols. (New York: New York Historical Society, 1934), vol. 8, 251–52. A second version, dated 1734, with the author designation as given here survives in the manuscript collection of the New York Public Library, Miscellaneous Papers, Songs (Cosby 21). The Colden manuscript is indented into quatrains, revealing the stanzaic form of the song. The second manuscript is a later version of the song, unindented, and incorporating two additions; these appear in the manuscript as marginal interpolations in a different hand. The NYPL manuscript contains the following variants:

Line	Variant			
9	ye]the	York] [blank]		
10	Two]two	Appear]appear		
11	No Parent Careing]no parent careing		own]own	
12	For Reasons]for reasons			
13	As]as	ye]the		
14	Naked]naked			
15	Arbitrary Power]arbitrary power		Cried]cryed	
16	Knaves]knaves			
17	ye]the	of ye]and the		
18	Of]of	Ministers of ye State]M————rs of S————te		
19	Who]who	and Common Right]& common right		
20	Scheemes]Schemes			
29	ye Great Men Come]the great men came			
30	The Cries]the Crys			
31	Least]least	ye Vulgar Charmed]the vulgar charmed		
32	Would]would	Rise]rue	Villany]villany	
33	haste]hast	Convene]Conveen		
34	A]a	Number]number	Men]men	
35	And]& in	Terms Commanded]terms commanded		
36	To]to	which]whence	Arose]arose	
37	But]but	Good]good	Could]could	
38	The Parent]the parent		ye]the	
39	brought]brought them			
40	Judges]judges	Great Pomp]great pomp		

41   o[r] Remorse]or remorse
42   O]Oh!   Arbitrary]arbitrary   Course]course!
43   Instead]instead
44   Condemn'd]condemned
45   The]the
46   When]when   two]poor   Alass]alass
47   At]at   Innoscence]innocence
48   Brutes]brutes
49   is]is,   Great Mens]great mens
50   Just]just   Unjust]unjust   Obey'd]obeyd
51   For]for   Warbling Tuneful]warbling tunefull
52   Those]those   end]End   Days]days
53   Without]without Tender Years]tender years
54   Beholders Cries]beholders cries   Tears]tears
55   They]they   ye Hangmans]the hangmans
56   In to ye]into the   O]Oh   Bless'd]blest
[After 56 the NYPL ms interpolates the following:]
                                      Oh Cruelty unknown before,
                                      to any barbarous savage shoar
                                      much more where men so much profess
                                      humanity and Godlyness
57   did Cry]Did cry
58   Behold]behold
59   A]a   Great Mens Ire]great mens ire
60   We perrish]we perish   Scorching]scortching
61   But ah Dear]but Ah dear   do Ake]Do ake
62   To]to   Mistake]mistake
63   Purifie]purifie
64   Our]our   Shall Never Die]shall never die
65   But]The   Kind and]kind &
66   About This Town]about this town
67   Blooming]blooming
68   To]with   Love]love   Truth]truth
69   In]in   Revenge]revenge
70   Defend]defend   and]&
71   From Abitrary]from arbitrary   Might]might
72   Pull]pull   ye]the   ye Right]the right

61. Silverman, *A Cultural History of the American Revolution*, 82–87.

62. Thomas Dale, "Prologue to the Orphan, acted at Charlestown, Febr 7, 1734–5," *South Carolina Gazette*, 54 (8 February, 1734/35). Archibald Home, "Prologue: intended for the second opening of the Theatre at New-York Anno 1739," "Poems on Several Occasions By Archibald Home. Esqr. late Secretary, and One of His Majestie's Council for the Province of New Jersey: North America," Laing Manuscripts III, 452, University of Edinburgh Library. Draft sketch of an speech introducing *The Orphan* for a private theatrical performance [ca. 1752], John Barrell Letterbook, The New-York Historical Society.

63. Samuel Stelle Smith, *Lewis Morris Anglo-American Statesman*, 182.

64. Lewis Morris, Jr., "Copy Instructions to Col. Morris for his Conduct in England," 19 November, 1734, Rutherfurd Collection, II, 71, The New-York Historical Society.

65. Robert Hunter Morris' lively diary of the journey was printed as Beverly McAnear,

ed., "R. H. Morris: An American in London, 1735–1736," *Pennsylvania Magazine of History and Biography*, 64 (1940), 164–217, 356–406.

66. "The Dream, A Riddle," ll. 57–60, Robert Morris Papers, Special Collections and Archives, Rutgers University Libraries. For a discussion of this poem, see Richard Cook, "Lewis Morris—New Jersey's Colonial Poet-Governor," *Journal of the Rutgers University Library* (Winter 1964), 100–113.

8. EMPIRE OF EVIL

1. R. A. Stradling, *Europe and the Decline of Spain* (London: George Allen & Unwin, 1981), 45.

2. Perez sought asylum in England in 1593 and there became a friend of Francis Bacon. G. Ungerer, ed., *A Spaniard in Elizabethan England: The Correspondence of Antonio Perez*, 2 vols. (London, 1974–76).

3. Hans-Georg Gadamer,*Philosophical Hermeneutics*, ed. David E. Linge (Berkeley: University of California Press, 1976), 44.

4. William S. Maltby, *The Black Legend in England: The Development of Anti-Spanish Sentiment, 1558–1660* (Durham: Duke University Press, 1971), 16.Henry Raup Wagner and Helen Rand Parish, *The Life and Writings of Bartolomé de las Casas* (Albuquerque: University of New Mexico Press, 1967), 195–208.

5. John H. Elliott, "Renaissance Europe and America: A Blunted Impact?" *First Images of America: The Impact of the New World on the Old*, ed. Fredi Chiappelli, 2 vols. (Berkeley: University of California Press, 1976), vol. 1, 16.

6. Ibid., vol. 1, 12.

7. Benjamin Keen, "The Vision of America in the Writings of Urbain Chauveton," *First Images of America*, vol. 1, 116.

8. William Byrd, *Histories of the Dividing Line*, 120.

9. Maltby, *The Black Legend in England*, 118.

10. For Ralph's career, see Robert W. Kenny, "James Ralph: An Eighteenth-Century Philadelphian in Grub Street," *Pennsylvania Magazine of History and Biography*, 64, 2 (April 1940), 218–42; Elizabeth R. McKinsey, "James Ralph," *Proceedings of the American Philosophical Society*, 117 (1973), 59–78; unpublished material concerning his career during the 1720s and 1730s may be found in the Rev. Thomas Birch correspondence, British Library.

11. *The History of England during the Reigns of King William, Queen Anne, and George I. By a Lover of Truth and Liberty*, 2 vols. (London, 1744–46), was particularly esteemed for its employment of primary resources in private archives.

12. James Ralph, *Zeuma: or the Love of Liberty. A Poem. In Three Books* (London: Billingsley, 1729), v.

13. The history of the Chilean invasion is related in Book 2, Chapters xix–xxii. The *Royal Commentaries* were sufficiently famous to be generally available in Europe throughout the eighteenth century. Garcilaso de la Vega, El Inca, *Royal Commentaries of the Incas and General History of Peru*, trans. Harold V. Livermore, 2 vols. (Austin: University of Texas Press, 1966), xv–xxxi.

14. Joel Barlow, *The Vision of Columbus* (1787), *The Works of Joel Barlow*, ed. William K. Bottorff and Arthur L. Ford, 2 vols. (Gainesville: Scholars' Facsimiles & Reprints, 1970), 177–91, 195–226. The matter is of such importance to Barlow's argument that he presents a prose synopsis of Capac's career before supplying his verse narration in Book III.

15. Britannicus, "A Letter from Don Thomas Geraldino, in Answer to Don Blas de Lezo's, at Carthagene. Faithfully translated by Britannicus," ll. 63–70, *The General Magazine*, 1 (February, 1741), 138–43. See also, Gentleman at Jamaica, "A Letter from Don Blas de Lezo, the Spanish Admiral at Carthagena, to Don Thomas Geraldino, late Agent for the King of Spain in London," *The Boston Evening Post*, 271 (13 October, 1740).

16. *The Negotiators* (London, 1740), broadside.

17. Britannicus, "Letter from Don Thomas Geraldino," l. 71.

18. [A Bostonian], "On the taking Porto-Bello by Admiral Vernon," ll. 14–27, *The General Magazine*, 1 (March 1741), 208–9.

19. H. T. Dickinson, *Liberty and Property: Ideology in Eighteenth-Century Britain* (London, 1977). Also B. A. Goldgar, *Walpole and the Wits* (Lincoln: University of Nebraska Press, 1977).

20. "Caetera descent," "Epistle to Admiral Vernon, on his success in the West Indies, in imitation of Waller's style," *Gentlemans Magazine*, 14 (February, 1744), 99–100.

21. J. Leitch Wright, Jr., *Anglo-Spanish Rivalry in North America* (Athens: University of Georgia Press, 1971), 89–100.

22. Tobias Smollett, *The Adventures of Roderick Random*, ed. Paul-Gabriel Bouce (Oxford: Oxford University Press, 1972), 188.

23. [Joseph Green?], *Some Excellent Verses on Admiral Vernon's taking the Forts and Castles of Carthagena, In the Month of March, last* ([Boston], {1741]). The connection of these verses to the Byles circle is attested by their reprinting in *A Collection of Poems* (Boston: B. Green, 1744), 31–34. None of the satires in this collection carry the ascriptions that are attached to the serious verses. Nonetheless, Green alone of the Byles circle, so far as I can determine, made a poetic habit of practicing verse parody.

24. For some British analogues, see the poems contained in the miscellany, *The New Ministry. Containing A Collection of all the Satyrical Poems, Songs, &c. 1742* (London, 1742). Two additional parts were published in subsequent months.

25. Son of a famous Boston baker noted for meat pies, Thomas Kilby (1706–1746) graduated from Harvard College in 1723. He attempted to make a career in commerce, but failed. Subsequently he became a placeman, securing the post of customs collector at Canso in Canada. His extensive correspondence with John Hancock is preserved in manuscript in the collections of the Graduate Business School library at Harvard. He apparently maintained a literary correspondence with many of his friends in Boston. His famous satire on the Land Bank survives in a number of manuscripts: Ephraim Eliot Commonplace Book, vol. 3, Boston Atheneum; Pemberton Poetry Manuscript, Massachusetts Historical Society Collection, fols. 8–15; fragment, Benjamin Lynde [II] poetry collection, Oliver Papers, Massachusetts Historical Society. A rejoinder to the satire by Joseph Green also has survived among the Gay Papers, Massachusetts Historical Society. Kilby lacked Green's sympathy for the Land Bank; since anti-Land Bank sentiments appear in "Carthegena's Downfall," it seems more likely to be from Kilby than Green.

26. [Thomas Kilby?], "Carthegena's Downfall," ll. 11–32, *A Collection of Poems. By Several Hands*, 35–36.

27. [William Smith], "A Poem: Being a serious Address to the House of Representatives," *Some Thoughts on Education with Reasons for Erecting A College in this Province, and fixing the same at the City of New-York* (New York: Parker, 1752), 22.

28. Larry E. Ivers, *British Drums on the Southern Frontier; The Military Colonization of Georgia, 1733–1749* (Chapel Hill: University of North Carolina Press, 1974), 125–50.

29. Phinizy Spalding, "Oglethorpe and Philanthropos," *Georgia Historical Quarterly*, 56, 1 (1972), 137–45.

9. GALLIC PERFIDY

1. The *OED*'s citation of usage for the seventeenth century conveys the point well. "1607 Sir E. Hoby in Ellis *Orig. Lett.* Ser. I. III. 86 Many other things he reporteth of the perfidy of the French nation."

2. John Williams, "Some Contemplations of the Poor and Desolate State of the Church at Deerfield," ll. 7–22, *The Redeemed Captive Returning to Zion*, in *Puritans Among the Indians;*

Accounts of Captivity and Redemption 1676–1724, ed. Alden T. Vaughan and Edward W. Clark (Cambridge, Mass.: Belknap Press, Harvard University Press, 1981), 197–98.

3. Donald P. Wharton, *Richard Steere Colonial Merchant Poet* (University Park, Pa.: The Pennsylvania State University Press, 1979), 14–17.

4. Richard Steere, *The History of the Babylonish Cabal; Or The Intrigues, Progression, Opposition, Defeat, and Destruction of the Daniel Catchers; In a Poem* (London, 1682), ll. 22–26.

5. Richard Steere, "Antichrist Displayed," *The Daniel Catcher. The Life of the Prophet Daniel: In a Poem* (Boston, 1713), 77.

6. Richard Steere, "The Daniel Catcher," *The Daniel Catcher*, 20–21.

7. John Saffin, "A Thankfull Memoriall October 6th 1704," ll. 24–32, *John Saffin His Book*, 86–87.

8. Benjamin Harris, ["Of the French Kings Nativity, &c."], ll. 1–20, *Seventeenth-Century American Poetry*, 455–56. Harris was long thought to have been the author of *The New England Primer*, but current scholarship casts doubt upon the attribution. See David H. Watters, "'I Spake as a Child': Authority, Metaphor and *The New-England Primer*," *Early American Literature*, 20, 3 (Winter 1985/86), 208–10. For Harris's career, see Worthington Chauncery Ford, "Benjamin Harris, Printer and Bookseller," *Proceedings of the Massachusetts Historical Society*, 57 (1924), 34–68.

9. For the forms and effects of the advice-to-the-painter genre, see Mary Tom Osborne, "Introduction," *Advice-to-a-Painter Poems, 1633–1856: An Annotated Finding List* (Austin: University of Texas Press, 1949). For its adoption by American poets, see Robert L. Pincus, "Pictures of New England's Apocalypse: Benjamin Tompson's Transformation of the British Advice-to-a-Painter Poem," *Early American Literature*, 19, 3 (Winter, 1984/85), 268–78.

10. John Gyles, *Memoirs of Odd Adventures, Strange Deliverances, Etc.*, in *Puritans Among the Indians*, 93–129. All quotations will be drawn from this edition.

11. The problems attending the Puritan mission to the Indians are thoroughly reviewed in Francis Jennings, *The Invasion of America: Indians, Colonialism, and the Cant of Conquest* (Chapel Hill: University of North Carolina Press, Institute of Early American History and Culture, 1975), 228–53.

12. Given the emphasis that Richard Slotkin and others have given to violence as a mode of "regeneration," it is instructive to note the absolute revulsion from Indian violence in Gyles; Richard Slotkin, *Regeneration Through Violence: The Mythology of the American Frontier, 1600–1860* (Middletown: Wesleyan University Press, 1973), 174–76. Here there is no "reconciliation with the Indian" or "initiation" and "self-creation" into a new identity. The total alienation from "Indian cruelty" is a hallmark of the "polite style" of discourse on the French and Indian threat. The groundbreaking anthropological discussion of Indian cruelty is Nathaniel Knowles, "The Torture of Captives by the Indians of Eastern North America," *American Philosophical Society Proceedings*, 82 (1940), 151–225.

13. Gyles, *Memoirs of Odd Adventures*, 155.

14. Vaughan and Clark, *Puritans Among the Indians*, 24.

15. Gyles, *Memoirs of Odd Adventures*, 127–28.

16. Mather Byles, "To Pollio, on his preparing for the Press a Treatise against the Romish Church," ll. 1–12, *Poems on Several Occasions*, 79–81.

17. Mather Byles, "To the Memory of a young Commander slain in a Battle with the Indians, 1724," ll. 37–52, *Poems on Several Occasions*, 34–38.

18. See news report, *Boston Gazette*, 248 (29 June, 1724).

19. Edward Wheelock, ed., *Penhallow's Indian Wars: A Facsimile Reprint of the First Edition, Printed in Boston in 1726 with the Notes of Earlier Editors and Additions from the Original Manuscript* (Williamstown, Mass.: Corner House Publishers, 1973), v.

20. Ibid., vi.

21. J. A. Leo Lemay advanced this attribution (private conversation, October 1985);

though the subject of frequent mention in the 1720s and 1730s, little concrete information survives concerning Law's career. The entire quotation runs

> How many pris'ners in they drew,
>   say, spirit of *Tom Law*!
> Two French-men, and papooses two,
> three sannops, and a squaw.
> The squaw, and the papooses, they
> are to be left alive:
> Two French, three Indian men must die:
> which makes exactly five.
> (Thus cypher, Sirs, you see I can,
> and eke make poetry:
> In common-wealth, sure such a man,
> how useful must he be!)

"A full and true Account of how the lamentable wicked French and Indian Pirates were taken by the valient English Men," *A Collection of Poems*, 30.

22. Phillips Barry, "Songs of the Pigwacket Fight," *Bulletin of the Folk Song Society of the Northeast*, 4 (1932), 3–9; 5 (1933), 17–19; 6 (1933), 3–4. Gail H. Bickford, "Lovewell's Fight, 1725–1958," *American Quarterly*, 10 (1958), 358–66.

23. Francis Parkman, "Sebastien Rale," *A Half-Century of Conflict: France and England in North America*, 2 vols. (Boston: Little, Brown, and Co., 1902), vol. 1, 212–49.

24. [Tom Law], *The Rebels Reward: Or, English Courage Display'd. Being a full and true Account of the Victory obtain'd over the Indians at Norrigiwock, on the Twelfth of August last, by the English Forces under Command of Capt. Johnson Harmon* (Boston: J. Franklin, 1724), ll. 23–36.

25. "A full and true Account," *A Collection of Poems*, 28–31. The poem also satirizes the almanac writer, Nathaniel Whittemore, and W. G. [William Goff?], author of *A Brief Narrative, or Poem, Giving an Account of the Hostile Actions of some Pagan Indians towards Lieutenant Jacob Tilton, {and his} brother Daniel Tilton, both of the town of Ipswich, as they were on board of a small vessel {traveling north?}ward; which happened in the summer-time, in the year 1722. With an Account of the Exploits of the said Tiltons, and their victorious Conquest over their insulting enemies* (Newburyport: W. J. Gilman, 1834), broadside. Gilman's is the earliest surviving printing of the piece that was probably published first in 1722.

26. William R. Mueller, *Spenser's Critics: Changing Currents in Literary Taste* (Syracuse: Syracuse University Press, 1959), 18–72.

27. William Byrd, *Histories of the Dividing Line*, 120.

28. Ibid.

29. Cadwallader Colden, *The History of the Five Nations* (New York, 1727), I, xxi.

30. By the Author of the American Fables [William Smith], *Indian Songs of Peace*, 11.

31. John A. Schutz, *William Shirley: King's Governor of Massachusetts* (Chapel Hill: University of North Carolina Press, Institute of Early American History and Culture, 1961), 90–91.

32. Henry Lincoln, ed. *The Correspondence of William Shirley* 2 vols. (New York, 1912) vol. 1, 162–63; cited in Schutz, *William Shirley*. See also John Schutz, "Imperialism in Massachusetts during the Governorship of William Shirley, 1741–1756," *The Huntington Library Quarterly*, 23 (1960), 217–36.

33. Samuel Niles, *A brief and plain essay on God's wonder-working Providence for New-England, in the reduction of Louisburg, and fortresses thereto belonging on Cape-Breton* (New London: T. Green, 1747), 18.

34. G. A. Rawlyk, *Yankees at Louisbourg* (Orono, Maine: University of Maine Press, 1967), University of Maine Studies, 2nd ser., 85, 44–45.

35. Ibid., 131–52.

36. "A Poetical Essay on the Reduction of Cape Breton on June 17, 1745," *Gentleman's Magazine*, 16 (1745).

37. An Officer that went on the Expedition against Carthagena, "On the Taking of Cape-Breton," *New York Weekly Post-Boy*, 131 (22 July, 1745).

38. An honest Tar [Charles Hansford], "On the Conquest of Cape-Breton," *Boston Weekly Post-Boy*, 566 (7 October, 1745).

39. An Officer, "On the Taking of Cape-Breton," 131.

40. Over the course of the eighteenth century, a literary camp culture developed in the British and American armies. No history has been undertaken of this development. It remains a desideratum for future investigation. Expressions of the animosities are contained in the myriad diaries that survive from participants in the expedition.

41. J. A. Leo Lemay, "The American Origins of 'Yankee Doodle'," *William and Mary Quarterly*, 3d ser, 33 (July, 1976), 443.

42. "Directions to the French King's Painter," *South Carolina Gazette*, 684 (25 May, 1747).

43. S.N. [Samuel Niles?], "A Short Hint by Way of Lamentation on restoring Cape-Breton to the French," *Boston Weekly News-Letter*, 2447 (11 May, 1749).

10. THE TENUOUSNESS OF IMPERIAL IDENTITY

1. [Adam Thomson], "An Ode, In Honour of New-England, (on their important Conquest of Cape-Breton from the French,) of ever glorious Memory," *Maryland Gazette* (14 January, 1746). Dr. Adam Thomson (1712?–1767) was born in Edinburgh and educated at the university. Shortly after graduation he published a ballad opera, *The Disappointed Gallant: or, Buckram in armour* (1738). Sometime before March, 1742, Thomson emigrated to Maryland, where he settled in Upper Marlborough, then Nottingham. There he came into contact with the wits of the Tuesday Club of Annapolis. In 1748 he moved again, to Philadelphia, where he gained notoriety for his advocacy of inoculation in *A discourse on the preparation of the body for the small-pox: and the manner of receiving the infection* (1750). His method provoked a paper war in the gazettes pitting him against Drs. John Kearsley and John Redman. History would eventually prove Thomson's medicine superior to that of his adversaries. While advancing his medical career, he continued to pursue the muses, publishing items under the pseudonyms "Town-side" and "Philo Musus." An imperial zealot, he provoked one of Franklin's more brilliant meditations on the meaning of Americanism, with publication of an "Extract of a Letter from a Gentleman in General Abercrombie's army, dated Camp at Lake George, August 24" in the *London Chronicle*. Thomson made several transatlantic journeys during the late 1750s. He died on September 18, 1767.

2. Adam Thomson, "An Ode, humbly inscribed to the Associators of Pennsylvania," *Pennsylvania Gazette* (1 September, 1748).

3. Lewis Morris, Jr., "Mr Gales Letter To his constituents in answer To on They wrote To him that he would Inform them what The assembly were Doing—put into verse by a Deacon at Goshen," Lewis Morris Literary Writings. Courtesy of The New-York Historical Society. Goshen is located in eastern Long Island, so the usual New England associations apply. The manuscript is undated, though 1754 seems a likely date. Lewis Morris, Jr., (1726–1798) lived in Westchester County as an aristocratic landholder. In later life he became increasingly Whiggish in politics.

4. Benjamin Franklin, "Short hints towards a Scheme for a General Union of the British Colonies on the Continent," *Papers*, vol. 5, 361–64.

5. Benjamin Franklin, "Reasons and Motives for the Albany Plan of Union," *Papers*, vol 5, 399.

6. Benjamin Franklin, "A Plan for Settling Two Western Colonies," *Papers*, vol. 5, 457.

7. Jonathan Beveridge, *Epistoles Familiares* (Philadelphia: Bradford, 1765); Benjamin Young Prime, *The Patriot Muse, or Poems on Some of the Principal Events of the Late War; Together with A Poem on the Peace* (London: Bird, 1764); George Cockings, *The Conquest of Canada; or the Siege of Quebec. An Historical Tragedy in Five Acts* (London: Cooke & Haysell, 1766); John Duncombe, *The Works of Horace, in English Verse . . . To which are added, Many Imitations, now first published* (London: White, 1767).

8. John Maylem, *Gallic Perfidy* (Boston: B. Mecom, 1758). *The Conquest of Louisbourg* (Boston, 1758).

9. George Cockings, *Arts, Manufactures, and Commerce: A Poem* (London: for the author, [1765]), 3. Cockings held a minor imperial post in Boston during the 1750s; he was serving as register of the Society of Arts, Manufactures, and Commerce when he composed this poem.

10. Philip Freneau, "The Village Merchant," *The Newspaper Verse of Philip Freneau: An Edition and Bibliographical Survey*, ed. Judith Hiltner (Troy, N. Y.: Whitson, 1986), 485–89, 492–96. Freneau's note that he wrote the poem in 1768 is specious, as Hiltner indicates. See also Freneau's "On the Too Remote Extension of American Commerce," *Time-Piece* (24 March, 1797).

11. Robert A. Ferguson, *Law and Letters in American Culture* (Cambridge, Mass.: Harvard University Press, 1984), 110.

12. Philip Freneau, "Ode. To the Americans. That the progress of liberty in the world, considering the present state of things, cannot be impeded, or its complete establishement prevented," *Newspaper Verse*, 615.

13. Jacob Bailey, "America," Bailey Papers, Public Archives of Nova Scotia. For an assessment of Bailey's verse, see Bruce Granger, "The Hudibrastic Poetry of Jacob Bailey," *Early American Literature*, 17 (Spring, 1982), 54–64.

14. Bryan Edwards, *Poems, Written Chiefly In the West-Indies* (Kingston, Jamaica: Aikman, 1792). Edwards lived on Antigua, and his antislavery verses may have influenced Freneau's West Indian verses.

15. Consult Martin Kallich, *British American Poetry: A Bibliographical Survey of Books and Pamphlets, Journals and Magazines, Newspapers, and Prints 1755–1800* (Troy, N.Y.: Whitson, 1988) for the ranks of Tory poets.

Bibliography of Primary Sources

At the request of early readers of this study I have organized by region a bibliography of primary sources consulted in the preparation of this history. The Lemay number following a printed poem refers to the verse's listing in J. A. Leo Lemay, *A Calendar of American Poetry in the Colonial Newspapers and Magazines and in the Major English Magazines Through 1765* (Worcester, Mass.: American Antiquarian Society, 1972). The Evans number following an imprint refers to the work's listing in Clifford K. Shipton and James E. Mooney, *National Index of American Imprints Through 1880: The Short-Title Evans,* 2 vols. (Worcester, Mass.: American Antiquarian Society & Barre Publishers, 1969). Items listed below bearing an Evans number may be read in the Readex Mircroform Edition of the Early American Imprints.

CANADA

Manuscripts

Bailey, Jacob. "America." Bailey Papers. Public Archives of Nova Scotia. This Harvard-trained Tory poet composed the most acerbic assessments of the patriot leadership committed to verse. Much of his output remains unpublished.

Kilby, Thomas. Correspondence. 1740s. John Hancock Papers. Special Collections. Harvard Graduate School of Business Library.

Published Works

Poetry

Beveridge, Jonathan. *Epistoles {sic} Familiares.* Philadelphia: Bradford, 1765.

Cockings, George. *The Conquest of Canada; or the Siege of Quebec. An Historical Tragedy in Five Acts.* London: Cooke & Haysell, 1766.

"Directions to the French King's Painter." *South Carolina Gazette,* 684 (25 May, 1747). Lemay #836.

[Hansford, Charles.] An honest Tar. "On the Conquest of Cape-Breton." *Boston Weekly Post-Boy,* 566 (7 October, 1745). Lemay # 792. Lemay attribution.

Maylem, John. *The Conquest of Louisbourg.* Boston: [B. Mecom], 1758. Evans # 8193.

————. *Gallic Perfidy.* Boston: B. Mecom, 1758. Evans # 8194.

Niles, Samuel. *A brief and plain essay on God's wonder-working Providence for New-England, in the reduction of Louisburg, and fortresses thereto belonging on Cape-Breton.* New London: T. Green, 1747. Evans # 6037.

————. [?]. S. N. "A Short Hint by Way of Lamentation on restoring Cape-Breton to the French." *Boston Weekly News-Letter,* 2447 (11 May, 1749). Lemay # 933.

An Officer that went on the Expedition against Carthagena. "On the Taking of Cape-Breton." *New York Weekly Post-Boy,* 131 (22 July, 1745). Lemay # 780B.

"A Poetical Essay on the Reduction of Cape Breton on June 17, 1745." *Gentleman's Magazine,* 16 (1745).

[Thomson, Adam.] "An Ode, In Honour of New-England, (on their important Conquest of Cape-Breton from the French,) of ever glorious Memory." *Maryland Gazette* (14 January, 1746). Lemay # 802.

NEW ENGLAND

Manuscripts

Barrell, John. Letterbook, 1730s–1750s. The New-York Historical Society. Correspondence and poetry of one of the principal Boston merchants. Also includes satirical verse by Joseph Green and Ruth Green Barrell.

Byles, Mather. Letterbook. New England Genealogical Society. A microfilm edition is available through the Massachusetts Historical Society. The Massachusetts Historical Society has recently purchased additional letters dating from the 1760s and 1770s.

Collins, Thomas. Notebook. American Antiquarian Society. A British officer's jottings and commonplaces compiled 1758–62. Includes poems by Collins, Nathaniel Gardner, Jr., and Joseph Green.

Eliot, Ephraim. Commonplace Book. 3 vols. Boston Atheneum. Manuscript compendium of a Boston antiquarian. Contains satirical verse by Thomas Kilby, Joseph Green, John Fenno, Benjamin Church. A treasury of information on subjects such as the Boston mob, tavern signs, Boston's military companies, and the puns of Mather Byles.

Fiske, Nathan. Notebook, 1750s–1780s. American Antiquarian Society.

Begun while Fiske was a Harvard undergraduate. Contains pieces by
Mather Byles and Nathaniel Gardner, Jr., as well as copies of the student
satires circulating in the 1750s.

Freeman, Enoch. Diary 1729–85. Special Collections, Portland Public Library. Good documentary source for New England culture by a Harvard
graduate.

Green, Joseph. "Answer to ye Govr Speach to ye Assembly New Hamp in
Verse." 17 January, 1733/34. Smith-Carter Papers, Massachusetts Historical Society. Another copy: F. L. Gay Papers, Box 1 1374–1823. Massachusetts Historical Society.

———. "Belchers Answer to an Answer of the House of Representatives of
N H in Verse." Smith-Carter manuscripts, Massachusetts Historical Society.

———. "Govr Belchers Speach to Assembly N:Hampshire in Verse."
Smith Townsend manuscripts, Massachusetts Historical Society. Another copy: F. L. Gay Papers, Box 1 1374–1823. Massachusetts Historical Society.

———. "A True & Impartial Accot. of the Celebration of the Prince of
Orange's Nuptials at P--------." 3, June, 1734. Smith-Carter manuscripts, Massachusetts Historical Society.

Lynde, Benjamin, Jr. Lynde Poetry Collection. Oliver Papers. Massachusetts Historical Society. Loose poems from the 1740s–80s including un-
attributed works by Nathaniel Gardner, Jr., Peter Oliver, and perhaps
Lynde himself.

Morris, Lewis, Sr. "On the word that in the Boston Poem." Robert Morris
Manuscripts. Archives and Special Collections. Rutgers University Libraries.

Pemberton, Thomas. Poetry Collection. Massachusetts Historical Society.
Begun late in the eighteenth century and kept into the 1820s. Includes
manuscript transcriptions of colonial works by Samuel Quincy, Joseph
Green, Thomas Kilby, and others.

Walker, Benjamin. Diary. 4 vols. Massachusetts Historical Society. Important and thorough diary kept by a Boston shopkeeper. Loose papers include copies of the pasquinades and political poems circulating through
Massachusetts from 1710s to 1740s.

Published Works

Poetry

"An Account of the Procession of the General Court into Salisbury, in the
Year 1736, when the Affair of the Boundary Line was debated between
the two Provinces of the Massachusetts and New-Hampshire." *A Collec-*

tion of Poems. By several Hands. Boston: Gookin & Green, 1744, 45–55. Evans # 5365.

Adam, Hugh. "March 20, 1722." *Proceedings of the Massachusetts Historical Society,* 1st ser., 3 (1797), 326.

[Adams, Matthew.] "A Gratulatory Poem received from a Friend the Day after the Arrival of His Excellency Governour Burnet." *Boston Weekly News-Letter,* 91 (25 July, 1728), 1–2. Lemay # 91. Shields attribution.

———. "A Poetical Lamentation, occasioned by the Death of His Late Majesty King George the First." *New England Weekly Journal* (12 February, 1727/28). Lemay # 83.

"Boston's First Play." Ed. Robert E. Moody. *Proceedings of the Massachusetts Historical Society* (1980), 111–40.

Bradford, William. "Of Boston in New England." *Seventeenth-Century American Poetry.* Ed. Harrison Meserole. New York: Anchor Books, Doubleday, 1968.

Bradstreet, Anne. *The Works of Anne Bradstreet in Prose and Verse.* Ed. John Harvard Ellis. Gloucester: Peter Smith, 1962.

Byles, Mather. *On the Death of the Queen. A Poem. Inscribed to His Excellency Governor Belcher.* Boston: Draper & Henchman, 1738. Evans # 4229.

———. *A Poem on the Death of His late Majesty King George, Of glorious Memory: And the Accession of our present Sovereign King George II. To the British Throne.* [Boston, 1727.] Evans # 2846.

———. "A Poem on the Death of King George I, and Accession of King George II." *New England Weekly Journal* (4 September, 1727). Lemay # 69.

———. *A Poem Presented To His Excellency William Burnet, Esq; On his Arrival at Boston, July 19, 1728.* [Boston]: By Order of his Excellency the Governour, 1728. Evans # 3004.

———. "To the Memory of a young Commander slain in a Battle with the Indians, 1724." *Poems on Several Occasions.* Boston: Kneeland & Green, 1744. 34–38. Evans # 5355.

[Franklin?, Benjamin.] "The Rats and the Cheese, a Fable." *Pennsylvania Gazette* (24 September, 1730). Lemay # 161. Lemay speculative attribution.

"A full and true Account of how the lamentable wicked French and Indian Pirates were taken by the valient English Men." *A Collection of Poems. By several Hands.* Boston: Green & Gookin, 1744, 28–31. Evans # 5365.

[Goff?, William.] W. G. *A Brief Narrative, or Poem, Giving an Account of the Hostile Actions of some Pagan Indians towards Lieutenant Jacob Tilton, {and his} brother Daniel Tilton, both of the town of Ipswich, as they were on board of a small vessel {traveling north}ward; which happened in the summer-time, in the year 1722. With an Account of the Exploits of the said Tiltons, and their vic-*

torious Conquest over their insulting enemies. Broadside. Newburyport: W. J. Gilman, 1834.

Green, Joseph. *A Mournfull Lamentation for the Sad and Deplorable Death of Mr. Old Tenor.* Boston, [1750]. Evans # 6512.

Harris, Benjamin. ["Of the French Kings Nativity, &c."] *Seventeenth Century American Poetry.* Ed. Harrison Meserole. New York: Anchor Books, Doubleday, 1968.

[Harrison?, Francis.] "An Elaegy upon His Excellency William Burnet, Esq; who departed this Life Sept. 7th 1729 Aetat 42." *New York Gazette,* 206 (13 October, 1729). Lemay # 127. Shields speculative attribution.

"The Introduction." *The Loyal American's Almanack for the Year 1715.* Boston, 1715. Evans # 39624.

[Kilby?, Thomas.] "Carthegena's Downfall." *A Collection of Poems. By Several Hands.* Boston: Green & Gookin, 1744. 35–36. Evans # 5365.

[Law, Tom.] *The Rebels Reward: Or, English Courage Display'd. Being a full and true Account of the Victory obtain'd over the Indians at Norrigidwock, on the Twelfth of August last, by the English Forces under Command of Capt. Johnson Harmon.* Boston: J[ames] Franklin, 1724. Evans # 39818. Lemay attribution.

"Lines put over the Door of the General Court." *New York Gazette* (2 November, 1730). Lemay # 164.

[Mather, Samuel.] S. M. *A Country Treat Upon the Second Paragraph in His Excellency's Speech, Decemb. 17. 1730.* Broadside. [Boston], 1730. Evans # 39957.

The Origin of the Whale bone-petticoat. A Satyr. Boston, August 2d, 1714. Boston, 1714. Evans # 1709.

Saffin, John. *John Saffin His Book, 1665–1708.* Ed. Carolina Hazard. New York: Harbor Press, 1928.

Steere, Richard. *The Daniel Catcher. The Life of the Prophet Daniel: In a Poem.* Boston, 1713. Evans # 1650.

———. *The History of the Babylonish Cabal; Or The Intrigues, Progression, Opposition, Defeat, and Destruction of the Daniel Catchers; In a Poem.* London, 1682.

Tompson, Benjamin. *Benjamin Tompson Colonial Bard: A Critical Edition.* Ed. Peter White. University Park, Pa.: Pennsylvania State University Press, 1980.

Winthrop IV, John. "Ad Regem." *Boston Weekly News-Letter* (22 August, 1723). Lemay # 45.

Wolcott, Roger. "A Brief Account of the Agency of the Honourable John Winthrop, Esq; in the Court of King Charles the Second, Anno Dom 1662." *Poetical Meditations.* New London, 1725. Evans # 2722.

Prose

Belcher, Jonathan. "The Speech of His Excellency Jonathan Belcher, Esq; Captain General & Governour in Chief, to and over His Majesty's Province of the Massachusetts-Bay in New-England." *Boston Gazette,* 562 (14 September, 1730).

Calef, Robert. *More Wonders of the Invisible World.* Salem: Carlton, 1796. Evans # 30149.

Checkley, John. *Choice Dialogues Concerning Election and Predestination.* Boston, 1720. Evans # 2100.

————. *A Modest Proof of the Order and Government Settled by Christ and His Apostles in the Church.* Boston: Fleet and Eliot, 1723. Evans # 2417.

[Cooke, Elisha, Jr.] *New News from Robinson Cruso's Island, in a Letter to a Gentleman at Portsmouth.* [Boston, 1720.] Evans # 2153.

————. *Reflections upon Reflections: Or, More News from Robinson Cruso's Island in a Dialogue between a Country Representative and a Boston Gentleman, July 12, 1720.* Cruso's Island [Boston], 1720. Evans # 2111. Evans attribution

Dudley, Joseph. Letter to Increase and Cotton Mather. *Massachusetts Historical Society Collections,* 1st ser., 3 (1794), 135–37.

[Dudley, Paul.] *News from Robinson Cruso's Island: With an Appendix relating to Mr. Cook's late Pamphlet.* [Boston], 1720. Evans # 39730.

Dummer, Jeremiah. *A Defence of the New-England Charters.* Boston: Kneeland, 1721. Evans # 2216.

Letter from a London Merchant upon the appointment of Jonathan Belcher as Governor, February 6, 1729/30. *Boston Gazette,* 546 (25 May, 1730).

A Letter to an Eminent Clergy-Man in the Massachusett's Bay. Containing some Just Remarks, and necessary Cautions, relating to Publick Affairs in that Province. Boston, 1720. Evans # 2230.

"The Massachusetts Charter of 1691." *The Glorious Revolution in America; Documents on the Colonial Crisis of 1689.* Ed. Michael G. Hall, Lawrence H. Leder, and Michael Kammen. Chapel Hill: University of North Carolina Press, Institute of Early American History and Culture, 1964. 76–79.

Mather, Cotton. *A Pillar of Gratitude.* Boston, 1700. Evans # 930.

————. "Political Fables by Cotton Mather." *The Andros Tracts.* Publications of the Prince Society, 2. Boston: Prince Society, 1869.

————. *Selected Letters of Cotton Mather.* Ed. Kenneth Silverman. Baton Rouge: Louisiana State University Press, 1971.

Mather, Increase. "The Autobiography of Increase Mather." Ed. Michael G. Hall. *American Antiquarian Society Proceedings* 71, 2 (1962), 307–8.

Penhallow, Samuel. *Pennhallow's Indian Wars; A Facsimile Reprint of the First Edition, Printed in Boston in 1726 With the Notes of Earlier Editors and Addi-

tions from the Original Manuscripts. Ed. Edward Wheelock. Williamstown, Mass.: Corner House Publishers, 1973.

Thomas, Isaiah. *The History of Printing in America with a Biography of Printers & an Account of Newspapers.* Ed. Marcus A. McCorison. New York: Weathervane Books, 1970.

NEW YORK AND NEW JERSEY

Manuscripts

[Alexander, James, et al] ["An Epistle to a Friend."] "The last words and testament of the song on the election condemn'd to be burnt by the c-----t partie." "A mournfull Elegy on the funeral pile & Execution of the ballad or ballads burnt by publick authority before a great crowd in a small town in a certain Country under the Northern hemisphere on a certain day since the year 1600 To the tune of Chevy chase or the two chldren in the wood or any other that you like best." "Of a merry sing song burnt by sound of ding dong why made, and what after befel it." Miscellaneous Papers, Songs (Cosby 19, 20, 21, 23.) New York Public Library.

Home, Archibald. "Poems on Several Occasions By Archibald Home. Esqr. late Secretary, and One of His Majestie's Council for the Province of New Jersey: North America." Laing Manuscripts III, 452. University of Edinburgh Library.

Morris, Lewis, Sr. Misc. Verse and Prose: "The choice of the forrest taken out of an antient manuscript Kept in the library of christs church colledge Oxford by D. M--ter." "Dialogue Concerning Trade." "The Dream & Riddle A Poem." "The Last Prophetick Speech of Mr. Zengar's Journalls Condemn'd to be burnt by ye g---r & C----le." "In the Garb of old Gaul with the Fire of old Rome." "The Mock Monarchy or the Kingdom of Apes A Poem by a gentleman of New Jersey in America." "On the Death of a Late Valorous and Noble Knight." "On the Essex Riots." "A Song made upon the Election of New magistrates for this Citty to the Tune of to you fair Ladies now at Land etc." "A song to the tune of ne'r a barrell better herring or Ask my fellow if in a [thirst?] Inscrib'd to the congress of Loan officers appointed to Stat. & Examine the Accounts of Loan Officers in the Province of New Hampshire." "To his Excellency The Governour of New Jersie, upon the Assembly's Disiring him to fix his own Seat." Robert Morris Papers. Rutgers University Library.

Morris, Lewis, Jr. "Copy Instructions to Col. Morris for his Conduct in England [19 November 19, 1734]." Rutherfurd Collection, II, 71. The New-York Historical Society.

———. "Mr. Gales Letter To his constituents in answer To one They wrote

To him that he would Inform them what The assembly were Doing—
put into verse by a Deacon at Goshen." Lewis Morris Literary Writings.
The New-York Historical Society.

Published Works

Poems and Plays

D., Z. "The Tuneful Muse in lofty strains." *New York Gazette,* 487 (25 February, 1734/35). Lemay # 358. Satire on the Morris faction.

"Expostulation." *New York Gazette,* 554 (14 June, 1736). Anti-Morris satire.

Freneau, Philip. "The Pictures of Columbus." *The Poems of Philip Freneau Poet of the American Revolution.* 3 vols. Ed. Fred Lewis Pattee. Princeton: Princeton University Library, 1902.

[Harrison, Francis.] ["Concerning the Purveyors of Scandal in New York."] *New York Gazette,* 442 (15 April, 1734). Lemay # 302. Shields attribution.

———. "Cosby the Mild, the happy, good and great." *New York Gazette,* 428 (31 December, 1733). Lemay # 283. Shields attribution.

———. [?] "An Elaegy upon His Excellency William Burnet, Esq; who departed this Life Sept. 7th 1729 Aetat 42." *New York Gazette,* 206 (13 October, 1729). Lemay # 127.

[Humphreys, David.] "The Lamentable Story of two Fatherless & Motherless Twins which Lately Appeared in ye City of N-w-Y-k who for their Phrophetick Cries were Condemn'd to be burnt by ye Common Hangman which was Accordingly Executed &c." *Cadwallader Colden Papers: Additional Papers 1715–1748.* Vol. 8. Ed. Alex J. Wall. New York: The New-York Historical Society, 1934, 251–52.

Hunter, Robert. "Androboros A Biographical Farce in Three Acts. VIZ. The Senate, The Consistory, and The Apotheosis By Governor Hunger." *Satiric Comedies. America's Lost Plays,* vol. 21. Ed. Walter J. Meserve and William Reardon. Bloomington: Indiana University Press, 1969.

[Martin, Alexander.] "An Ode." *New American Magazine* (November, 1759), 690–91.

Morris, Lewis, Sr. "'Dialogue Concerning Trade': A Satirical View of New York in 1726." Ed. Edmond Dale Daniel. *New York History* (1974), 199–229.

———. *A Song made upon the Election of the New magistrates for this Citty to the Tune of to you fair Ladies now at Land &c.* Broadside. [New York, 1734]. Evans # 3836. Shields attribution.

Non Ignotus. "The Masque of Life." *New York Weekly Journal,* 243 (10 July, 1738). Lemay # 504.

Prime, Benjamin Young. *The Patriot Muse, or Poems on Some of the Principal*

Events of the Late War; Together with A Poem on the Peace. London: Bird, 1764.

Right, Tho. "Poor Toby's Fate, Or, a Farewell to Courtiers, To the Tune of Daphne our dearest Bitch. O bone, o bone." *New York Weekly Journal,* 119 (16 February, 1735/36). Lemay # 399. Anti-Cosby satire.

[Smith, William.] *Indian Songs of Peace: with A Proposal, in a prefatory Epistle, for erecting Indian Schools.* New York: Parker and Wayman, 1753. Evans # 7217.

————. "A Poem: Being a serious Address to the House of Representatives." *Some Thoughts on Education with Reasons for Erecting A College in this Province, and fixing the same at the City of New-York.* New York: Parker, 1752. Evans # 6935.

Prose

Alexander, James. *A Brief Narrative of the Case and Trial of John Peter Zenger, Printer of The New-York Weekly Journal, by James Alexander.* Ed. Stanley N. Katz. Cambridge, Mass.: Belknap Press, Harvard University Press, 1963.

Colden, Cadwallader. *Cadwallader Colden Papers.* 8 vols. Ed. Alex J. Wall. New York: The New-York Historical Society, 1934.

Documents Relating to the Colonial History of the State of New Jersey. 10 vols. Ed. William A. Whitehead. Newark: Daily Advertiser Printing House, 1880–84.

Morris, Robert Hunter. "R. H. Morris: An American in London, 1735–1736." Ed. Beverly McAnear. *Pennsylvania Magazine of History and Biography,* 64 (1940), 164–217, 356–406.

Mulford, Samuel. *Samuel Mulford's Speech to the Assembly at New-York.* New York: [Bradford], 1714. Evans # 1705.

Smith, Samuel. *The History of the Colony of Nova-Caesara, or New-Jersey.* Burlington, 1765. Evans # 10166.

Smith, William, Jr. *The History of the Province of New-York.* 2 vols. Ed. Michael Kammen. Cambridge: Belknap Press, John Harvard Library, 1972.

PENNSYLVANIA

Manuscripts

Becket, William. Notices and Letters Concerning Incidents at Lewes Town 1727–1744. Manuscript Am .0165. Historical Society of Pennsylvania. A valuable miscellany by the S.P.G.A. missionary to Sussex County, reflecting upon religion, politics, and material conditions in Pennsylvania's lower three counties. Letters and poems reflect his involvement in the proprietary interest.

Brooke, Henry. Commonplace Book [poetry]. Peters Collection. Historical

Society of Pennsylvania. Collection of verse by the principal poet of the anti-Quaker faction in Pennsylvania. The material dates from 1702 through 1727 and contains satires against the Quaker-controlled city corporation of Philadelphia, invectives against several politicians, as well as a variety of belletristic compositions.

Lloyd, David. "A Further Vindication of the Rights and priviledges of the People of this Province of Pensilvania." Penn manuscripts, Assembly and Provincial Council. Philadelphia, March, 1725. Historical Society of Pennsylvania. A major statement of Quaker party principles.

Logan, James. Letterbooks I–III. Logan Papers. Historical Society of Pennsylvania. Logan, Penn's agent in Pennsylvania, was a scholastic, rigorous man with a taste for polite letters. His correspondence with Henry Brooke reveals the extent to which the press was becoming a political tool during the 1720s. Early literary manuscripts once located at Stenton, the Logan Estate, were lost before the transfer of the Logan papers to the Historical Society of Pennsylvania.

Norris, II, Isaac. Norris Commonplace Book. H. M. 164. Henry E. Huntington Library. Contains letters and verse from Isaac Norris, Sr., Joseph Norris, and Isaac Norris, Jr., dating from 1727 through 1736, including "The Choice wrote the Election day Morning 1727," elegies, and epigrams mocking anti-Quaker partisans including Andrew Hamilton.

Scull, Nicholas. Notebooks, 1732 & 1733 Jury registers. Am 1359. Historical Society of Pennsylvania. A surveyor and member of Franklin's Junto, Scull amused himself by penning poems in his field notebooks.

Watson, John F. Annals of Philadelphia. 2 vols. [scrapbooks]. Am .301. Historical Society of Pennsylvania. In the supplementary materials to his book, Watson included texts of a number of early poems, letters, and manuscript works reflecting on the political situation of the 1710–50 era.

Published Works

Poetry

[Breintnall, Joseph.] *The Death of King George Lamented in Pennsylvania: Being Part of a Letter to the Author's Country Friend.* Philadelphia: [Keimer?], 1728.

————. "To the Memory of Aquila Rose, Deceas'd." *Poems on several Occasions, by Aquila Rose: To which are prefixed, some other Pieces writ to him, and to his Memory after his Decease.* Philadelphia: [B. Franklin], 1740. Shields attribution.

————. [?]. "To the Memory of John Dommett, the unborn Poet, lately deceased." *Pennsylvania Gazette*, 556 (9 August, 1739). Lemay # 530. Shields speculative attribution.

"Congratulatory Verses, wrote at the Arrival of our Honourable Proprietary." *Pennsylvania Gazette* (21 August, 1732). Lemay # 234.

Frame, Richard. *A Short Description of Pennsilvania. Or, A Relation What things are Known, enjoyed, and like to be discovered in the said Province.* Philadelphia: William Bradford, 1692. Evans # 594.

[Franklin?, Benjamin.] Pennsylvanus. "Against Party-Malice and Levity, usual at and near the Time of Electing Assembly-Men." *The Pennsylvania Gazette*, 252 (28 September, 1733). Lemay # 272. Lemay attribution.

Holme, John. "A True Relation of the Flourishing State of Pennsylvania, 1686." *Bulletin of the Historical Society of Pennsylvania* (1845), 161–80.

[Hughes, Griffith.] Ruris Amator. "From Chester County in the Province of Pennsylvania. To a Friend at Oxford." *The American Weekly Mercury*, 794 (20 March, 1734/35). Lemay # 363. Shields attribution.

Hughes, John. "Utopia." *An Ephemeris For the Year of Our Lord, 1726.* Philadelphia: A. Bradford, [1725]. Evans # 2644.

Makin, Thomas. "A Discription of Pennsylvania [1728]." *Pennsylvania Magazine of History and Biography*, 32 (1913), 372.

———. "On the Arrival of the Honourable Thomas Penn, Esq; one of the Proprietors of the Province of Pennsylvania." *The American Weekly Mercury*, 659 (17 August, 1732). Lemay # 233. Lemay attribution.

Scull, Nicholas. "Nicholas Scull's "Junto" Verses." Ed. Nicholas B. Wainright. *The Library* (January, 1949), 82–84. Another draft: "The Junto." *Colonial American Poetry*. Ed. Kenneth Silverman. New York & London: Hafner Pub. Co., 1968, 372–73.

Smith, William. *A Poem on Visiting the Academy of Philadelphia, June 1753.* Philadelphia: [Franklin & Hall], 1753. Evans # 7122.

[Taylor, Jacob.] Enroblos. ["Pennsylvania."] *The American Weekly Mercury*, 1051 & 1052 (19, 26 February, 1739/40). Lemay # 557. Shields attribution.

[Thomson, Adam.] "An Ode, humbly inscribed to the Associators of Pennsylvania." *The Pennsylvania Gazette* (1 September, 1748). Lemay # 886. Lemay attribution.

"To the most Ingenious Pamphleteer, author of the He-Monster." *The American Weekly Mercury* (28 July, 1726). Lemay # 62. An anti-Keithian satire.

[Webb, George.] Oxf. Schol. Exit. ["A Memorial to William Penn."] *The Genuine Leeds Almanack For the Year of Christian Account, 1730.* Ed. Titan Leeds. Philadelphia: David Harry, 1730. Evans # 3295. Lemay attribution.

———. T. Z. ["The New Athens."] *The American Weekly Mercury*, 495 (3 July, 1729). Lemay # 122. Shields attribution.

———. ["A Prospect of Philadelphia."] *The Pennsylvania Gazette*, 125 (8 April, 1731). Lemay # 182. Shields attribution.

Prose

The Conspiracy of Catiline; Recommended to the Serious Consideration of the Authors of Advice and Information. [Philadelphia, 1727.] Evans # 2858. Anti-proprietary fulmination.

Fisher, Joshua Francis. "Narrative of Sir William Keith's Coming to the Government of Pennsylvania, with his Conduct in it (1726)." *Memoirs of the Historical Society of Pennsylvania.* Vol. 2. Philadelphia: E. Littel, 1830.

Franklin, Benjamin. *Benjamin Franklin's Autobiography.* Ed. J. A. Leo Lemay & P. M. Zall. New York: W. W. Norton, 1986.

———. *The Papers of Benjamin Franklin.* Vols. 1–5. Ed. Leonard W. Labaree & Whitfield J. Bell, Jr. New Haven & London: Yale University Press, 1959–62.

Keith, William. *A Just and Plain Vindication.* [Philadelphia], 1726. Evans # 2754.

———. *A Letter from Sir William Keith, Bart. to Mr. James Logan.* Philadelphia, 1725. Evans # 2646.

———. *A Modest Reply to the Speech of Isaac Norris.* [Philadelphia, 1727.] Evans # 2890.

———. *Remarks upon the Advice to Freeholders.* [Philadelphia, 1727.] Evans # 2951. Wendel attribution.

[Keith?, William, and John Hughes?.] *The Life and Character of a Strange He-Monster, Lately arrived in London from an English Colony in America and is often to be seen upon the Royal Exchange.* [London], 1726. Evans # 2757.

Lloyd, David. *A Vindication of Legislative Power.* [Philadelphia: Bradford?, 1725.] Evans # 2649.

Logan, James. *The Antidote.* Philadelphia, 1725. Evans # 2650. Reprinted in *Pennsylvania Magazine of History and Biography,* 38 (1914), 463–86.

———. *A More Just Vindication.* [Philadelphia, 1726.] Evans # 2759.

———. *Remarks on Sir William Keith's Vindication.* Philadelphia: Bradford, 1726. Evans # 2808.

Penn, William. *Correspondence between William Penn and James Logan, Secretary of the Province of Pennsylvania, and Others, 1700–1750.* 2 vols. Philadelphia: Historical Society of Pennsylvania, 1870–72, Memoirs of the Historical Society of Pennsylvania, vols. 9 & 10.

———. *The Papers of William Penn.* 4 vols. Ed. Mary Maples Dunn and Richard S. Dunn. Philadelphia: University of Pennsylvania Press, 1981–87.

Pennsylvania Archives, Selected and Arranged from Original Documents in the Office of the Secretary of the Commonwealth. 1st ser. 12 vols. Ed. Samuel Hazard. Philadelphia: Severns & Co., 1852–56.

Rawle, Francis. *Some Remedies Proposed, for the Restoring the sunk Credit of the Province of Pennsylvania, with Some Remarks of its Trade. Humbly offer'd to the*

Consideration of the Worthy Representatives in the General Assembly of this Province, By a Lover of this Country. Philadelphia, 1721. Evans # 2287. The first paper-money tract. Rawle was a Quaker follower of David Lloyd.

A Revisal of the Intreagues of the Triumvirate, with the rest of the Trustees of the Proprietor of Pennsylvania, and also, of a Warning to the Inhabitants of the said Province, against the Guiles of the Devil and Men. Philadelphia, 1729. Evans # 3210.

The Triumvirate of Pennsylvania. In a Letter to a Friend in the Country. [Philadelphia, 1725?] Evans # 2712. Anti-proprietary tract attacking Andrew Hamilton, Jeremiah Langhorne, and James Logan.

THE CHESOPEAN COLONIES

Manuscripts

Callister, Henry. Callister Papers: Letter books and Correspondence. Maryland Diocesan Society Library at Maryland Historical Society. Important source of commentary for cultural life in Maryland during the 1740s, including poem by Thomas Bacon and informative letters on a variety of political subjects.

Cook, Ebenezar. "An Elegy on the death of the Honourable William Lock, Esq. 1732." MS letter. Bozman-Kerr Papers, Manuscript Division, Library of Congress.

Lewis, Richard. "Verses to the memory of his Excell'y Benedict L. Calvert, Late Governor of Maryland Who died at Sea, June —— 1732." MS notebook E3 V4. U. S. Naval Academy Library, Annapolis.

[Mercer, John.] Poetry Collection. Mss 5345 a 522 (1–3). Virginia Historical Society.

William and Mary College Collection. Shelf # 16,470. Manuscript Division, Library of Congress. Contains poetry, essays of students, and correspondence from William Dawson.

Wood, Henry. Poetic epistles to Benjamin Waller, 2 February, 1745/46, 25 December, 1752, 4 December, 1753, 9 July, 1754. Waller Family Papers, 1737–1912. Folder 2. Colonial Williamsburg Foundation.

Published Works

Poetry

Cooke, Ebenezer. *The Maryland Muse.* Annapolis: [Parks], 1731. Evans # 3407.

————. *The Sot Weed Factor: or, A Voyage to Maryland.* London, 1708.

————. *Sotweed Redivivus: Or the Planters Looking-Glass.* Annapolis: [Parks], 1730. Evans # 3266.

Fox, John. "The Publick Spirit." *The Wanderer.* London, 1718.

Hansford, Charles. "My Country's Worth." *The Poems of Charles Hansford.* Ed. James A. Servies and Carl R. Dolmetsch. Chapel Hill: University of North Carolina Press, for the Virginia Historical Society, 1961.

Lewis, Richard. *Carmen Seculare, for the Year, M, DCC, XXXII To the Right Honourable Charles, Lord Baron of Baltimore.* [Annapolis: Parks, 1732.] Evans # 39994.

————. "An Elegy on the much lamented Death of the Hnourable Charles Calvert, Esq; formerly Governour in Chief of the Province of Maryland; and at the time of his Decease, Commissary-General, Judge of the Admiralty, Surveyor-General of the Western Shore, and President of the Council, Who departed this Life, February 2, 1733–4." *Maryland Gazette* (15 March, 1733/34). Lemay # 294. Carlson Attribution.

————. "To His Excellency Benedict Leonard Calvert, Governour, and Commander in Chief, in and over the Province of Maryland." *The Mouse-Trap, or the Battle of the Cambrians and Mice. A Poem. Translated into English.* Annapolis: Parks, 1728, vii–viii.

————. "To Mr. Samuel Hastings, (Ship-wright of Philadelphia) on his launching the Maryland-Merchant, a large Ship built by him at Annapolis." *Pennsylvania Gazette* (13 January, 1729/30).

————. "Verses. To the Memory of His Excelly Benedict Leonard Calvert; Late Governor of the Province of Maryland." "Some Recently Found Poems on the Calverts." Ed. Walter B. Norris. *Maryland Historical Magazine,* 32 (1937), 121–27.

Markland, John. "To the Right Honourable Charles, Lord Baron of Baltimore, Absolute Lord and Proprietary of the Province of Maryland and Avalon." *A poem by John Markland 1733.* Ed. J. A. Leo Lemay. Williamsburg: William Parks Club, 1965.

Mercer, John. "O Dinwiddianae or Select Poems Pro Patria." *The Colonial Virginia Satirist; Mid-Eighteenth-Century Commentaries on Politics, Religion, and Society.* Ed. Richard Beale Davis. Transactions of the American Philosophical Society. New ser., vol. 57, 1. Philadelphia: American Philosophical Society, 1967.

Mossom, David. "Imitation of the 15th Ode of the 4th Book of Horace . . . humbly addressed to the Honourable William Gooch, Esq; Governor of the Colony." *The Virginia Gazette* (3 December, 1736).

"A Rapsody, occasioned by a Review of the Common Misery of Human Kind, especially in that Part of the World called Great-Britain." *Virginia Gazette* (10 December, 1736). Lemay # 433.

Sterling, James. *An Epistle to the Hon. Arthur Dobbs, Esq.; In Europe From a Clergyman in America.* Dublin, 1752.

————[?]. "Verses Occasioned by the Success of the British Arms in the Year 1759." *The Maryland Gazette,* 765 (3 Jan., 1760). Reprinted in *Colonial American Poetry.* Ed. Kenneth Silverman. New York & London:

Hafner Pub. Co., 1968. Lemay # 1695. Lemay's speculative attribution.

Prose

Byrd, William. *Histories of the Dividing Line betwixt Virginia and North Carolina.* Ed. William K. Boyd. New York: Dover Publications, 1967.

Eddis, William. *Letters from America.* Ed. Aubrey C. Land. Cambridge, Mass.: The Belknap Press, John Harvard Library, Harvard University Press, 1969.

Mason, George. Letter, June 6, 1766. "To the Committee of Merchants in Lond[on]." *The Papers of George Mason, 1725–1792.* Ed. Robert A. Rutland. Chapel Hill: University of North Carolina Press, 1970.

Reid, James. "The Religion of the Bible and Religion of K[ing] W[illiam] County Compared." *The Colonial Virginia Satirist.* Ed. Richard Beale Davis. Transactions of the American Philosophical Society. New ser., vol. 57, 1. Philadelphia: American Philosophical Society, 1967, 43–71.

[Spotswood, Alexander.] [Letter and Fable signed John Spotswood.] *Virginia Gazette* (17 June, 1737).

[Tennent, John.] *Every Man his own Doctor or, the Poor Planter's Physician.* Williamsburg: Parks, 1734. Evans # 3843.

THE CAROLINAS

Manuscripts

Dale, Thomas. Letters to Rev. Thomas Birch. Thomas Birch Papers. British Library. 1730s correspondence of physician-poet-politician resident in Charleston. The most informative unpublished source for information on the culture of Charleston for the decade.

Dobbs, Arthur. "Proposals and Plans concerning the administration of the British Colonies in America." Dobbs Papers. Reel 2, # 5. Microfilm copy, Southern Historical Society Collection. University of North Carolina. [1740s and 1750s.] Important meditations on trade and production by the governor of North Carolina. The collection is drawn from materials at the National Library of Ireland, Irish Public Record Office, and Dobbs Castle.

Murray, John. Letters and reports. Murray of Murraythwaite muniments. Scottish Records Office. Correspondence of the secretary of South Carolina and letters of two brothers resident in Charleston, offering reports on politics and commentaries on society.

Ogilvie, George. Letters. Ogilvie-Forbes Papers. Queens College Library, University of Aberdeen. Includes detailed meditations on rice culture and South Carolina politics, including letters reflecting on the contents of his major poetic work, *Carolina; or, The Planter.*

Rugeley, Roland. Letters re settlement of South Carolina. 1740–1810. Rugeley papers. X 311/1-242. Bedfordshire County Record Office. Correspondence of the Tory poet and official. Also included are the letters of Henry Rugeley, the famous Tory militia commander during the Revolution.

Woodmason, Charles. Sermon Books. 3 ms volumes. The New-York Historical Society. Extracts published as Richard J. Hooker, *The Carolina Backcountry on the Eve of the Revolution.* Includes his writings as spokesman for the South Carolina Regulators. The manuscript of Woodmason's "Indico" has been lost.

Published Works

Poems

Dale, Thomas. "Prologue spoken to the Orphan, upon its being play'd at Charlestown, on Tuesday the 24th of Jan. 1734/5." *South Carolina Gazette,* 54 (8 February, 1734/35). Lemay # 354.

Dumbleton, Joseph. "A Rhapsody on Rum." *Gentleman's Magazine,* 19 (September, 1749), 424. Lemay # 942.

Kirkpatrick, James. *The Sea-Piece; A narrative, philosophical and descriptive Poem. In Five cantos.* London: Cooper and Buckland, 1750.

Ogilvie, George. *Carolina; or, the Planter* (1776). Ed. David S. Shields. *Southern Literary Journal,* special issue (1986). Reprint of 1791 edition.

Rugeley, Rowland. *Miscellaneous Poems and Translations from LaFontaine and Others.* Cambridge, U.K., 1763.

[Woodmason, Charles] C. W. "C. W. in Carolina to E. J. at Gosport." *Colonial American Poetry.* Ed. Kenneth Silverman. New York & London: Hafner Pub. Co., 1968.

―――. "Indico." "A Colonial Poem on Indigo Culture." Ed. Hennig Cohen. *Agricultural History,* 30 (1956), 42–43.

Prose

de Crevecoeur, Hector St. John. "Letter IX; Description of Charles Town; Thoughts on Slavery; On Physical Evil; A Melancholy Scene." *Letters From an American Farmer.* New York: Signet Classics, 1963, 150–73.

Dale, Thomas. *The Case of Miss Mary Roche.* Charlestown: Peter Timothy, 1738. Evans # 40139.

―――. *The Puff; or, A Proper Reply to Skimmington's last Crudities.* Charleston: Peter Timothy, 1739. Evans # 40157.

Garden, Alexander. Letter of July 24, 1789 to George Ogilvie describing Otranto Plantation, Goose Creek, South Carolina. *Southern Literary Journal,* special issue (1986), 129.

Killpatrick, James. *A Full and Clear Reply to Doct. Thomas Dale.* Charleston: Peter Timothy, 1739. Evans # 4373.

———. [Kirkpatrick, James.] *The Analysis of Inoculation: comprizing the History, Theory, and Practice of it: With an occasional Consideration of the Most Remarkable Appearances in the Small Pox.* London: Millan, Buckland, and Griffiths, 1754.

Pinckney, Eliza Lucas. *The Letterbook of Eliza Lucas Pinckney 1739–1762.* Ed. Elise Pinckney. Chapel Hill: University of North Carolina Press, 1972.

Woodmason, Charles. *The Carolina Backcountry on the Eve of the Revolution.* Ed. Richard J. Hooker. Chapel Hill: University of North Carolina Press, Institute of Early American History and Culture, 1953.

———. C. W. [Indigo Culture in South Carolina.] *Gentleman's Magazine,* 25 (May, 1755), 201–3; (June, 1755), 156–59.

GEORGIA

Published Works

Poetry

[Browne?, Moses.] "To the honourable James Oglethorpe, Esq, On his Return from Georgia." *Gentleman's Magazine,* 4 (September, 1734), 505. Lemay # 329. Richard C. Boys attribution.

[Fitzgerald, Thomas.] "Tomo Chachi, an Ode." *Georgia, And Two Other Occasional Poems on the Founding of the Colony, 1736.* Ed. John Calhoun Stephens, Jr. Emory University Publications, Sources & Reprints, ser. 6, # 2. Atlanta: The Library, Emory University, 1950, 12–16.

Incognito. "The Petition of some of the inhabitants of the Province of G——a, to the P—— of S. C——." *South Carolina Gazette,* 38 (19 October, 1734). Lemay # 330.

[Kimber, Edward.] "A Letter From a Son, in a distant Part of the World, March 2, 1743." *The London Magazine,* 13 (July; August, 1744), 355–57, 405–6. Lemay # 737.

[Kirkpatrick?, James.] A muse from India's savage plain. "An Address to James Oglethorpe, Esq; on his settling the colony in Georgia." *The South Carolina Gazette* (10 February, 1732/33). Lemay # 245. Reprinted in "Two Colonial Poems on the Settling of Georgia." Ed. Hennig Cohen. *Georgia Historical Quarterly,* 27 (1953), 131–34.

Philanthropos. "To His Excellency, James Oglethorpe, Esq; On his Success in having defeated the Spaniards in their attack upon Georgia. *New York Weekly Journal,* 474 (20 December, 1742). Lemay # 666.

"To James Oglethorpe Esq; on His late Arrival from Georgia (London, October 5)." *Pennsylvania Gazette,* 327 (20 March, 1735). Lemay # 362.

Wesley, Samuel. "Georgia, A Poem." *Georgia, and Two Other Occasional Poems on the Founding of the Colony, 1736.* Atlanta: The Library, Emory University, 1950.

Prose

[Martyn, Benjamin.] *Reasons for Establishing the Colony of Georgia, With Regard to the Trade of Great Britain, The Increase of our People, and the Employment and Support it will afford to great Numbers of our own Poor, as well as foreign persecuted Protestants.* London: W. Meadows, 1733. Reprinted in *The Most Delightful Country of the Universe.* Ed. Trevor Reese. Savannah: Beehive Press, 1972.

————. *Some Account of the Designs of the Trustees for establishing the Colony of Georgia in America.* London, 1733. Reprinted in *The Most delightful Country of the Universe.* Ed. Trevor Reese. Savannah: Beehive Press, 1972.

Montgomery, Robert. *A Discourse Concerning the design'd Establishment of a New Colony to the South of Carolina, in the Most delightful Country of the Universe, 1717.* Reprinted in *The Most Delightful Country of the Universe.* Ed. Trevor Reese. Savannah: Beehive Press, 1972.

Oglethorpe, James. *A New and Accurate Accounte of the Provinces of South-Carolina and Georgia.* Reprinted in *The Most Delightful Country of the Universe.* Ed. Trevor Reese. Savannah: Beehive Press, 1972.

Reese, Trevor. Ed. *The Clamorous Malcontents; Criticism and Defenses of the Colony of Georgia, 1714–1743.* Savannah: Beehive Press, 1973.

Stephens, William. *A Journal of the Proceedings in Georgia, Beginning October 20, 1737.* 2 vols. London: Meadows, 1742.

Tailfer, Patrick. *A True and Historical Narrative of the Colony of Georgia by Pat. Tailfer and Others with Comments by the Earl of Egmont.* Ed. Clarence L. Ver Steeg. Wormsloe Foundation Publications, 4. Athens: University of Georgia Press, 1960.

WEST INDIES

Manuscripts

[Banks, John?]. John Stewart Poetry Book, 1770s–1780s. Perkins Library. Duke University. Contains poetic ruminations of an Irish overseer to a Jamaican sugar plantation. The author of the manuscript may be the merchant who entered Charleston in 1782. The manuscript is named for a child who wrote his signature on the end sheets a number of times, and not for the author of its contents.]

Hope, John Bruce. Letterbook, 1722–27. MS Rawl A 484. Bodleian Library. Oxford University. Hope was the governor of Bermuda. Valuable commentary on conditions in that island.

Martin, Samuel. Martin Papers. Add Mss 41348-53. British Library. Correspondence from Antigua of the major defender of the slave system in the West Indies. Also of interest in Add MS 41,352 are the letters of Josiah Martin, particularly his writings of 1736 describing the slave revolt in Jamaica.

Walduck, Thomas. Letters, 1708–12, to James Petiver. Sloane Ms 2302. British Library. Informative discussions of customs, commerce, government, and natural history of Barbados. Includes "An Acrostick upon ye Island of Barbadoes & ye Inhabitants thereof."

Published Works

Poetry

A Bostonian. "On the taking Porto-Bello by Admiral Vernon." *The General Magazine*, 1 (March, 1741), 208–09.

Britannicus. "A Letter from Don Thomas Geraldino, in Answer to Don Blas de Lezo's, at Cathagene. Faithfully translated by Britannicus." *The General Magazine*, 1 (February, 1741), 138–43. Lemay # 614. Possibly by Samuel Martin who used the pseudonym on occasion.

Caetera descent. "Epistle to Admiral Vernon, on his success in the West Indies, in imitation of Waller's style." *Gentleman's Magazine*, 14 (February, 1744), 99–100. Lemay # 724.

Edwards, Bryan. *Poems, written chiefly in the West Indies*. Kingston, Jamaica: Aikman, 1792.

Gentleman at Jamaica. "A Letter from Don Blas de Lezo, the Spanish Admiral at Carthagena, to Don Thomas Geraldino, late Agent for the King of Spain in London." *The Boston Evening Post*, 271 (13 October, 1740). Lemay # 577.

Grainger, James. *The Sugar-Cane. A Poem in Three Books*. London: [J. & R. Dodsley], 1764.

[Green?, Joseph.] *Some Excellent Verses on Admiral Vernon's taking the Forts and Castles of Carthagena, In the Month of March, last*. Broadside. [Boston, 1741]. Evans # 4810.

Jamaica, a poem, in three parts. Written in that island, in the year MDCCLXXVI. To which is annexed, A poetical epistle from the author in that island to a friend in England. London: W. Nicoll 1777. Volume also includes, "A Poetical Epistle, from the Island of Jamaica, to a Gentleman of the Middle-Temple." A microfilm version is available through Columbia University Library.

Majoribanks, J[ohn]. *Slavery: an essay in verse inscribed to planters and others concerned in the sale of negro slaves*. Edinburgh, 1792.

More, Hannah. *Slavery: a poem*. London, 1788.

"A native of the West Indies." *Poems, on subjects arising in England and the West Indies*. London: R. Faulder, 1783. Of particular interest is the poem "The Field Negroe; or the Effect of Civilization." The author was the rector of St. John's, Nevis.

An Ode Pindarick on Barbados. [London, 1710?].

Querard, I. *Melodies Indiennes*. Cape Francais, 1736.

Roscoe, William. *Wrongs of Africa*. London, 1788. A metropolitan poem on the African slave trade written by an abolitionist.

Rushton, Edward. *West Indian Eclogues*. London: W. Lowndes & J. Phillips, 1787.

[Shervington, William.] *The Antigonian and Bostonian Beauties*. Boston: Fowle, [1751?] Evans # 7317.

Singleton, John. *A Description of the West Indies. A Poem in blank Verse in Four Books*. London, 1767.

Stanfield, James Field. *The Guinea voyage: a poem in three books*. London: J. Phillips, 1789. The major poem describing the middle passage. Stanfield claims to have worked in the slave trade.

"Timothy Touchstone." *Tea and sugar; or, the nabob and the creole: a poem in two cantos*. London, 1792.

Tucker, Nathaniel. *The Bermudian: A Poem*. London: By the Author, 1774.

[Wagstaffe, A.] *The Politicks and Patriots of Jamaica A Poem*. London: T. Warner, 1718. The author's name, found in the body of the poem, is a pseudonym.

Prose

Abbad y Lasierra, Inigo. *Historia Geografica, civil y politica de la Isla de S. Juan Bautista de Puerto Rico*. Madrid: A. Espinosa, 1788.

Atwood, Thomas. *The History of the island of Dominica. Containing description of its situation, extent, climate, mountains, rivers, natural productions, &c. Together with an account of the civil government, trade, laws, customs, and manners of the different inhabitants of that island. Its conquest by the French, and restoration to the British dominions*. London: J. Johnson, 1791. Microform edition available: Selected Americana from Sabin's Dictionary of Books Relating to America, group 9, supplement # 18. Lost Cause Press, Louisville, Ky.

Belgrove, William. *Treatise on Husbandry, or Planting*. Boston: D. Fowle, 1755. Written in Barbados.

Clark, Samuel. *A True and Faithful Account of the Four Chiefest plantations in America*. London, 1670. Barbados.

Edwards, Bryan. *An historical survey of the French colony in the island of St. Domingo: comprehending a short account of its ancient government, political state, population, productions, and exports; a narrative of the calamities which have desolated the country ever since the year 1789 and a detail of the military transactions of the British army in that island to the end of 1794*. London: J. Stockdale, 1797.

———. *The history, civil and commercial, of the British colonies in the West Indies* (London: J. Stockdale, 1793).

An Essay concerning Slavery, and the Danger Jamaica is expos'd to from the too great number of Slaves, and the too little care that is taken to manage them. London: C. Corbett, [1746].

Estwick, S. *Considerations on the Negroe Cause.* London, 1764. About Barbados.

Frere, George. *A Short History of Barbados, from its first discovery and settlement, to the end of the year 1767.* London: J. Dodsley, 1768. Largely cribbed from Oldmixon.

Graves, John. *A memorial, or, a short account of the Bahama-Islands; of their situation, product, conveniency of trading with the Spaniards . . . deliver'd to the Lords, proprietors of the said Islands, and the Honourable Commissioners of Her Majesty's Customs.* [London, 1707?]

The Groans of Jamaica express'd in a Letter from a Gentleman residing there, to his friend in London. London, 1714. A literate attack on "the triumvirate" who ruled the island: Deputy Governor Rigby, Attorney General Brodrick, and Dr. John Stuart.

Hughes, Griffith. *The Natural History of Barbados.* 10 books. London, 1750.

[Keimer, Samuel.] *Caribbeana: containing letters and dissertations, together with poetical essays on various subjects and occasions.* 2 vols. London: T. Osborne, 1741. A valuable compilation of the contents of the *Barbados Gazette* for the 1730s, containing many important political essays and a substantial quantity of poetry.

Littleton, Edward. *The Groans of the Plantations: or, A true account of their grievous and extreme sufferings by the heavy impositions upon sugar, and other hardships. Relating more particularly to the island of Barbados.* London: M. Clark, 1689.

Lufman, J. *Brief Account of the Island of Antigua, together with the Customs and Manners of its inhabitants, as well white as black.* London, 1789.

Martin, Samuel. *Essay on Plantership humbly inscribed to His Excellency George Thomas, esq.* London: A. Millar, 1765. Also, London: T. Cadell, 1773. 5th ed. with "A Preface upon the slavery of the negroes in the British Colonies." The most articulate defense of the slave system in the Sugar Islands. Antigua.

Sancho, Ignatius. *Letters of an African. To which are prefixed memoirs of his life.* 2 vols. London, 1784.

Smith, William. *Natural history of Nevis and the Rest of the Charibee islands.* Cambridge, U. K., 1745.

Smollet, Tobias. *The Adventures of Roderick Random.* Ed. Paul-Gabriel Bouce. Oxford: Oxford University Press, 1972.

Some Considerations humbly offered to both Houses of Parliament concerning the Sugar Colonies. London, 1701.

Some Memoirs of the First Settlement of the Island of Barbados and other the Carribbee Islands with the Succession of the Governours and Commanders in Chief of Barbados to the Year 1741. Barbados: William Beeby, 1741.

Suckling, George. *An Historical Account of the Virgin islands in the West indies From their being settled by the English near a century past, to their obtaining a legislature of their own in the year 1773; and the lawless state in which His Majesty's subjects in those islands have remained since that time, to the present.* London: B. White, 1780.

[Ward, Edward "Ned".] "A Trip to Jamaica." *The Second Volume of the Writings of the Author of the London-Spy.* London: J. How, 1704.

METROPOLITAN WRITINGS

Published Works

Poetry

Arnold, Cornelius. *Commerce.* London, 1751.

Aston, Miles. *An Heroick Poem on the Weaving Trade setting forth its Antiquity and Use.* Dublin: Gowan, [1734].

Brailsford, John. *Derby Silk-Mill. A Poem.* Nottingham: Ayscought, 1739.

Cockings, George. *Arts, Manufactures, and Commerce: A Poem.* London: For the author, [1765].

Denham, John. "Cooper's Hill." *Expans'd Hieroglyphicks; A Study of Sir John Denham's Coopers Hill with a Critical Edition of the Poem.* Ed. Brendan O Hehir. Berkeley & Los Angeles: University of California Press, 1969.

Dyer, John. "The Fleece." *Poems by John Dyer, L. L. B.* London: R. & J. Dodsley, 1761.

Goldsmith, Oliver. "The Deserted Village." *The Collected Works of Oliver Goldsmith.* Ed. Arthur Friedman. 4 vols. Oxford: Oxford University Press, 1966.

Herbert, George. "The Church Militant." *The Collected Writings of George Herbert.* Oxford: Oxford University Press,

Lord, George deF. Ed. *Poems on Affairs of State: Augustan Satirical Verse, 1660–1714.* 8 vols. New Haven: Yale University Press, 1963–1978.

The New Ministry. Containing A Collection of all the Satyrical Poems, Songs, &c. London, 1742.

Ralph, James. *Zeuma: or the Love of Liberty. A Poem. In Three Books.* London: Billingsley, 1729.

Thomson, James. *Britannia.* London, 1729.

———. *A Poem Sacred to the Memory of Sir Isaac Newton.* London, 1727.

Young, Edward. "Imperium Pelagi. A Naval Lyric. Written in Imitation of Pindar's Spirit. Occasioned by His Majesty's Return, September 10th, 1729 and the Succeeding Peace: THE MERCHANT. Ode the First. On the British Trade and Navigation." *The Complete Works Poetry and Prose.* Ed. James Nichols. Hildesheim: George Olms Verlagsbuchhandlung, 1968.

Prose

Abercromby, James. "An Examination of the Acts of Parliament Relative To the Trade and Government of our American Colonies (1752)." *Magna Carta for America*. Memoirs of the American Philosophical Society, 165. Ed. Jack P. Greene, Charles F. Mullett, and Edward C. Papenfuse, Jr. Philadelphia: American Philosophical Society, 1986.

Bacon, Francis. *Advancement of Learning and Novum Organum*. New York: Colonial Press, 1899.

Hale, Matthews. *Sir Matthew Hale's The Prerogatives of the King*. Ed. D. E. C. Yale. Publications of the Selden Society, 91. London: Selden Society, 1976.

Johnson, Samuel. *Lives of the English Poets*. Ed. George Birkbeck Hill. 3 vols. Oxford: Oxford University Press, 1905.

————. Review of Grainger's *The Sugar-Cane. Critical Review* (October, 1764), 170.

Keymer, John. "John Keymer's Observations touching Trade and Commerce, 1618–1620." *Seventeenth-Century Economic Documents*. Ed. Joan Thirsk and J. P. Cooper. Oxford: Clarendon Press, 1972. 464–71.

[Ralph, James.] *The History of England during the Reigns of King William, Queen Anne, and George I*. 2 vols. London, 1744–46.

Royal Instructions to the British Colonial Governors 1670–1776. Ed. Leonard W. Labaree. 2 vols. New York: Appleton-Century, 1935.

Smith, Adam. *An Inquiry into the Nature and Causes of the Wealth of Nations* (1776). Ed. R. H. Campbell, A. S. Skinner, and W. B. Todd. 2 vols. Oxford: Oxford University Press, 1976.

Steele, Richard. *The Tatler*, 38 (1709).

Index